French Renaissance
and Baroque Drama

French Renaissance and Baroque Drama

Text, Performance, and Theory

Edited by
Michael Meere

UNIVERSITY OF DELAWARE PRESS
Newark

Published by University of Delaware Press
Copublished by The Rowman & Littlefield Publishing Group, Inc.
4501 Forbes Boulevard, Suite 200, Lanham, Maryland 20706
www.rowman.com

Unit A, Whitacre Mews, 26-34 Stannary Street, London SE11 4AB

British Library Cataloguing in Publication Information Available

Library of Congress Cataloging-in-Publication Data

French Renaissance and baroque drama : text, performance, theory / edited by
Michael Meere.
   pages cm
   Includes bibliographical references and index.
   ISBN 978-1-61149-548-5 (cloth : alk. paper) — ISBN 978-1-61149-549-2
(electronic : alk. paper) 1. French drama—17th century—History and criticism.
2. Baroque literature—History and criticism. I. Meere, Michael, editor.
   PQ528.F74 2015
   842'.409—dc23
                                                                        2014046949

∞™ The paper used in this publication meets the minimum requirements of
American National Standard for Information Sciences—Permanence of Paper
for Printed Library Materials, ANSI/NISO Z39.48-1992.

Printed in the United States of America

Contents

~

Illustrations

~

Notes on Sources and Translations

In general, primary sources that exist in modern editions have been used. Otherwise, the punctuation and spelling of the transcriptions for the original texts have not been modified except for the letters *u* and *i*, which have been changed to *v* and *j*, respectively, when appropriate, and ampersands have been converted to the words *and* or *et*. Nearly all translations are the authors' own renderings, keeping as close to the original French as possible. Most of the verse has not been translated poetically but rather in prose form; thus the line distinctions have not been maintained in the translations. If contemporaneous translations exist, as is the case for Théodore de Bèze's *Abraham sacrifiant* or Montaigne's *Essais*, for example, they have been included as the primary translation, with the modern translation in the notes.

Several articles engage with Montaigne's *Essais*. Therefore, in order to maintain consistency between them, all French quotations are taken from Pierre Villey and V.-L. Saulnier's edition (Paris: PUF, 1965). We have also included John Florio's contemporaneous translations in *The Essayes or Morall, Politike and Millitarie Discourses of Lord Michaell de Montaigne* (London: Val. Sims, 1603), available online at http://www.luminarium.org/renascence-editions/montaigne/. Finally, we have relied on Donald Frame's modern translations in *The Complete Essays of Montaigne* (London: Everyman's Library, 2003), unless otherwise noted. We thank Stanford University Press for permission to reproduce Frame's translation in this volume.

~

Acknowledgments

This volume of fifteen essays grew out of a two panels at the Renaissance Society of America's annual convention, "French Renaissance Drama: Poetics and Performance," held in Washington, D.C., in 2012. I would like to thank those who participated on these panels as well as the Renaissance Society of America for providing us with the opportunity to share and exchange ideas. I am especially grateful to Kathleen P. Long, whose support made the panels possible, and to Gary Ferguson, who has followed the project since its inception. I would also like to thank all of the authors for their contributions, the external readers who provided insightful and helpful comments on each article, the editors at the University of Delaware Press, and the staff at the Getty Research Institute and the Bibliothèque nationale de France for their help in providing the figures for Antónia Szabari's and Ellen R. Welch's articles, respectively. Finally, I would like to express my thanks to my family, friends—notably Annelle Curulla, Helen Dunn, Caroline Gates, and Rivka Swenson—and generous colleagues at King's College London, College of the Holy Cross, and Wesleyan University.

Christian Biet's chapter, "Red and Black, Pink and Green: Jacques de Fonteny's Gay Pastoral Play," is a modified translation (by Cécile Dudouyt) of an essay that originally appeared in French in a festschrift for Madeleine Alcover, titled "Le Rouge et le noir, le rose et le vert, ou la pastorale homosexuelle de Jacques de Fonteny (1587)" (in *Dissidents, excentriques et marginaux de l'Age classique: Autour de Cyrano de Bergerac*, ed. Patricia Harry, Alain Mothu, and Philippe Sellier [Paris: Honoré Champion, 2006], 265–88). I thank the editors at Honoré Champion for their permission to translate and reproduce this essay.

M. M., Paris, July 2014

~

Introduction

The essays presented in this volume demonstrate the variety and diversity of drama written in French from the late fifteenth to the early seventeenth centuries, as well as the various methodologies used in this scholarly field. Conventional French theater histories of this period tend to privilege (humanist) tragedies and comedies over other types of drama, and they also tend to consider these plays' textual elements from philological and poetic perspectives in order to locate models and to establish a French dramatic canon. This volume, however, attests to the inventiveness, suppleness, and creativity not only of the plays, play-texts, and performances themselves, but also the dynamism of current drama studies.[1] In turn, this volume seeks to deepen and complicate our knowledge of the textual, co-textual,[2] and poetic aspects of French Renaissance and baroque drama in new ways by highlighting notions of performance. Indeed, if it is indeed true that many humanist "plays were probably never performed,"[3] and even if some playwrights struggled to find an audience (Noirot), Garnier's humanist tragedies were (and continue to be) performed (Szabari, Usher), Calvinist plays were successfully put on stage in Geneva and in other Protestant areas (Beam, Lyons), and numerous mystery plays (Marculescu, Chevallier-Micki) and other types of drama continued to be written and performed well into the seventeenth century (Calhoun, Chevallier-Micki, O'Hara, Hillman, Welch). Many of the chapters in this volume also show how we can think theoretically about this drama, which the French critical canon has been slow to accept. This volume thus urges scholars and students to rediscover this drama on its own terms, to experiment with it as their creators did, and even, perhaps, to put these plays back where they belong: on the stage.

From multiple vantages, the chapters presented here examine an array of dramatic forms including farce, tragedy, the mystery play, comedy, the pastoral play, royal entrances, and court ballets, as well as meta- and para-theatrical writings from the period. These studies shed light on and inform us about pressing issues of the time, such as sacrifice (Lyons, Szabari), possession (Marculescu), war (Biet, Cavaillé, Chevallier-Micki, Noirot, Usher), religious conversion (Beam), law (Usher), international relations (Calhoun, Guild, Hillman, Welch), gender (Marculescu, O'Hara), sexuality (Biet), memory (Guild, Chevallier-Micki), and community (Beam, Cavaillé, Gates and Meere, Noirot, Welch). Moreover, many of the chapters engage with contemporary theory and methods such as psychoanalysis (Guild), anthropology and performance theory (Cavaillé, Gates and Meere), intertextuality (Hillman), stage design (Chevallier-Micki), gender studies (Biet, Marculescu, O'Hara), post-structuralism (Marculescu), and the history of emotions (Calhoun). The diversity of the essays in their methodologies and objects of study—none of which are privileged over any other—attests to the variety of this multifaceted drama and the many ways that we may study it.

In this introduction, I first delineate the parameters of this volume, beyond that which is reflected in the main title, *French Renaissance and Baroque Drama*. In the second half, synopses of the chapters show how, cumulatively and in separate ways, they can help us re-see those seemingly stale—and, for a long time, critically neglected—categories. In the end, we hope that this volume will find a wide readership in order to stimulate further research on this rich and complex drama, not only in the realm of early modern French studies, but also in disciplines and subject areas ranging from English, history, and performance studies, to gender studies and critical theory.

French

This adjective does not so much refer to the geopolitical boundaries of the French kingdom, especially since they were in flux during this time period and they are not the same today as they were then. This term refers rather to the French language and French-speaking regions, including but not limited to Paris, the provinces, and Geneva.[4] Language certainly unifies the dramatic production; however, depending on the region and religious divide, the types of drama, its causes and effects, and the goals of such productions can be quite diverse. Sara Beam, for instance, analyzes Calvinist *comedie* as a strategy for conversion and community building in francophone Geneva, while Richard Hillman shows how French dramatists at the courts of Marie de' Medici and Gaston d'Orléans were adapting English pastoral narratives onto the French stage with political intentions.

The term "French," however, as a linguistic delineation does not preclude the study of dramas written or performed in Latin, at court or in the schools, especially since the learned men (and some women) understood Latin. Ellen R. Welch's essay on the *Ballet des Polonais* opens up possibilities of further inquiry into the presence of neo-Latin spectacles in French-speaking regions by offering insights into the use of Latin in court ballets for diplomatic purposes.[5] Indeed, Welch's essay investigates the use of Latin in an international setting in the French court, a hybrid and multicultural space, which in turn "raises a fundamental question about the legibility of court entertainments' political meanings."

Renaissance and Baroque

These terms are generally considered chronological bridges between the Middle Ages and what is known in French studies as "classicism," which raises the very thorny question of periodization. In contrast to the English, Italian, or Spanish contexts, for example, intellectual historians of France tend to use the term "Renaissance" for the stretch of time between the beginning of Charles VIII's reign (1483) to the year of Henri IV's assassination (1610). This is a period during which ancient sources, and for our purposes dramatic texts and poetics by ancient Greek and Roman writers, were rediscovered and adapted into French, while the Italian models were imported into French letters.[6] As for the "baroque," in French literary and theater studies at least, it tends to delineate the time period from roughly the late 1570s to the 1650s, or from Montaigne's *Essais* to the Fronde—a series of civil wars in France between 1648 and 1653, more or less contemporaneous with the second and third English Civil Wars (1648–1651)—and the coronation of Louis XIV (1654). There is thus much chronological overlap between the "Renaissance" and the "baroque," yet there are important distinctions to be made between these two concepts.

The term "Renaissance" derives from the nineteenth century and has been defined as a "construction of elite culture rather than a global historical phenomenon."[7] As for the term "baroque," though it derives from the Portuguese *barroco* to designate imperfectly formed pearls and was introduced into French in the 1530s,[8] it appeared as a critical category for literary and theater studies only in the early twentieth century. Though the men and women of the sixteenth century did not use these exact terms, we can assert nonetheless that the "Renaissance" was a self-conscious movement of mainly humanist writers and artists, while the "baroque" is an a-posteriori descriptor for works of art and literature that favor movement, instability, metamorphosis, illusion, and ostentatious spectacles such as death and torture.

Many of the essays in this volume undermine the elitist aspect of the "Renaissance" to show how texts and performances, which have tended to be marginalized in conventional literary histories of the sixteenth and seventeenth centuries—the medieval heritage, for example—were central to the establishment and production of culture, knowledge, sociopolitical institutions, religion, and communities. The "baroque" was, for many years, used pejoratively to designate irregularity, imperfection, crudeness, or the grotesque. The chapters in this volume, on the contrary, do not offer these types of value judgments; rather, they analyze "baroque" drama on its own terms in a context that is specific to it.

In French studies, moreover, the term "baroque" has often been used in contradistinction to "classical."[9] According to John D. Lyons, "classical" has been used as "a historical and descriptive term . . . to associate seventeenth-century textual and cultural production with political absolutism and a related *épistemè*," while "baroque" is a descriptive term to distinguish certain seventeenth-century works from "classical" ones.[10] In turn, "baroque" drama is one that predates and resists "classical" ideologies, even if it has neither canonical, formal rules nor a systematic poetics. Chevallier-Micki, Calhoun, O'Hara, and Hillman, in the latter part of the volume, trace the sociopolitical stakes of shifting from the "baroque" stage to a "classical" one, from a France torn apart and fragmented during and after years of civil wars, to the rise of the absolutist rule.

Finally, there has been a resurgence of interest in the production of drama during the sixteenth and at the turn of the seventeenth centuries, which makes this volume especially timely. "Renaissance" and "baroque" drama has been relatively neglected in literary and theater studies, whereas there is a tremendous body of scholarship on classical theater.[11] This disparity in scholarship also explains why we have not chosen the expression "early modern" to describe the dramatic productions analyzed in this volume, as this term would indicate coverage from the sixteenth and seventeenth centuries, including French classical drama.[12] By keeping the terms "Renaissance" and "baroque," we do not mean to imply, however, that there were clean breaks and seamless transitions between the "Middle Ages," the "Renaissance," the "baroque," and "classicism"; indeed, many essays in this volume show that an incredible variety of genres and practices coexisted with one another between the fifteenth and seventeenth centuries. To take the example of medieval theater again, the Paris *parlement*'s decision to ban the mystery play in 1548 did not put an end to the production of medieval drama. On the contrary, medieval forms and practices continued throughout the French-speaking world well into the sixteenth and seventeenth centuries, as the chapters by Marculescu, Beam, Chevallier-Micki, and O'Hara demonstrate,[13] and the "baroque" aesthetic existed concurrently with the burgeoning "classical" one, as O'Hara's and Hillman's chapters show. Still, to avoid ambiguity, and in order not to mislead the reader, we have found that "Renaissance" and "baroque" are the most precise and appropriate terms to describe the current volume of essays for on the one hand, they underscore the particularity of the French context, and on the other, they provide a chronological framework in which to place the drama that was written and performed from the late fifteenth to the mid-seventeenth centuries.

Drama

This term entered the English vernacular in Alexander Barclay's *The Boke of Codrus and Mynalcas* (ca. 1521), and it has since come to designate, in literary criticism, a story written in verse or in prose that is acted on a stage with scenery, props, gestures, and costumes. Figuratively, "drama" rejoins the French usage, as a "series of actions or course of events having a unity like that of a drama, and leading to a final catastrophe or consummation" (*OED*, "drama"). In French, however, the word *drama* did not appear until the Abbé d'Aubignac's *Pratique du Théâtre*, which d'Aubignac began writing in the 1630s at the Cardinal de Richelieu's request but did not have printed until 1657.[14] "Ce Poëme [tragedy]," writes d'Aubignac, "est nommé *Drama*, c'est à dire, *Action*, et non pas *Récit*" ["'Tis called a *Dramma*, which signifies an Action"].[15] He employs *drama* as a Greek neologism to underscore tragedy as an action and not a narrative, but does not continue to use the term, preferring instead "poëme dramatique." In the eighteenth century, the *Encyclopédistes* challenged d'Aubignac's usage: "Un *drame*, ou comme on dit communément, une pièce de théâtre, est un ouvrage en prose ou en vers, qui ne consiste pas dans un simple récit comme le poëme épique, mais dans la représentation d'une action. Nous disons *ouvrage*, et non pas poëme; car il y a d'excellentes comédies en prose" ["A *drama*, or as we commonly call it a play, is a work in prose or in verse, which is not a simple narrative like the epic poem, but rather the performance of an action. We say *work*, and not poem, for there are excellent comedies written in prose"].[16] The authors of the *Encyclopédie* maintain d'Aubignac's basic definition of *drame*, an action as opposed to a narrative, yet they counter the "classical" view of plays as poems by endorsing dramas written in prose. This observation about the presence of prose in drama is explored in Hillman's chapter, which focuses on the 1620s and 1640s, a key period of debate as to whether plays should be written in verse or in prose. For the "classical" period, even though some *réguliers* (i.e., promoters of plays that follow Aristotelian rules outlined in his *Poetics*) such as Jean Chapelain—in the name of *vraisemblance* [verisimilitude]—were in favor of prose, those who insisted on the *poème dramatique* won the battle until the eighteenth, and particularly the nineteenth, centuries.[17]

Denis Diderot and Beaumarchais adopted the term *drame* to establish a new theatrical genre, the *drame bourgeois*, which designated a type of play that fell between tragedy and comedy. The *drame bourgeois* challenged the classical conventions of time and place and preferred plotlines that turned around the private lives of ordinary people.[18] In the nineteenth century, Romantic poets and playwrights, particularly Victor Hugo, also used the *drame* in opposition to the rigidity of the "classical" generic boundaries of tragedy and comedy, similar to Diderot a century before. Yet the Romantics provided a new theoretical and conceptual framework for the *drame*. Hugo, in his *Préface de Cromwell* (1827), promotes an arguably freer, more fluid, and liberated theatrical genre in which "le laid y existe à côté du beau, le difforme près du gracieux, le grotesque au revers du sublime, le mal avec le bien, l'ombre avec la lumière" ["the ugly exists beside the beautiful, the unshapely beside the graceful, the grotesque on the reverse of the sublime, evil with good, darkness with light"].[19] Or, put more succinctly toward the end of the preface, "le drame, c'est le grotesque avec le sublime, l'âme sous le corps, c'est une tragédie sous une comédie" ["drama is the grotesque in conjunction with the sublime, the soul within the body; it is tragedy beneath comedy"].[20] In this sense, albeit in a very different context, Hugo's definitions of the *drame* is in accordance with the types of drama that this volume addresses: the drama of possession (Marculescu), Rabelais's violent farce (Gates and Meere), the burlesque ballet (Calhoun), the tragicomic pastoral (Biet, Hillman), and the stages of cruelty in Rouen at the turn of the seventeenth century (Chevallier-Micki).[21]

Finally, "drama" is a very useful concept for our purposes in this volume. An alternative term such as "theater" would be too restrictive for the scope of the volume for, while the bulk of the studies do consider "drama" in terms of a conventional stage play, to limit the study of these texts to staged plays alone would eclipse the fact that culture and politics at this time were deeply imbued with spectacle, as we are today, whether it were a traditional play, a royal entrance, a court ballet, or a wedding ceremony.[22] As Fabien Cavaillé reminds us in his chapter, sixteenth- and early seventeenth-century audiences and dramatists "perceived theater less as a textual product or as an art and more as an event," while the term *"théâtre"* was "understood first and foremost an architectural structure (tiers or stage)." To corroborate Cavaillé's claim that *"théâtre"* designated the place where plays were performed, rather than the play-texts themselves, we might return to d'Aubignac, who, just after his use of the word *"drama,"* provides a definition of the *"Theatre"*: "[l]e Lieu qui sert à ces Representations est dit *Theatre* et non pas *Auditoire,* c'est à dire, *un Lieu où on Regarde ce qui s'y fait,* et non pas, où l'*on Ecoute ce qui s'y dit"* ["The place where these performances take place is called the theater, and not the auditorium; that is to say, the theater is a place where we watch what is happening, and not where we hear what is being said"].[23] Therefore, taking a cue from the etymology of the term from the Greek word $\delta\rho\tilde{\alpha}\mu\alpha$, meaning "deed, action, play," this volume considers "drama" in its broadest sense, from the literal play acted on a stage in front of an audience that is aware of the fiction taking place (Beam, Biet, Hillman, Lyons, Noirot, Szabari, Usher) to the metaphorical drama of exorcisms (Marculescu), executions (Chevallier-Micki, O'Hara), exposure (and exploitation) of the Amerindian during a royal entrance (Guild), ritual (Cavaillé, Gates and Meere, Lyons, Szabari), and social drama (Gates and Meere). What is more, the chapters not only examine plays or performances that took place on a stage, but also narratives depicting performance (Gates and Meere, Guild), meta-theatrical discourse (Cavaillé, Guild), para-theater (theater in which the audience directly participates; Calhoun, Gates and Meere, Guild, Welch), and dramas that blur the lines between actor and spectator, thus highlighting the porosity between the stage and the audience (Calhoun, Gates and Meere, Hillman, Usher, Welch).

As a result, the essays contained in this volume take into account the "dramatic" text or event as a base, then extend analyses to the ways in which these dramas interact with and inform the ethics, politics, religions, and communities of the Renaissance and baroque French-speaking world. To achieve this, many chapters consider drama less as a poetic (i.e., self-contained) text and rather as a play-text that was performed; these dramas are cultural artifacts that help us understand the multiple roles and the power of performance during this turbulent time in French and European history.

Organization of Chapters

The chapters have been organized more or less chronologically, though this is not to suggest that there was a certain evolution of French drama from decade to decade. On the contrary, this arrangement is simply a practical way to arrange the material coherently and to give the reader—particularly the nonspecialist—points of reference. To order the essays generically,[24] thematically, or methodologically would risk downplaying the crossovers and connections between them, overlaps that the volume wishes to highlight and nurture. Indeed, the ideological intention that underpins this volume is to open up the study of this drama in all its complexity. Moreover, some chapters discuss the role of community formation (Beam, Cavaillé, Gates and Meere, Noirot), while others discuss the notion of dignity (Calhoun, Szabari), the porosity between the page and the stage (Hillman, Marculescu, Hillman, Usher), or even the transnational aspects of drama (Beam, Calhoun, Hillman, Welch), yet they address very different kinds of drama and employ different methods.

Andreea Marculescu opens the volume with a study on the representations of demonic possession in the late medieval mystery play and its afterlife in the possession narratives of the mid-sixteenth century, particularly in Jean Boulaese's *Le miracle de Laon en Launoys* (1566). Given its means of dissemination as spectacle and through printed editions, medieval theater enters the realm of public memory fueling the collective imaginary with an archive of demonic potentialities consisting of certain gestures, behavioral patterns, and particular forms of speech. When this image of the possessed gets surreptitiously immersed into the new types of narratives on possession, it loses the ethical component conferred by mystery plays, in which the demoniac had enough agency to narrate his or her encounter with demons. In the demonic narratives, though the possessed uses a vocabulary about possession developed in mystery plays, we no longer have access to the excessive self-production of the possessed, but rather to an abject demoniac reduced to pure bodily materiality, whose physical presence is meant to serve an ideological purpose: the veracity of the case of possession and, thus, the effectiveness of the Catholic doctrine.

John D. Lyons continues the discussion about ethics from a Calvinist perspective in his chapter on Théodore de Bèze's *Abraham sacrifiant* (1550) [*A Tragedie of Abrahams Sacrifice*, 1577], which stages the founding ritual of Judaism and subsequently of Christianity and Islam: the binding of Isaac in preparation for his slaughter and for the burning of his corpse as an offering to God. The most striking thematic and formal characteristic of the play is Abraham's solitary, forward-looking deliberation about killing his son. This deliberation does not consist of *stances* (lyrical stanzas), as in many later French plays, nor does it have the entirely clear-cut form of a soliloquy. Instead, Satan, disguised as a monk, seems to serve as a prompter to suggest themes of reflection for Abraham. More radical than plays such as *Iphigenia*, in which paternal hesitation about killing a child is seen as entirely human in a positive sense, *Abraham sacrifiant* seems to represent all ethical deliberation as diabolical in origin. The monkish disguise points to Catholicism as the source of diabolical moral deliberation, against which a Protestant anti-ethical and theocratically absolutist doctrine is shown to be figured within the founding moment of the covenant.

In the following chapter on Rabelais's *Quart Livre*, Caroline Gates and Michael Meere revisit the Chiquanous episode (chapters 12–16) to consider drama, particularly farce, and the performativity of violence as constitutive forces in community building within the intercalated narratives about the Seigneur de Basché and François Villon. However, at the end of this episode, the constructive creativity of violence is turned on its head. Indeed, the Chiquanous's bleak and oppressive community is starkly contrasted with the joyful *communitas* in the Basché household and in the Villon story.[25] Gates and Meere approach the Chiquanous episode from anthropological and performance theory perspectives to show, then, how the relations between performative violence and laughter subtend the problematic complexities of communal life and collective joy, on the one hand, and on the other, to what extent laughter and violence constitute organizing principles of identity and community, at the risk of becoming potentially detrimental to this very act of community building.

Sara Beam, a historian, examines theological questions in Calvinist theater (echoing Lyons) as well as notions of community building via theater (recalling Gates and Meere) during the Reformation. To achieve this, she considers the role of theater, in particular the role of comic theater, in rapidly converting the French to the Reformed faith, which has until now been underplayed. In fact, evidence that Calvinist comedies, farces, and morality plays were performed in both Geneva and France confronts us with the possibility that new converts were first exposed to the Reformed faith on the comic stage. This essay thus explores the print and archival evidence that comic morality plays were performed in Geneva under Jean Calvin and analyzes the theological messages explored in two of these plays: Conrad Badius's *La comédie du pape malade* and Jacques Bienvenu's *Comedie du monde malade et mal pensé*.

Corinne Noirot's chapter also deals with community and theater, but rather than proposing that theater was successful at bringing people together, she investigates external and internal factors to explain why French humanist comedy, particularly that of Jean de La Taille, had difficulty securing an audience at all. Focusing on *Les corrivaux* and *Le négromant*, Noirot examines

how these plays incorporate contemporary national issues and political allusions, following the French and neo-Latin tradition, suggesting that they do
so in a veiled and oblique fashion, thus raising the question of address and
the possibility of tiered audiences. In the midst of serious empirical hazards
and uncertainties, a clash of expectations ultimately reveals in La Taille the
compelling yet powerless clear-sightedness of a soldier-poet who painfully
understood that his dramatic ambition, especially in the "comic" genre, blossomed at a time when war and politics were no laughing matter.

While French humanist comedy had difficulty in securing an audience,
the court ballet flourished under Catherine de' Medici's regency. Ellen R.
Welch considers the performance of this hybrid drama in terms of its role
in foreign diplomacy, showing that the diplomatic context requires us to
revise our understanding of the relationship between representation and
politics in court entertainments. Indeed, entertainments appear as a genu-
ine space of politics in which creators, performers, and multiple types of
spectators all played a role in negotiating meaning. To this effect, Welch
examines how the textual traces of the 1573 *Ballet des Polonais*, staged in
honor of an extraordinary embassy from Poland (and the Duke of Anjou's
election as Polish king), reveal how court artists anticipated that spectators would use multiple strategies for "reading" the performance. Welch
demonstrates that it requires the individual observer to negotiate her or his
own interpretive path through a rich combination of emblematic images,
descriptive texts, and poems in both French and Latin. This case study thus
suggests a range of more flexible approaches to theorizing the politics of
court spectacle in early modern Europe.

The next two chapters deal with the most celebrated tragic playwright
of the sixteenth century, Robert Garnier. Antónia Szabari's essay recalls
Lyons's analyses of sacrifice and ethics, by looking closely at Garnier's Greek
plays, *Hippolyte* (1572) and *La Troade* (1578). However, rather than thinking about sacrifice in religious terms, Szabari draws on art historian Rebecca
Zorach's work to examine the physicality of the body on stage, the shedding
of blood, the burning of flesh, and the functions of ritual in theatrical performance. Phillip John Usher's chapter considers a very different aspect of
Garnier's tragedies by investigating the relations between the fictional world
of theater and the real world legal institution of the *parlement*[26] in an attempt
to problematize the traditionally accepted allegorical readings, in which
the plays "represent" the Wars of Religion. For his part, Usher sketches out
approaches that emphasize the proximity between Garnier's expression of
inquiétude [worry] and the roles played by, and discourses of, magistrates and
the French *parlement* during the *troubles* [civil wars]. The article builds on

recent work in social and religious history (especially that relating to the *paix de religion* [religious peace]) and on archival research in order to develop, in particular, two concrete traces of how Garnier's tragedies situate themselves "on the threshold of *parlement*," in particular via the figures of Barnabé Brisson and Guy du Faur de Pibrac.

The following two chapter focus on Montaigne's *Essais*. Fabien Cavaillé analyzes the ways in which Montaigne conceived of *jeux* [play or games] and their social and political ramifications during a time of upheaval and crisis. Cavaillé offers a panorama of political philosophy on the notion and risks of leisure, from Etienne de La Boétie and Jean Bodin to Giovanni Boterò and Montaigne himself, to suggest that the French essayist's ideas on space and "play" bring to mind Victor Turner's ideas on the "liminal" and the "liminoid" (recalling Gates and Meere), and the useful functionalities of drama within society. For Elizabeth Guild, Montaigne, who was unusually able to acknowledge his failures to live up to his own preferred version of himself or what others wanted him to be and exceptionally curious about what it meant to be human, was well-placed to try to engage differently with the savage "other," when he had the chance. His encounter with savages—three cannibals—in Rouen in 1562, happened within a political performance, celebrating the city's return to legitimate rule after months under Huguenot control. Guild's essay draws on psychoanalysis to explore questions to do with being human that are dramatized by Montaigne's representation in "Des cannibales" ["Of Cannibals"] of that remembered encounter. In turn, Guild considers Montaigne's famous essay in terms of the relation between self and other, the temporality of human understanding, the desire for knowledge, and the significance of what is missing or will remain unknown.

Christian Biet's chapter offers a look into the pastoral play, a new type of theater imported from Italy that was gaining prominence in France during the last decades of the sixteenth century. He focuses on the melancholic and agonistic aspects of pastoral drama, in order to analyze the ways same-sex love could operate with the sylvan grove. Taking as a case in point Jacques de Fonteny's *Le beau pasteur* (1587), which would become *Le beau berger* [*The Fair Shepherd*] in later editions (the last one printed in 1624), Biet shows on the one hand how Fonteny's play underscores the generic limitations of the Italian and Spanish models, which are based on heterosexual desire, and supplants this schema with same-sex love, thus subverting the foreign pastoral "genre." On the other, Biet suggests that Fonteny's *bergerie* (not *pastorale*) offers an alternative space that allows men to embrace one another and live, albeit in an a-/u-chronic state, in harmonious community.

Just how were sets designed at the turn of the century? This is the question Sybile Chevallier-Micki attempts to answer, in the context of Rouen from 1600 to 1620. By focusing on two types of stage design, the tent and the elevated stage, Chevallier-Micki offers an array of analyses of many plays printed (and presumably) performed in Rouen, to show that the same types of settings were recycled and that it appears, as a result, that the playwrights were aware of these mechanisms and modalities of performance. She further suggests that the audience, too, was aware of the kinds of settings, and that there existed a kind of common, communal memory not only of theatrical practices, but also of the previous decades of religious wars, shared by the playwright, the actors, and the audiences.

From the physicality of stage design in urban provincial spectacles of cruelty, the next chapter, by Alison Calhoun, returns to the court ballet, but rather than thinking about dance, music, and dialogue in terms of foreign diplomacy (Welch), she considers the stakes of royal and courtly dignity within domestic politics. Calhoun examines closely the *Bal de la douairière de Billebahaut* [*The Royal Ballet of the Dowager of Bilbao's Grand Ball*, 1626], in which, rather than constructing an allegory of power and control, each leader, Louis included, acts out his own weaknesses and failures. Indeed, as Calhoun shows, we watch parade before us a series of monarchs who candidly struggle to balance their feelings (both sensorial and emotional) and their duties as sovereign. As a critical, even satirical mode of representation coming from the official power (Louis and his favorites at court), by preempting any possibility for public dissent, the burlesque ballet under Louis XIII might help us locate a period of regression in the development of dignity and a dignified public sphere.

The penultimate chapter, by Stephanie O'Hara, considers the performances of poison in French tragedy from 1600 to 1636 in order to relate them to contemporaneous tragic stories of poison. As does Marculescu, O'Hara investigates the porosity between the stage and the page by examining, on the one hand, plays by Alexandre Hardy, Pierre Corneille, Jean Mairet, Jean de Rotrou, and La Calprenède, and on the other, stories of poison that appear in tragic stories and newspapers, or the *canards*. O'Hara demonstrates how the stylized versions of poison on stage are very different from the narrative accounts, notably in terms of gender, as the imaginary poisoner on stage tends to be a woman, whereas men were often guilty of the murderous crime.

The final chapter opens the field of study both temporally and spatially. Indeed, Richard Hillman offers an intertextual study of two French plays, Puget de la Serre's tragedy in prose *Pandoste* (1631) and André Mareschal's tragicomedy *La cour bergère* (*The Pastoral Court*, 1640), which the dramatists adapted from Elizabethan pastoral narratives: Robert Greene's *Pandosto* (and perhaps even Shakespeare's *The Winter's Tale*) and Philip Sidney's *Arcadia*, respectively. Not only does Hillman's essay place French drama in a pan-European context (recalling Welch), but he also considers them in political terms. Indeed, he argues that the French adaptations were composed, performed, and published in circumstances involving fraught relations between England and France and turbulent domestic politics on both sides, particularly in the context of Marie de' Medici's involvement in Anglo-French circles on the one hand, and on the other, the tensions between Gaston d'Orléans, the Queen Mother, and the Cardinal de Richelieu.

M. M., Paris, July 2014

Notes

1. Benoît Bolduc has edited a special edition titled *Texte et représentation: Les arts du spectacle* (*XVIe s.–XVIIIe s.*), *Texte* 33/34 (2003), in which a few essays are dedicated to Renaissance drama. Other recent volumes of essays include Marie-France Wagner and Claire Le Brun-Gouanvic, eds., *Les arts du spectacle au théâtre (1550–1700)* and *Les arts du spectacle dans la ville (1404–1721)* (Paris: Champion, 2001); Jean-Claude Ternaux, ed., *Le théâtre du XVIe siècle et ses modèles*, *XVIe Siècle* 6 (2010); and Jan Clarke, Pierre Pasquier, and Henry Phillips, eds., *La ville en scène en France et en Europe (1552–1709)* (Oxford: Peter Lang, 2011), with essays by Christian Biet, Anne Surgers, and Jean-Claude Ternaux. For a comprehensive volume on the spectacle of the royal entrance, see Nicolas Russell and Hélène Visentin, eds., *French Ceremonial Entries in the Sixteenth Century: Event, Image, Text* (Toronto: Centre for Reformation and Renaissance Studies, 2007).

2. In new historicism, the term "co-text" has often replaced "context"; "co-text" refers to interrelated nonliterary texts from the same time period. In effect, many of the essays in this volume adopt in some form or another a new historicist approach to this drama, for the literary text is not privileged over other types of discourse in a kind of hierarchy. Rather, the "literary" and the "nonliterary" texts are examined in parallel, as equally valuable kinds of discourse. See notably Stephen Greenblatt, *Renaissance Self-Fashioning. From More to Shakespeare* (Chicago: University of Chicago Press, 1980). Other essays, however, take a cultural materialist approach, as this drama is interpreted not only in terms of the cultural production at this particular time in history, but also in how the texts have evolved, how they have been interpreted according to various critical and theoretical paradigms, and how this drama has been performed in our contemporary world. For the English context in Shakespeare studies, see Jonathan Dollimore and Alan Sinfield, eds., *Political Shakespeare: Essays in Cultural Materialism* [1994], 2nd rev. ed. (Manchester, UK: Manchester University Press, 2012).

3. Gillian Jondorf, "Sixteenth-Century Theatre," in *The Cambridge History of French Literature*, ed. William Burgwinkle, Nicholas Hammond, and Emma Wilson (Cambridge, UK: Cambridge University Press, 2011), 204–10, 205. This is the type of generalization that the essays in this volume challenge. Though Jondorf must be applauded for challenging traditional approaches to French humanist tragedy, there is much more to say about other forms of sixteenth- and early seventeenth-century drama.

4. Recent studies in French have adopted the phrase *théâtre d'expression française* [theater of French expression] to include plays written in the French language rather than *théâtre français*, which would intimate plays written in France. For a recent monograph on theater being written and produced in the northern Franco-Flemish provinces, see Kattel Lavéant, *Un théâtre des frontières. La culture dramatique dans les provinces du Nord aux XVe et XVIe siècles* (Orléans: Paradigme, 2011).

5. Besides, several very recent volumes of essays have appeared that include chapters on neo-Latin drama in early modern Europe. See Philip Ford and Andrew Taylor, eds., *The Early Modern Cultures of Neo-Latin Drama* (Leuven: Leuven University Press, 2013), especially essays by Oliver Pédeflous ("Ravisius Textor's School Drama and its Links to Pedagogical Literature in Early Modern France"; 19–40) and Carine Ferradou ("George Buchanan's Sacred Latin Tragedies Baptistes and Iephthes: What Place for Humankind in the Universe?"; 41–62); and Jan Bloemendal and Howard B. Norland, eds., *Neo-Latin Drama in Early Modern Europe* (Leiden: Brill, 2013), especially essays by Jean-Frédéric Chevalier ("Jesuit Neo-Latin Tragedy in France") and Mathieu Ferrand ("Humanist Neo-Latin Drama in France"). On neo-Latin comedy, see Céline Candiard's essay "The Reception of Roman Comedy in Early-Modern Italy and France," in *A Cambridge Companion to Roman Comedy*, ed. Martin Dinter (Cambridge, UK: Cambridge University Press, forthcoming).

6. Robert J. Knecht, *The Rise and Fall of Renaissance France* (London: Fontana Press, 1996; repr. 2008). The importation of Italian models into French did not take place without resistance, as Christian Biet argues in his chapter. Moreover, the Pléiade's manifesto by Joachim Du Bellay, *La deffence et illustration de la langue françoise* (1549), which only cursorily addresses theater, also had its critics, such as Barthélemy Aneau's *Quintil Horatian* (Lyons, ca. 1550).

7. Terence Cave, "Locating the Early Modern," *Paragraph: A Journal of Modern Critical Theory* 29, no. 1 (2006): 12–26. For a discussion of theory in the early modern French context, see Michael Moriarty, "Theory and the Early Modern: Some Notes on a Difficult Relationship," *Paragraph: A Journal of Modern Critical Theory* 29, no. 1 (2006): 1–11. For the French Renaissance specifically, and for theoretical readings of discrete texts, see John O'Brien and Malcolm Quainton, eds., *Distant Voices Still Heard: Contemporary Readings of French Renaissance Literature* (Liverpool, UK: Liverpool University Press, 2000). It is important to note, however, that neither the special issue of *Paragraph* (2006) nor the book collection *Distant Voices* includes theoretical readings of dramatic texts.

8. The term appeared in an inventory of Charles V's treasures, in 1531 (*Trésor de la langue française*: "baroque"). According to the *Oxford English Dictionary*, the term

did not appear in English until 1765, in H. Fuseli's translation of J. J. Winckelmann's *Reflections on the Painting and Sculpture of the Greeks* (OED: "baroque").

9. Some scholars have seen the *Essais* as a manifestation of the crisis and decline of Renaissance humanism in France. See, for example, Philippe Desan, ed., *Humanism in Crisis: The Decline of the French Renaissance* (Ann Arbor: University of Michigan Press, 1991). 1580 is also the date Jean Rousset selected in his seminal *La littérature à l'âge baroque en France* (Paris: José Corti, 1953).

10. John D. Lyons, "What Do We Mean When We Say 'Classique'?" in *Racine et/ou le classicisme*, ed. Ronald Tobin (Tübingen: Narr; 2001), 497–505, 499. Lyons offers four ways to define "classique": besides the two explained above, it is also used, according to Lyons, as "an evaluative term selecting certain aesthetic and moral values as the preferable ones without regard to historical periods" (e.g., as in a survey literature course in which students read "classics" such as Flaubert's *Madame Bovary* or Shakespeare's *Romeo and Juliet*) and "as a neutral period marker of the seventeenth (and also eighteenth) century" (ibid.). We are not using the term in these ways here.

11. Most recently, in France, Christian Biet has fostered much scholarship on the theater of the turn of the century, with theses by Sybile Chevallier-Micki on stage design in Rouen, Charlotte Bouteille-Meister on drama and *actualité* [current events], and Corinne Meyniel on biblical drama. François Lecercle has also directed important comparative work by Clotilde Thouret on the monologue, Enrica Zanin on the dénouement, and Zoé Schweitzer and Adrien Walfard on the figures of Medea and Caesar, respectively. Richard Hillman's intertextual scholarship has greatly contributed to these comparative studies. Biet and Lecercle, along with Marie-Madeleine Fragonard, have also edited volumes that place French "baroque" theater within a European context, particularly in terms of violence. Christian Biet and Marie-Madeleine Fragonard, eds., *Le théâtre, la violence et les arts en Europe (XVIe–XVIIe s.)*, *Littératures Classiques* 73 (2011); François Lecercle, ed., *Réécritures du crime: L'acte sanglant sur la scène (XVIe–XVIIIe s.)*, *Littératures Classiques* 67 (2009). Finally, Anne Teulade's comparative work on drama from the early seventeenth century recuperates baroque religious drama to place it at the center of the aesthetic and ideological debates taking place in France and Spain. *Le saint mis en scène. Un personnage paradoxal* (Paris: Cerf, 2012).

12. There is no equivalent in French for the expression "early modern," though some scholars have recently used the expression *première modernité*. Besides, as Terence Cave has suggested, the term "early modern" presents its own complications, not least because it is implicitly "teleological and evolutionary, since there can be no 'early modern' unless it leads to the 'modern'" ("Locating the Early Modern," 13).

13. One of the first scholars to underline the continuity between the medieval period and the Renaissance, particularly in terms of humanist tragedy, is Donald Stone Jr., in *French Humanist Tragedy: A Reassessment* (Manchester, UK: Manchester University Press, 1974), esp. ch. 2, "Old and New Drama."

14. The English translation of d'Aubignac's *Pratique du théâtre*, *The Whole Art of the Stage*, renders d'Aubignac's terminology "Poëme dramatique" and "Piéce de The-

atre" (2:1, 77; 78) as *"Drama"* (2:1, 61, 62; 2:4, 89; emphasis in original); however, in the original French, d'Aubignac uses the term "drama" only once, in book 4, chapter 2. Abbé d'Aubignac, *La pratique du théâtre: Œuvre tres-necessaire a tous ceux qui veulent s'appliquer a la composition des poëmes dramatiques* (Paris: Antoine de Sommaville, 1657); *The Whole Art of the Stage*, trans. William Aglionby (London, 1684).

15. Ibid., 4: 2, 370; 3: 2, 11 (emphasis in both originals).

16. [Denis Diderot et al.], *Encyclopédie, ou Dictionnaire raisonné des sciences, des arts et des métiers*, vol. 11 (Lausanne and Bern, 1782), "drame," 352 (emphasis in original).

17. See Giovanni Dotoli, *Temps de préfaces. Le débat théâtral en France de Hardy à la Querelle du "Cid"* (Paris: Klincksieck, 1996), esp. 114–15. On the general debates surrounding dramaturgy, the three unities, verisimilitude, *bienséance(s)* [decorum], and the general shift from Renaissance and baroque to "classical" tragedy, see Georges Forestier, *La tragédie française. Passions tragiques et règles classiques* (Paris: Armand Colin. 2010), esp. part one, "La crise des genres: Mort et renaissance de la tragédie"; on the codification of "classical" tragedy, see John D. Lyons, *Kingdom of Disorder: Theory of Tragedy in Classical France* (West Lafayette, IN: Purdue University Press, 1999).

18. For more on the *drame bourgeois*, see Diderot's theoretical essay in the form of a dialogue, "Les entretiens sur *Le fils naturel*," in *Œuvres complètes* (Paris: Garnier Frères, 1875), 7:85–168. For studies on the *drame bourgeois* in the eighteenth century, see Béatrice Didier, *Beaumarchais, ou la passion du drame* (Paris: PUF, 1994); Martine de Rougemont, *La vie théâtrale en France au XVIIe siècle* (Paris: Honoré Champion, 2001); Marc Buffat, ed., *Diderot, l'invention du drame* (Paris: Klincksieck, 2000); David Marshall, *The Surprising Effects of Sympathy. Marivaux, Diderot, Rousseau, and Mary Shelley* (Chicago: University of Chicago Press, 1988); and Julie Candler Hayes, *Identity and Ideology: Diderot, Sade, and the Serious Genre* (Amsterdam: J. Benjamins, 1991).

19. Victor Hugo, Préface to *Cromwell, drame* [1827] (Paris: Ambroise Dupont, 1828), I–LXIV, XI; "Preface to Cromwell" [1910], in *Prefaces and Prologues to Famous Books*, trans. Andrew Motte (New York: Cosimo, 2009), 39:354–409, 363.

20. Hugo, Préface to *Cromwell, drame*, LIX; "Preface to Cromwell," 403.

21. Today, the *drame* has come to be used in opposition to classical tragedies and comedies, as a theatrical genre in which the action is generally tense and made of risks and catastrophes, including realistic and familiar elements, common in the eighteenth and nineteenth centuries. Figuratively, a *drame* designates a grave and tragic event or situation, often presenting violent or mortal characteristics (*Trésor de la langue française*, "drame").

22. An alternative title could be "theater and spectacle," for instance, but this seems to us a bit heavy and inelegant.

23. D'Aubignac, *La pratique du theatre*, 4:2, 370. Curiously enough, Aglionby, the translator of d'Aubignac's treatise, does not translate this quotation, as this precision may have seemed too obvious for an English reader. The translation is mine.

24. Besides, the notion of "genre" was fluid at this time: the pastoral play could slip into the tragic or tragic-comic modes (Biet, Hillman), court ballets border comedy and the burlesque (Calhoun), mystery plays contain comical characters (Marculescu), and so forth.

25. In *The Ritual Process: Structure and Anti-Structure*, Turner prefers the Latin term *communitas* to "community," "to distinguish this modality of social relationship from an 'area of common living'" (London: Routledge and Kegan Paul, 1969, 96). *Communitas* is thus more than simply living together. It is, as he would make more explicit in 1982,

> the liberation of human capacities of cognition, affect, volition, creativity, etc., from the normative constraints incumbent upon occupying a sequence of social statuses, enacting a multiplicity of social roles, and being acutely conscious of membership in some corporate group such as family, lineage, clan, tribe, nation, etc., or of affiliation with some pervasive social category such as a class, caste, sex, or age-division. (*From Ritual to Theatre: The Human Seriousness of Play* [New York: Performing Arts Journal Publications, 1982], 44)

26. The *parlements* were regional judicial, government bodies in Old Regime France that were primarily the courts of appeal for trial courts. This term will recur throughout the volume in several essays, which underlines the multiple interconnections between and the stakes of drama and politico-judicial institutions during this time.

CHAPTER ONE

∿

Mystery Plays Reloaded

Performing Demonic Possession in the Histoires véritables

ANDREEA MARCULESCU

Older and contemporary histories of early modern French theater privilege the idea of an organic development that postulates its theater's own aesthetic evolution among genres, authors, and periods.[1] For such perspectives, humanist drama, for instance, is preceded by a religious and comic type of theater that had a great popular appeal despite its aesthetically unsatisfactory qualities. The same humanist drama is by far more complex than its medieval dramatic antecedents but cannot compete with the seventeenth-century theater canon. In fact, contemporary theater scholars do not hesitate to refer overtly to this model in Darwinian terms. Such is the case with Gillian Jondorf, the author of *French Renaissance Tragedy*:

> The notion of evolution is one which is very hard to exclude. We are all post-Darwinians, and the Darwinian model is now firmly fixed in our mental landscape. . . . In the case of French tragedy, this ascent is deemed to falter somewhat in the first decades of the seventeenth century, and then to find its direction again, to culminate in what we grandly call French classical tragedy.[2]

The evolutionary model might be very useful in allowing us to notice how national literary canons get constituted, but it does not satisfactorily explain why a particular author and/or genre resisted and survived more than others if we judge from the standpoint of narrowly defined aesthetic criteria alone.

1

Moreover, from a post-structuralist perspective, we know that texts produce effects, and that they do not reside in a continuum validated by canonical norms. On the contrary, texts are consumed and, thus, displaced and then restructured in heterogeneous circuits. They enter into and impact different social orbits, different formations of tense, and different political regimes.

This chapter aims to analyze these types of metamorphosis undergone by mystery plays, extensive dramatic productions performed throughout France and French-speaking territories during roughly the fifteenth and mid-sixteenth centuries. Instead of reading them in terms of the organic metaphor proposed by theater historians, I investigate the effects that mystery plays produced once they went beyond their typical circuit of dissemination, namely that of actual staging and printing.

I refer to the metamorphosis of only a particular scenario contained in mystery plays: the figure of the demoniac. This figure is a very potent framework and trope that allowed medieval and early modern subjects to problematize issues such as the relation between the divine and the demonic, body and soul, and material and spiritual. In addition to giving voice to a purely theological construction of the demoniac, I argue that mystery plays provided a rhetorical, poetic, and conceptual framework that fueled possession narratives, or *histoires véritables* as their authors also call them. These possession narratives constituted a genre in itself that came into existence roughly during the first decades of the sixteenth century (ca. 1528) and continued throughout the seventeenth century. It consisted of accounts whose length would range from the size of a booklet to as long as eight hundred pages. Scholars have acknowledged that the main function of these narratives,[3] usually published on poor quality paper and written for a wide audience comprising both literate and illiterate people, was to defend Catholicism itself in a context when the latter,[4] both as a doctrine and as a system of practices, was contested by Huguenot movements.[5] Critics have also recognized the inherent theatricality of possession narratives. Michel de Certeau, in his *Possession de Loudun*, points out that the whole phenomenon of demonic possession and its attendant arsenal (exorcisms, trials, medical assessments of the possessed subjects) represent a form of theater that brings together a significant number of spectators [*curieux*] from both France and Europe.[6] Recently, Brian Levack has argued for a recognition of possession as a theater in which everyone involved has to play his or her assigned role.[7] Theater scholars such as Jelle Koopmans, however, turn around de Certeau's idea about the theatricalization of the demoniac world and interpret mystery plays as a "literary fiction" that stages larger historical fictions.[8] Marianne Closson also mentions the *diableries*—scenes in the mystery plays exclusively based on the presence of devils—as the comic fuel that inspires both canonical authors such as Rabelais in his *Quart Livre* and the new genre of the possession narratives.[9]

Mystery plays, however, represent more than simply a comic intervention, as Closson asserts. They can hardly be regarded as mere fiction, as Koopmans has conceived of medieval theater. Indeed, we can think of theater and, implicitly, of mystery plays, as a set of discursive and embodied practices that derive from other discursive practices and that generate new forms of knowledge, embodied practices, and representation. My question then is: What happens to the representations of the demoniac epitomized in theater once they mark their exit from the economy of mystery plays? The latter are a mass media phenomenon,[10] which undoubtedly shaped public reception of the demonic element—the Rabelais case is an instance. But to what extent do the new narratives on possession, themselves a mediated phenomenon, engendering their own codes of representation on the possessed, incorporate the discourse on possession? And more important, how do they incorporate it? By incorporation, I do not mean simply a systematic and direct influence exerted by "fiction," that is, mystery plays, on "history," represented by narrativized cases of possession and exorcism that happened in "real life." Instead, I argue that mystery plays seeped into what scholars call the realm of collective memory, which, in Svetlana Boym's words, designates "the common landmarks of everyday life. . . . [They] constitute shared social frameworks of individual recollections. They are folds in the fan of memory, not prescriptions for a model tale."[11] Similarly, I argue, mystery plays created a textual and representational network that contributed to the formation of collective memory with respect to the notion of demonic possession. My essay, therefore, first analyzes the scenario of possession encompassed in mystery plays and then looks at the displacement of this scenario into possession narratives and the effects that this metamorphosis produces.

Staging Possession in Mystery Plays

Mystery plays roughly consisted of two large categories: passion plays, centered on the life of Jesus Christ, and hagiographical mystery plays, narrating the lives of saints. Composed and staged during the fifteenth and the first half of the sixteenth centuries throughout France, the former give particular attention to the scenes of the scourging of Jesus and the cruelty of his tortures. In terms of authorship, the passion plays were written by authors who had a minimum amount of theological instruction and who used diverse sources such as moral, theological, encyclopedic, or hagiographical writings that were widely known in the Middle Ages, disseminated by texts such as the *Elucidarium* by Honorius of Auntun, *Legenda aurea* [*The Golden Legend*] by Jacobus de Voragine, *Speculum historiale* by Vincent of Beauvais, the *Glossa ordinaria*, and pseudo-Bonaventure's *Meditationes Vitae Christi* [*Meditations on the Life of Christ*].[12] Such is the case with Eustache Mercadé (ca. 1380–1440), provost of Dampierre, who in 1420–1430 wrote the twenty-five-thousand-line *Passion d'Arras*.[13] His work was continued by Arnoul Gréban, who in 1456 was a student at the Faculty of Theology in Paris and who, around this time, composed the thirty-thousand-line *Mystère de la Passion* [*Mystery of the Passion*].[14] In 1486 Jean Michel, a doctor in medicine and regent at the University of Angers, adapted Gréban's text into a new passion play of about thirty thousand verses,[15] which was printed and disseminated in a variety of early-printed editions, both *deluxe* and of poor quality,[16] at the end of the fifteenth century and throughout the sixteenth century. These editions were also employed in staging dramatic representations in other northern French cities such as Mons or Valenciennes.[17]

However, the theological content of these plays and the scholarly background of their authors do not transform them into purely religious productions. The passion plays definitely aim at strengthening the audience's edification and respect for Christian values, but they possess a strong secular dimension as well. Indeed, they are public events of great scale for whose staging town authorities would invest significantly large financial and logistic resources. For example, Jean Michel's play, *Mystère de la Passion*, was staged in the city of Angers at the end of August 1486. The hagiographical *mystères* display formal similarities to passion plays: they are lengthy compositions, divided into *journées* [days], and follow the same sociocultural circuit that situates them at the crossroad of the secular and religious dimensions. They contributed to the social, cultural, and religious cohesion of the identity of a particular geographical area. Such is the case of *Mystère de saint Remi*, staged sometime between 1520 and 1528 in Reims,[18] or *Mystère des Actes des Apostres* [*Mystery of the Acts of the Apostles*], staged in 1536 in Bourges and in 1541 in Paris.

As far as the demonically possessed in *mystères* are concerned, they are relatively less numerous in comparison to the other characters that populate the mystery plays, such as devils, Christ, saints, apostles, Jews, and angels. So what discourse and status does the demoniac have in the mystery plays? At the heart of the medieval discourse on possession is the idea that demons can inhabit human bodies. Such a conception triggered certain theological complexities that presupposed the existence of a particular schema in which the soul, the spirit, and the body enter a hierarchical relation. Thus medieval theologians established that demons, as aerial creatures, cannot reside in the soul, but in the lower parts of the body.[19] Almost unanimously, the accounts of the demoniacs in theater follow this theological trajectory: the devil is an exterior entity that occupies the human body in its mass and not substance abusively. In their speech, both the possessed and the devils themselves assert and reassert this aspect of the phenomenon of possession. In Jean Michel's *Passion*, one of the devils, Astaroth, complains that Jesus evicted him out of the body of a young girl.[20] Similarly, in *Mystère de saint Remi*, Sathan mentions the case of Belzebus, which Jesus manages to "bouter hors" ["drive out"] of Floquart's body.[21] In the same play, one character notices that the devil made its "habitacle" ["house"] in the body of the demoniac Floquart.[22] Not surprisingly then, mystery plays construe the possessed as an open body in which demons are lodged and from which, by means of exorcism, they are evicted, as Fergalus, one of the demons, states in Arnoul Gréban's *Passion*.[23]

What codes of representation do mystery plays use to enact such an aspect of the possessed as a subject whose interior and exterior bodily boundaries are disrupted by the demonic presence? An effective way of recuperating these codes is to take a close look at the numerous stage directions that accompany the scenes of possession in the mystery plays, together with the existing archival information that refers directly to this type of scene and/or the props used in them. Indeed, in all passion plays the stage directions immediately following the scene of Christ healing the possessed girl are quite substantial and thus allow us to reconstitute the actual staging of scenarios of possession. In *Mystère de la Passion*, the directions read: "Icy sort une fumee et ung canon de dessoubtz la fille et Astaroth sort de la fille" ["Here smoke and a cannon exit from underneath the girl and Astaroth gets out from within the girl"].[24] The hagiographical mystery plays are also rich in such details. From these paratextual details, we see that possession scenes in theater are articulated around the conception of presence or, rather, the making of presence. What might sound like an abstraction in the theologians' opinions about demons inhabiting the humans' bodies is materialized in mystery plays. Props like the cannon and the other *secrets* [machines, or special effects], together with the performing body of the actors, confer materiality and hence credibility, to otherwise rather abstract notions.

The mimesis that mystery plays propose is, however, not simply a representation of a common scenario of a possessed person healed by an exorcism. Indeed, more than representation, mimesis can be interpreted as presence. I follow Michael Taussig's definition of mimesis here, which is based on James Frazer's concept of sympathetic/imitative magic. In this perspective, the copy and, additionally, any mimetic/representational act "affect the original to such a degree that the representation shares in or acquires the properties of the represented."[25] Thus a copy is not just a copy, a simple signifier arbitrarily connected to its signified. Rather, in this logic, the referent and the sign are intrinsically connected in the sense that the representation extracts the characteristics of the original and, hence, acquires its power and aura. Similarly, the devils that are eliminated from possessed people's bodies are not effigies standing for an abstract concept, but become live entities whose presence makes their whole trajectory within the human bodily boundaries believable. In other words, it is precisely within this framework of theater, as an aesthetic territory composed of presence, materiality, and reality over invisibility, abstraction, and illusion, that demonic possession is reenacted.

The demonically possessed subjects perform in this regime of demonic materiality. Indeed, for the theatrical demoniac, demons are a vivid presence and an exterior entity that violently enrapture their bodily boundaries. The possessed in theater declare that the devil is around them and that they can palpably feel its presence. Fleurie in *Mystère de saint Remi* overtly expresses her seeing the demon: "Veez le ci, je y vois" ["Look at it (the devil), I can see it there"].[26] The same happens to the *fille demoniacle* [possessed girl] in the passion plays, who states that she actually sees the devil: "je voy tous les dyables en l'air" ["I can see all the devils in the air"]; "j'ay veu Lucifer et Sathan" ["I saw Lucifer and Satan"].[27] The devil is therefore not simply an exterior presence but also an entity that leaves visible traces that can be deciphered and heard by both the audience and the demoniac himself or herself. Indeed, in the mystery plays, the possessed does exhibit agency that allows him or her to narrate what it effectively means to be possessed by the devil. The possessed refer to their condition in terms of *destresse* [distress], *tristesse* [sadness], *merencholie* [melancholia], *maladie* [illness], and *angoisse* [anguish]. Fleurie, for instance, in *Mystère de saint Remi*, conveys her clear sense of suffering, mobilizing the vocabulary of disgust in addition to that of pain:

> Que l'ennemi soit absens
> Et mis hors
> De mon corps
> Car il est puant et ors
>
> . . . .
>
> Ce larron me vient agrapper,
> Ce larron, ce faulx ennemi.
> N'attendez plus jour ni demi,
> Laissiez moy coucher, haro, lasse!
> Le cuer me part, le col me quasse![28]

[May the enemy be absent and taken outside my body for it is smelly and dirty .
. . . This rascal has just grabbed me, this crook, this perfidious enemy. Wait no
longer, let me go to sleep, ah, let me go! I am dying, I am choking!]

The demoniac's discourse then acquires an evaluative dimension, and the
words signifying disgust that are associated with the devil are crucial in helping the demoniac pondering the physiological and psychological effects that
the proximity of demons produces upon her personality. By pondering, I do
not mean a rational, controlled, reflexive act, but a middle ground in which
the possessed expresses a certain degree of consciousness—he or she knows
that demons attacked—combined with an experience of epidermic intensity.

Moreover, the performance of the possessed in mystery plays equally involves an overt access to the rationale of gestures that the demoniac makes
and to the speech that he or she actually utters. In other words, thanks to
theater's capacity for unmediated connections with the spectator, we understand the whole mechanics of possession in its minute details and thus
empathize with the victims' mental and physiological reactions. For instance,
Fleurie in *Mystère de saint Remi* states that the demon made her body move
backward and forward, provoking a series of disruptive movements and
gestures: "Avant, avant! Ariere, ariere! / Esgratiner, mordre, estrangler, /
Trembler, haro, haro, trembler!" ["In front, in front! In the back, in the
back! / Scratch, bite, choke, / tremble, help, help, tremble!"].[29] The scenario
of possession in mystery plays appears, then, as a framework in which the
demoniac is not simply shut down and being spoken for, as de Certeau put
it, by both the devil and the exorcists.[30] Surely these two instances exist,
but the demoniacs themselves occupy the centrality of the phenomenon of
possession. Mystery plays construct a scaffold in which the patterned bodily
movements, the psychological reactions, the feelings of disgust and pain that
the possessed experience are displayed overtly. In other words, instead of
having access to a normative set of behavioral and mental features that are
predicated upon what the a demoniac should look like, mystery plays offer
us access to a zone where the persona of the demoniac is being formed in
terms of gestures, of speech, of psychosomatic reactions. Fleurie, Floquart,
the Canaanite woman's daughter, and other demoniacs perform their condition in such a way that possession is no longer "pathological." To a great
extent, mystery plays offer the playground for what a cultural theorist such
as Ann Cvetkovich has called "the depathologization of negative feelings."[31]
Indeed, for these characters, possession is not simply an inferior condition
with which they need to live and about which they must feel ashamed. The
depathologization occurs precisely through the agential capacity that the

mystery plays allow to demoniacs to be able to ponder on all the complexities and consequences of their state.

In the rest of this chapter, I analyze how the performance of the theater demoniac, consisting of verbal speeches and of bodily movements, alludes to the flux of events in daily life, to physical and mental suffering, or to a vocabulary that the demoniac uses, but is displaced within the possession narratives. As already mentioned in my introduction, I do not employ the term "displacement" as an indirect way of saying direct influence in a positivist fashion. Thus, I do not use it in the sense of capturing the exact circumstances and date in which particular mystery plays entered into contact with particular possession narratives. The two genres do share common channels of dissemination, such as printing. Moreover, there are temporal overlaps between the two genres. For instance, Jean Michel's *Mystère de la Passion* circulated in numerous printed editions between 1486 and 1560s.[32] One of the earliest possession narratives, Adrien de Montalembert's *La merveilleuse histoire de l'esperit* [*The Marvelous Story of the Spirit*], was published as early as 1528. Nevertheless, despite these commonalities, a positivist approach would not explain how we could acknowledge that the scenarios of possession like those that I have just analyzed are recognizable in possession narratives. A fruitful way to make sense of the dynamics of this type of metamorphosis, I think, would employ Joseph Roach's notion of "genealogy of performance," which

> draw(s) on the idea of expressive movements as mnemonic reserves, including patterned movements made and remembered by bodies, residual movements retained implicitly in images or words (or in the silences between them), and imaginary movements dreamed in minds, not prior to language but constitutive of it, a psychic rehearsal for physical actions drawn from a repertoire that culture provides.[33]

Mystery plays are also a territory that elicits these "mnemonic reserves." They display images, words, and behavioral patterns in connection to demonic possession that are "memorized" and then reproduced. That is to say, they float, become ingrained in public behavior, and once "remembered," are culturally retransmitted and thus reinvented and displaced. How does this process take place?

The Demoniac in the *Histoires véritables*: The Case of Nicole Obry

The genre of possession narratives emerges out of both secular and ecclesiastic anxieties concerning the necessity of discerning spirits, fighting off religious skepticism, and reinforcing the strength of Catholic faith, especially in the context of Protestant attacks.[34] Scholars dealing with the spiritual movements of the sixteenth century have pointed out that during this period Catholic representatives would feel the need to document cases of demonic possession closely, which subsequently led to the emergence of a new style of writing about this phenomenon.[35] Moshe Sluhovsky underscores that this tendency on the part of Catholic representatives was motivated by two factors. First, anxieties concerning the identity of the spirits, whether they were of demonic or of divine origin, played an important role in designing this type of narrative.

Second, the development of the printing press facilitated the dissemination of such stories on demonic possession. We witness what Sluhovsky calls "sensational printed records of possession and exorcism" that focus on the veracity of the possession story that they narrate.[36] The titles of these publications provide precise details about the exact location and the date on which possession and exorcism took place. Such is the case with Jean Boulaese's *Manuel de l'admirable victoire du corps de Dieu sur l'esprit maling Beelzebub* (1575) [*Manual of the Admirable Victory of the Lord's Body over the Malign Spirit Beelzebub*], Michel Marescot, *Discours veritable sur le faict de Marthe Brossier, pretendue demoniaque* (1599) [*The True Story of the Case of Marthe Brossier, a So-Called Demoniac*] and François Buisseret, *Histoire admirable et veritable des choses advenues a l'endroict d'une religieuse* (1586) [*The Admirable and True Story of What Happened in a Convent to a Nun*].[37]

Among these titles, Boulaese's *Manuel* exerted a great deal of influence on the genre, also being used as propaganda material against Protestants.[38] Its central character is Nicole Obry of Vervins, from the diocese of Laon, a region in northeastern France. Nicole, sixteen and recently married, was allegedly mesmerized by the spirit of her dead grandfather, Joachim Vuillot. The spirit, dressed all in white, appeared to her when she was praying at her grandfather's tomb on a Saturday in November 1565. Scared by this incident, she went home, after which, during the night, the spirit took possession of her body. Subsequently, she felt both physically and mentally sick and was taken by her in-laws to see a number of local priests in order to be exorcised. Despite their efforts, they were not successful in healing her and sought help from a Dominican priest, Pierre de la Motte. He performed a series of exorcisms in Vervins that were only partially effective. At the order of Beelzebub, one of the thirty demons inside Nicole, in 1566 she was taken to Laon to be healed by the Bishop of Laon, Jean de Bours. A scaffold was built in the Cathedral of Laon, where the crowd of about twenty thousand people could see how the bishop exorcised Nicole. Boulaese was a theologian, Hebraist, director of the Collège de Montaigu in Paris, and last but not least, a witness himself at some of the exorcisms of 1566.[39] In the same year, on the occasion of the royal visit, he published a pamphlet in various languages—French, German, Spanish, Italian, and Latin—titled *Le miracle de Laon en Lannoys*,[40] which he dedicated to the king of Spain, and another version to the pope.[41] During the same period, Boulaese collaborated with Guillaume Postel,[42] who published his account about Laon in Latin with the same printer (Pierre Lombard) in Cambray.[43] In 1569, Boulaese compiled a detailed narrative of the Laon miracle under the title *Manuel de l'admirable victoire du corps de Dieu sur l'esprit maling Beelzebub*, which he managed to publish only in 1575 in Liège. The *Manuel*, a three-hundred-page narrative, represents the core of Nicole Obry's story. In 1578, Boulaese incorporated the *Manuel* into an even larger narrative about the events in Laon, under the title *Le thresor et entiere histoire de la triomphante victoire du corps de Dieu sur l'esprit maling Beelzebub, obtenuë à Laon l'an mil cinq cens soixante six* [*The Treasure and the Entire History of the Triumphant Victory of the Lord's Body over the Malign Spirit Beelzebub, Obtained in Laon in the Year 1566*].[44] In the *Thresor*, in addition to the *Manuel*, Boulaese also included existing documents and minutes,[45] as well as the eyewitness testimonies of a canon, Nicolas Despinoys, and of the royal notary, Guillaume Gorret.[46] Boulaese published his *Thresor* at a printer's shop specializing in Catholic propaganda, namely that of Nicolas Chesneau,[47] having obtained the permission of King Charles IX.[48]

On a formal level, the resemblance of the *Manuel* to theatrical forms is quite evident. Boulaese himself explains the reason for which he wrote his narrative using terms from the vocabulary of theater. In his view, the audience that witnessed Nicole Obry's numerous exorcisms "ont esté spectateurs des choses passées, tant à Vreuin, qu'aillieurs hors ceste ville de Laon" ["were spectators of things that happened both in Vervins and somewhere else outside this city of Laon"].[49] Moreover, the idea of spectatorship is not just a simple rhetorical device, but deeply informs Boulaese's enterprise. In this sense, the possessed and the exorcisms inflicted upon them are meant to be seen and heard. The identity of the possessed is dependent on the public gaze, which explains the rationale for which Nicole Obry's exorcist had a scaffold built.

In Nicole's case, the scaffold in the cathedral of Laon was just one of the many instances when the possessed were displayed in public. Nicole was very often captured in the act of being gazed at, whether by ecclesiastical, medical, or royal officials or by simple folks from the crowd. Indeed, in Boulaese's description of her case, there is always an implied theatricality—an aesthetics of vision meant to construe her diagnostic and, hence, her identity as a demoniac. Thus, Nicole was quite often portrayed as being carried to church, exhibited on a small bed, or on a scaffold either inside the church or outside it: "[E]lle estoit portée à l'Eglise environ la fin de la grand Messe, et posée sur l'eschaffault. . . . [S]elon la coustume fut elle apportée sus son bas eschafaut, au pied de la chaire du Predicateur. . . . [I]l (Despynoys) la tira avec son lict en tel estat qu'elle estoit, et la meist sur une table, pour la y porter" ["She was carried to church toward the end of the High Mass and placed on the scaffold. . . . According to the custom she was brought on her small scaffold, at the foot of the Preacher's pulpit. . . . He (Despynoys) pulled her with her bed in the state she was and put her on a table to carry her there (to the procession)"].[50] Nicole's persona revolves around the notion of the *theatron*[51] designating a place for seeing. Her own ontological status, which is reduced to a simple body, is created, assessed, and contested within the space of "theater." In fact, Nicole Obry, the possessed, cannot be imagined outside her exhibition in the public space.

In this sense, Boulaese becomes very precise in describing the reactions that her presence engenders when she is being gazed at in the open: "Le peuple d'autre costé esmerveillé, estonné, et affrayé de la veoir et ouir ainsi horriblement mugler cryoit, voire les uns avec grosses larmes, redoublans Iesus misericorde!" ["On the other side, the crowd, marveled, astounded, and scared at seeing and hearing her squealing horribly, was crying, some people with big tears, imploring Jesus's pity"].[52] Her condition as a possessed figure therefore provokes horror, sympathy, and, most important for someone like Boulaese, edification and the concomitant strengthening of Catholic doctrine.

Moreover, as de Certeau notes, the body of the possessed becomes a theater in which the theologians and/or doctors inquire, observe, approve, or disapprove, and the devil, speaking through the possessed person's mouth, responds to or disobeys them.[53] Nicole is also in a similar situation. During the innumerable scenes of exorcism, the devils that possess her, mainly Beelzebub, Astaroth, and Cerberus, obey or revolt against the theological authorities. Her body thus represents an open stage where various authorities—human, demonic, secular, ecclesiastical, Catholic, and/or Huguenot—inscribe their idiom of power. Possession is precisely this anomaly that becomes theatricalized and, in this sense, de Certeau's assertion that horror is transformed into spectacle is confirmed.[54] The horrific spectrum of the possessed body is de facto that unrepresentable element that is exhibited, assessed, felt, examined, carried out in the public space, and, ultimately, inflicted on everybody's gaze.

Doctors are probably those who are most keen in transforming the grotesque of the possession scenes into an object of study with the alleged purpose of healing that body. Whether they are Huguenots or Catholics, they need to palpably encounter Nicole who, for them, is a body that acquires materiality once it is looked at. The medical gaze is just another way of inflicting violence by trying to unmake what the demonic element made, which in turn unmade the initial "human" nature of Nicole. In other words, Nicole is doubly tortured: by demons and by doctors.

In her book about the tortured body, Elaine Scarry argues that in the process of torture, the world is unmade: what is created is reduced to the sheer matter, a form of nothingness that exists in the moment before matter's inception as a recognizable form.[55] Similarly, after some of Nicole's exorcisms, doctors assess and alleviate her condition. But the core of their endeavor is to mark their own traces on Nicole's body, while attempting to decipher the marks that demons left on the possessed body. Tools, gestures, and artifacts meant to heal are deviated from their initial purpose and reinscribed into an economy of violence based on looking, on interpreting what lies in front of the eyes, of what is a *theatron*: "[L]e Chirurgien la lia fort estroictement pres des jonctures des bras et jambes. La frotta fort, mais principalement les deux jambes, avec gros linge chaud. Luy tira les poils des temples et autres parties, que la honte naturelle nous defend nommer autrement" ["The surgeon fastened her tightly close to the joints of the arms and feet. He rubbed her, but especially the legs, with a thick hot piece of linen. He pulled hairs out of her temples and from other parts, which shame defends us to name otherwise"].[56] Nicole's body is reduced therefore to its pure materiality. It can be pinched, rubbed, pulled. The body is important only as long as it proves something: either the power of the Eucharist, for the Catholics, or the real presence of the devil, for the Huguenots and, frequently, for Catholics as well. In other words, the body becomes a site for the production of truth. Therefore, it (the body) needs to be searched in all its parts.

Doctors are not the only ones to inscribe their gaze into a language of sovereignty. Nicole's abandoned body is equally gazed at and surveilled by other secular and religious authorities. For instance, royal counselors, army people, and lawmen are equally involved in assessing Nicole's case.[57] Thus one of the lieutenants, narrates Boulaese, "contempla la patiente" ["contemplated the patient"] and eventually, at Nicole's mother's insistence allowed the girl to receive the Eucharist.[58] Nicole's story becomes an example of how a subject in pain is created at the intersection of various discourses: medical, theological, political. Her diagnosis is always accomplished in the open, through the strict observance and "contemplation" of her body, which is nothing else but a *theatron*, a place to see.

Apart from the inherent theatricality of Boulaese's narrative, there is also a surrogated theatrical element generated, among other media, by the afterlife of mystery plays. To begin with, the devils that attack Nicole and her exorcists, together with the way in which they are evicted out of the human body, take us back to *Mystère de la Passion*. Indeed, the devil Astaroth is a constant presence that vexes Nicole but that, eventually, is chased out of the girl's body through exorcism. At the end of the fourth chapter of his *Manuel*, Boulaese accounts for this event in a type of language reminiscent of the mystery plays: "Nicole fut delivrée de sa dureté . . . et Astaroth fut chassé comme on le cogneut par les effectz d'iceluy en la pauvre creature, et signe donné ce matin du Dimanche vingt septisieme jour de Janvier" ["Nicole was healed from her tightness (of her body) . . . and Astaroth was chased out as one could see from the effects that he had on the pour soul (Nicole) and after the sign that was given this Sunday morning, the 27th day of January"].[59] We remember the numerous stage directions from various passion plays in which props render devils visible and material, allowing the audience to see how they are actually located underneath. We notice a strikingly similar modality in which the two types of texts converge to "stage" the cleansing of the human body from the presence of Astaroth/Fergalus (called Astaroth in Jean Michel's version as well). Nevertheless, the theatrical scenario that the possession narrative is reminiscent of produces different effects when it percolates into Boulaese's narrative.

We saw above that mystery plays construe the idea of the demonic by making use of the rhetorical strategies of mimesis, in Taussig's sense—that is, as imitation that produces the presence of the imitated object. Fergalus/Astaroth becomes a real presence that through special effects colonizes the visual imaginary of the audience. In exchange, Boulaese's account elaborates on the structure of the stage directions. The effects are those of the rationalization of the demonic phenomenon. Thus the time framework (Sunday morning, January 27, 1566) situates us on the territory of forensic investigation. The devil was eradicated on that particular day, which means that the devil was physically in Nicole's body. In turn, it (the devil) can actually be defeated, and the sacraments are crucial in this process.

Both mystery plays and the possession narrative, therefore, aim at the same thing: to unwrite the demonic element from the human body. But the effects produced are different: Boulaese's account inscribes the phenomenon of possession in the area of control and surveillance. By contrast, mystery plays reinforce the idea of individual agency: by means of special effects the devil as presence is propagated within the space of the stage, and everyone can perceive it. What also exits the contours of theater is Nicole's representation as possessed. Just like the demoniac girl in Arnoul Gréban and Jean Michel's plays, who described what was happening to them while the devil was attacking, Nicole does the same thing. On her bed or scaffold, always in the presence of a person representing the law (whether religious, secular, or medical), Nicole exhibits both the mental and physical reactions triggered by the immersion of devils within her.

Similar to demoniacs in mystery plays, Nicole declares the symptoms she has when the devil is taking possession of her: "[P]arce que lors elle voyoit, comme un homme noir, maigre et fort laid ayant de grand dentz, les yeulx grandz et enfoncez en la teste et de granz mains seiches, duquel elle se disoit estre tenue et estranglée et suffoquée" ["Because she was seeing how a black man, thin and very ugly having big teeth, big eyes pushed in the head and with big dry hands, with which she felt herself being held and choked and suffocated"].⁶⁰ We see how Nicole's testimony contains standard elements from the medieval discourse of possession: the devil resides in the throat. But the way in which this detail is appropriated in the narrative comes from the mediation of mystery plays that fashioned models of suffering and physical pain. The discourse that Nicole is employing to make sense of her own suffering caused by the attacks of devils is routed through dialogues, snapshots from mystery plays. Just like Floquart or other demoniacs, Nicole becomes aware of the destructive effects that the demonic presence has upon her and speaks up, almost visualizing the moment of her death: "'Je di [sic] adieu à Monsieur l'Evesque, et à vous tous. Je me meurs. Priez Dieu pour moy. Je m'en vois [sic] mourir.' Et puis inclina la teste, et ne parla plus. Elle demeura comme morte sans pouls ne sentiment" ["'I say good-bye to the Bishop, and to all of you. I am dying. Pray to God for me. I am going to die.' Then she lowered her head and stopped speaking. She was like dead with neither pulse nor sensation"].⁶¹

Mystery plays, nevertheless, allow more room to the demoniac to understand his or her condition and to construe the source of his or her pain, namely the devil. In exchange, Boulaese's narrative confiscates the autonomy that the possessed had in theater and channels it into the web of political, religious, and medical complexities that the concept of possession enters in the sixteenth century. Nicole becomes a vessel that reproduces the demonic idiom. She needs to repeat whatever the devil tells her. In this sense, her humanity is challenged and needs to be restored through a re-Christianization, hence, reeducation of her persona within the spirit of Catholicism. Nevertheless, Boulaese remains tributary to a model of behavior—the theatrical one—that offers recognizable gestural and discursive patterns by means of which one can qualify a person as possessed.

Such a conceptual schema is evident when Boulaese refers to Nicole's behavior as possessed in the public space. For instance, during a procession, she is dancing and uttering a series of interjections performed by similar characters in the mystery plays: "Car comme la Demoniacle en la procession baguenauldant, caquetant, chantant, siflant, huppant hou hou, ha ha, he he, he, disoit: Ce n'est pas ce que l'on pense: J'ay gaigné un jour: aussi de vray l'experience le demonstra" ["As during the procession the Possessed behaving frivolously, prattling, singing, whistling, shrieking hou hou, ha ha, he, he, she was saying: It is not what you think: I have gained one day; the real event will show it, too"].[62] In mystery plays, the demoniacs' "irrational" behavior and discourse are a prolongation of their own self, a territory marked by their inner thoughts and personal fragments of reality materialized as snapshots. From this fragment we notice that Nicole's movements as possessed and her apparently incoherent speech are similar yet distinct from those of the possessed people present in the mystery plays. Indeed, Nicole is depossessed of her identity as possessed. Her discourse does not belong to herself, but is part of a binomial composed, on the one hand, of salient figures of Christianity such as Jesus, and on the other, of the devil. In other words, she speaks and behaves like a possessed exhibiting the impossibility of gripping with reality. Yet this is just a false incapacity, because she is integrated within a rational schema in which Christianity (more specifically Catholicism) triumphs over demons or other "corrupted" versions of Christians such as Huguenots.

To sum up, mystery plays leave visible material patterns of representation within the corpus of possession narratives that emerges in the sixteenth century. These theatrical productions being disseminated into the public space of the sixteenth century become part of the collective memory. In turn, Boulaese's audience, including himself, already has an image of what a possessed looks like and how she or he behaves. Yet in this endeavor, demonically possessed characters like Nicole lose the agential capacity that similar characters in theater display. Various conflicting secular and religious groups manipulate both her body and mind. We can say that with theater *representatio*, Boulaese built his case and asserted his Catholic credo, transforming Nicole from a person into a manipulated body of knowledge that triggered tremendous religious and cultural capital.

Early modern judges and exorcists who faced devils mediated them through representations in mystery plays rather than any abstract idea of "real" devils. To align with a key point made by post-structuralists, this

second-order representation structures a field of the "real." Positivist accounts of demonic possession often do not take this structuring of the "real"
by representation into account. But what does this mean for the field of early
modern French drama? First and foremost, it involves an analysis of this domain outside canonical boundaries. The old Darwinian/canonic approach, in
which certain theatrical genres have more endurance than others, presents
at least two major risks. First, early modern French theater would continue
to encompass the voice of certain canonic characters and silence the others. The pain, humiliation, and depression represented by the performance
of theatrical subjects such as Fleurie or Nicole, for instance would be lost
in favor of analyzing how certain literary genres such as the *fantastique* appeared,[63] or how classical drama replicated monarchic ideological concerns.[64]
Second, the notion of theater means much more than a series of authors and
literary periods (medieval, humanist drama, French classicism). Theater has
always been a lived experience translating an epoch's desires, obsessions,
anxieties, and modes of remembering and of forgetting. Borrowing heuristic
tools from other fields such as performance studies would show how early
modern French drama was linked to these minutiae of daily life, how different discursive and performative frameworks morph into one another. In this
chapter, I have shown how the history of somebody like Nicole, belonging
undoubtedly to a rather cruel period in French history, can be deconstructed
following the logic of "genealogies of performance" in which knowledge fil-
tered in one genre such as mystery plays is reshaped in another. Nicole's case
is not singular, however—the role of other demoniacs from "real life" await
to be reevaluated in a theatrical tradition and a historical context.

Notes

1. This chapter was assisted by a New Faculty Fellows award from the American
Council of Learned Societies, funded by the Andrew W. Mellon Foundation. I also
thank Walter Stephens and Moshe Sluhovsky for their suggestions and comments.

2. Gillian Jondorf, *French Renaissance Tragedy: The Dramatic Word* (Cambridge,
UK: Cambridge University Press, 1990), 2.

3. D. P. Walker, *Unclean Spirits: Possession and Exorcism in France and England in
the Late Sixteenth and Early Seventeenth Centuries* (Philadelphia: University of Pennsylvania Press, 1981); Irena Backus, *Le miracle de Laon: Le déraisonnable, le raisonnable,
l'apocalyptique et le politique dans les récits du "Miracle de Laon" (1566–1578)* (Paris: Vrin,
1994); Sarah Ferber, *Demonic Possession and Exorcism in Early Modern France* (London:
Routledge, 2004); Moshe Sluhovsky, *Believe Not Every Spirit: Possession, Mysticism, and
Discernment in Early Modern Catholicism* (Chicago: University of Chicago Press, 2007).

4. Sluhovsky, *Believe Not Every Spirit*, 23.

5. See Barbara B. Diefendorf, *Beneath the Cross: Catholics and Huguenots in Sixteenth-Century Paris* (New York: Oxford University Press, 1991); Denis Crouzet, *La genèse de la Réforme française, 1520–1562* (Paris: SEDES, 1996).

6. Michel de Certeau, *Possession de Loudun* (Paris: Julliard, 1970), rev. ed. 2005, 16–17.

7. Brian P. Levack, *The Devil Within: Possession and Exorcism in the Christian West* (New Haven, CT: Yale University Press, 2013), 30.

8. Jelle Koopmans, *Le théâtre des exclus au Moyen Âge: hérétiques, sorcières et marginaux* (Paris: Imago, 1997), 33.

9. Marion Closson, *L'imaginaire démoniaque en France (1550–1560)* (Geneva: Droz, 2000), 163–210, 209. For more on Rabelais's *Quart Livre* and François Villon's *diablerie*, see Gates and Meere, chapter 3.

10. Koopmans, *Le théâtre des exclus*, 34.

11. Svetlana Boym, *The Future of Nostalgia* (New York: Basic Books, 2001), 53.

12. Jean-Pierre Bordier, *Le "Jeu de la Passion": Le message chrétien et le théâtre français (XIIIe-XVIe s.)* (Paris: Honoré Champion, 1998).

13. Eustache Mercadé, *Passion d'Arras*, ed. Jules-Marie Richard (Arras: Société du Pas-de-Calais, 1893).

14. Arnoul Gréban, *Mystère de la Passion*, ed. Gaston Paris and Gaston Raynaud (Paris: F. Vieweg, 1878).

15. Jean Michel, *Mystère de la Passion*, ed. Omer Jodogone (Gembloux: J. Duculot, 1959).

16. Graham Runnalls, "Les mystères de la Passion en langue française: tentative de classement," *Romania* 114 (1996): 494–506.

17. Ibid., 491–492.

18. *Mysère de saint Remi*, ed. Jelle Koopmans (Geneva: Droz, 1997), 60.

19. Nancy Caciola, *Discerning Spirits: Divine and Demonic Possession in the Middle Ages* (Ithaca, NY: Cornell University Press, 2004).

20. Michel, *Passion*, v. 8369–8375.

21. *Saint Remi*, v. 2119–25. Otherwise indicated, all translations are mine.

22. Ibid., v. 2238.

23. "il m'en a fallu desloger" ["I needed to leave the shelter"] (Gréban, *Passion*, v. 12, 346).

24. Michel, *Passion*, 112.

25. Michael Taussig, *Mimesis and Alterity: A Particular History of the Senses* (New York: Routledge, 1993), 47–48.

26. *Saint Remi*, v. 5105.

27. Michel, *Passion*, v. 8043, 8156.

28. *Saint Remi*, v. 6299–6302, 6323–27.

29. Ibid., v. 5166–68.

30. Michel de Certeau, *L'écriture de l'histoire* (Paris: Gallimard, 1975), 249–73.

31. Ann Cvetkovich, *Depression: A Public Feeling* (Durham, NC: Duke University Press, 2012), 5.

32. Graham Runnalls, *Les mystères français imprimés: Une étude sur les rapports entre le théâtre religieux et l'imprimerie à la fin du Moyen Âge* (Paris: Honoré Champion, 1999), 173.

33. Joseph Roach, *Cities of the Dead: Circum-Atlantic Performance* (New York: Columbia University Press, 1996), 26.

34. For the question of skepticism in sixteenth-century Catholic thought and practices see Walter Stephens, *Demon Lovers: Witchcraft, Sex, and the Crisis of Belief* (Chicago: University of Chicago Press, 2002) and Ferber, *Demonic Possession*.

35. Walker, *Unclean Spirits*; Backus, *Le Miracle de Laon*; Ferber, *Demonic Possession*; Sluhovsky, *Believe Not Every Spirit*.

36. Sluhovsky, *Believe Not Every Spirit*, 23.

37. For an exhaustive list of possession narratives see Closson, *L'imaginaire démoniaque*, 481–508; Ferber, *Demonic Possession*, 198–206.

38. Sluhovsky, *Believe Not Every Spirit*, 34–35.

39. For a full account of his life and activities, see Backus, *Le miracle de Laon*, 55–82.

40. The full title is *Le miracle de Laon en Launoys representé au vif et escript en latin, françoys, italien, espagnol et allemant* (Cambray: Pierre Lombard, 1566).

41. Ferber, *Demonic Possession*, 35.

42. Postel's title is *De summopere consyderando miraculo victoriae corporis Christi, quod Lauduni contigit 1566 a creatione mundi anno deque eius fructu Opusculum* (Cambray: Pierre Lombard, 1566).

43. Backus, *Le miracle de Laon*, 12; Ferber, *Demonic Possession*, 35.

44. The full title is *Le thresor et entiere histoire de la triomphante victoire du corps de Dieu sur l'esprit maling Beelzebub, obtenuë à Laon l'an mil cinq cens soixante six . . . recueillie des œuvres et actes publics cy apres specifiez et de mot à mot entièrement couchez, et par ce notoire, par les heretiques impugnee, et publiquement aueree par la veüe, l'oyë et le toucher de plus de cent cinquante mil personnes, et selon la foy et selon le fait de double lettre patente et de double seel public authentiques, comme vray instrument de foy publique, auquel on croira en tout jugement. Ainsi presentee au Pape, au Roy, au Chancelier de France, et au premier Président, et selon le vouloir d'iceux faicte imprimer, Par Jehan Boulaese Prebstre, professeur des sainctes Lettres Hebraïques* (Paris: Nicolas Chesneau, 1578).

45. Backus, *Le miracle de Laon*, 57.

46. Ferber, *Demonic Possession*, 35.

47. For his printing activities in the context of Huguenot-Catholic conflict see Luc Racaut, *Hatred in Print: Catholic Propaganda and Protestant Identity during the French Wars of Religion* (Aldershot, UK: Ashgate, 2002), 38–51.

48. Backus, *Le miracle de Laon*, 71.

49. Boulaese, *Le manuel de l'admirable victoire du corps de Dieu sur l'esprit maling Beelzebub* (Paris: Denis Duval, 1575).

50. Ibid., 40, 82, 273.

51. From which the modern word "theater" derives. See Carol Symes, *A Common Stage: Theater and Public Life in Medieval Arras* (Ithaca, NY: Cornell University Press, 2007), 2.

52. Boulaese, *Manuel*, 255.

53. de Certeau, *Possession*.

54. Ibid.

55. Elaine Scarry, *The Body in Pain: The Making and Unmaking of the World* (New York: Oxford University Press, 1985).

56. Boulaese, *Manuel*, 133.

57. Ibid.: "le Doyen, le Lieutenant, et plusieurs autres notables personages s'en allerent" ["the dean, the lieutenant, and several other official characters left]".

58. Ibid., 134.

59. Ibid., 136.

60. Ibid., 227–28.

61. Ibid., 277.

62. Ibid., 231.

63. See Closson, *L'imaginaire demoniaque*.

64. Mitchell Greenberg, *Baroque Bodies: Psychoanalysis and the Culture of French Absolutism* (Ithaca, NY: Cornell University Press, 2001).

CHAPTER TWO

⁓

Abraham sacrifiant
and the End of Ethics

John D. Lyons

Abraham sacrifiant (1550) is an original and ambitious work at the boundaries of humanism and the Protestant Reformation. Its author, Théodore de Bèze (or Theodore Beza), was a widely respected scholar of ancient languages in France before his conversion to the reformed religion and his emigration to Geneva, in 1548. It was there, two years later, that he published his only dramatic work, which was translated into English in 1577 as *A Tragedie of Abrahams Sacrifice*[1] and into Latin in 1599 as *Abrahamus Sacrificans*.[2] The play can be seen as a turning point in Bèze's own thought, as he moved away from classical humanism toward a theocratic absolutism, and the play, which "connut un vif succès chez les protestants jusqu'à la fin du XVIe siècle" ["was a great success with Protestants up until the end of the sixteenth century"],[3] can be read as an apology for the abrogation of all human law in favor of divinely ordained homicide.

As a playwright, working on the basis of the very succinct story of what is known in the Jewish tradition as the *akedah* [binding], Bèze built into his text suspense and depth of character. These two dramaturgic efforts come together in a long, deliberative passage, a quasi-monologue by Abraham, that is entirely Bèze's invention and is without foundation in Genesis 22. To see how important this moment of deliberation is, we need only consider that it occupies close to a fifth of the play (17.5 percent of 701 verses). The play is structured in a way that makes this passage stand out, but the structure is one that readers accustomed to seventeenth-century, five-act tragedies may have some initial difficulty perceiving.[4]

Bèze modulates the emotional tone of moments in the story to promote suspense.[5] The exposition correspondingly serves not only to provide background information (a lesson in biblical history), but also to establish a confident and happy starting point. Sara and Abraham rehearse Abraham's wanderings, his discovery of the true God, and the covenant with God. This crescendo of confidence in God's benevolence peaks just before the first of the angel's two appearances. The protagonist has just declared, "Que Dieu jamais ne se fâche / De m'aider, pourquoi je ne tâche / A ne me fâcher point aussi / De reconnaître sa merci. . . ." ["That seeing God is never tyrde / In helping me, yea undezyrde: / I also likewise doe not streyne / My selfe, unweerie to remain / In dew and trew acknowledgment, / Of his great mercie to me sent. . . ."].[6] Against this peaceful confidence, the angel's call in v. 282 marks a brutal turning point. Within a few verses Abraham is given the command to burn his son, a command that Abraham immediately accepts: "Brûler! Brûler! Je le ferai" ["burne him! burne him! wel I wil do so"].[7]

This moment of sudden and horrifying command and even more startling and terrifying acquiescence is followed by a long period of numb resignation. Abraham shares the news of the angel's command offstage with Sara. They reappear ("Abraham sortant avec Sara" ["Abraham coming out with Sara"]) as Abraham is insisting that once God has ordered something, one must obey without any hesitation, "Sans étriver aucunement" ["Without resisting at all"].[8] Sara makes a small number of relatively subdued quibbles, the strongest of which is simply the announcement that she finds the command distressing: "Je vous prie ne vous ébahir, / Si le cas bien fâcheux je trouve" ["But yit I pray you thinke not straunge, that I / Doe take this matter somewhat heavily"].[9] Otherwise she only points out that traveling to the designated place to offer the sacrifice will be dangerous, that it would be better to kill Isaac right where they are, and that if Isaac is dead they will be in a difficult position ("S'il meurt, nous voilà demeurés" ["If he should dye, then farewel our good dayes"]).[10]

Two "pauses" span the time leading to the expected killing. The first "pause" marks the end of the three days that it takes Abraham and his escort of shepherds to reach the designated place, where Isaac takes up the burden of the material necessary for the ceremony, with the exception of the fire and the knife, which Abraham himself carries.[11] The second "pause" indicates Abraham's and Isaac's arrival at the top of the mountain, the specific place for the sacrifice.[12] So far, Isaac has no idea how the sacrifice is going to be carried out, since, as he points out, they have brought wood, fire, and knife but no animal.

In a setup that resembles modern cinematic parallel montage, Bèze momentarily shifts the action of the play back to Sara at exactly the same moment,[13] the third day of the six that she expects Abraham to be absent,[14] three days that already seem like three years, she says. During this time, Abraham, standing apart from Isaac, plunges into a long monologic scene of deliberation.[15] This is the moment of dramatic crisis. One could even say that it is, in one sense of the term, the *only* "dramatic" moment (*OED*: "characteristic of, or appropriate to, the drama; often connoting animated action or striking presentation, as in a play"), the moment when there is apparent uncertainty of the outcome within the horizon of the play's characters and the only moment when there is conflict. Up until this point everyone agrees with everyone else. Abraham immediately agrees to kill and burn his son; Sara makes only essentially technical objections about the practicality and effect of killing Isaac; Isaac shows himself to be entirely obedient, though he does not know what awaits him. So it is only now, when the killing is imminent and all is in place—Isaac is busy piling up the wood for the burnt offering—that Abraham shows any struggle with the deed that is before him.

This is the crux of the play, and before considering what happens here, it would be good to ask what kind of play this is. Bèze himself pondered this question. He writes in the address to the readers: "Or, pour venir à l'argument que je traite, il tient de la tragédie et de la comédie, et pour cela ai-je séparé le prologue et divisé le tout en pauses à la façon des actes des comédies, sans toutefois m'y assujettir. Et pource qu'il tient plus de l'une que de l'autre, j'ai mieux aimé l'appeler tragédie" ["But to come to the matter that I have in hand, it is partly tragicall and partly comicall: and therefore I have separated the prologue, and divided the whole into pawses, after the manner of actes in comedies, howbeit without binding of myself therto. And because it holdeth more of the one then of the other: I thought best to name it a tragedie"].[16] Noteworthy first of all is that Bèze gives as his criterion for generic classification the "argument" of the play, what is sometimes called the "subject" or the "story." The close identification of story and argument is indicated by the fact that Bèze simply quotes the relevant passage from Genesis rather than constructing his own summary of the principal actions of the plot. As a result there are major differences between what the author provides as the *argument* and what he shows in the verses and stage directions of the drama itself.

From the standpoint of today's literary theory, we would say that Bèze's argument corresponds to what formalists call the *fabula* rather than the *sujet*, that is, to the events and circumstances considered to be part of the world of reference rather than to the selection and construction of those events in the literary work. The *sujet* is what the author does to represent a *fabula*, and this is the point at which Bèze's originality as a dramaturge appears, for instance, the roles he gives to Sara and to Satan, both of which are absent from Genesis 22.[17]

A second important feature of the playwright's two-sentence comment on the genre of his play is the frank declaration of arbitrariness. While Bèze perceives elements of two contrasting genres (and here he does not tell us whether he finds those elements in the Genesis story or in the play that he has made), there is more of one than the other, he says. He does not tell us what makes tragedy preponderant, and he concludes by asserting his arbitrary right, as an author, to impose a generic descriptor: "I preferred to call it. . . ." Bèze is not alone in hesitating about the boundaries of what constitutes a tragedy. One might suppose that in the following century, after the flurry of quarrels, pamphlets, treatises, and Academy decisions, there would be a consensus about generic standards, but we need only think of Rotrou's *Bélisaire* (1643)—on the title page of the first edition it is called a "tragedy," but a few pages later, between the list of dramatis personae and the first scene, it is called a "tragicomedy."[18] And of course that cornerstone of the literary canon, Corneille's *Le Cid*, was first a tragicomedy (in 1637) and then, with minor changes, a tragedy (1648).

It is difficult to fault Bèze on this matter of the genre of his drama, because *Abraham sacrifiant* is a puzzling case by any standard. If we consider only the *argument*—essentially God's order, Abraham's acceptance and implementation of that order, and the *peripeteia* of the second, contrary order from God—then the story appears to anticipate what Corneille called the "tragédie à visage découvert" ["tragedy with the face unmasked"], that is, the fourth type of tragic configuration of knowledge and action theorized by Aristotle—theorized and rejected by Aristotle, but rehabilitated in *Le Cid* according to the author of the latter.[19] We recall the schema in the *Poetics*, where it is foreseen that a killing can occur first, with full knowledge and understanding of the identity and kinship of the person killed, for example, *Medea*; second, in ignorance of this identity and kinship, which is discovered too late. Or, the third possible configuration, the mortal act may be at the last minute averted by a person "who is on the point of committing an incurable deed in ignorance" and who comes "to a recognition before he has done it."[20] And the fourth and final possibility is "the worst . . . where the agent, in full knowledge, is on the point of acting, yet fails to do so: for this is repulsive and untragic."[21]

Abraham sacrifiant belongs to this fourth configuration. Both Bèze and Corneille operate in a blind spot of Aristotle's poetics, for the Greek supposed that the only variables in play with regard to knowledge concerned kinship, or *philia*. More specifically, Aristotle focused solely on the identity of the victim or potential victim. In the case of *Abraham sacrifiant*, Bèze shows that there is another crucial category of knowledge that can bend the plot back toward Aristotle's third type, the type he preferred above all others, the just-in-time rescue. This category concerns the source of authority governing our actions toward friend and foe alike.

If we continue to focus, as Bèze does in his address to the readers, on the quality of the *argument* as justification for calling this play a tragedy, then what is implied is that not only the play, *Abraham sacrifiant*, but Genesis 22 itself, has tragic qualities. This view has been presented by Sherryll Mleynek, who finds in the *Poetics* a central emphasis on mortal violations of "natural affections."[22] For Mleynek, even though the *akedah* itself is "incomplete" in Aristotelian terms because first, the killing does not take place, and second, there is no new recognition of the intended victim, the story in Genesis 22 concerns an act that is "shocking" and "morally repulsive."[23] And this act arouses pity and fear, as those are defined by Aristotle in the *Rhetoric*: "Let fear be defined as a painful or troubled feeling caused by the impression of an imminent evil that causes destruction or pain. . . . Let pity then be a kind of pain excited by the sight of evil, deadly or painful, which befalls one who does not deserve it; an evil which one might expect to come upon himself or one of his friends, and when it seems near."[24] Mleynek goes on to argue, however, that although the *akedah* takes the form of tragedy, it "is not definable as tragedy for there is no *katharsis*, no purgation, no closure. There is, however, a saturation of pity and fear sufficient to puzzle and trouble and inspire readers with the mystery of the myth."[25] For Mleynek, this lack of a proper Aristotelian conclusion is a valuable feature of the *akedah* precisely because the inconclusiveness makes Genesis 22 an appropriate founding myth for a new religion. Fear and pity are generated but not purged. What Abraham learns is to *fear* God. The fundamental relationship between Abraham and God and between Isaac and Abraham is forever changed because there is no telling what God will ask for next. When a person knowingly and willingly undertakes to kill friend or kin, argues Mleynek, "surely there is no return to ordinary, trusting filial relations. The relationship between Abraham and Isaac is now defective, just as the relationship between God and Abraham is contaminated because the instrument of Abraham's faith is his fear of God."[26]

While this discussion concerns Genesis 22, what Bèze calls his "argument," rather than Bèze's developed play, it does show that readers other than Bèze have found reason to consider the story of the *akedah* troubling and unresolved. On the other hand, for readers of the Hebrew Bible generic clas-sification need not be a problem. "Tragedy" is not a Hebrew word and was not an Israelite concept. However, readers of Genesis who live in European cultures, including Jewish writers, find it difficult to resist the term "tragic" when describing this situation.[27] Bèze himself felt the need to classify his play and at the same time the difficulty of doing so. His formation as a human-ist brought him directly in contact, more, indeed, than most readers, with both Greek and Hebrew traditions and texts. It is the difference between his quotation of Genesis 22 and his own dramatic version with its supplementary passages that can help us see how he recasts the story as tragic.

He does this by putting into the play what, for a modern reader, is "miss-ing": the thoughts and feelings of the protagonist. Abraham finds himself required to do something that appears both evil and absurd—absurd because there seems to be no cause or goal for this killing. It is often noted that an important characteristic of tragedy is the disproportionate quality of the suffering of the protagonist. Aristotle comments upon this,[28] but translators and commentators amplify the concept of disproportion, as does Corneille: "Nous avons pitié . . . de ceux que nous voyons souffrir un malheur qu'ils ne méritent pas" ["We feel pity . . . for those whom we see suffer unhappiness that they do not deserve"].[29] However, all such reasoning about the character is based on the idea that in tragedy there is a cause that can be located in the acts of the human being who suffers. This assumption is so deeply embedded in theorization about tragedy that the belief in a cause of what happens is taken for granted and overlooked in the midst of debates about what kind of cause this might be: a moral failure, a lack of skill, a temporary distraction, etc. Bèze takes the biblical Abraham and makes him think like a man who is aware of the assumptions that undergird the tragic vision.

For the characters of Greek tragedies, there seems to be no doubt that ac-tions have consequences and that effects have causes. In the Greek tragedy that is most compared to the *akedah*, Euripides's *Iphigenia in Aulis*, it is clear that Artemis, demanding the death of Iphigenia, sought satisfaction in the pain of Agamemnon, who had offended her. In the text of Genesis 22, there is no such clear indication of God's purpose. Bèze supposes, however, that the modern viewer—the viewer of tragedy—will expect a protagonist to ask why things are happening. So the protagonist of *Abraham sacrifiant* interprets the angel's command as a punishment: "Ah, bien connais-je ouvertement / Qu'envers moi tu es courroucé! / Las, Seigneur! je t'ai offensé" ["I well per-ceive and plainly now doe find, / That thou art angrie with me in thy mind. / Alas my Lord I have offended thee"].[30] These words are Bèze's invention.

In Genesis 22 Abraham gives no interpretation whatever of God's motives or purpose. In *Abraham sacrifiant*, however, he explains for himself God's demand according to his own, human, logic. No one would make such a hideous request, such an outrageous demand, if not as punishment for a heinous crime. Likewise, later in the play, it seems to Isaac that the God of Abraham acts to be compensated for some offense, which he imputes to himself rather than to his father: "qu'ai-je fait pour mourir?" ["what deeds of mine deserve / This death"].[31] Abraham's attempt at an explanation comes after the angel's stark command, which, as represented in the play (though not in the scripture) informs the father that Isaac will be burned for God's pleasure:

> Ton fils bien aimé,
> Ton fils unique Isac nommé,
> Par toi soit mené jusqu'au lieu
> Surnommé la "Myrrhe de Dieu"[32]
> Et tout entier le brûleras
> Au mont que je te montrerai.[33]
> [Goe take thyne onely deerebeleoved sonne
> Even Isaac, and bring him to the place
> Which hight the myrrhe of God: which being done,
> Slea him in sacrifice before my face:
> And burne him whole upon a hill which
> I will shew thee there.[34]

In the text of the play Bèze does not give the name Moriah to the mountain on which the sacrifice is to take place, though the translation of Genesis 22 that he gives says "t'en va au pays de Moria et l'offre là en holocauste sur une es montagnes laquelle te dirai" ["goe into the country of Moria, and there offer him up for a burnt sacrifice upon one of the hills that I wuill sheuw thee"].[35] So the expression in quotation marks that specifies a name for the place stands out strikingly. Juxtaposed with the following verse that commands that Isaac be *entirely* burned, this expression makes it clear, in Bèze's version, that this killing and burning is done uniquely for God's pleasure. The burning corpse will smell good to God—this is Bèze's addition to the Genesis text. In the same brief speech, the angel stresses twice, as he does in the biblical text, Isaac's value to his father, both as "unique" ["onely"] and as "bien aimé" ["deerebeloved"] son. Thus, what is stressed in this message from the transcendent being is that God's pleasure will come at what could be assumed to be the expense of Abraham's intense suffering.

After Abraham's statement to the angel that he feels that he must have committed some offense, he does not utter any further comments on God's motivation or express any hesitation to sacrifice Isaac until he reaches the place of sacrifice. Here Bèze is at his most inventive, since the Abraham of Genesis makes only five brief utterances. Upon each of the two appearances of the angel, who calls out the name "Abraham," the protagonist of Genesis 22 simply says "Me voici" ["Here I am"]. And he speaks to his servants and to Isaac, first to say that he and his son will walk to the top of the mountain unaccompanied; next to respond to his son "Me voici, mon fils" ["Here I am, my son"]; and then to tell Isaac that "Dieu se pourvoira d'agneau pour l'holocauste" ["God will provide the lamb for the holocaust"]. Bèze's Abraham is far more talkative. In what seems to be an echo of Jesus withdrawing to Gethsemane to pray (Matthew 26:36), Abraham tells Isaac that he is going off by himself to pray.[36] What follows is one of the strangest deliberative scenes in the French theater, one that is difficult to classify, formally.[37] Is it a monologue or a dialogue?

Bèze had already introduced the character Satan in a very long monologue addressed to the theatrical public, in which Satan explains who he is,[38] that he dominates earth while God governs heaven,[39] and that the monk's costume that he wears, though unknown in the epoch of Abraham, will some day be widely recognized and will bring great harm to the world. Despite Bèze's education as a humanist, he borrows from the medieval theater this grotesque figure of the devil, traditionally the source of comic effects.[40] Devils made frequent appearances in Catholic passion plays. One scholar writes of the "prédominance du profane sur le sacré, marquée par l'extension du rôle des diables" ["the dominance of the profane over the sacred, as shown by the extended role of the devils"].[41] These were decidedly theatrical and comical figures, noted for their entertaining contortions, "une pratique du geste comme *gesticulatio*, attachée tradionellement à l'histrion, mais aussi à la prostituée et au diable" ["a practice of gesture as gesticulation, traditionally associated with players, but also with prostitutes and the devil"].[42] We know that the public can see and hear Satan in his monk's costume, but Abraham apparently cannot see him. He can, however, hear him, though it is not clear to what extent Abraham perceives the devil as an external entity, instead of a voice representing his own thoughts. Though Bèze is clearly using a figure from medieval mystery plays and thus seems to be rearguard or archaizing with regard to late sixteenth-century, classically inspired drama, in some ways he is also anticipating twentieth-century devices for externalizing a character's thoughts (e.g., voice-over in film, novelistic stream-of-consciousness). Whereas Corneille's characters such as Rodrigue in the *stances* (lyrical stanzas as opposed to alexandrines) of *Le Cid* take both sides of an argument as they debate in solitude, Abraham seems to be receiving conceptual impulses from Satan that his soliloquy is meant to counter.

Abraham sacrifiant thus represents Abraham's struggle against the temptation to spare his son. Addressing God, Abraham refers to this temptation as a weakness, and indeed, as a sickness: "Tu vois, hélas, tu vois ma maladie! / Tu peux tout seul guérison m'envoyer, / S'il te plaisait seulement m'octroyer / Un tout seul point que demander je n'ose" ["Thou seest, alas thou seest my wofull care. / Thou onely canst me rid of my diseaze / By graunting me (if that it might thee pleaze) / One onely thing the which I dare not crave"].[43] The stakes of this internal argument are not simply the life of Isaac, but the whole relationship between God and man. Can man judge God? Abraham denounces this deviation in himself: "Est-il raisonnable / Que moi qui suis pécheur tant misérable, / Vienne à juger les secrets jugements / De tes parfaits et très saints mandements?" ["Is it right / That I so sinfull and so wretched wight / Should fall to scanning of the judgements / Of they most perfect pure commaundements?"].[44] This internal struggle against the urgings of Satan shows that Satan represents human judgment and human values. While it seems, from a human point of view, that a man should not kill his son, this belief and the value placed on human life and on any temptation to fatherly affection that can stand in the way of a divinely ordered homicide are literally satanic in Bèze's drama. Even the idea that God is not cruel appears to be driven by Satan's influence:

ABRAHAM.   . . . tant plus j'examine
                    Ce cas ici, plus je le trouve étrange.
                    C'est quelque songe, ou bien quelque faux ange
                    Qui m'a planté ceci en la cervelle:
                    Dieu ne veut point d'offrande si cruelle.
                    Maudit-il pas Caïn n'ayant occis
                    Qu'Abel son frère? Et j'occirai mon fils!
SATAN.   Jamais, jamais![45]

[ABRAHAM.   . . . the more it is examined,
                    The more the case seemes straunge. It was perchaunce
                    Some dreame or wicked feend that at a glaunce
                    Did put this matter in my head for why,
                    So cruell offrings please not God perdye.
                    He curses Cayne for killing of his brother:
                    And shall I kill myne Isaac and none other?
SATAN.   No no. Never doe soe.][46]

Satan, in a monk's habit, does not clearly represent any specific person or order in the Catholic church, but the juxtaposition of the monkish garb with a rationalistic approach to understanding God's intentions is consonant with a condemnation of such medieval Catholic philosophers as the Dominican Thomas Aquinas and the Franciscan Duns Scotus. Abraham supposes that one can deduce God's wishes on the basis of some idea of his character (merciful) and of his dealings with mankind (consistent through time and bound by precedents), and that reason forms a basis for decisions concerning mankind's conduct both toward God and toward other human beings. Bèze's play seems to promote a much different idea, one that is consistent with what has been said about his religious doctrine: "For Beza, if we can establish that it is, in fact, God who speaks in Scripture, the individual mysteries revealed therein must be granted, regardless of how absurd they may seem to human reason."[47]

In Abraham, Bèze has portrayed a man who stifles both paternal affection and the temptation to reason. In this, the protagonist differs from heroes like Lucius Junius Brutus, a founder of the Roman republic and consul in 509 BCE who ordered and witnessed the execution of his sons Titus and Tiberius. In this case, as reported by Livy, the father saw clearly the need for his sons to die and suffered for a cause that he and all those around him understood: "All men gazed at the expression on the father's face, where they might clearly read a father's anguish, as he administered the nation's retribution."[48] And Abraham differs also from Agamemnon, to whom he is often compared, because in the case of the Achaean general, there are multiple converging reasons for killing his daughter Iphigenia.[49] Her death is, first of all, required as penalty or compensation for her father's transgression against Artemis. And Agamemnon must also, as general, appease the goddess so that the fleet can sail against Troy. In Abraham's case, on the contrary, the father is expected to act without any understanding whatever of the reason for God's demand. He speculates that God is punishing him, because this is the only logical cause that he, with human reason, can suppose, but by the end of the play he finds that this supposition was false. According to the angel, God's purpose was to demonstrate that Abraham would violate the most intense human bond if ordered to do so:

Or puis-je voir tout clairement
Quel amour tu as au Seigneur,
Puisque lui portes cet honneur
De vouloir pour le contenter
Ton fils à la mort présenter.[50]

[For now I see before mine eyes
What love thou bearst to the Lord,
And honor unto him avord (afford)
In that thou doost so willingly
Thy sonne thus offer even to dye.][51]

Since multiple passages in the play indicate that Abraham believes God to be all-powerful, there is no reason to suppose that God is in suspense to know if Abraham will obey or not. So it is not God but the protagonist who has learned something by the end of the play: that he will not function according to human laws and logic but as a tool in the hands of the divine.

Let us return to the question of what kind of play this is, the question that seems to have puzzled Bèze himself. If it is, finally, more tragic than comic, why? Is it simply because the serious character of Abraham is more important than the grimacing devil? One might argue that in the loose terms used to describe tragedy in the sixteenth century, the apparently happy ending would authorize the denomination "comic." Almost a century later, in the *Poetics*-obsessed epoch of *Le Cid*, Corneille felt called upon to justify the use of the adjective "tragic" to describe his major play on the grounds that even Aristotle permitted "happy" endings.[52] There are at least two answers to that question. The first is, simply, that Bèze fully accepted the idea that tragedy can have a "happy" ending. His education in the literature of Greek antiquity makes this supposition entirely plausible and fits the historical moment. It is probable that Bèze perceived his play as ending happily. Another answer, which is anachronistic but not necessarily less valuable, is that Bèze anticipated the tragedy of dehumanization that appears in such later plays as *Horace*.[53] On this reading, Abraham is a tragic hero precisely because he has killed himself—that is, he has purged himself of his human affections— rather than his son.

In the most general terms, Bèze's approach to making a tragedy out of Genesis 22 is first to make Abraham more human and then to show that humanity disappear. The playwright took a man without character and made him a believable human being, one who, like Agamemnon, would be horrified at the thought of killing his child. But then that human feeling is conquered, so that Abraham resists the diabolic (i.e., human) feelings of pity in order to become an obedient, unquestioning killer, the true believer of what became the "Abrahamic" religions. Having learned to kill even his own son, for no humanly apparent reason, Abraham models the ruthless killer (without "ruth"; *OED*: "the quality of being compassionate; the feeling of sorrow for another; compassion, pity") that will be so admired in such figures as Joshua, who, following similar divine instructions, defeated Jericho and "utterly destroyed all in the city, both men and women, young and old, oxen, sheep, and asses, with the edge of the sword."[54]

In Bèze's construction and then deconstruction of Abraham's character, there is an emphatic anti-ethical stance. The word *éthique* did not appear in the Academy dictionary until the fourth edition, in 1762, but it was widely used in the sixteenth century. Montaigne wrote in "Des cannibales" ["Of Cannibals"] about the moral instruction of the Americans that "toute leur science ethique ne contient que ces deux articles, de la resolution à la guerre et affection à leurs femmes" ["all their moral discipline containeth but these two articles; first an undismaied resolution to warre, then an inviolable affection to their wives"].[55] Scipion Dupleix defined *éthique* in his *Logique ou l'art de discourir et raisonner* (1607): "Ethique, c'est à dire, Morale, concernant les mœurs, du mot Ethos qui signifie mœurs" "[Ethics, that is to say, Morality, concerning conduct, from the word Ethos that means conduct"].[56] Dupleix, tutor to the son of Henri IV, conceived ethics as the pursuit of the supreme good by the use of reason. As he wrote in his *Ethique ou philosophie morale* (1610),

> Le souverain bien s'acquerant par l' exercice de la vertu Morale il sera bien à propos qu'au troisiéme livre nous commencions à traiter d'icelle. Premiere-ment donc nous monstrerons que la vertu ne nous est point innée, ains qu'elle s'acquiert par l'exercice et frequentes actions honnestes, à quoy nous adjousterons une belle deduction touchant la difference des actions vertueuses et vicieuses.[57]

> [The highest good being acquired by the practice of Moral virtue, it is entirely proper that in the third book we begin dealing with this. First we will show that virtue is not innate in us but rather than it is acquired by practice and by frequent decent actions, to which we will add a corollary concerning the dif-ference between virtuous actions and vicious ones.]

When, much later, Ralph Waldo Emerson wrote "Ethics and religion differ herein; that the one is the system of human duties commencing from man; the other, from God," he was only expressing an opposition that existed plainly in the sixteenth and seventeenth centuries.[58] The English poet William Warner wrote in his *Albions England* (1586) about the opposition between ethics, clas-sified with physics as the work of human reason, and religion:

> The pompious Prelacie of Rome, and lives lycentious thear,
> Italian Driftings, and such Sinnes to *Mandeuil* appeare,
> That then Devinitie seem'd thear for Atheisme but a Stayle,
> And wheare Religion most had boaste Religion most to fayle.
> Nor wanted thear (may now and here we wish) that did relye
> On Physickes and on Ethickes, and (O sinne) a God deny.[59]

In *Abraham sacrifiant* we can see the playwright playing with *ethos* in both rhetorical and philosophical senses. In the first sense, as "character," Bèze takes the biblical figure, a man without character, and imagines for him thoughts and feelings that are verisimilar for a man in such a situation. And then, those thoughts and feelings, which incline him to pity, are suppressed. In the philosophical sense, Bèze has shown ethics, as a creation of human reason, as the enemy of God. Given the moment of the play's creation, in 1548, one year after Henri II's decree establishing a *chambre ardente* to try suspected heretics,[60] the play may well represent dramatic encouragement for a dehumanized holy war against the country in which, as Bèze writes in the opening sentence in his address to the readers, God is persecuted.[61]

Notes

1. Théodore de Bèze, A *Tragedie of Abrahams Sacrifice*, trans. Arthur Golding (London: Thomas Vautroullier, 1577). In the main body of this chapter, I cite translations from this text, found in Malcolm W. Wallace's edition (Toronto: University of Toronto Press, 1906). In this edition, Wallace has chosen to number separately the verses of the Prologue, the play, and the Epilogue (or "Conclusion"), which explains the disparity in verse numbers between the original French and the English translation. When the sixteenth-century English could be considered unclear or ambiguous for a twenty-first-century reader, I provide my English translations in the notes. I refer only to verse numbers, as the play is not divided into acts and scenes. All other translations are mine unless otherwise noted.

2. Théodore de Bèze, *Abrahamus Sacrificans*, trans. Johann Jakob Barrensi (Geneva: Jacobus Stoer, 1599).

3. Editors' introduction to Théodore de Bèze, *Abraham sacrifiant. Tragédie française*, in *Théâtre français de la Renaissance: La tragédie à l'époque d'Henri II et de Charles IX (1550–1561)*, 1st series, vol. 1., ed. Enea Henri Balmas and Michel Dassonville (Florence; Paris: Leo S. Olschki; PUF, 1986), 13.

4. The text consists of 1,015 verses of varying lengths (but primarily ten-syllable verses), inclusive of the prologue, in which a presenter speaks directly to the audience to explain that the action staged does not take place in Lausanne but in Palestine, "ici est le pays / Des Philistins" (v. 27) ["this is the land of Palestine"] There is also an "Aux Lecteurs" ["Address to the Readers"] in which the author, writing in Lausanne, explains his theatrical and orthographic principles, and an *Argument* that consists of a quotation of the 1546 edition of the Olivétan Bible. Bèze's play is not divided into acts or scenes, but there are two *pauses* (after v. 524 [v. 484] and in the midst of v. 650 [v. 606]). In addition to the "Prologue" (v. 1–48; v. 1–54) there are three *cantiques* [songs] (of Sara and Abraham, v. 111–176 [v. 68–133], and of the *troupe* [Shepherds] v. 337–423 [v. 299–378] and 575–650 [v. 497–606]), and an epilogue (v. 973–1016; v. 1–49). The action of the play itself—exclusive of prologue and epilogue—is 923 verses long (v.49–v. 972; in the English translation v. 1–946). The exposition comprises the first 221 verses, or almost a third.

5. Bèze was representative of the rise of suspense as an aesthetic value. See on this point Terence Cave, "Towards a Pre-history of Suspense," in *Retrospectives: Essays in Literature, Poetics and Cultural History*, ed. Neil Kenny and Wes Williams (London: Legenda, 2009), 158–167.

6. Bèze, v. 277–80; Golding, v. 242–47. My translation: "That God is never tired of helping me, which is why I try never to be tired of recognizing his mercy."

7. Bèze, v. 290; Golding, v. 256. Only 415 verses later, of 701 that constitute the action of the play, does Abraham begin to think critically about this act.

8. Bèze, v. 427. The translation is mine. Golding gives a periphrastic translation: "if God will us any thing to doe / We must streyt wayes obedient be thereto" (v. 387–88).

9. Bèze, v. 430–31; Golding, v. 391–92. My translation: "Please don't be surprised if I find this very upsetting."

10. Bèze, v. 455; Golding, v. 415. My translation: "If he does die, we'll be in a quandary." The demand that Abraham kill his son was not especially unusual among Israelites: "The *mlk*-sacrifice was a rite in which children were indeed sacrificed and burned, a practice probably known and partly tolerated by the prophets of the 8th century (Isa 30:33; Mi 6:7). If there was child-sacrifice similar to the Punic customs, it must have been practised on a regular basis primarily during the 8th and 7th centuries." Edward Noort and Eibert J. C Tigchelaar, *The Sacrifice of Isaac: The Aqedah (Genesis 22) and Its Interpretations* (Leiden: Brill, 2002), 12.

11. The first *pause* appears after Bèze, v. 524; Golding, v. 484.

12. The second *pause* appears in the midst of ibid., v. 650; v. 606.

13. Ibid., v. 670–704; v. 626–58.

14. Ibid., v. 689–90; v. 637–38.

15. Ibid., v. 705–844; v. 659–791.

16. Ibid., 18; 7. My translation: "Now, as for the subject of my play, it is somewhat like a tragedy and somewhat like a comedy, and that is why I separated the prologue and divided the whole with pauses like the acts of comedies, but without being entirely systematic. And because it is more like one than the other, I preferred to call it a tragedy."

17. Johannes Willem Bertens, *Literary Theory: The Basics* (2nd ed., London· Taylor and Francis, 2008), 29.

18. Jean de Rotrou, *Bélisaire*, in *Théâtre complet*, ed. Georges Forestier and Marianne Béthery (Paris: Société des textes français modernes, 1998), 1:69–199. The play was first published in 1644.

19. Pierre Corneille, *Trois discours sur le poème dramatique* [*Three Discourses on Dramatic Poetry*] [1660], ed. Bénédicte Louvat and Marc Escola (Paris: Ed. Flammarion, 1999), 110.

20. Aristotle, *The Poetics of Aristotle : Translation and Commentary*, ed. and trans. Stephen Halliwell (Chapel Hill: University of North Carolina Press, 1987), 46.

21. Ibid.

22. Ibid., 14.1453b.

23. Sherryll Mleynek, "Abraham, Aristotle, and God: The Poetics of Sacrifice," *Journal of the American Academy of Religion* 62, no. 1 (Spring 1994): 109.

24. Aristotle, *Poetics*, 2.5.1.1282a; 2.8.1–2.1285b, as quoted by Mleynek, "Abraham, Aristotle, and God," 110.

25. Ibid., 112.

26. Ibid., 116.

27. See, for example, Ruth Kartun-Blum, "'Where Does This Wood in My Hand Come From?' The Binding of Isaac in Modern Hebrew Poetry," *Prooftexts* 8, no. 3 (September 1, 1988): 303.

28. Aristotle, *Poetics*, 13.

29. Corneille, *Trois discours*, 95.

30. Bèze, v. 296–98; Golding, v. 262–64. My translation: "Now I see clearly that you are angry toward me! Alas, Lord! I have offended you."

31. Ibid., v. 865; v. 828–29. My translation: "What have I done to deserve to die?"

32. "As to the meaning of the name, the Rabbis advanced various interpretations, e.g.: 'the teaching-place' [מורה], in allusion to the Temple as the seat of the Sanhedrin; 'the place of fear' [מורא], the Temple causing fear to the heathen; 'the place of myrrh' [מור; comp. הר המור, Cant. iv. 6], referring to the myrrh and other spices which were burned on the altar" ("Moriah," in *The Jewish Encyclopedia*, 12 vols. (New York [u.a.]: Funk and Wagnalls, 1906).

33. Bèze, v. 285–89.

34. Golding, v. 250–54. My translation: "Your well beloved son, your only son named Isaac, may he be brought by you to the place called the 'Myrrh of God' and you will burn him completely on the mountain that I will show you."

35. Bèze, "Argument du XXII Chapitre de Genese," 20; Golding, "The Argument of this Tragedy taken out of the two and twentidth chapter of Genesis," 11. My translation: "Go to the land of Moria and offer him there as a holocaust on one of the mountains that I will tell you of."

36. One important absence from Bèze's play is any typological reference that would make Isaac a prefiguration of Jesus. Thus, the literal killing of Isaac by his father is focused upon in brutal human terms, unrelieved by the thought that this is simply a metaphor for the subsequent death of Jesus.

37. Bèze, v. 705–844; Golding, v. 659–791.

38. Ibid., v. 195–270; v. 152–235.

39. "Règne le Dieu en son haut firmament, / Mais pour le moins la terre est toute à moi. . . ." (Bèze, v. 198–99) ["Reigne God aloft above the firmament, / The earth at least to me doth wholly draw. . . ."] (Golding, v. 155–56).

40. John D. Cox, *The Devil and the Sacred in English Drama, 1350–1642* (Cambridge, UK: Cambridge University Press, 2000).

41. Véronique Dominguez-Vignaud, "De la morale à l'esthétique. La danse et le rondeau dans les mystères de la Passion du XVe siècle," in *Le mal et le diable: Leurs figures à la fin du Moyen Age*, ed. Nathalie Nabert (Paris: Beauchesne, 1996), 53.

42. Ibid., 54.

43. Bèze, v. 708–11; Golding, v. 662–65. My translation: "You see, alas, you see my sickness! You alone can cure me, if it pleased you only to grant a single thing that I dare not ask."

44. Ibid., v. 721–24; v. 675–78. My translation: "Is it reasonable that I, a poor miserable sinner, undertake to judge the secret judgments of your perfect and holy commandments?"

45. Bèze, v. 728–35.

46. Golding, v. 681–89. My translation:

ABRAHAM.	The more I consider this case, the more I find it strange. It's a kind of dream, or else a false messenger that has put it in my brain. God would not wish such a cruel offering. Did he not curse Cain who only killed Abel, his brother? And I will kill my son!
SATAN.	Never, never!

47. Jeffrey Mallinson, *Faith, Reason, and Revelation in Theodore Beza: 1519–1605* (Oxford: Oxford University Press, 2003), 176.

48. This is the Brutus whose heroic act was depicted by Jacques-Louis David in 1789, *Les Licteurs rapportant à Brutus les corps de ses fils* (Louvre).

49. For instance, Philip L. Quinn, "Agamemnon and Abraham: The Tragic Dilemma of Kierkegaard's Knight of Faith," *Literature and Theology* 4, no. 2 (July 1990): 181–93.

50. Bèze, v. 944–48.

51. Golding, v. 917–21. My translation: "Now I can see clearly what love you have for the Lord, because you do him the honor of being willing, in order to please him, to expose your son to death."

52. Corneille, *Trois discours*, 70, 73–74.

53. On the importance of anachronism in proper literary interpretation see T. Cave, "Towards a Pre-history of Suspense" and John D. Lyons, "Retrospectives: Essays in Literature, Poetics and Cultural History (review)," *French Studies: A Quarterly Review* 65, no. 1 (2011): 93–94.

54. Herbert G. May and Bruce Manning Metzger, *The New Oxford Annotated Bible with the Apocrypha* (New York: Oxford University Press, 1973), 269.

55. Michel Montaigne, *Les essais*, ed. Pierre Villey and V.-L. Saulnier (Paris: Presses universitaires de France, 1965), I.31.208; Translation by John Florio, *The Essayes or Morall, Politike and Millitarie Discourses of Lord Michaell de Montaigne* (London: Val. Sims, 1603), I.30, http://www.luminarium.org/renascence-editions/montaigne/1xxx.htm, last accessed June 24, 2013. Frame's translation: "Their whole ethical science contains only these two articles: resoluteness in war and affection for their wives." *The Complete Essays of Montaigne*, trans. Donald Frame (London: Everyman's Library, 2003), I.31.187.

56. Scipion Dupleix, *La logique ou art de discourir et raisonner*, 1607 ed., Corps de philosophie de langue française (Paris: Fayard, 1984), 36.

57. Scipion Dupleix, *Ethique ou philosophie morale* (Chicago: ARTFL Electronic Edition, 2009), 33.

58. Emerson, *Nature* (Boston, 1836), vi, 72.

59. William Warner, *Albion's England* (1586), 313.

60. Literally, burning chamber. It refers to an extraordinary court of justice in Old Regime France, mainly held for the trials of heretics. R. J. Knecht, *The French Wars of Religion, 1559–1598* (London; New York: Longman, 1989), 3.

61. "Il y a environs deux ans, que Dieu m'a fait la grâce d'abandonner le pays auquel il est persécuté, pour le servir selon sa sainte volonté" (Bèze, 17) ["It is now a two yeares, since God graunted me the grace to forsake the countrie where he is persecuted, to serue him accordinge to his holy will"] (Golding, 3).

~

CHAPTER THREE

Farce, Community, and the Performativity of Violence in Rabelais's *Quart Livre*

The Chiquanous Episode

CAROLINE GATES AND MICHAEL MEERE

In Rabelais's *Quart Livre* [Fourth Book], Pantagruel and his group of friends set out on a sea voyage, on a quest for the *Dive Bouteille* [Divine Bottle] that will take them to a series of fantastic islands and past monstrous creatures.[1] From the travelers' first stop—Medamothi Island, the place of "nowhere" with its absent rulers—to their last—the island of the world sovereign Gaster, who personifies the tyrannical rule of the stomach over all other faculties—the drama of human interaction intensifies: initial portrayals of interpersonal strife culminate in final accounts of humankind's agonistic nature that sunders the fabric of society. The *Quart Livre*'s hostile social interactions coincide with scenes of physical violence, ranging from murder and war to, as in the French sense of the word, *violences*, transgressions against individuals or groups of people.[2] The travelers themselves react with increasing horror to the world that they witness. Indeed, deemed by Alice Fiola Berry to be Rabelais's "season in hell," the *Quart Livre* conveys a bleak vision of human nature and society through fabulous tales of physical consumption and social strife,[3] underscoring economic struggles, religious impasses, and territorial wars that allude to current social realities.[4]

Still, as violent as these images of conflict may be, they also take on various comic guises,[5] such as, and this is our focus here, in the Chiquanous episode (chapters 12–16).[6] These chapters are especially informative in regard to Renaissance drama, as they are the only ones in the *Quart Livre* that explicitly depict theatrical performance. Many critics have commented on the violent and comedic elements of this episode, from Mikhail Bakhtin and François Rigolot to Barbara Bowen and Lawrence Kritzman,[7] and M. A. Screech was the first to dub it a "comedy of cruelty."[8] André Tournon has abstained from providing a moralizing interpretation of these chapters, precisely to show how violence, drunkenness, and humor can be intertwined and complementary without being contradictory, though he does not discuss the episode's performative aspects in detail.[9] E. Bruce Hayes does approach the episode from the vantage point of drama, but he privileges the ethical implications of farce as a theatrical "genre" rather than the modalities of performance, concluding that "farce functions in an entirely destructive fashion, suggesting that Rabelais reevaluated its utility and arrived at a rather negative view of the genre."[10] We want to counter this view by adopting Tournon's "amoralizing" approach to the episode and to investigate how farce, or rather *jeux* ("play" or "games"), can be a creative and productive force that strengthens community and social bonds, by creating what the an-thropologist Victor Turner has called *communitas*.[11] In this chapter, then, we show how the relations between performative violence and laughter subtend the problematic complexities of communal life and "collective joy,"[12] on the one hand, and on the other, to what extent laughter and violence constitute organizing principles of identity and community, at the risk of becoming potentially detrimental to the very act of community building.

Nowhere is the concomitance of violence and laughter more present than in the 1552 version of the Chiquanous episode, the *Quart Livre*'s first extensive allegory about society.[13] In this elaborate, comic, theatrical, and most violent episode, three intercalated stories shape a wide-ranging satire that takes as its starting point a social injustice—the serving of slanderous summonses, a type of chicanery—and extends its portrayal of social antagonisms in all possible directions.[14] Each of the four narratives includes graphic depictions of vio-lence inflicted on certain characters, as a reward and as punishment (for the Chiquanous, told by the translator), in retaliation (on the part of the Seigneur de Basché, told by Panurge), as revenge (by the poet François Villon, told by Basché), and as a test (Frère Jan, told by the main narrator Alcofrybas).

Upon the travelers' arrival at Procuration Island, they first learn about the Chiquanous people from an interpreter, who associates their seem-ingly illogical occupation of getting beaten for money with a real-life one. Chiquanous—none of them has a given name, and so they are all called Chiquanous, in the singular and in the plural—resembles a legal official who serves summonses, thus satirizing legal and church officials. In this world, however, Chiquanous wants to be attacked by those to whom he delivers summonses. In fact, Chiquanous profits doubly from his occupation, for the "moine, prebstre, usurier, ou advocat" ["monk, priest, usurer, or lawyer"] hire him to deliver a summons to a nobleman and to serve a writ on him, but Chiquanous insults the gentleman to such an extent that the latter cannot help but beat the former or even throw him out the chateau windows ["le jecter par les creneaulx et fenestres de son chasteau"]. In doing this, Chiquanous is rich for months, thanks not only to the good fee from the one who requests Chiquanous's services, but also to "reparation du gentilhome aulcunefois si grande et excessive" ["damages so huge and excessive against the nobleman"] that the said nobleman may lose everything he possesses.[15] In structural terms, the Chiquanous community adheres to a mechanism of animosity and violence to provide social cohesion, livelihood, sustenance, and even wealth.

We return to the depiction of the Chiquanous community at the end of the chapter, but first we look closely at the second narrative layer, which begins when Panurge, in response to the interpreter's description of the Chiquanous, tells the story of Seigneur de Basché, who "par chascun jour estoit adjourné, cité, chiquané, à l'appétit et passetemps du gras prieur de sainct Louant" ["every day was cited, summoned, wrangled with, to the taste and for the sport of the fat prior of Saint-Louant"].[16] Basché's elaborate ruse involves staging a feigned wedding as a pretense to give crippling blows to the Chiquanous who have come to cite him, in the name of a wedding custom of giving playful taps and jabs to all present.[17] The lengthy Basché story consists of three visits by different Chiquanous to Basché's home—with the repetition of the mock wedding and murderous assaults on the Chiquanous, which intensify with each performance—before Basché is finally left alone.

Before examining the actual proceedings of each Chiquanous's visit, let us first establish the modalities of performance. Basché acts as producer, paying his "actors," giving them "cent escuz d'Or" ["a hundred gold crowns"] for the upkeep of their "beaulx accoutremens" ["finery"],[18] and providing the setting, his home; as director, as it is he who conceives of the idea and explains to his players what to do; and as actor. It is significant that Basché does not play a passive role, for it shows that the lord of the estate is involved and on an equal footing—if only for a moment—with his subordinates.[19] To complete his cast, Basché recruits three actors and a musician: his curate and wine steward, named Oudart, will perform the fake wedding; his baker, named Loyre, and his wife will play the engaged couple; and his drummer, Trudon, will play his flute and drum.[20] The porter will play a small part by opening the door to Chiquanous, leading him "courtoisement" ["courteously"] to Oudart's chambers, and ringing the bell to announce Chiquanous's arrival and to allow the actors to get ready.[21] There is also a silent group of extras who will put on "guanteletz de tous coustez" ["gauntlets on all sides"] and partake in the beating of each Chiquanous.[22]

As for costumes, Oudart will "*comparoistre*" ["*appear*"] in his "beau supellis et estolle" ["fine surplice and stole"], and Loyre and his wife will "*representer*" ["*appear*"] in his great hall in their "belles robbes nuptiales, *comme si* l'on vous fiansoit, et *comme* premierement feustez fiansez" ["fine wedding clothes, *as if* you were just getting married, *just as* you were married in the first place"].[23] In terms of props, Oudart will bring "l'eau beniste, *comme* pour les fianser" ["holy water, *as if* to marry them"], and all the actors (save Trudon, it appears) will carry "jeunes guanteletz de jouste, couvers de chevrotin" ["young jousting gauntlets covered with kid leather"].[24]

When Chiquanous arrives in the great hall and the "paroles dictes, et la mariée baisée, au son du tabour" ["words are pronounced and the bride kissed to the sound of the drum"], Basché explains to his actors how they must play "la Tragicque comedie" ["the tragic comedy"],

"vous tous baillerez l'un à l'aultre du souvenir des nopces, ce sont petitz coups de poing. Ce faisans vous n'en soupperez que mieulx. Mais quand ce viendra au Chiquanous, frappez dessus comme sus seigle verde, ne l'espargnez. Tappez, daubez, frappez, je vous en prie. . . . Donnez luy coups sans compter à tors et à travers. Celluy qui mieulx le daubera, je recongnoistray pour mieulx affectionné. N'ayez paour d'en estre reprins en justice. Je seray guarant pour tous. Telz coups seront *donnez en riant*, selon la coustume observée en toutes fiansailles."[25]

["You will each give one another momentos of the wedding: those are little punches with your fist which are reminders of wedlock. So doing, you will sup ony the better for it. But when it comes to the Chiquanous, lay it on him as green on rye, don't spare him, rack him, bash him, I beseech you. . . . Keep on striking countless times at random. The one who hits hardest I'll recognize as the one who loves me most. Don't be afraid of being taken to court for it; I'll stand warrant for you all. Such blows must be *given laughingly/fleeringly*, according to the custom observed at weddings."][26]

Several important points must be made at this juncture. First, Basché's choice of actors is significant. His wine steward and baker parallel the blood and body of Christ, and the Eucharistic associations, as Berry has pointed out, are clear from the outset.[27] Second, the wedding ceremony itself is a sacrament, a ritual, which dramatic representations were not to depict on stage.[28] If this were in fact a wedding, it would thus be highly sacrilegious. But then, is not playacting a wedding, with *real* holy water and a *real* priest in this "comedy" or "farce" equally blasphemous? Whatever the case, that

Rabelais chose to merge the Eucharistic ritual and the wedding sacrament into this play has further significance. In anthropological terms, although the wedding ceremony, as a liminal entity, is "both earnest and playful,"[29] it is nonetheless a sacred ritual that enacts changes in social status that relate directly to the everyday world. It transforms its participants, in this case, through speech acts ("les parolles dictes" ["the words pronounced"]), gestures (the bride is kissed, the exchange of punches), and sounds (the drum). The performance theorist Richard Schechner uses this very example of the wedding ceremony to illustrate the liminality of ritual: the "bachelor," to borrow Schechner's example, is transformed into the "husband," while his status as "groom" is liminal and limited to the ceremony.[30] Hence, though wedding ceremonies include playful acts, such as the friendly wedding jabs, they are not mere leisure activities. They have important social, political, and religious functions, all of which are undermined and subverted in Bas-ché's mise-en-scène [staging].

For in this play, the wedding ceremony is completely faked; it is not fulfill-ing a "liminal" role but rather a "liminoid" one.[31] "Liminoid" performances resemble ritual processes, but they are not such processes themselves. As Victor Turner claims, the "liminoid" is a commodity that can be taken or left as individual preference; such performances adhere to activities of leisure ("play") and entertainment.[32] However, as Schechner has argued, using his "efficacy-entertainment braid," "no performance is pure efficacy or pure en-tertainment."[33] *Pace* Turner, Schechner suggests that liminoid performances have "transformative" potential, both for the actors and for the spectators, even though they have no "proper" ritual function.[34] Reading Basché's com-edy in this light is useful, for it offers a theoretical framework in which to interpret the transformative power of the fake wedding and its relationship between fiction and reality, between "art" and "life."

Yet the question remains: What is *real?* This question has several answers. Keeping in mind that we are in a fictional world (i.e., Panurge is telling this tale about Basché), so nothing is actually "real" within this fictional space, we can nonetheless consider the spectacle (or performance) real, but not the wedding ceremony itself. Sure, Oudart is *really* a priest, Loyre and his wife are *really* married, and Trudon is *really* a drummer, so they (presumably) do not have to try too hard to act well, but the fact remains that they are doing *as if* ("comme," "comme si," cited above) for the purposes of the per-formance. They remain in the subjunctive, liminoid space where anything could happen. They are not *really* getting married. On the other hand, the violence is very real. The verb mood shifts in the passages cited above from a subjunctive "as if" to the indicative future ("baillerez," "soupperez" ["you will give," "you will sup"]), and especially the forceful series of imperatives ("tappez, daubez, frappez" ["don't spare him, rack him, bash him"]), highlight the make-believe nature of the spectacle and the realness of the violence inflicted on the Chiquanous.

Still, like the experimental theater of the 1980s about which Schecher writes,[35] the lines between illusion (spectacle) and reality (violence) are blurred, and only the actors and the readers know what is going on, creating dramatic irony that would, according to narrative's logic, induce laughter.[36] Basché and his players are in on the joke and joyfully, laughingly, and/or contemptuously beat up the Chiquanous. This joy and laughter, combined with violence, in turn creates and reinforces a sense of community among the players by alienating the Chiquanous and shattering their bodies. One could see this as cruel, yet the Chiquanous, we have already been told, *enjoy* being beaten, which, besides the fact that the wedding jabs are part of a sacred ritual and thus legally tolerated, exculpates Basché and his household.

Let us turn, then, to the three Chiquanous's beatings. The first Chiquanous's visit goes according to plan: Chiquanous enters Basché's estate, "le portier luy feut courtoys, le introduict honestement: joyeusement sonne la campanelle" ["the porter was courteous to him, brings him in honorably, joyfully rings the bell"].[37] At the sound of the bell, Loyre and his wife "se vestirent de leurs beaulx habillemens, comparurent en la salle faisans bonne morgue" ["dressed in their finery and, with a straight face, appeared in the hall"].[38] Meanwhile, Oudart puts on his surplice and stole; he meets Chiquanous and "le mene boyre en son office longuement" ["takes him to drink a long time in his sacristy"].[39] (It is notable that Chiquanous is presumably quite intoxicated by the time he actually arrives in the great hall.)

It is in the sacristy that the first lines of direct speech of the play occur. "'Vous ne poviez à heure venir plus oportune. Nostre maistre est en ses bonnes: nous ferons tantoust bonne chere: tout ira par escuelles: nous sommes ceans de nopces: tenez, beuvez, soyez joyeulx'" ["'You couldn't have come at a better time. Our master is in the best of moods. You'll soon have a great time, nothing will be spared; we're having a wedding in here. Here, drink up, be merry'"].[40] Oudart's words are steeped with irony and wordplay, as the blows will rain down on Chiquanous ("nothing will be spared"). Moreover, Oudart prepares the scene for Chiquanous, who of course does not know that the wedding is fake. Once everyone is ready in the great hall, Basché sends for Oudart and Chiquanous to come.

Oudart arrives, carrying the holy water, while Chiquanous makes numerous humble bows and serves the summons on Basché. The latter shows him signs of friendship—even gives him a golden coin (an *angelot*)—and asks

Chiquanous to stay for the ceremony. Then the wedding punches begin; however, our narrator Panurge tells us that

"quand ce vint au tour de Chiquanous, ilz le *festoierent* à grands coups de guan-teletz si bien, qu'il resta tout eslourdy et meurtry: un œil poché au beurre noir, huict coustes freussées, le brechet enfondré, les omoplates en quatre quartiers, la maschouere inferieure en trois loppins: et *le tout en riant.* . . . Ainsi retourne à l'Isle Bouchard Chiquanous acoustré à la Tigresque: bien toutesfois satisfaict et content du seigneur de Basché: et moyennant le secours des bons chirurgiens du pays vesquit tant que vouldrez.[41]

["when Chiquanous's turn came, they *feted* him with great blows with the gauntlets, so roundly that it left him all punchy and bruised, with one eye poached in butter sauce, eight broken ribs, his breast bone knocked in, his shoulder blades each in four corners, his lower jaw in three pieces, and *all this done laughing.* . . . So Chiquanous goes back to L'Isle Bouchart, striped like a tiger but quite satisfied and content with the lord of Basché; and with help from the good surgeons of the region he lived as long as you like."][42]

Concomitant with the rather graphic description of Chiquanous's violent beating is the lexical field of festival and joy, in both metaphorical and literal terms ("festoierent" ["feted"], "le tout en riant" ["all this done laughing"]), thus linking "play" [*jeux*] with feasting, celebration, and leisure. Moreover, Chiquanous is happy with Basché and perhaps lives for a long time thereafter, not needing, it would seem, to have to work again, since "'depuis n'en feut parlé. La memoire en expira avecques le son des cloches, lesquelles quarrilonnerent à son enterrement'" ["'there was no talk of him from then on. The memory of him expired with the sound of the bells that pealed out at his burial'"],[43] thus establishing a connection with the festive bells that welcomed him to the Basché estate and his funeral bells.

The leitmotiv of festival and banquet continues in the next chapter when Basché gathers his wife and all his people in his "jardin secret" ["private garden"] to drink wine, eat pastries, hams, fruits, and cheeses, while telling the story of François Villon.[44] We are now in a *hortus conclusus* [enclosed garden], whose biblical connotations must not go unnoticed. The term *hortus conclusus*, derived from the Vulgate Bible's Song of Solomon 4:12, has al-legorical significance, referring to King Solomon's nuptial song to his bride, which was later reinterpreted as the love and union between Christ and the church.[45] Besides the "Vineyard of Dionysos,"[46] another subtext to this gar-den that Bakhtin, Berry, and others have analyzed, this enclosed garden and its indirect references to marriage and the church link the mock wedding to the Villon story that Basché will tell. The performative space (the garden) of

Basché's narrative about Villon (diegesis), in other words, lines up with the performative space (the great hall) of drama (mimesis).

In this third, mise-en-abyme narrative layer, Basché gives a rather detailed and accurate account of the operations of theater during the fifteenth century.[47] In Saint Maixent of the Poitou region, once the roles were distributed, the players rehearsed, and the theater structure and decor prepared ["les rolles distribuez, les joueurs recollez, le theatre preparé"]—note that the *theater* is an architectural structure, not the text or performance of a play—the mayor and the aldermen granted Villon permission to put on a passion play "pour donner passetemps au peuple" ["to entertain the people"].[48] All that remained was to find the costumes. Villon, with the authorization of the mayor and the aldermen, requests a cope and a stole from Estienne Tappecoue, the sacristan of the Cordeliers of Saint Maixent, to dress up an old peasant to play the role of God. Tappecoue refuses to lend his cope and stole, on the grounds that the rules of his order forbade it.

To get revenge on Tappecoue, Villon and his actors, dressed as devils, decide to scare Tappecoue's horse and, as Villon expects, the filly drags the sacristan to his dismemberment.[49] Tappecoue's gruesome death is narrated with great effervescence. The horse's frantic movements, "multipliante en ruades" ["multiplying the kicks against him"], are buoyantly rhythmed: "au trot, à petz, à bonds, et au gualot; à ruades, fressurades, doubles pedales, et petarrades" ["at a trot, with farts, and jumps, and at a gallop, kicking up her heels, stepping high, bucking, and farting"] "par les hayes, buissons, et fossez" ["through the bushes, hedges, and ditches"]. As Tappecoue gets ripped apart, his body parts disperse in order—head, brain, arms, legs, entrails—until there is just one foot left. "[U]n long carnage" ["(O)ne long carnage"] of human remains marks the horse's sprint home.

Villon's original plan was to have a passion play performed as a leisure activity ("passetemps," cited above), in which all spectators would understand that they were attending a theatrical production with actors, props, stage settings, costumes, special effects, and so forth. When this fictional play is not possible, Villon decides to improvise another kind of spectacle, one in which only the actors are aware of the roles they are playing, while Tappecoue remains in the dark. This mirrors the Basché comedy, since Chiquanous is the only one not aware that the marriage is fake. However, what is most ridiculous (and perhaps most convincing) about the Villon story is that it is the horse that is scared—we never hear Tappecoue's reaction to the devils—and that is what causes Tappecoue's demise. Nonetheless, the slipperiness between what is fiction (i.e., the devils) and what is real (i.e., Tappecoue's death) echoes Basché's comedy, as does the fact that both Tappecoue's and the Chiquanous's deaths transform into comic spectacles.

After watching Tappecoue's heroicomic death, Villon proclaims "'Vous jourrez bien, messieurs les Diables, vous jourrez bien, je vous affie. O que vous jourrez bien. . . . O que vous jourrez bien'" ["'You'll play well, Sir Devils, you'll play well, I promise you. O how well you'll play. . . . O how well you'll play!'"].[50] These words end the Villon tale, and Basché says to his listeners: "'Ainsi (dist Basché) prevoy je mes bons amys, que vous dorenavant jouerez bien ceste tragicque farce'" ["'So,'" said Basché, "'I foresee, my good friends, that from now on you will play this tragic farce well'"].[51] The point of the Villon story, then, far from being a moralizing one, at least in Basché's eyes, is simply to serve as an exemplum about playing one's role well, to create such a perfect illusion of reality that it is difficult to tell what is real and what is not, which will essentially allow them to fool the Chiquanous and be rid of the pestilence that is threatening their community's well-being. Basché, overcome with excitement, exudes generosity and liberality, as he decides to double wages, give gifts, and open his coffers to his wife; promises not to beat his pages for three months; and so forth, as long as they play well the "tragicque farce."[52] The joy of performing and listening to stories about acts of violence have, in turn, increased and solidified the sense of community within the Basché household.

This strong social cohesion continues as the second Chiquanous—a young, tall, and thin one—arrives at the Basché estate, four days after the first, and the tone of the estate is dominated by "play": while the main actors of the farce are working—"Loyre poitrissoit sa paste, sa femme belutoit la farine. Oudard tenoit son bureau" ["Loyre was kneading his dough. His wife was sifting the flour. Oudart was minding his office"]—the others are all engaged in some sort of game: "les gentilzhomes jouoient à la paulme. Le seigneur Basché jouoit aux troys cens troys avecques sa femme. Les demoiselles jouoient aux pingres, les officiers jouoient à l'imperiale, les paiges jouoient à la mourre à belles chinquenauldes" ["the gentlemen were playing tennis. Lord Basché was playing three hundred and three with his wife. The younger ladies were playing spillikins. The officers were playing *impériale* (a card game). The pages were playing mourra with vigorous finger-snaps"].[53] It is significant that the gentlemen were playing *à la paulme*, since theater was often performed in the *jeux de paume* buildings, indoor precursors to tennis courts that were very popular during the sixteenth and seventeenth centuries; the reference is not accidental. Meanwhile, the others are playing various card games, idle, dispersed in discrete units, waiting for Chiquanous to arrive to supplant their games for a more interesting one, the "farce," which brings them all together in one collective unit of choreographed play: joyful *communitas*. Thus, upon the ringing of the bell, "tout le peuple du chasteau entendit le mystere" ["all the folk in the castle were privy to the mystery"]; they drop what they are doing to come together, making, moreover, another link to the Villon tale and intimating the violent spectacle (*mystere*) that is about to take place.[54]

Once Basché and his people hear the bell, then, they all get ready as before. This is, in Turner's nomenclature, normative *communitas*, for it is neither spontaneous nor ideological.[55] Indeed, the ephemeral, fleeting moment of togetherness is planned and organized in order to achieve a certain goal: to rid the Basché household of the Chiquanous. However, this time, the unraveling of the action is a bit different, as it is Basché himself who greets Chiquanous in the courtyard, not Oudart. Chiquanous drops to his knees and begs Basché not to take it amiss if he cites him on behalf of the fat prior ["'ne prendre en mal, si de la part du gras Prieur il le citoit'"].[56] Basché announces to him that there is a wedding, and that Chiquanous should not serve a summons on him without having a drink, and then orders Oudart to see to it that Chiquanous drinks his Quinquenais wine ["vin de Quinquenays"] and has a chance to freshen up ["refraischir"]. Again, Chiquanous drinks a lot before coming into the great hall; the wedding is performed as before (Oudart pronounces mysterious words, hands are clasped, the bride is kissed, everyone is sprinkled with holy water).

And then the jabs begin. Chiquanous gives a few to Oudart, and then Oudart, from under his surplice, pulls out his hidden gauntlet. The description of Chiquanous's beating is stark and total from here on: "Il feut si bien acoustré que le sang luy sortait par la bouche, par le nez, par les aureilles, par les oeilz . . . en fin il tombe par terre" ["He was so well attended that blood was coming out of his mouth, his nose, his ears, his eyes . . . finally he falls to the ground"]. To describe the violence, the narrator makes reference to carnival and the young men playing a game of dice: "Croyez qu'en Avignon on temps de Carneval les bacheliers oncques ne jouerent à la Raphe plus melodieusement, que feut joué sus Chiquanous" ["Believe me, even in Avignon at Carnival time, the young men never played more harmoniously at Winner-grabs-all than was played there that day at the expense of Chiquanous"].[57] The narrator (Panurge) ironically contrasts the beating of the Chiquanous with a nonviolent game of dice, just as the members of the Basché household were playing nonviolent games before he arrived. In this sense, the infliction of violence is placed on the same level with the pleasure derived from a peaceful game of cards or dice.

At the end of the story, Panurge simply says that "on luy attacha à la manche de son pourpoinct belle livrée de jaulne et verd: et le mist on sus son cheval morveulx. Entrant en l'isle Bouchard, ne sçay s'il feut bien pensé et traicté tant de sa femme, commes des Myres du pays. Depuis n'en fust parlé" ["(they) fastened to the sleeve of his doublet a fine green and yellow costume, and put him on his sniffling horse. Back in L'Isle Bouchard, I don't know whether he was well tended and treated by his wife and local doctors. There has nothing been heard from him since"].[58] Chiquanous is thus doubly humiliated—not only do they throw wine in his face while he lies on the floor, but the yellow and green are also the traditional colors worn by fools and jesters—and his outcome as well as his reaction to the violence (Did he welcome it?), as opposed to the first Chiquanous, remain unknown. Whatever the case may be, the violence has certainly intensified.

The third and final Chiquanous arrives the very next day, after having found the summons in the thin Chiquanous's pouch, but he arrives with two "Records pour sa sceureté" ["two witnesses/bailiffs for his security"].[59] This time, the Basché household is not playing but eating dinner, and the ringing of the bell "rejouit toute la famille" ["gladdened the whole family"]. The image of the banquet and fête is reintroduced, though Basché invites Chiquanous and his bailiffs to join him and his family and noblemen. At dessert, Chiquanous serves his summons on Basché while the others leave the room to get ready for the farce. Basché gives Chiquanous and the bailiffs four sun-crowns, and Trudon begins to beat his drum, indicating the beginning of the wedding show. It is again Basché who invites Chiquanous to attend the wedding, and the same process repeats, but with some stage directions made more explicit.

In this scene, the "stage" is in the middle and only Oudart is present in his priestly dress, until Loyre enters from one side and his wife [femme] from the other, both of them dressed in their wedding clothes. The entire ceremony takes place: from Oudart taking their hands and asking about their vows, to the sprinkling of holy water and the signing of the contract. While the wine, spices, and ribbons are brought out, so are the gauntlets, secretly.[60] After guzzling a big glass of wine, Chiquanous laments that there are no wedding taps ["nopces"] being given, and so he goes around the room and strikes Basché and his wife, the young ladies, and Oudart. In return, Basché's household pull out their secret gauntlets and "Chiquanous feut rompue la teste en neuf endroictz: à un des Records feut le bras droict defaucillé, à l'aultre feut demanchée la mandibule superieure, de mode qu'elle luy couvroit le menton à demy, avecques denudation de la luette, et perte insigne des dens molares, masticatoires, et canines" ["Chiquanous had his skull cracked in nine places;

one of the witnesses had his right arm banged out of joint, the other had his upper jaw dislocated, so that it half covered his chin, baring the uvula and knocking out a lot of the teeth: molars, masticators, and canines"].[61]

In the pages that follow this violent scene, Basché's actors all claim to be hurt, too, using implausible, fantastical, and imaginary words to describe their injuries. For example, Oudart alleges that one of the witnesses has "desincornifistibulé" ["disincornifistibulated"] his shoulder; Loyre complains that the de-armed witness hit him so hard on the other elbow with his fist that he has got him "tout esperruquancluzelubelouzerirelu" ["all shrdlucripplogrillachortlificated"] way down in his heel; Trudon, hiding his eye with his handkerchief, accuses them for having "lourdement morrambouzevezengouzequoquemorguatasacbacguevezinemaffressé" ["roughly nuzzlefizzledtizzledackbacksocked"] his eye; Loyre's wife simultaneously laughs and cries, making a lewd joke, claiming that Chiquanous "luy avoit trepignemampenillorifrizonoufressuré les parties honteueses" ["had treacherously swattwotchinkkinkbruisedabused her private parts"].[62]

Now, Berry claims that Chiquanous and the witnesses *fight back*, but the text does not suggest that this is the case.[63] It appears instead that Chiquanous give the friendly wedding jabs before the players strike Chiquanous and the witnesses, but there is no indication that the victims retaliate. As François Rigolot argues, moreover, Chiquanous and the witnesses are really hurt, while Basché's household *pretend* to be injured, which is conveyed in their language, Loyre's wife's manipulation of tears and laughter, and other props such as the handkerchief and the steward's sling ["escharpe"].[64] Furthermore, if we are to follow Elaine Scarry's central thesis, that "physical pain has no voice, . . . [it] does not simply resist language but actively destroys it," we notice that while Basché and his household make up words (and injuries), their mastery of language in the moment highlighting the fact that they are not really hurt at all.[65] Chiquanous and the witnesses, on the other hand, have great difficulty uttering a word: Chiquanous only speaks briefly to apologize to Trudon, offering him a large royal letters patent to patch up his drum, and to ask for forgiveness. One witness "joingnoit les mains, et tacitement luy demandoit pardon. Car parler ne povoit il" ["clasped his hands and tacitly asking his (Oudon's) pardon, for speak he could not"]. When the other witness does attempt to speak, he simply murmurs "'mon, mon, mon, vrelon, von, von': comme un Marmot" ["'My, my, fly, fie, bye, bye,' like a little monkey"], thus reverting to a prelinguistic phase.[66] The Basché household dominates, therefore, not only in the originality and creativity of language, but also by the sheer act of speaking; their effusive use of language betrays their physical injuries. On top of that, their acting is superb, as Chiquanous and the witnesses believe them, returning to L'Isle Bouchard and praising Basché's qualities, his honorable household, and putting the blame on themselves for starting the banging.[67] As a result of Basché's stratagem—the mock wedding—and the actors' mastery of playacting, inspired by the Villon story and Basché's gifts to them, order is finally restored to his home and estate: the Chiquanous no longer serve him summonses, and he is left at peace ["en repous"].[68]

In the structures of both the Basché wedding and Villon's diablerie emerges what Turner has described as a "social drama." First there is a breach of some sort: in Basché's case, it is the unjust attacks of the fat prior; for Villon, it is Tappecoue's refusal to lend his vestments for the mystery play. Then there is crisis: the Chiquanous serve Basché a summons every day, thus depleting his resources and causing instability in his home; for Villon, this means that the play will not go on. Third, there is a redressive action: Basché uses the *tragicque farce* and the fake wedding to beat the Chiquanous without getting into trouble (as the jabs after a wedding ceremony were part of the sacred rite); Villon stages his diablerie, which ends up killing Tappecoue. Finally, there is reintegration: the Chiquanous leave Basché alone and order is restored in the household; in the Villon story, with Tappecoue out of the picture, the play presumably goes on as planned.[69] What is more, theatrical performance during social dramas, according to Turner, comes out of the third stage, the "mode of redress," "which always contained at least the germ of self-reflexivity, a public way of assessing our social behavior."[70] To be sure, both Basché and Villon use fictional drama (the wedding and the diablerie) as methods to rid their communities of the crisis in order to regain peace and stability. In the Basché and Villon stories, then, the infliction of violence, tantamount to murder, resolves the conflict and causes rejoicing. Levity and comic references also embellish these violent acts, whose depictions are explicit, detailed, and unforgiving toward the victim. The Basché and Villon stories thus provide "successful" acts of violent resistance against persecution, demonstrating that violence, play, and laughter are not incompatible.

However, the violent performances are mediated through Panurge's narrative, as it is he who tells the Basché and Villon stories, which some critics have seen as a way for him to justify revenge in the Dindenault episode (chapters 6–8).[71] Thus, as constructive as this use of violence may be, its ambiguity and ambivalence is nonetheless exacerbated once his narrative ends. For it is unlikely that the reader overlooks the ethical (not moralizing) dimension of the Basché and Villon stories. Indeed, while the internal characters in the Basché and Villon stories find this violence funny, Pantagruel does not laugh, pointing instead to the brutality of these acts: "'Ceste narration, dist Pantagruel, sembleroit joyeuse, ne feust que davant nos oeilz fault la craincte de Dieu continuellement avoir'" ["'This story,' said Pantagruel, 'would seem merry, were it not that we must continually have the fear of God before our eyes'"].[72] In effect, that Villon is preparing a passion play is highly significant, especially as this is a focal point that lies at the center of these nestled narratives. The passion evokes Christ's suffering and death on the cross, a story that provides an answer to the repeated examples of persecution and revenge in this episode. Christ, the suffering subject, does not retaliate against his oppressors. Even if he must also bear his "passion" and experience society's omnipresent violence, he frees himself (or is freed) from this continuous cycle. He offers a truly exemplary model as the scape-goat figure who accepts suffering, instead of passing it on. And unlike the Chiquanous and Tappecoue, he does not represent an oppressive force. His story illustrates the inequity of persecution and the hope for peace in accor-dance with his teachings. It would appear, then, that Pantagruel's reaction suggests that the only solution to the cycle of violence, in the *real* world, is through mercy and forgiveness, even if it appears to resemble submission. Offense and reprisal are temporary forms of appeasement that may satisfy one, or many, but they perpetuate discord.

To conclude this chapter, let us turn briefly to the final depiction of the Chiquanous. Here we see the Chiquanous gathered together, allowing us to observe their community's structure. Frère Jan, to see for himself whether all these stories are true, decides to test whether the Chiquanous will accept being beaten for money. He takes out twenty sun-crowns in front of "une grande tourbe" ["great mob"] of Chiquanous people and asks who would like to be beaten in exchange.[73] They all run toward him and beg to be beaten, but Frère Jan chooses "de toute la trouppe . . . un Chiquanous à rouge muzeau: lequel on poulse de la main dextre portoit un gros et large anneau d'argent: en la palle du quel estoit enchassée une bien grande Crapauldine" ["of the whole rabble . . . one red-snouted Chiquanous, who wore on the thumb of his right hand a great broad silver ring, in the bezel of which was set quite a big toadstone"].[74] The Chiquanous are described like animals—or actors ["trouppe"]?—and Frère Jan chooses the most clown-like member of the crowd who, with his silver ring with the talisman against headaches (the toadstone), recalls the first Chiquanous to enter the Basché estate.

Frère Jan then proceeds to beat Red-Snout: "Frère Jan daubba tant et trestant Rouge muzeau, dours et ventre, braz et jambes, teste et tout, à grand coups de baston, que je le cuydois mort assommé. Puis luy bailla les vingt escuz. Et mon villain debout, ayse comme un Roy ou deux" ["Frère Jan drubbed Red-Snout so much, back and belly, arms and legs, head and all, with great blows of his stick, that I thought he was beaten to death; then he gave him twenty crowns; and here's my lout on his feet, cherry as a lark or a king or two"].[75] Red-Snout resembles several stock characters from French and Italian drama: Hellequin, the devilish figure from passion plays, thus recalling the Villon story; Harlequin, the commedia dell'arte *zanni* whose mask could be that of a pig (red snout) or a monkey, reminiscent of the third Chiquanous's visit; or a commonplace character from French farce such as the fifteenth-century Triboulet, René d'Anjou's famous fool.[76] As in many slapstick French farces and in the commedia dell'arte (known as the *comédie des masques*, which was gaining prominence in France after the 1548 performance of *La calandra* in Lyon during a royal entrance of King Henri II),[77] Red-Snout is beaten repeatedly with a stick and falls to the ground, only to jump up again as if nothing happened, ready to be beaten again.

The expected reaction from the audience, in the context of farce, would be laughter, but nobody here even grins. On the contrary, the sudden irruption of the first-person pronoun *je* [I] during this scene highlights the spectacularity of the scene, as it removes Frère Jan from an omniscient narrative mode to a subjective one, thus reinforcing the narrator Alcofrybas's shock at having witnessed such a violent beating. What is even more surprising, perhaps, is that the other Chiquanous approach Frère Jan and request to be beaten for less money, but Red-Snout cries out against them only to ask Frère Jan, turning his "face riante et joyeuse" ["smiling, joyous face"], to beat him again.[78] The other Chiquanous beg Panurge, Epistemon, and Gymnaste to beat them for fear of long fasting, but the travelers are not interested. Ultimately, then, as farcical and ridiculous as Red-Snout and his fellow Chiquanous may be at first glance, they are in actuality deprived figures, unable to evoke the slightest pity in Pantagruel's friends, who will not participate further in this exchange based on the infliction of violence.

The Chiquanous thus represent a bleak and depressing community that contrasts sharply with the joyful *communitas* shared by Basché's and Villon's entourages. Although Frère Jan's beating of Chiquanous is depicted in a dramatic and farcical way, there is no laughter. Even Red-Snout's "smiling, joyous face" seems forced, unnatural, like a mask worn as a means or ruse to make more money. This is not a leisurely game for the Chiquanous, but a dreary and oppressive way of life, as Red-Snout shows when he yells at and insults his fellow Chiquanous, threatening to cite and scratch them for taking away his business. The Chiquanous community, built and structured on physical violence, is thus not productive but destructive. After Frère Jan chooses Red-Snout, for example, the surrounding Chiquanous enviously protest that only one, Red-Snout, always gets most of the wealth.[79] In this final characterization, the Chiquanous resemble those at the bottom rung of society whose physical survival determines their choices, as they need this money to survive.

Moreover, violence is not only a way to make money (and therefore survive), but it also, performatively, in a Butlerian sense, forms their identity, as physical violence is the principal defining feature of both their individual selves and their community as a whole. Whereas Basché and Villon utilize violence temporarily as a (dramatized) tool to eradicate the evil that is threatening their well-being, the Chiquanous only know violence as an intrinsic, ontological, structural element of their culture, and by extension, of their community. They perform their role of the buffoon, desperately searching to be beaten because it is this role that their community imposes on them. There is no escape for them. And there is no joy, no play. In its farcical portrayal of the social relationship as one of violence, the Chiquanous episode signals the repressive aspects of social practices, structures, and systems, when they do not uphold the well-being of the community as a whole.[80]

In the end, the intercalated stories of Basché and Villon transpose the Chiquanous and their bizarre customs from the imaginary and alien Procuration Island to France, first to the Touraine region where the Basché story takes place, then to a Poitou town, Saint Maixent. The violence committed against the French Chiquanous and Tappecoue, the Cordelier sacristan, is woven into scenes of domestic tranquility and village life in a further amplification of the French countryside setting. In the Basché episode, there is a dinner in the garden, and the playing of cards and other household activities. The Villon episode sketches out the existence of a French village: the mayor and the townspeople eagerly anticipate the performance of Villon's passion play; Villon's actors disguised as devils make the adults laugh and the children cry. By means of these nestled narratives, France punctures through the surreal fabric of the distant, fictional voyage. The *Quart Livre* tales identify with a more recognizable world, the France that is the readers' home, and its systems of authority. Just as the mock wedding blurs with the sacred ritual and Villon's diablerie is indistinguishable from real devils running in the streets, the conflation of Procuration Island with France obscures the boundaries of the *Quart Livre*'s fictional and real realms. Ultimately, perhaps, these multiple obfuscations gesture toward the spectacle of human society, this *tragicque farce* being played out during a time of profound and often violent political, religious, and social changes taking place in mid-sixteenth-century France.

Notes

1. François Rabelais, *Quart Livre*, in *Œuvres complètes*, ed. Mireille Huchon with François Moreau (Paris: Gallimard, 1994). Rabelais, *The Fourth Book of the Heroic Deeds and Sayings of the Good Pantagruel*, in *The Complete Works of François Rabelais*, trans. Donald Frame (Berkeley: University of California Press, 1991). Quotations from the Huchon edition are abbreviated *H* followed by the page number(s). Quotations from the Frame translation are abbreviated *F* followed by the page number(s). Frame's translation is the base text, though M. A. Screech has also recently translated the text (*Gargantua and Pantagruel* [London: Penguin, 2006]), quotations from which are abbreviated *S* followed by the page number(s). All other translations are ours unless otherwise noted.

2. Guy Demerson questions why Rabelais's works, so long criticized for their obscenities, have not provoked greater reactions for their inordinate displays of violence ("Rabelais et la violence," *Europe* 757 [1992]: 67–77, 67). Gérard Defaux and Lawrence Kritzman interpret the *Quart Livre*'s violence as the literary expression of overt (Defaux) or latent (Kritzman) frustrations on the part of the author, Rabelais, who thereby asserted himself against various authorities, especially the Roman Catholic Church. Defaux, "Introduction," in *Le Quart Livre* (Paris: Livre de Poche, 1994), 58–59; *Rabelais Agonistes, Etudes Rabelaisiennes* no. 32 (Geneva: Droz, 1997), 463–79; Lawrence D. Kritzman, "Sexuality and the Political Unconscious in Rabelais' *Quart Livre*: Three Case Studies," in *The Rhetoric of Sexuality and the Literature of the French Renaissance* (Cambridge, UK: Cambridge University Press, 1991), 171–213.

3. Alice Fiola Berry, *The Charm of Catastrophe: A Study of Rabelais's "Quart Livre"* (Chapel Hill: University of North Carolina Press, 2000), 11.

4. See, among many others, Frank Lestringant, "L'espace maritime du *Quart Livre*," in *En relisant le Quart Livre de Rabelais*, ed. Nathalie Dauvois and Jean Vignes, *Cahiers textuel* no. 35 (2012), 29–42.

5. Critical perspectives on Rabelais's humor offer a variety of interpretations. Some of Rabelais's contemporaries found his writings not only impious, but also distasteful. Defaux reproduces Gabriel du Puy-Herbault's 1549 published tirade against Rabelais in the introduction to his edition of the *Quart Livre* (30–31). Twentieth- and twenty-first-century scholarship has viewed the *Quart Livre*'s comic violence as irreverent comedy in the carnival tradition, where conventional orders are reversed. Bakhtin's seminal study of Rabelais's comedy identifies Rabelais's fictions as the literary expression of a universal and essential form of popular, subversive humor whose social manifestations would be suppressed soon thereafter. *Rabelais and His World*, trans. Helene Iswolsky (Cambridge, MA: MIT Press, 1968), 101–20; on the Chiquanous episode, see especially 196–208 and 263–70. See also M. A. Screech, *Rabelais* (London: Duckworth, 1979), 336. Barbara Bowen's *Enter Rabelais Laughing* (Nashville, TN: Vanderbilt University Press, 1998) is another important study of Rabelais's humor that emphasizes his humanist background, though she does not discuss violence much—she refers the reader to Demerson's article "Rabelais et la

violence"—and her remarks on farce and the Chiquanous in this book are quite minimal ("Laughter on Stage," 53–67). Natalie Zemon Davis's essay "The Reasons of Misrule" explains the social and political function and origins of the widespread tradition of "misrule" such as charivaris, plays, and festivals, arguing that "rather than being a mere 'safety valve,' deflecting attention from social reality, festive life can on the one hand perpetuate certain values of the community (even guarantee its survival), and on the other hand criticize political order." In *Society and Culture in Early Modern France* (Stanford, CA: Stanford University Press, 1965), 97–123, 97.

6. In Frame's translation, the "Chiquanous" are called "Shysteroos," as he seems to be making the semantic connection with the English word "shyster." Screech prefers the term "Chicanous," a choice that maintains the semantic correlation with chicanery, deriving etymologically from the sixteenth-century French term *chicanerie* [legal quibbling, sophistry]. Randle Cotgrave translates *chiquanous* or *Chiquanous* as "a litigious pleader, a pettifogger." He defines *chicaner* as "to wrangle, or pettifog it; to spoyle, or perplex a cause with craftie, and litigious pleading; also, to write a very fast hand," while *chicanerie* translates as "wrangling, pettifogging; litigious, or craftie pleading; the perplexing of a cause with trickes; or the pestering thereof with (sub-tile, but) impertiment [*sic*], words." Randle Cotgrave, *A Dictionarie of the French and English Tongues* (London, 1611). In this chapter we have chosen to keep the original French term, "Chiquanous."

7. François Rigolot analyzes the Chiquanous episode in terms of the generative force of the language of farce (*Les langages de Rabelais* [Geneva: Droz, 1972, 1996], 126–30). Echoing Rigolot, Bowen suggests that Rabelais's interest in farce stems from his attraction to wordplay, particularly playing with clichés (*Enter Rabelais*, 62–63), but in terms of the Chiquanous, she simply describes the laughter induced in these chapters as "bad" (i.e., mocking, vengeful, mad, or treacherous) laughter. "Laughing in Rabelais, Laughing with Rabelais," in *The Cambridge Companion to Rabelais*, ed. John O'Brien (Cambridge, UK: Cambridge University Press, 2011), 31–41, 35. Berry compares the 1548 and the 1552 versions of the episode and considers the violence in terms of allegorical satire against the corrupt clergy, concluding that the "impera-tive of deferred vengeance . . . gives the ending of the episode its tonality of tension and dissatisfaction, for in the present, al actions are blocked and all remedies fail" (*Charms of Catastrophe*, 91). Margaret Broom Harp, in her study *The Portrayal of Community in Rabelais's "Quart Livre"*, contrasts the violent behavior with the trav-elers' *pantagrueliste* ethos. She distinguishes communal types among the islands and the travelers to suggest that the "theme of community" is "embodied in the concept of *Pantagruelistes*" (New York: Peter Lang, 1997, 2). Thus, her reading of the Chi-quanous episode, "the most perverse community" (83), rests on a series of contrasts between the travelers and the Chiquanous (35–42), ultimately to argue for Rabelais's repudiation of utopia (80–87). Finally, Edwin Duval contends that "the physical brutality that tends to impress modern readers is not all the point of the episode," and chooses to concentrate on the "insidious aspect[s]" of *anticaritas*, concluding that "the anticaritas of Procuration is . . . double. It lies first in the chicanry that allows

the wicked to ruin the just with impunity, and second in the false face of caritas put on [. . .] to provoke even the innocent and good to self-destructive acts of physical violence" (*The Design of Rabelais's "Quart Livre de Pantagruel"* [Geneva: Droz, 1998], 71–72). Duval, however, does not analyze the performative aspects of the episode, limiting—even reducing—his analyses to the sole notion of *anticaritas*.

8. See Screech, *Rabelais*, 335–40, and Kritzman, *Rhetoric of Sexuality*, 187–201.

9. André Tournon, "Jeu de massacre. La 'tragique farce' du seigneur de Baské," in *Rabelais-Dionysos: Vin, carnaval, ivresse*, ed. Michel Bideaux (Marseille: Jean Lafitte, 1997), 43–50; "Discussion," 364–66. Screech, too, points out that the chapters are "unimpeded by irrelevant moral worries or by any contact with pity, an emotion which successfully puts and stop to so much laughter" (*Rabelais*, 336). However, Screech hardly analyzes the actual episodes themselves in order to focus on a moralizing interpretation (337–41).

10. E. Bruce Hayes, *Rabelais's Radical Farce: Late Medieval Comic Theater and Its Function in Rabelais* (Farnham, UK: Ashgate, 2010), 168. Bernd Renner, though he focuses on the hermeneutic relations between the farce and satire, while Hayes considers the internal dynamics of farce and its ethical implications, reaches a similar conclusion, gesturing toward Rabelais's waning interest in farce as a useful theatrical "genre." *Difficile est saturam non scribere. L'herméneutique de la satire rabelaisienne* (Geneva: Droz, 2007), 279–83.

11. In *The Ritual Process: Structure and Anti-Structure*, Turner prefers the Latin term *communitas* to "community," "to distinguish this modality of social relationship from an 'area of common living" (London: Routledge and Kegan Paul, 1969, 96). Communitas is thus more than simply living together. It is, as he would make more explicit in 1982,

> the liberation of human capacities of cognition, affect, volition, creativity, etc., from the normative constraints incumbent upon occupying a sequence of social statuses, enacting a multiplicity of social roles, and being acutely conscious of membership in some corporate group such as family, lineage, clan, tribe, nation, etc., or of affiliation with some pervasive social category such as a class, caste, sex, or age-division. (*From Ritual to Theatre: The Human Seriousness of Play* [New York: Performing Arts Journal Publications, 1982], 44)

The overlap of Bakhtin's and Turner's ideas is not coincidental, as the Turners had read and were very much influenced by Bakhtin's *Rabelais and His World* (Edith Turner, *Communitas: The Anthropology of Collective Joy* [New York: Palgrave Macmillan, 2012], 32). Zemon Davis also discusses Bakhtin and Turner as a complementary pair ("Reasons for Misrule," 103). For a Turnerian approach to *jeux* in Montaigne and others, see Fabien Cavaillé's chapter (9) in this volume.

12. The expression is borrowed from the subtitle of Edith Turner's recent book, cited in note 11.

13. In the original version of 1548, the Chiquanous episode is comprised of only one short chapter. In the 1552 expanded version, which included five chapters,

Rabelais added the Basché and Villon intercalated tales. For the 1548 version, see Huchon's edition, or Jean Plattard, ed., *Le Quart Livre de Pantagruel (edition dite partielle, de Lyon, 1548)* (Paris: Champion, 1909).

14. While it is not the focus here, it is worth pointing out that different internal narrators tell stories throughout this episode, which not only reinforces the hybrid modes of the diegetic and the mimetic, but also highlights the act of narrative itself as a performative gesture.

15. *H*, 565; *F*, 462.

16. Ibid. As critics have noted, the surname Basché echoes the Basoche, a guild of legal clerks in Paris that would put on satirical plays throughout the sixteenth century (see Tournon, "Discussion," 364–66). The semantic similarity is certainly not accidental. On the Basosche and theater, see Sara Beam, *Laughing Matters: Farce and the Making of Absolutism in France* (Ithaca, NY: Cornell University Press, 2007), 77–110; Marie Bouhaïk-Gironès, *Les clercs de la Basoche et le théâtre politique (Paris, 1420–1550)* (Paris: Honoré Champion, 2007).

17. Bakhtin reminds us:

> In Touraine, where the [Basché] episode took place, as well as in Poitiers and other French provinces, there existed the custom of the so-called *nopces à mitaines* (gauntlet weddings). During the wedding feast the guests cuffed each other jokingly. The person who was subjected to these light blows could not complain; they were consecrated and legalized by custom. And so each time a slanderer came to Basché's castle, a mock wedding was celebrated, and the plaintiff inevitably had to join the guests. (200)

18. *H*, 566; *F*, 463.

19. In order for *communitas* to occur, the members of the community must be on equal footing, because *communitas* "transgresses or dissolves the norms that govern structured and institutionalized relationships and is accompanied by experiences of unprecedented potency" (Turner, *Ritual Process*, 128).

20. *H*, 565–66; *F*, 463.

21. *H*, 566; *F*, 463.

22. *H*, 567; *F*, 464.

23. *H*, 566; *F*, 463 (emphasis added).

24. Ibid. (emphasis added).

25. *H*, 566 (emphasis added).

26. *F*, 463 (translation slightly modified; emphasis added).

27. Berry, *Charm of Catastrophe*, 87.

28. In fact, one will never see a wedding take place on the stage in French theater as late as Beaumarchais's *Le Mariage de Figaro*. We may see the fiancés before and after the ceremony, but the ceremony itself, a religious sacrament, occurs offstage.

29. Turner, *From Ritual to Theatre*, 35.

30. Richard Schechner, *Performance Theory*, rev. ed. (New York: Routledge, 2003), 193.

31. "Liminality may involve a complex sequence of episodes in sacred space-time, and may also include subversive and ludic (or playful) events," while the "liminoid" events include, for Turner, charivaris, fiestas, Halloween masking, and mumming (*From Ritual to Theatre*, 27–28). During Rabelais's time, which Turner would call the proto-industrial era, the "liminal" would be a sacred ceremony such as a wedding, and the "liminoid" would be the mock wedding. What is at stake in this episode is, as we will see, the inability to distinguish the sacred ritual from the profane performance.

32. Turner, *From Ritual to Theatre*, 20–59.

33. Schechner, *Performance Theory*, 112–69, 130. See also James Loxley, *Performativity* (London: Routledge, 2007), 154–61.

34. Schechner, *Performance Theory*, 128, 192–93.

35. Richard Schechner, *Between Theater and Anthropology* (Philadelphia: University of Pennsylvania Press, 1985), 304–5.

36. Bakhtin (*Rabelais*, 264) and Kritzman (*Rhetoric of Sexuality*, 191) have both commented on this aspect of the episode.

37. *H*, 567; *F*, 464. As mentioned previously, none of the Chiquanous are given names; rather, they are designated by their appearance. This one is fat, ruddy, and old ["viel, gros, et rouge"] (*H*, 566; *F*, 463). The third Chiquanous is called "monsieur le Roy," but it is unclear whether all Chiquanous go by this name or if this is this particular Chiquanous's surname (*H*, 575; *F*, 471).

38. *H*, 567; *S*, 700.

39. *H*, 567; *F*, 464.

40. Ibid. (translation slightly modified).

41. *H*, 567.

42. *F*, 464 (emphasis added; translation modified).

43. Ibid. These bells also announce the ornaments that two Chiquanous have stolen from the church and hid under the bell tower, for which they are hanged (*H*, 578; *F*, 473–74). This part of the story, however, is beyond the scope of this study.

44. *H*, 568; *F*, 465.

45. In Latin: "Hortus conclusus soror mea, sponsa, hortus conclusus, fons signatus" ["A garden enclosed is my sister, my spouse; a garden enclosed, a fountain sealed up"].

46. Berry, *Charm of Catastrophe*, 87.

47. On the historical aspects of this passion play and Villon's presence in Poitou, see Jelle Koopmans, "Maistre Françoys Villon, sur ses vieux jours, se retira à Saint-Maixent en Poictou," in *En relisant le "Quart Livre" de Rabelais*, ed. Nathalie Dauvois and Jean Vignes, *Cahiers textuel* no. 35 (2012), 59–69.

48. *H*, 568; *F*, 465.

49. *H*, 569–70; *F*, 466–67.

50. *H*, 570; *F*, 467.

51. Ibid.

52. Ibid.

53. *H*, 571; *F*, 467–68.

54. *H*, 571; *S*, 705.

55. Turner, *Ritual Process*, 132.

56. *H*, 571; *F*, 468.

57. I have modified Frame's translation, since there is no mention of slapping in the original. The *jeu de Raphe* is a game of dice, not a violent punching game (*S*, 706).

58. *H*, 572; *F*, 468.

59. *H*, 572; *F*, 469 (translation modified).

60. *H*, 573; *F*, 469.

61. *H*, 573; *F*, 470.

62. *H*, 574–75; *F*, 470–71.

63. Berry, *Charm of Catastrophe*, 88 (emphasis in original).

64. Rigolot, *Les Langages de Rabelais*, 129–30.

65. Elaine Scarry, *The Body in Pain: The Making and Unmaking of the World* (New York: Oxford University Press, 1985), 3–4.

66. *H*, 574; *F*, 470 (translation modified); Scarry, *Body in Pain*, 4.

67. *H*, 575; *F*, 471.

68. Ibid.

69. See Turner, *From Ritual to Theatre*, 10. For a more elaborate explanation, see Victor Turner, *Dramas, Fields, and Metaphors: Symbolic Action in Human Society* (Ithaca, NY: Cornell University Press, 1974), 37–42.

70. Turner, *From Ritual to Theatre*, 11.

71. Hayes has read the earlier case of Panurge and the sheep merchant Dindenault alongside the Chiquanous episode (*Rabelais's Radical Farce*, 158–69).

72. *H*, 576; *F*, 472. "Their feet are swift to shed blood: Destruction and misery are in their ways: And the way of peace have they not known: There is no fear of God before their eyes" (Romans 3:15–18). Paul warns the Romans against being unmerciful and passing judgment on others. As cited by Frère Jan to Panurge, only God can judge and punish; for such actions, one shall incur God's wrath.

73. *H*, 576; *F*, 472.

74. *H*, 577; *F*, 472.

75. *H*, 577; *F*, 473.

76. See, e.g., Bruno Roy, "Triboulet, Josseaume et Pathelin à la cour de René d'Anjou," *Le Moyen Français* 7 (1980): 7–56. Of the many publications on French farce, see Beam, *Laughing Matters*; Barbara Bowen, *Les Caractéristiques essentielles de la farce française et leur survivance dans les années 1550–1620* (Urbana: University of Illinois Press, 1964). On commedia dell'arte, see Robert Henke, *Performance and Literature in the Commedia dell'Arte* (Cambridge, UK: Cambridge University Press, 2002).

77. Bernard Jolibert, *La commedia dell'arte et son influence en France du XVIe au XVIIIe siècle* (Paris: L'Harmattan, 1999), 51.

78. *H*, 577; *F*, 473.

79. Ibid.

80. Violence is not, of course, a purely symbolic construct in a society whose legal system sanctioned violence. Lucien Febvre describes that when approaching a town,

one would be greeted with heads on stakes as a warning against criminal activity. *Life in Renaissance France*, trans. Marian Rothstein (Cambridge, MA: Harvard University Press, 1979), 4. Henri II's suppression of the revolt against the salt tax in western France (November 1548) included the executions of at least a couple hundred people, and the presumed leaders were put to death in particularly cruel ways. Didier Le Fur, *Henri II* (Paris: Tallandier, 2009), 220–25, 247–48.

~

CHAPTER FOUR

Calvinist "Comedie" and Conversion during the French Reformation

La comedie du Pape malade (1561) and La comedie du Monde malade et mal pensé (1568)

Sara Beam

Historians of the "popular" Reformation, that is to say the reception of religious reform among the common people, struggle to understand what the average European actually believed. Although during the Reformation the *menu peuple* [common people] expressed their enthusiasm for religious reform in acts of iconoclasm and riot, it is not always clear what they thought they were fighting for. Because the private religious experience of the vast majority of illiterate Europeans is inaccessible to us, historians are able to approach this question only indirectly. Cultural historians have examined the media by which reformed religion was disseminated to the general population: pamphlets, vernacular Bibles, and woodcuts, for example.[1] Scholars have also looked at music, public rituals, and theater in order to better understand communal religious identity. Andrew Pettegree writes persuasively about the importance of what he calls "badges of belonging": owning a Protestant book that one did not or could not read, listening to a reform-minded public sermon, or attending a heretical theatrical performance.[2] Such activities could help to form new communal solidarities, loyalties that were perhaps just as important as a commitment to a specific set of theological tenets.

Recent emphasis on the performative aspect of early modern subjectivity underlines the importance of these kinds of social rituals to an individual's sense of self. Whereas some historians claim for early modern selves an interior life as rich as that posited by Freud, most argue that early modern identity was highly "performative": embedded in conceptions of honor and communal and family allegiances expressed in public performances of self.[3] During a moment of religious transition, when individuals were flirting with or committing themselves to a new confessional identity, participation in ritual performances—in mass (or communion), in religious processions, or in theater-going—was an important way of consolidating and expressing their religious identity.[4]

Reformation France presents an interesting case for historical investigation because of the rapidity of the Huguenot explosion in the 1550s and early 1560s. By the time the Wars of Religion erupted in 1562, possibly 10 percent of the population had joined reformed congregations.[5] How can this sudden Protestant surge be explained? It has been variously attributed to the long-standing humanist tradition of *évangélique* reform, the flooding of the French market with reformed propaganda, and the disciplined energy of Genevan-trained pastors.[6] Scholars have also argued that music played a role in establishing reformed solidarity: drawing on the rich psalm-singing tradition established in Geneva, French Huguenots joined together in song to signal their adherence to the true church.[7]

In contrast, historians have downplayed the importance of the theater, particularly comic plays, in the French conversion process. This tendency is no doubt due to Jean Calvin's image as a humorless, legalistic reformer who tried to eliminate all traditional entertainments and festivals.[8] Unlike Martin Luther, who is famous for his willingness to use scatological allusion to satirize Catholic practice,[9] Calvin developed a polemical style that demeaned Catholicism as a material religion without being grotesque.[10] The idea that Calvin would spread his message through bawdy theater seems incongruous, and certainly Calvin himself never wrote a farce.[11] Nevertheless, between the mid-1540s and mid-1560s, Calvin and the Genevan city council did in fact authorize the performance of reform-minded *comedies*, and this tradition in due course passed on via Genevan-trained pastors into France. Comic theater was performed to spread a Protestant message to the French and may have helped to forge new religious loyalties during this period of confessional boundary-making.

Not that the French needed material imported from Geneva in order to air religious polemic on stage.[12] Religious reform had always been a central theme in late medieval *sotties*,[13] morality plays, and *sermons joyeux*.[14] These genres take for granted that humanity is fallen and corrupt and that exposing folly is both a form of entertainment and of ribald moral instruction. As early as the fifteenth-century *Concile de Basle*, French plays satirized the corruption of the clergy and criticized the power of the pope. This tradition continued during the first decades of the sixteenth century, when several plays implying the need for religious reform were published in France;[15] archival evidence demonstrates that performances of other religiously polemical plays, which have since been lost, also occurred.[16] Such performances often took place during the intermissions of mystery plays, at religious festivals, as well as at royal entries, and were an accepted element of popular culture. One did not need to be a schismatic to laugh at the hypocritical and selfish behavior of the clergy at the turn of the sixteenth century.

With Luther's break from Catholicism and the reform efforts in the diocese of Meaux in the 1520s, however, satire of the Catholic church became dangerous. The persecution of "Lutherans" within France and the establishment of Protestant churches elsewhere raised the stakes for this kind of polemical humor. As early as 1529, the humanist noble Laurent Berquin—translator of Erasmus, scathing critic of the Sorbonne, and author of the satirical *Farce des Théologastres*—was condemned as a heretic and burned at the stake.[17]

Although as far as we know no other playwright was executed for penning a farce, by midcentury the practice of mocking the church on stage had come under attack. Traditional youth groups and *sociétés joyeuses* [companies of fools] that performed at the Feast of Kings, at carnival, and during Mayday celebrations were brought under closer surveillance and censorship: in Rouen, as early as 1545, the Conards, a well-established confraternity that performed satirical plays each year, were chastised for making fun of a cathedral canon even though there is no evidence that this performance was in any way schismatic.[18] Students at the University of Paris and those attending provincial *collèges*, institutions often suspected of being sympathetic to religious reform, were also disciplined and sometimes imprisoned for performing comic plays that touched on religious questions.[19] In the town of Agen, the city council was made aware that "farces et moralitez . . . pleines d'erreurs, scandale, doctrine reprouvee" ["farces and morality plays . . . full of errors, shocking material, perverted doctrine"] were being performed in the city streets;[20] in 1553, the *parlement* of Bordeaux outlawed such activities and ordered that all theatrical performances be vetted by magistrates to assess whether the plays contained "aucune chose scandaleuse ou reprouvee contre la foy et religion chrestienne" ["anything scandalous or reprehensible against the faith or the Christian religion"].[21] Two years later, *farceurs* and members of the *enfans de sans soucy* in Libourne were imprisoned for having performed plays that sparked acts of iconoclasm—a clear indication that the *menu peuple* were responding actively to such performances.[22] Also in 1555, civic authorities in the northern city of Amiens began to censor theatrical performances to ensure that they were "honneste et non sentant aucun point d'hérésie" ["morally sound and not containing even a hint of heresy"].[23] Actors and playwrights who transgressed these rulings were in real danger of being fined, beaten, imprisoned, or even banished. Members of the audience were not imprisoned, but they were seen to be in danger of contamination or even conversion. Although few new farces, morality plays, or *sotties* were published in France after 1550, the existence of theatrical censorship demonstrates the continued vitality of these genres for spreading religious reform.

Both French and Genevan civic authorities were aware that comic theater had the power to change hearts; it is for this reason that Genevan authorities tolerated the performance of reform-minded plays and French authorities so often condemned them. Was French officials' wariness of *comedie* justified?

Historians, having in mind the bloody conflicts that tore France apart between 1562 and 1598, have traditionally imagined the conversion experience as a black-and-white transformation: attracted to the message of God's grace or the sociability of the new reformed congregations, a minority of French subjects abruptly abandoned the Catholic church to jump onto the Protestant bandwagon. This narrative of decisive change is reinforced by the martyrologies published by both Catholics and Protestants and by fiery sermons that urged French subjects to purge their communities of heretics or face damnation.[24] After 1555, when France was flooded with reformed pastors, individuals in communities across the country were pressured to repudiate Nicodemism and openly declare their allegiance to the new faith.

In recent decades, however, historians have become aware that many Europeans did not experience their conversion in such polarized terms. Raised in a Catholic faith that was steeped in ambiguity, they had a more elastic understanding of Christianity than was being propagated in Catholic or Protestant polemic. As late as 1552, some Lutheran reformers, including Philip Melanchthon, still hoped to reach a compromise with the Catholic church. Historians have recently been looking into the "moderate reformation": the attitudes of those who converted but were not willing to kill or die for their faith, or those, in France in particular, who hoped for reform while remaining Catholic.[25] Although civil war erupted on eight separate occasions in France during the second half of the sixteenth century, at the end of each conflict a measure of religious coexistence was imposed on the population, with some success.[26] This more nuanced understanding of religious allegiance can help to explain why some Catholics chose to protect and hide their Huguenot neighbors during the St. Bartholomew's Day massacres of 1572.[27] Historians now characterize the period between 1555 and 1572 both as a time of aggressive boundary-making and also as a time when many French subjects were sitting on the confessional fence. At such a moment in history, attending a reform-minded theatrical performance could be a means of cementing one's loyalty to the Protestant faith, but it could also be a means of exploring new ideas or of confirming a commitment to reform within the Catholic fold. The moment was ripe for a social ritual that created the feeling of belonging to a new and improved community but without specifying very clearly exactly what this involved doctrinally. Calvinist *comedie* seems to have met these criteria, although, as we will see, its normalization of religious conflict between Catholics and Protestants also reinforced confessional boundaries.

Traditionally, Calvin has been considered hostile to the theater, and certainly he did nothing to promote theatrical performances during his time in Geneva. However, he did not fear them as much as did some of his fellow pastors. When in 1546 the Genevan preachers disagreed about a proposed performance of the mystery play *Les actes des Apostres* [*The Acts of the Apostles*], Calvin at first hesitated, then eventually decided to support his colleague Michel Cop and discourage the city council from permitting the performance.[28] But when the council defied his recommendation, Calvin sought to downplay the conflict, writing in a letter to Guillaume Farel that "je vois qu'on ne peut refuser aux hommes tous les divertissements" ["I see that one cannot refuse all diversions to man"].[29] Whereas some pastors feared that watching plays would distract Genevans from more pious activities, Calvin's main concern was that the performances be doctrinally sound. In subsequent decades, the council followed Calvin's lead, demanding assurances from performers that their plays contained nothing "contre Dieu" ["against God"],[30] sometimes granting permission only "si Monsieur Calvin est de ce avis" ["if Monsieur Calvin is of this opinion"][31]—a condition that assured that no play ridiculing Calvin himself would ever make it to the stage. The city council continued to sanction the performance of *comedies* and *hystoires* throughout the 1550s and 1560s and even helped on some occasions to defray the costs of costumes and staging.[32] Calvinist *comedie* was by no means an oxymoron; indeed, it was seen as an effective means of communicating the reformed message to "les simples" ["the simple folk"].[33] What was being performed in Geneva was precisely what was being censored in France.[34]

The two plays that I discuss in this chapter were written, published, and performed in Geneva during the 1560s, and there is no direct evidence that either was ever performed on French soil. We do know, though, that reformed pastors in France permitted the performance of comic plays in the late 1550s and early 1560s. Those plays are lost, but the Genevan *comedies* I examine here suggest what those French performances might have contained.

In Geneva as in France, there had been since at least the late fifteenth century a tradition of performing comic plays to celebrate peace treaties and to mark important festivals, and these plays often criticized political and religious authorities.[35] They were customarily composed by members of the urban elite, as are the two *comedies* I discuss. Their authors, Conrad Badius and Jacques Bienvenu, were well-educated humanists, members of the Genevan intellectual elite, and both had previously published Protestant-leaning works. Archival evidence demonstrates that Badius's play was performed at the Genevan *collège* in 1561 and Bienvenu's at civic celebrations in 1568.[36]

When Conrad Badius wrote *La comedie du Pape malade* in 1561, he was a well-respected member of the French émigré population of Geneva and had been writing and publishing Protestant polemic for over a decade.[37] Having fled France in 1549 due to his religious convictions, Badius was a friend of theologian Théodore de Bèze, related by marriage to the printer Robert Estienne, and known to most Swiss and south German Protestant reformers. In addition to his Calvinist *comedie*, Badius wrote treatises in favor of reform, edited a satire by Bèze, and helped to publish the 1555 French-language Bible. He might have continued to write comic plays in a Reformed vein had he not returned to France in early 1562 and succumbed to the plague soon afterward.[38] His compatriot, Jacques Bienvenu, author of *La comedie du Monde malade et mal pensé* (1568), had a less internationally visible career but was well-respected locally.[39] Born and bred in Geneva, son of a cloth merchant, Bienvenu was a citizen and a member of the Council of 200. A notary by profession, Bienvenu demonstrated his solid humanist credentials in numerous publications: he wrote a polemical response to a treatise by arch-Catholic Artus Désiré and translated into French a satirical comedy by John Foxe and a history of the Spanish Inquisition.[40] Throughout the 1550s and 1560s, Bienvenu wrote and helped to produce comic theater in Geneva.[41] Both authors were thus seasoned Reformed polemicists whose aim in writing these plays was to reinforce loyalty to the Protestant cause. However, neither play elucidates theological concepts or contains doctrinal instruction; evidently the authors aimed at something other than intellectual persuasion.

Both these plays adapted the traditional *malade* [ill, sick] topos, in which an allegorical character representing worldly corruption seeks aid from fools and rogues. Although these two plays were published as *comedies*, they in no way engaged with the generic experiments in neo-Latin theater occurring in France at this time. In his prologue, Badius makes the distinction explicit. Unwilling to trouble his popular audience with scene divisions and sophisticated vocabulary, Badius defines *comedie* simply as a play that has "commencement fâcheux et issue joyeuse" ["that which starts unbearably and ends joyously"].[42] A broad definition of this kind allows both authors to label as a *comedie* what was in fact a form very much like that of the late medieval farce, morality play, or *sottie*. Apparently the term *comedie* rendered a comic play respectable in Calvin's Geneva, whereas farces and *sotties* were associated with carnival, a festival that had been outlawed since the 1530s.[43]

In earlier plays, the *malade* figure is triumphantly cured by right doctrine, but these two *comedies* are less optimistic. Badius opens with *Pape* [Pope] lamenting that he is ill and that his days are numbered, the potency of his "vent de derrière" ["wind from the rear"] testifying to his internal rot.[44] Concerned for his salvation but more worried about losing his temporal power, *Pape* asks Satan to help him gather a great army to fight his archenemies, the followers of "ce faux apostat de Luther" ["that false apostate Luther"].[45] In the second half of the play, Satan interviews potential papal allies, most of whom he finds lacking due to their greed and selfishness. In Bienvenu's *comedie*, the target is more general: the *malade*, Monde [World], represents sinful mankind as a whole. Attended to first by an incompetent doctor, *Monde* then seeks help from a band of fools led by a blind lawyer. The lawyer, Bridoye, wearing glasses with gold lenses, examines *Monde*'s body but takes his head for his shoes, his knee for his torso, and his stomach for his back;[46] needless to say, he does not succeed in curing his patient. In both plays, an allegorical character named *Vérité* [Truth] points out the path of godliness, but she convinces neither *Pape* nor *Monde* and leaves, having failed in her mission. The happy ending of both plays is a qualified one: *Pape* is not yet defeated, and *Monde* has not yet acknowledged the truth. In promoting virtue by dramatizing the cost of vice, both *comedies* were part of a long-standing theatrical tradition. But their somewhat pessimistic message about the threat of religious violence and the dangers of straying from the reformed path is explicable by the fact that they were produced during the 1560s, a period of religious war.

Polemical though they are, these two Genevan plays do not say much about Protestant theology. True, comic plays would not be the ideal medium for articulating complex theological positions, but these *comedies* contain even less discussion of the principles of religious reform than do earlier *malade* plays. In the 1520s and 1530s, characters unsubtly named *Parole* [Speech, Word], *Chrestienté* [Christianity], or *Medecin* [Doctor] relieve the sufferings of *Malade* by teaching Christ's true message of grace and reverence for the scriptures.[47] Acceptance of Christ's true teachings is portrayed as leading to personal salvation and a purified church in these *évangélique* plays, but the healed *Malade* figure does not always abandon Rome. In contrast, Badius and Bienvenu are more skeptical about the immediate curative power of scripture; neither of them sees conversion as an inevitable result of exposure to the Protestant message. Additionally, they both insist that salvation requires that the *Malade* character abandon the Catholic church.

In Badius's play, *Pape* briefly alludes to Luther's teaching—"Jesus Christ / Pour seul Sauveur et moi pour Antéchrist" ["Jesus Christ as only Savior and me as Antichrist"]—but expends much more verse describing the Protestants' criticisms of the abuses of the church, such as purgatory, indulgences, and simony.[48] When Satan goes out looking for supporters, he encounters several individuals, most of whom are identified, such as Catholic polemicist Artus Désiré and Nicolas Durand de Villegaignon, a French nobleman who had recently engaged in theological debate with Calvin and whom Jean de Léry would criticize in his *Histoire d'un voyage faict en la terre du Brésil* (1578) [*History of a Voyage to the Land of Brazil*]. Désiré and Villegaignon are mocked as hypocrites eager to minimize their suffering and to fill their own bellies, but the actual theological issues at stake are not articulated. Sebastian Castellio, for example, the well-known defender of religious toleration, is represented as obsessed with wealth, fame, and personal perfection,[49] but the substantive issues over which he clashed with Calvin, including Castellio's opposition to the execution of the heretic Michael Severtus, are never mentioned.

In Bienvenu's *comedie*, the fools propose several remedies to cure *Monde*: the "jus du Concile de Trente" ["juice of the Council of Trent"], rejected as too violent a medicine for *Monde* (though a useful enema for dogs);[50] a dose of *Athéisme*, which even the fools realize would leave the soul like "un bel oison" ["a sitting duck"] on Judgment day;[51] or a massage with oil of the *Interim*, a failed religious compromise imposed by Charles V after his victory against the Protestants in 1547. Catholic remedies are thus mocked as debased and worthless, but the truth offered by the reformed alternative is taken for granted rather than expounded in any detail.

In short, both plays represent the reformed faith as an alternative to Catholic corruption rather than as a specific set of beliefs or practices. In his address to the readers, Badius explains that he aims to highlight "les abus du Pape et les complots de ses suppôts, afin que les pauvres fidèles s'en donnent garde et détestent cet ennemi de Jésus Christ et de sa vérité" ["the pope's abuses and the plots of his supporters, so that the poor faithful guard against and detest this enemy of Jesus Christ and of his truth"].[52] These texts are more anti-Catholic than pro-Calvin: indeed, Calvin is not named in either play.[53] Like Huguenot polemical songs, broadsheets, and woodcuts more generally, Calvinist *comedie* was a blunt instrument for damning Catholics as servants of the devil and pointing in a rather general way to the alternative path. It encouraged audiences to think of Protestants as a community of the righteous without specifying exactly what this new allegiance would entail.

Engaged in making clear that the Catholic church is a sinking ship, Badius and Bienvenu present the Catholics as broken and the Protestants as unified. Satan remains skeptical about *Pape*'s health, announcing that *Pape* "est près de sa ruine" ["is close to his ruin"].[54] *Pape* seems to agree when he complains that he is surrounded by a united front of heretics in Germany, in England, in Savoy, and now even in France.[55] In Bienvenu's version, *Monde* and the fools decide at the end of the play to arm themselves against *Vérité*, but their directionless and ineffective behavior up until then suggests that they will fail.[56] Misguided, ill, scattered, and lost to God, Catholics it seems cannot win. In contrast, the ethereal *Vérité* characters represent the Protestants' unity of purpose and their clear message: follow God or be damned. This oversimplification occludes the many theological quarrels that divided contemporary Protestants, notably Calvin's differences with his fellow reformers, for example over such central issues as communion and double predestination.[57] As propaganda supporting the reformed cause, these *comedies* take care not to mention the failures of Protestants to unite militarily in the 1530s and exaggerate their ability to fight off their Catholic foes. Performed in the 1560s, when Geneva faced military threats from France and Savoy, and when their alliance with more powerful Protestant cities such as Berne were made vulnerable by Calvin's theological intransigence, these comic plays were an urgent call to come together against the Catholic enemy. The plays make it clear that religious war is inevitable and that everyone, even fools, will have to take a stand.

Yet although both these plays imagine a world divided in two camps, with the Protestants on the winning side, they also present conversion to the reformed faith as an ongoing internal struggle for each individual. This might seem surprising in Geneva, the very birthplace of the reformed religious movement, where, beginning with Calvin's return in 1541, citizens were overseen by a well-organized reformed church and disciplined by the consistory, a church court staffed by pastors and lay elders. At the height of the Reformation, as many as one adult in fifteen was summoned by the consistory each year for infractions that ranged from blasphemy to giving one's child a nonbiblical name.[58] In such an environment, one might expect that the local population would already have internalized the basic principles and practices of Protestantism and that Badius and Bienvenu would not need to elucidate them. Unlike the French, many of whom were first exposed to the reformed message only in the 1550s, Geneva residents should have long since converted to the true faith.

But both historical research and the content of these two plays belie such a conclusion. Calvin's sermons make it clear that he was dissatisfied with the piety of most Genevans: he constantly urged them to reform their ways and, as late as the 1550s, railed that they were no better than Romans in their religious commitment. In his prefaces to Calvin's printed sermons, Conrad Badius agreed, noting that most Genevans were ignorant of scripture and even of the Ten Commandments.[59] Historians analyzing the records of the consistory have reached similar conclusions: many Genevans failed to attend church regularly, participated in the Catholic mass outside the city walls, and engaged in practices considered idolatrous by the reformed church.[60] Although Calvin and his fellow pastors were determined to stamp out such transgressions, they apparently had not done so by the 1560s, when Badius's and Bienvenu's plays were performed.

Conversion is presented as being a lifelong project, a constant effort to overcome temptation. In Bienvenu's *comedie*, Bridoye and his fools represent the common people of Geneva and Bern, who evidently require spiritual guidance, as their first reaction to *Vérité* when she arrives on stage is "Dame, nous ne vous cherchons pas!" ["Madam, we are not looking for you!"].[61] When Vérité explains that they will be lost unless they heed her words, their refusal to accept her message becomes a comic refrain. Though confronted with the truth, the fools refuse to change their ways: exposure to reformed teaching does not inevitably lead to conversion. As a result, at the end of the play, the more reasonable character *Le Temps* [Time] appeals to the civic leaders of Bern and Geneva, "pleins de grande prudence" ["full of great prudence"], to remain faithful to their military alliance and to lead both communities through this period of impending war.[62] Bienvenu concludes that the common man would not fight for *Vérité* without the leadership of the urban elite.

In Badius's play, the idea of conversion is ironized in the struggles of *Pape*. Unlike his minions, who care only for creature comforts, *Pape* is aware of his own corruption and knows he should recognize the truth of Luther's teachings: after dreaming that he is the Antichrist, he confesses "je n'ai eu plaisir ne repos" [I had neither pleasure nor rest].[63] He realizes that he has been tricked by Satan into a life of worldly pleasure and that the result will be "misère éternelle" ["eternal misery"],[64] yet Satan has little trouble convincing him that examining his conscience too closely will do him no good, as his fate is already sealed.

In both plays, the bad choices made by the characters represent the easier path, a "mensonge agréable" ["pleasant lie"] that will lead to eternal damnation.[65] Unlike earlier reform-minded *malade* plays, in which the protagonist is cured by a quick infusion of faith and Bible study, these two later plays both depict conversion not as a joyous moment but as a long-term endeavor that requires constant renewal and an ever-active conscience. Both Badius and Bienvenu belonged to the second generation of religious reformers, who had lived through the first euphoric decades of reform but now realized that the path to God was fraught with dangers. Intermittent civil war undermined the Huguenot leaders' hopes that the king himself might convert and the true faith prevail throughout France, and they increasingly came to see themselves as a beleaguered but committed minority of true believers.[66] During the 1560s, the message that the faithful must constantly fight against temptation was as relevant to Genevans as it was to French subjects faced with an entrenched Catholic church and threatened by political authorities hostile to reform.

Yet though Badius's and Bienvenu's plays are similar in many ways, they are quite different in tone. Bienvenu's lighthearted *comedie* is more like earlier Genevan comic plays.[67] *Monde malade* was written and performed in 1568 to mark the renewal of a military alliance between Geneva and Bern just before war broke out again within France for the third time in a decade. Yet the play is less bitter than it is rueful about mankind's fallen state and hopeful that unity among Protestants and sound political guidance will enable truth to prevail.

Monde malade has been called a *sottie*, a comic play in which the central character is a fool or *sot*. Like many *sotties*, this play contains less polemic than revelry: there are song, dance, and more slapstick humor than in Badius's play, with many stage directions specifying the actors' physical movements.[68] Much of the humor is violent or scatological: Bridoye threatens to beat his fools when they refuse his unreasonable requests; when Jean, the fool priest, is scolded for disobedience, he shows his rear end to Bridoye; the *sots* strip *Monde* of his clothes, his jewels, and even his beard in order to lighten his temporal load—all in a Rabelaisian spirit of comedy and derision.[69] The play deals only tangentially with Protestant concerns. When Bridoye asks his fool students to translate homilies from Latin and assigns to each individual a passage about how to live his life, the lazy priest is given an appropriate moral—"A pastor of the people must take care of his flock"—but renders it thus: "*Pastor populi curam gregis fideliter habeto: curam* / Un curé, *habeto* fort habile, *fideliter* fit des / Lanternes, *populi* pour pouvoir lire, *pastor* / Sa patenotre, *gregis* à la gregesque" ["*Pastor populi curam gregis fideliter habeto: curam* a priest, *habeto* very capable, *fideliter* made some lanterns, *populi* to be able to read, *pastor* his Paternoster, *gregis* like a Greek"].[70] The point is a familiar one—that many priests are ignorant of Latin and are more preoccupied with ritual than with spreading the Word of God—but the joke is as much silly wordplay as a serious satire of the Catholic clergy. Because the fools are revealed to be residents of Geneva and Bern, the audience is asked to identify with them—to recognize their weakness and folly as being common to all mankind. Written in the hope that war might end and Genevans survive the fray, Bienvenu does not advocate violence, but rather mocks the pathetic efforts of Monde and his fools to prepare for war. Though the world Bienvenu depicts is divided into saints and sinners, the sinners seem to predominate, and it is not clear who will be saved.

Badius's play, on the other hand, represents much more virulent Protestant polemic. His comedie has been classified as a moralité polémique [polemical morality play]: the characters are allegorical, the satire is biting, and there is little action.[71] The various characters are identified by name, and their blindness to Vérité is unambiguously condemned. It is an aggressive play, written in 1561 when the Huguenots still hoped to win the French monarchy to their cause. In his address to the readers, Badius says that though some might be shocked by the satire, the time for pussyfooting is over: "il n'est plus question de médicaments lénitifs, ains de cautères et incisions" ["it is no longer a question of calming medicine, but instead of cauterizations and incisions"].[72] The faithful need such violent remedies because, as L'Église [Church] explains, they are like sheep "traînés à la boucherie" ["led to the butchers"];[73] they are under violent attack and need to trust in God to survive. In the opening remarks of Pape malade, Old Testament vengeance is evoked with a measure of satisfaction. Badius expects his audience to laugh at the foolish Catholics "pas d'un ris profane et sans science" ["not with profane and ignorant laughter"] but rather "de ce ris sobre et saint" ["with sober and saintly laughter"], produced by good conscience and knowledge of the grace of Jesus Christ.[74] Badius's comedie is a play about boundary-making, about the hardening of lines between Catholics and Protestants in the middle decades of the sixteenth century. Yet it is no more vehement than comparable French morality plays defending the Catholic faith.[75]

The contempt for the Catholic church expressed in Badius's comedie resonated with the Swiss and French alike. Pape malade, first performed in Geneva at the local collège, an institution founded by Calvin as a training school for pastors, was possibly performed elsewhere in the years that followed. Published with the permission of the city council in the fall of 1561, the play was republished four more times before 1600, including editions produced in Neuchâtel and in Rouen.[76] Although it is likely that the Rouen address is fictive and that this edition was actually published in Geneva, the fact that a nominally French edition exists reveals the publisher's ambitions to make the play known internationally.[77] In the early 1560s, Rouen was a city renowned for its lively theatrical culture, so it is possible that Badius's *comedie* was indeed performed there.[78]

The audience of these plays would have come away with neither a detailed understanding of reformed doctrine nor a vivid apprehension of the moral discipline that a Calvinist church might impose on its community.[79] For an individual sitting on the confessional fence, however, the effect of these plays might have been to intensify contempt for the Catholic hierarchy, strengthen the resolve to combat corruption, or evoke a sense of satisfaction or even joy at the idea of belonging to the party of truth.

Historians have traditionally understood Calvinism to be more like Badius's play than like Bienvenu's: confident that the reformed path will bring the faithful righteousness and ready to damn the rest with Old Testament resolution. Indeed, judging by the number of editions published, Badius's polemical satire may have resonated more with Calvinists than Bienvenu's gentler fare. By the 1570s, faced with religious riots, warfare, and massacre, the Protestants in both Geneva and France needed tougher propaganda than a lighthearted *sottie* like *Monde malade*, a play that refuses to condemn anyone outright. Not surprisingly, Bienvenu's 1568 play was the last known *comedie* to be performed in Geneva in the sixteenth century.[80] In French Huguenot communities, too, the reformist farces and morality plays performed during the first half of the 1560s largely died out thereafter and were replaced by biblical tragedies. As early as 1572, a Huguenot synod explicitly banned all theatrical performances "comme apportans corruptions de bonnes mœurs" ["as corrupting to good manners"], and subsequently only the most somber student theatricals were permitted.[81]

Though the period when Calvinists laughed together to learn about their faith was a brief one, the existence of these Calvinist *comedies* shows that reformers were, for a time at least, ready to use any means at their disposal to reach and convert the common people. Calvinist *comedies* were performed during a period of fluid confessional boundaries, but their message, about Catholic corruption and the urgency of committing to the true faith, may have contributed, along with Protestant sermons and martyrologies, to the hardening of those boundaries in subsequent decades. Most French authorities, eager to bring Protestants back into the fold, were right to be wary of Calvinist *comedies*, because these plays sought to forge confessional divisions and fortify the resistance of true believers to perceived Catholic corruption.

Notes

1. Natalie Zemon Davis, *Society and Culture in Early Modern France: Eight Essays* (Stanford, CA: Stanford University Press, 1975); Robert W. Scribner, *For the Sake of Simple Folk: Popular Propaganda for the German Reformation* (Oxford: Clarendon Press, 1994); Jacques Tortorel and J. Perrisin, *Graphic History: The Wars, Massacres and Troubles of Tortorel and Perrissin*, vol. 1, ed. Philip Benedict (Geneva: Droz, 2007).

2. Andrew Pettegree, *Reformation and the Culture of Persuasion* (Cambridge, UK: Cambridge University Press, 2005). For France, see Denis Crouzet, *Les guerriers de Dieu: la violence au temps des troubles de religion*, 2 vols. (Seyssel: Champ Villon, 1990); Barbara B. Diefendorf, *Beneath the Cross: Catholics and Huguenots in Sixteenth-Century Paris* (New York: Oxford University Press, 1991); Henri Léonard Bordier, *Le chansonnier huguenot du XVIe siècle* (1870; repr., Geneva: Droz, 1969); and Larissa Taylor, *Heresy and Orthodoxy in Sixteenth-century Paris: François Le Picart and the Beginnings of the Catholic Reformation* (Leiden: Brill, 1999).

3. Lyndal Roper, *Oedipus and the Devil: Witchcraft, Sexuality and Religion in Early Modern Europe* (London: Routledge, 1994); Susan Crane, *The Performance of Self: Ritual, Clothing, and Identity during the Hundred Years War* (Philadelphia: University of Pennsylvania Press, 2002); Kristen B. Neuschel, *Word of Honor: Interpreting Noble Culture in Sixteenth-Century France* (Ithaca, NY: Cornell University Press, 1989); Natalie Zemon Davis, "Boundaries and the Sense of Self," in *Reconstructing Individualism: Autonomy, Individuality and the Self in Western Thought*, ed. Thomas C. Heller and Christine Brooke-Rose (Stanford, CA: Stanford University Press, 1986), 53–63; Jonathan Dewald, *Aristocratic Experience and the Origins of Modern Culture: France, 1570–1715* (Berkeley: University of California Press, 1993).

4. John Bossy, "The Mass as a Social Institution 1200–1700," *Past and Present* 100 (1983): 29–61; David Warren Sabean, "Production of the Self During the Age of Confessionalism," *Central European History* 29 (1996): 1–18; Pettegree, *Reformation and the Culture of Persuasion*.

5. Philip Benedict and Nicolas Fornerod, "Les 2,150 'églises' réformées de France de 1561–1562," *Revue historique* no. 651 (2009): 529–60.

6. Denis Crouzet, *La genèse de la Réforme française: 1520–1560* (Paris: SEDES, 1996); Francis M. Higman, *La diffusion de la Réforme en France: 1520–1565* (Geneva: Labor et Fides, 1992); Philip Benedict, *Christ's Churches Purely Reformed: A Social History of Calvinism* (New Haven, CT: Yale University Press, 2002); Augustin Renaudot, *Préréforme et humanisme à Paris pendant les premières guerres d'Italie (1494–1517)* (Paris: Champion, 1916); Robert M. Kingdon, *Geneva and the Consolidation of the French Protestant Movement, 1564–1572* (Geneva: Droz, 1967).

7. Bordier, *Chansonnier*; Bénédicte Louvat-Molozay, "Le théâtre protestant et la musique (1550–1586)," in *Par la vue et par l'ouïe. Littérature du Moyen Age et de la Renaissance*, ed. Michèle Gally and Michel Jourde (Fontenay Saint Cloud: ENS Editions, 1999), 135–58; *Théâtre et musique: Dramaturgie de l'insertion musicale dans le théâtre français (1550–1680)* (Paris: Honoré Champion, 2002), 219–55; Rebecca

Wagner Oettinger, *Music as Propaganda in the German Reformation* (Aldershot, UK: Ashgate, 2001).

8. William G. Naphy, *Calvin and the Consolidation of the Genevan Reformation* (Manchester, UK: Manchester University Press, 1994); Christian Grosse, *Les rituels de la Cène: le culte eucharistique réformé à Genève (XVIe–XVIIe siècles)* (Geneva: Droz, 2008).

9. Heiko Oberman, "Teufelsdreck: Eschatology and Scatology in the 'Old' Luther," *Sixteenth Century Journal* 19 (1988): 435–50; Eric W. Gritsch, "Luther on Humor," *Lutheran Quarterly* 18 (2004): 373–86.

10. Francis M. Higman, *The Style of John Calvin in his French Polemical Treatises* (London: Oxford University Press, 1967), 123–52; T. H. L. Parker, *Calvin's Preaching* (Edinburgh: T & T Clark, 1992), 114–28. Other Calvinists were less restrained. See Jeff Persels, "'The Mass and the Fart Are Sisters': Scatology and Calvinist Rhetoric against the Mass, 1560–63," in *Fecal Matters in Early Modern Literature and Art: Studies in Scatology*, ed. and introd. Jeff Persels and Russell Ganim (Aldershot, UK: Ashgate, 2004), 38–55.

11. Considerations of genre have preoccupied scholars of sixteenth-century Francophone comic theater. Farces, *sermons joyeux*, morality plays, *sotties*, and even the *comedies* fall into a broad category of comic fare that is often difficult to disentangle. It is clear that contemporaries, from publishers to authorities who sought to censor these plays, did not make clear or consistent distinctions between them. Jelle Koopmans, "Genres Théâtraux," *Fifteenth-Century Studies* 16 (1990): 131–42; André Tissier, "Sur la notion de 'genre' dans les pièces comiques: De La Farce de 'Pathelin' à La Comédie de 'L'Eugène' de Jodelle," *Littératures Classiques* 27 (1996): 13–24; Alan E. Knight, *Aspects of Genre in Late Medieval French Drama* (Manchester, UK: Manchester University Press, 1983).

12. Rather, plays written and performed throughout Francophone Europe are generally assumed to be part of the French tradition. Émile Picot, *Recueil général des sotties*, 3 vols. (Paris: Firmin Didot, 1902); Werner Bernard Helmich, *Moralités françaises: Réimpression fac-similé de vingt-deux pièces allégoriques imprimées aux XVe et XVIe siècles* (Geneva: Slatkine, 1980); Jonathan Beck, Estelle Doudet, and Alan Hindley, eds., *Recueil général de moralités d'expression française* (Paris: Garnier, 2012).

13. Short satirical plays common in France in the fifteenth and sixteenth centuries.

14. A comic form of theater that appeared in the fifteenth century and that parodies the sermon from Catholic mass.

15. *Eglise, Noblesse et Povreté*; *Sottie des sots ecclésiastiques qui jouent leurs benefices*; *Le maistre d'escolle*; Jelle Koopmans, *Recueil de sermons joyeux: Édition critique avec introduction, notes et glossaire* (Geneva: Droz, 1988); Jonathan Beck, ed., *Théâtre et propagande aux débuts de la Réforme: Six pièces polémiques du Recueil La Vallière* (Geneva: Slatkine, 1986); Pierre Gringore, *Le jeu du prince des sotz et de Mère Sotte*, ed. Alan Hindley (Paris: Champion, 2000); Christopher Pinet, "Monks, Priests, and Cuckolds: French Farce and Criticism of the Church from 1500 to 1560," *Stanford French Review* 4 (1980): 453–73; Alan Hindley, "Théâtre antipapal: Trois textes

dramatiques du début du XVI siècle," in *Le théâtre polémique français: 1450–1550*, ed. Marie Bouhaïk-Gironès, Jelle Koopmans, and Katell Lavéant (Rennes: Presses Universitaires de Rennes, 2008), 109–22; Jody Enders, "Of Protestantism, Performativity, and the Threat of Theater," *Mediaevalia: An Interdisciplinary Journal of Medieval Studies Worldwide* 22 (1999): 55–74.

16. Louis Petit de Julleville, *Histoire du théâtre en France* (Paris: Le Cerf, 1885); Émile Picot, *Les moralités polémiques ou la controverse religieuse dans l'ancien théâtre français* (1887–1906, repr., Geneva: Slatkine, 1970); Raymond Lebègue, "Théâtre et politique religieuse en France au XVIe siècle," in *Culture et politique en France à l'époque de l'humanisme et de la Renaissance*, ed. Franco Simone (Turin: Academica della Scienze, 1974), 427–37.

17. Claude Longeon makes a strong case that the farce was written by Berquin or by one of his close associates. Introduction to *La farce des Théologastres* (Geneva: Droz, 1989), 11–17.

18. A. Floquet, "Histoire des Conards de Rouen," *Bibliothèque de l'École des Chartes* 1 (1839): 117; Dylan Reid, "Carnival in Rouen: A History of the Abbaye De Conards," *Sixteenth Century Journal* 32 (2001): 1027–55; Samuel M. Carrington, "Censorship and the Medieval Comic Theatre in France," *Rice University Studies in French Literature* 57 (1971): 17–39.

19. Sara Beam, *Laughing Matters: Farce and the Making of Absolutism in France* (Ithaca, NY: Cornell University Press, 2007), 95–110; Jelle Koopmans, "Polémiques universitaires sur la scène," in *Théâtre polémique*, 77–87; L.-V. Gofflot, *Le théâtre au collège du Moyen Age à nos jours* (Paris: Champion, 1907).

20. Archives Départementales de la Gironde (ADG) 1 B 226, 201a, September 16, 1553.

21. Ibid., 201c; René Bonnat, "Une représentation protestante à Agen, en 1553," *Revue de l'Agenais* 29 (1902): 75–77; Henri Patry, "La Réforme et le théâtre en Guyenne au XVIe siècle (Agen 1553, Libourne 1555)," *Bulletin Historique et Littéraire de la Société de l'Histoire du Protestantisme Français* 50 (1901): 524. All translations are mine.

22. ADG 1 B 158, 93r-96r, May 14, 1555.

23. Georges Lecocq, *Histoire du théâtre en Picardie depuis ses origines jusqu'à la fin du XVIe siècle* (Paris: Menu, 1880), 143.

24. Brad S. Gregory, *Salvation at Stake: Christian Martyrdom in Early Modern Europe* (Cambridge, MA: Harvard University Press, 1999); David El Kenz, *Les bûchers du Roi: La culture protestante des martyrs (1523–1572)* (Seyssel: Champ Vallon, 1997); Diefendorf, *Beneath the Cross*; Luc Racaut, *Hatred in Print: Catholic Propaganda and Protestant Identity During the French Wars of Religion* (Aldershot, UK: Ashgate, 2002); Crouzet, *Genèse*.

25. Luc Racaut and Alex Ryrie, eds., *Moderate Voices in the European Reformation* (Aldershot, UK: Ashgate, 2005); C. Scott Dixon, Dagmar Freist, and Mark Greengrass, eds., *Living with Religious Diversity in Early-Modern Europe* (Farnham, UK: Ashgate, 2009).

26. Penny Roberts, *Peace and Authority during the French Religious Wars, c. 1560–1600* (New York: Palgrave Macmillan, 2013); Jérémie Foa, "Making Peace: The Commissions for Enforcing the Pacification Edicts in the Reign of Charles IX (1560–1574)," *French History* 18 (2004): 256–74; Mark Greengrass, *Governing Passions: Peace and Reform in the French Kingdom, 1576–1585* (Oxford: Oxford University Press, 2007).

27. Thierry Wanegffelen, *Ni Rome ni Genève: Des fidèles entre deux chaires en France au XVIe siècle* (Paris: Champion, 1997); Rosine A. Lambin, *Femmes de paix: La coexistence religieuse et les dames de la noblesse en France, 1520–1630* (Paris: Harmattan, 2003); Didier Boisson and Yves Krumenacker, eds., *La coexistence confessionnelle à l'épreuve: Etudes sur les relations entre Protestants et Catholiques dans la France moderne* (Lyon: Université Jean Moulin Lyon III, 2009).

28. Archives de l'État de Genève (AEG) Registres du Conseil (RC) 41, 142ʳ, July 12, 1546.

29. Jean Calvin translated from Latin in Émile Doumergue, *Jean Calvin: Les hommes et les choses de son temps* (Lausanne: G. Bridel, 1905), 3:584.

30. AEG RC 43, 67ʳ, April 16, 1548. See also AEG RC 48, 101r, August 9, 1554.

31. AEG RC 56, 249ʳ, October 13, 1561. See also AEG RC 54, 35v, January 6, 1558.

32. Christian Grosse and Ruth Stawarz-Luginbühl, "La pastorale (1585) de Simon Goulart," in *Simon Goulart: Un pasteur aux intérêts vastes comme le monde*, ed. Olivier Pot (Geneva: Droz, 2013), 431–40; AEG RC 44, 58ʳ, April 1, 1549.

33. Conrad Badius, "L'auteur au lecteur," in *Comedie du Pape malade*, in *Théâtre français de la Renaissance: La Comedie à l'époque d'Henri II et de Charles IX (1561–1568)*, 1st series, ed. Enea Balmas, Michel Dassonville, and Luigia Zilli (Florence; Paris: Leo S. Olschki; PUF, 1986), 7:181–273, v. 49.

34. Other cities on the French borderlands were also active in promoting religious reform through the theater. Jonathan Beck, ed., "*La maladie de Chrestienté* et *La Vérité cachée*: Deux moralités de polémique religieuse imprimées par Pierre de Vingle (Neuchâtel, 1533–1534)," in *Recueil général de moralités d'expression française*, ed. Jonathan Beck, Estelle Doudet, and Alan Hindley (Paris: Garnier, forthcoming); Glenn Ehrstine, *Theater, Culture, and Community in Reformation Bern, 1523–1555* (Leiden: Brill, 2002); Katell Lavéant, "Le théâtre et la Réforme dans les villes francophones des Pays-Bas méridionaux," in *Théâtre polémique*, 161–77.

35. Francis-Noël Le Roy, ed., *Deux sotties jouées à Genève l'une en 1523, sur la Place du Molard, dite sottie à dix personnages, et l'autre en 1524, en la Justice, dite Sottie à neuf personnages* (Geneva: J. Gay et fils, 1868); François Bonivard, *Chroniques de Genève*, ed. Micheline Tripet (Geneva: Droz, 2004), 2:191–95.

36. AEG RC 56, 224ʳ⁻ᵛ, August 5, 1561; AEG RC 63, 37r, April 20, 1568.

37. AEG RC 56, 242ʳ, September 22, 1561; Jean-Pierre Bordier, "Satire traditionnelle et polémique moderne dans les moralités et les sotties françaises tardives," in *Satira e beffa nelle commedie europee del Rinascimento*, ed. Maria Doglio Chiabò et al. (Rome: Torre d'Orfeo, 2002), 109–33; Claude Thiry, "Conrad Badius, Jacques

Bienvenu et leurs malades," in *Art de lire, art de vivre: Hommage au Professeur Georges Jacques*, ed. Myriam Watthée-Delmotte (Paris: Harmattan, 2008), 391–99; Jeff Persels, "The Sorbonnic Trots: Staging the Intestinal Distress of the Roman Catholic Church in French Reform Theater," *Renaissance Quarterly* 56 (2003): 1089–1111.

38. Helen Arnot Shaw, "Conrad Badius and the *Comedie du Pape malade*" (PhD diss., University of Pennsylvania, 1934); Enea Balmas and Monica Barsi, Introduction to *La comedie à l'époque d'Henri II*, 181–212.

39. Jacques Bienvenu, *Comedie du Monde malade et mal pensé*, ed. Rosalba Guerini, in *Théâtre français de la Renaissance*, 277–340; AEG RC 63, 37^r, April 20, 1568; Bordier, "Satire traditionnelle"; Thiry, "Conrad Badius"; G. Bonet-Maury, "'Le monde malade et mal pansé' ou la comédie protestante au XVIe siècle," *Bulletin Historique et Littéraire de la Société de l'Histoire de Protestantisme Français* 35, 3rd ser. (1886): 210–24.

40. Marcel Godet and Heinrich Türler, eds. *Dictionnaire historique et biographique de la Suisse* (Neuchâtel: Administration du Dictionnaire historique et biographique de la Suisse, 1921), 2:179; AEG RC 58, 121^r, November 19, 1563; AEG RC 54, 220^r, June 24, 1558; AEG (Mi B 109 p); Jacques Bienvenu, *Response au livre d'Artus Desire intitulé: Les grandes chroniques et annales de Passe-Partout* (Geneva: Jacques Berthet, 1558); *Le triomphe de Jesus Christ: Comedie apocalyptique, traduite du latin de Jean Foxus anglois, en rithme françoise, et augmentée d'un petit discours de la maladie de la messe, par Jacques Bienvenu citoyen de Geneve* (Geneva: Jean Bonnefoy, 1562).

41. Jacques Bienvenu, *Poesie de l'alliance perpetuelle entre deux nobles et chrestiennes villes franches, Berne et Geneve, faite l'an M.D.LVIII*; [Jacques Bienvenu], *Comedie facetieuse et tres plaisante, du voyage de frère Fecisti en Provence, vers Nostradamus: Pour savoir certaines nouvelles des clefs de Paradis et d'enfer, que le pape avoit perdues* (Nîmes [Geneva?], 1589).

42. Badius, *Pape malade*, "Auteur au lecteur," v. 56.

43. See AEG RC 56, 249^r, October 13, 1561; AEG RC 44, 58^r, April 1, 1549; AEG RC 48, 101^r, August 9, 1554; Grosse and Stawarz-Luginbühl, "La pastorale," 437.

44. Badius, *Pape malade*, v. 446.

45. Ibid., v. 277.

46. Ibid., v. 500–510.

47. *Farce des theologastres* (1526–1528); *La maladie de Chrétieneté* (1553–1535); *Sottie à neuf personnages, jouée en la Justice* (1524). Olga Duhl notes that Marguerite de Navarre makes a different choice in *La mallade* (1534–1535) by according the voice of faith to Chambrière. Olga Duhl, "La polémique religieuse dans le théâtre de Marguerite de Navarre," in *Théâtre polémique*, 189–97; Persels, "Sorbonnic Trots."

48. Badius, *Pape malade*, v. 287–88.

49. Ibid., v. 1047–84.

50. Bienvenu, *Comedie*, v. 540.

51. Ibid., v. 559.

52. Badius, *Pape malade*. "Auteur au lecteur," v. 59–61.

53. Geneva is only evoked as an "anglet en Savoie" ["corner in Savoy"] where heresy has taken hold. Badius, *Comedie*, v. 329.

54. Badius, *Pape malade*, v. 120.

55. Ibid., v. 321–35.

56. Bienvenu, *Comedie*, v. 805–38.

57. Bruce Gordon, *Calvin* (New Haven, CT: Yale University Press, 2009).

58. E. William Monter, "The Consistory of Geneva, 1559–1569," *Bibliothèque d'Humanisme et Renaissance* 38 (1976): 467–84; Isabella M. Watt, Introduction to *Registres du Consistoire de Genève au temps de Calvin*, vol. I, *1542–44*, ed. Thomas A. Lambert, Isabella M. Watt, Robert M. Kingdon, and Jeffrey R. Watt (Geneva: Droz, 1996), xiii.

59. Shaw, "Conrad Badius," 20–24.

60. Grosse, *Rituels*; Scott M. Manetsch, "Pastoral Care East of Eden: The Consistory of Geneva, 1568–82," *Church History* 75 (2006): 274–313; Thomas Lambert, "Cette loi durera guère: inertie religieuse et espoirs catholiques à Genève au temps de la Réforme," *Bulletin de la Société d'Histoire et d'Archéologie de Genève* 23 (1993): 5–24; Jeffrey R. Watt, "Women and the Consistory in Calvin's Geneva," *Sixteenth Century Journal* 24 (1993): 429–39.

61. Bienvenu, *Comedie*, v. 672, 680, 688, 692.

62. Ibid., v. 854.

63. Badius, *Pape malade*, v. 182.

64. Ibid., v. 200.

65. Bienvenu, *Comedie*, v. 720.

66. Arlette Jouanna, *La Saint-Barthélemy : Les mystères d'un crime d'état, 24 août 1572* (Paris: Gallimard, 2007), 231–81.

67. Grosse and Stawarz-Luginbühl, "La pastorale," 436–38; Le Roy, *Deux sotties*.

68. Jean-Claude Aubailly, *Le monologue, le dialogue et la sottie: Essai sur quelques genres dramatiques de la fin du Moyen Age et du début du XVIe siècle* (Paris: H. Champion, 1976); Heather Arden, *Fools' Plays: A Study of Satire in the "Sottie"* (Cambridge, UK: Cambridge University Press, 1980).

69. Bienvenu, *Comedie*, v. 192–94, 442–43, 588–664.

70. Ibid., v. 296–99.

71. Picot, "Moralités polémiques"; Bordier, "Satire traditionnelle,"; Beck, *Théâtre et propagande*.

72. Badius, *Pape malade*, "Auteur au lecteur," v. 37.

73. Ibid., *Pape malade*, v. 1617.

74. Ibid., *Pape malade*, "Prologue," v. 17–22.

75. Jonathan Beck, "De l'endoctrinement des enfants: les écoliers de la Gestapo antiprotestante d'après le théâtre aux débuts de la Réforme," *Fifteenth-Century Studies* 13 (1988): 471–83.

76. Balmas and Barsi, Introduction, 209–11.

77. Ibid., 188.

78. Beam, *Laughing Matters*; Reid, "Conards"; Dylan Reid, "Renaissance Printing and Provincial Culture in Sixteenth-Century Rouen," *University of Toronto Quarterly* 73 (2004): 1011–20.

79. Raymond Mentzer, ed., *Sin and the Calvinists: Morals Control and the Consistory in the Reformed Tradition* (Kirksville, MO: Sixteenth Century Journal Publishers, 1994); Benedict, *Christ's Churches*.

80. Grosse and Stawarz-Luginbühl, "La pastorale," *passim*; Émile Rivoire, ed., *Les sources du droit du Canton de Genève* (Arau: H.R. Sauerländer, 1933) 3:505.

81. Glenn S. Sunshine, "French Protestantism on the Eve of St-Bartholomew: The Ecclesiastical Discipline of the French Reformed Churches, 1571–1572," *French History* 4 (1990): 375, art. 18; Philippe Chareyre, "'The Great Difficulties One Must Bear to Follow Jesus Christ': Morality at Sixteenth-Century Nîmes," in *Sin and the Calvinists*, 63–96; Philip Conner, *Huguenot Heartland: Montaubon and Southern French Calvinism During the Wars of Religion* (Aldershot, UK: Ashgate, 2002), 78–82.

~

CHAPTER FIVE

French Humanist Comedy in Search of an Audience

The Case of Jean de la Taille

Corinne Noirot

Who watched, who heard, who read French Renaissance comedies? Whom were French humanist writers of the mid-sixteenth century and beyond (ca. 1552–ca. 1611) addressing when composing and—more seldom—publishing (neoclassical) comedies? Both Raymond Lebègue and Madeleine Lazard pose the question of reception and audience as they discuss the history of French "comic" theater and the enduring popularity of the farce.[1] The fact that the revival coincided with the tumultuous decades of the French Wars of Religion has a lot to do with its feeble success, they contend, since it became less possible to produce or even attend a staged play. External historical factors undoubtedly account in part for the limited impact of the genre, which includes roughly two dozen comedies. Complex internal, dramaturgical tensions heretofore hardly explored by critics, however, also explain the relative failure of French Renaissance comedy, understood in a narrow sense as imitating classical form, directly or indirectly. This relative literary failure is all the more striking given the future of the genre a few generations later with the likes of Pierre Corneille and Molière.

How did such a pioneering genre fail to find and perhaps define an audience for itself? This chapter highlights important theoretical as well as practical obstacles, by using Jean de la Taille de Bondaroy's *Les corrivaux* (*The Rivals*, 1573; composed ca. 1562) and *Le négromant* (*The Necromancer*, 1574;

likely written before 1562) as two cases in point.[2] La Taille's plays constitute an eloquent corpus both because his contribution has been overlooked—Lazard's original index even fails to list his plays—and because his writing arrestingly grapples with a genre whose normative definition often clashed both with "national" aesthetics and the author's complex pragmatic goal to both reunite and satirize, mobilize and pacify the nation and its leaders.[3]

I first examine the historic struggle to reach an audience that French humanist comedy encountered by summarizing its empirical (including editorial) and theoretical causes and outlining the main (sociopolitical, ideological, and aesthetic) reasons behind it.[4] I then analyze the complex case of La Taille's plays, focusing on the implications of the external and internal impediments delineated. Furthermore, *Les corrivaux* (to a large extent) and *Le négromant* (to a lesser extent, perhaps because it was translated from Ariosto) are fraught with contemporary national issues and political allusions—following the French and neo-Latin tradition—but in a covert fashion, which raises the question of indirect address and the possibility of tiered audiences. Could the new and hybrid genre of comedy capture the attention of unlearned, unconcerned, and often demobilized and impoverished noblemen? In La Taille's plays, a pragmatic and moral thrust conflicts with certain normative aspects of neoclassical comedy—a tension that stands out in *Les corrivaux* in particular. How can La Taille address those who "can" (i.e., the monarchy and the nobility) and those who "know" (i.e., Christian humanists and poets, if not persecuted Huguenots or affiliated souls) on the same level? And what if for La Taille, a playwright actively seeking to pacify his fellow countrymen, the technical features of the newly restored genre of comedy were primarily a means to an end?

French Humanist Comedy:
Struggling to Reach beyond Learned Audiences

Although it was a well-defined (yet not completely uniform) genre, French humanist comedy never quite reached a sizable audience. Let us first review the main reasons for that historical struggle, starting with internal obstacles. A summary of past research will also help us outline the chief external causes for such failure in the context of religious tensions during the tenure of Catherine de' Medici as queen and regent of France (1549–1588).

Internal Obstacles: The Precarious Status of Comedy
Let us begin by noting the philological, aesthetic, national/circumstantial, and theoretical tensions inherent to the genre. The lack of codification, the

existence of a national tradition, and an ambivalence toward Italian models are the principal internal points of resistance or instability within the genre. Comedy was assumed to be symmetrical to tragedy as the other subgenre of dramatic poetry embodying the mimesis of actions.[5] Yet humanist discussions of comedy suffered from a lack of Aristotelian precepts due to the loss of the Stagyrite's treatise on comedy.[6] Lack of generic codification therefore remained strong in spite of extended philological endeavors.

Generic categorization surrounding comedy in the mid-sixteenth century, moreover, appears particularly unstable in France due to conflicting uses of the adjective *comique* [comedic/comical]. On the one hand, *comique* referred to comedy as the codified classical genre that humanists strove to revive (and not to laughing matter in general). Humanist comedy was not particularly comical in nature. Erudite comedy distanced itself from laughter partly because of the continued blossoming of the farce on the French stage, and partly due to the lack of Aristotelian prescriptions on comedic matter. It featured overcomplicated plots, produced by emulators of the *commedia erudita*,[7] and an emphasis on wordplay and *facetiae*, that is, aspects of *festivitas* or linguistic gaiety distinct from the theory of *ridicula* [laughing matter], much criticized as licentious and potentially immoral, in the Ciceronian tradition.[8] On the other hand, and prior to that generic use, *comique* could designate a type of style or discourse—namely, "plain style," as epitomized by Clément Marot—imitating private conversations between *personae*, high or low. This private decorum entails that common usage be put in the mouth of characters;[9] in this respect, Donatus considered the iambic dialogue of Greek comedy to be best suited for mirroring daily exchanges.[10] Besides the fact that Charles Estienne had paved the way,[11] this meta-rhetorical meaning of the term *comique* explains La Taille's choice of prose in his comedies, while Pléiade poets wrote their comedies in octosyllabic verse. Such ties to rhetorical plain style also match prefatory statements underlining the fact that comedy is the dramatic genre representing *ethe* [character temperaments] and the ways of common people ("un chascun du populaire" [commoners]).[12] It similarly matches the definition of comedy as a mirror of life according to Aristotle's theory of mimesis, as disseminated by Donatus.[13] The latter incidentally dubbed the *Odyssey* "comedic/comical," after Longinus and the Ciceronian tradition.[14] Besides these two general traits—antitragic mimesis and private/conversational decorum[15]—practitioners of comedy rarely applied rigid rules; their works belie "a tension between formal theory and subjective response that remains unresolved."[16]

Another explanation of the dissonance felt in the revival is that much of the theory surrounding New Comedy more or less went against the national

tradition of narrative and dramatic satire, featuring lewd and physical comedy (medieval stage plays such as farces and sotties, fatrasies, fabliaux).[17] The
farce was alive and well in the sixteenth century, despite humanist contempt
and the development of more elaborate, mostly Italianate, court spectacles.
Critical consensus posits that humanist comedy intended to break with the
tradition of the farce, perceived as base and aimed at the ignorant masses, the
populace.[18] Yet all these writers grew up in an environment in which Gallic wit and bawdy comedy prevailed and all holidays were marked by farce
performances. In that sense, the rebellious spirit of Old Comedy was closer to
the French comedic mind-set than a tame domestic New Comedy centered
on innocuous amorous entanglements.

Neoclassical comedy came to be revived under Italian influence at a
time when ambivalence toward the Italians was pervasive, especially under
Francis I and Henri II. Adrianus Turnebus and Pierre de Larivey (the latter
Italian born), for instance, are described as belonging to two generations in
the short-lived tradition of humanist and post-humanist comedy, the second
one more prone to integrating the Italian theatrical and satirical tradition,
and closer in style to the French genre of bigarrures, discursive pieces of (often satirical) prose. French humanist comedy simply would not exist without
Ariosto and his followers,[19] and La Taille himself in his original prologue
refers to Ariosto and other "Italians."[20] He is nevertheless closer to Estienne's
position, striving to hark back more directly to Roman comedy and to revive
and "naturalize" the consummate art of the ancients[21] while praising Italian
playwrights.[22] Regarding characters, the author selectively imports new types
formalized and popularized in commedia erudita; even though Le négromant is
translated from Ariosto and its title character, the charlatan Necromancer,
is a "doctor" type (mixed with the Terentian parasite), none of his plays feature an authoritative and abusive Italian father of the ilk found in both the
commedia erudita and the newly imported commedia dell'arte: no Pantalone
populates La Taille's plays.

Regardless of the difficulty to emulate the success of Italian comedies,
humanists praised the new dignified genre, which explicitly aimed at super-
seding the farce, both aesthetically and morally. It is still commonly called
"erudite comedy," after the Italian commedia erudita (starting with Ariosto's
La cassaria in 1508).[23] It is to be understood as composed by erudite authors,
as opposed to literally learned in its content. Based on the model of Roman
comedy—that is, Plautus and Terence, imitated indirectly via Ariosto and
other Italian models—humanist comedy in the French Renaissance tended
to be apolitical in scope and to avoid religious undertones. This became truer
after the 1541 and 1548 decrees of the Paris parlement regulating theatrical

performances as part of Christian mystery plays. Indeed, in 1548 the Paris *parlement* officially banned *mystères de la passion* (although mystery plays continued to be performed well into the seventeenth century). In such a hostile context, Jacques Grévin's *La trésorière* (1558) deliberately eschewed religious topics, as did *Les ébahis*, an Italian imitation generally understood as not echoing contemporary political debates. On the contrary, *L'Eugène* by Etienne Jodelle was considered polemical. The play was published posthumously in 1574 (the same year as *Le négromant*) but was performed in 1552 or 1553 before Henri II, on the very same day as Jodelle's tragedy *Cléopâtre captive*, in the same venue and in front of the same set of spectators: royal attendees and courtiers, for the most part, that is, the audience implicitly criticized in the play(s). Most comedies were written by well-respected *Pléiade* poets to be heard by princes and national stakeholders, but few got produced at court, partly because authors writing during the French Wars of Religion were at risk of being prosecuted, if not persecuted. Censorship and retaliation were to be avoided. Such awareness of hazardous consequences tied to the act of addressing power is clear in the case of La Taille's published comedies. As we shall see, a more nuanced assessment of erudite comedy's apolitical stance is therefore necessary in order to understand this author's positioning.

External Obstacles: Farce and Court Tastes

External obstacles, well documented in past scholarly studies, help explain why French humanist comedy never found any significant resonance. These are mostly sociopolitical in nature, since the vitality of the farce, new trends in court plays and festivities, and a crisis of patronage all characterized the state of French theater during the French Wars of Religion.

In spite of *parlement* edicts and humanist contempt, the enduring popularity of the farce was conspicuous when it comes to actual staged plays. The Hôtel de Bourgogne and Hôtel de Reims had begun housing Italian companies,[24] while farces still prevailed in the provinces and on the street. The commedia dell'arte was deeply favored by Queen Catherine de' Medici, as evidenced by the installation of the Gelosi under Charles IX and Henri III. Due to its high level of physical engagement (acrobatics, *lazzi* [improvised comic dialogue or action], and so forth) and noisy live audience, commedia dell'arte was closer to the farce and its performative traits.[25]

Change in political leadership and Catherine's Tuscan taste further altered court festivities and limited humanist authors' chances at having their comedies produced, save for a self-selected, learned, limited audience. While "popular theater" took place in public (mostly urban) spaces during political and religious festivities (e.g., carnival, royal weddings), educated audiences all over Europe enjoyed staged drama in court theaters, universities, and schools (or *collèges*). Plays penned by humanist writers, including erudite comedy, were "performed by students in their colleges and occasionally in aristocratic houses or at court."[26] In Paris, new urban venues such as the Hôtel de Bourgogne and Hôtel de Reims were geographically independent but still tied to the court. Italian companies and Ariosto's plays were omnipresent in repertories throughout the sixteenth century,[27] with the commedia dell'arte gaining ground in the 1560s through the 1590s.

Finally, active patronage became (often drastically) limited starting in 1559, both for writers and patrons suspected of, persecuted for, or executed for heresy. Clientage and patronage fluctuated due to dynastic and religious tensions; Catherine, Henri II, and Charles IX did not particularly favor poetry.[28] If Jean de la Taille wrote, and then patiently waited for the opportunity to publish, two humanist comedies in this theoretically valorizing (since a revival of neoclassical dramatic forms was called for) but practically limiting context, due to a lack of authorities and royal interest, how did he view and shape his projected audience, and did he succeed in reaching the right eyes and ears?

La Taille's Precarious Address: Between Those Who "Can" and Those who "Know"

A follower of the *Pléiade* and affiliated Latinate humanists such as Charles Estienne, La Taille sought both to follow the new—normative and imitative—aesthetic ideal and fulfill the pragmatic goal of serving the common good. In this respect, his works, not least his comedies, are addressed to humanists and educated aristocrats, the royal family included. Reading them closely, however, leads one to detect arresting dissonant details and elements of resistance to certain set patterns and expectations of erudite comedy. Having to negotiate conflicting imperatives, such as those of caution and bravery, necessary concealment, and desired reach, it would seem that La Taille projected for his comedies a tiered audience, between like-minded thinkers and powerful doers. Perhaps he failed to be heard because, in trying to foster peace and reconciliation, he was attempting to speak the same language to the persecuted and the persecutors, to the disempowered and the powerful, to those who could (royals and aristocrats) and those who knew (poets, humanists, and possibly also persecuted Huguenots).

Addressing Those Who Can: The Crown and the French Nobility
La Taille emphasizes the dignity of the genre and his projected audience so as to orient the reception and elevate the message, first addressing those

who *can*, in times of turmoil—those who can make and read neoclassical plays of course, but first and foremost those who can take action and exert political power.

In La Taille's mind, erudite comedy was meant to reach a live audience. Numerous components pointing to staged performance can be inventoried. To begin with, direct address to the audience (by the prologue or characters) frames the plays. For instance, the prologue of *Les corrivaux* utters "Messieurs," a title reserved for noblemen.[29] Attendees are also urged to listen in silence and applaud at the end, eschewing the rowdy behavior for which farce viewers were known, even though the playwright, following Ariosto, aims to induce laughter ("vous donner matiere de rire" ["give you reason to laugh"]).[30] At the end of *Le négromant*, Maxime solicits applause from the "benins spectateurs" ["benevolent spectators"].[31] Classical form is followed by La Taille and taken to increase the pleasure of drama (after Estienne). Such formal conformity includes the tripartite Aristotelian plotline (*protasis-epitasis-catastrophe*[32]) and self-contained act-and-scene composition "selon l'art" ["following the (rules of) art"].[33] *Les corrivaux*, it is worth repeating, was the first neoclassically structured comedy (or *comédie régulière*) published in France.[34] Act 1 provides a domestic and intimate exposition in both of La Taille's comedies—a young woman in dire straits confides in her maid [*chambriere*], allowing the narrative deployment of the background and plot—while the denouement expectedly seals reconciliations and marriages. Learned audiences were more apt to appreciate classical form and structure, but La Taille nonetheless preferentially addresses educated gentlemen.

Within this meant-for-the-stage framework, theatrical elements serve to add antique luster, but none are sprinkled gratuitously. La Taille's *Négromant*, mirroring Ariosto's self-consciousness, uses dramatic action buttressed by theoretical notions to problematize the nature of *action*. Many types of practices (*pratiques* [practices], *œuvres* [works], *affaires* [affairs, business], *trafiquer* [trade, commerce]) are implemented, assessed, and criticized, as are ways of succeeding.[35] Moreover, La Taille conveys meta-dramatic discourse in his play through phrases such as "une trame" ["plot"], "la connoissance" ["acquaintance"] (i.e., *agnitio*), "grand meslange" [i.e., *imbroglio*],[36] or the allusion to the stone mask of the *hypokritès* [actor] to let the audience judge a character.[37] The responsibilities of the leading aristocrats addressed are front and center. Theirs is the field of action, and it behooves them to mobilize themselves for acts more noble than corrupt and deceitful ones, other than court intrigue and political scheming. When life is too close to comedy, then comedy should act as a deterrent and steer viewers back toward more befitting, dignified behaviors. Estienne believed it worked in ancient Rome, "[c]ar par ce moyen chascun mettoit peine à ne faire chose parquoy il peust estre joué aux comedies" ["for in that way, everyone strove to avoid any behavior that could potentially be acted out in comedies"].[38] Estienne means that even though Roman emperors and other notables became upset by drama as overt political commentary, it did have—or so humanists wanted to believe—preventive effects so as to preserve or rebalance the social order.

For all the (legitimate) fears that humanist writings on theater bespeak, ancient drama was no purely aesthetic venture, but an inherently political and civic affair. La Taille was keenly aware of the multiple forms and functions of theater. French humanists who set out to revive classical dramatic forms had underscored their public nature, both at the production and performance stages—"aux fraiz de la chose publique" ["at the cost of the *res publica*"], writes Estienne in his preface to Terence's *Andria*, which he translated into French.[39] For instance, in Rome, actors were free, rewarded, and well-regarded, and a tiered seating chart both distinguished and conjoined citizens of all ranks in the theater or amphitheater, from senators to the populace.[40] Conveying the political centrality of theater in ancient Rome is crucial to Estienne,[41] even when summarizing contemporary knowledge—partly conjectural, he admits—on ancient drama for the young *Dauphin* [heir apparent of France] and emphasizing "delectable" "recreation."[42] La Taille similarly declares that his goal as a playwright is to benefit the state, to act for the public good, the *res publica*.[43]

Addressing Neighbors-Turned-Strangers in *Les corrivaux*

La Taille dramatizes contemporary events and issues, exposing French struggles everywhere in his *œuvre*. Erudite comedy does carry political portent in his work, however discreet. As a case in point, illusory "strangeness" (unfamiliarity and foreignness) is enacted and exposed in multifarious ways in *Les corrivaux*.[44] In this singular play, three "bourgeois" families, one of which scattered a decade before because of continuous wars, end up converging in the same town and uniting into one clan, even though they are seemingly foreigners (from Lorraine and Picardy, especially), thus avoiding incest and repairing losses. This play shows that La Taille does not write merely to be read but for his voice and vision to resonate in a theater. At the level of spectacle, insistence on the reception of the performance, minimized contrast between (non-noble) *personae*,[45] and unwarranted antagonisms reflected in the dialogue, all speak to a strong dramatic vision, related to convergence and action, and the challenging goal of reuniting estranged parties.

Insistence on reception pervades *Les corrivaux*, a play in which misrecognition abounds. It is a play, a *jeu*, that the author proposes, and numerous cues underscore the dramatic genre,[46] including a contemporary plot line, deictics, tonal variations, important accessories and gestures, dramatic tension, dialogical ironies, lexical contrasts, and numerous comedic devices. The paratext, moreover, insists on the importance of theatrical seeing-and-hearing, following the etymology of *theatron* incidentally inscribed in the text itself, since the liminary sonnet by Jacques de la Taille, the author's deceased brother, presents a polyptoton on the verb *voir* at the beginning of each stanza: "Qui voudra voir," "Qu'il vienne voir," "On y verra," "Bref, on verra" ["Whoever wants to see," "Let them see," "Therein you'll see," "In short, you'll see"].[47] The prologue, moreover, addresses live audience members who came to *watch* and *hear* a comedy ("venus pour ouir une Comedie . . . une Comedie pour certain vous y verrez. . . . Escoutez donc" ["Having come to hear a comedy . . . A comedy you shall see, no doubt. . . . Listen up"]).[48] Theatricality is also emphasized through the participatory framing of Roman comedy: an initial introduction and a final request for applause are uttered by the prologue.[49] The stated necessity to listen carefully ["soigneusement"] additionally highlights the active reception and attention expected of the audience by linking the effects of theatrical performance to the core topic introduced in Jacques's liminary sonnet, namely, care ["la cure"], a virtue modeled on a father's affection toward his children.[50] The idea that a careless listener might miss certain elements if not the very point of the play[51] alerts the audience to the presence of subtle allusive meaning: they will hear what is said, provided they care.[52]

In an effort to lessen social divides, commoners are shown as potentially noble, in a strategy almost reverse to the "deterrent" intent of Roman tragedy underscored by Estienne.[53] The selection and organization of characters or *dramatis personae* also dramatizes the desired rapprochements. The types chosen conform to Aristotle's *Rhetoric* and Horace's *Ars poetica*—old and young, male and female characters harbor decorous passions and language—but differences appear, if not leveled out, at least strongly relativized. This favors identification on the part of the audience. Likewise, the author explicitly expects noblemen ("Messieurs," says the prologue) to hear or watch his play, but the characters in a comedy are all commoners ["du populaire"]. Social difference is marked by the use of prose in both comedies, while La Taille's tragedies are in verse; regional colloquialisms, physical comedy, and the kind of bawdy talk [*gauloiserie*] that was part and parcel of aristocratic (masculine) sociability at the time also favor commonality between distant groups or entities. Male solidarity is thus reinforced via the interactions of servants as well as suggestive jabs addressed by the author to his peers. The nobleman whom La Taille targets ideally shares his humanist education, as incidentally evidenced by a valet's joke involving Proserpina.[54] Tavern banter brings masters and servants closer as *men* while still extolling the higher status, the condition of masters. The double entendre put in the mouth of a governess evoking her young (secretly pregnant) mistress's projected religious seclusion and the "good fruit/fruition" it shall yield further illustrates this Gallic solidarity, while adding a religious allusion.[55]

In addition, the bourgeois depicted (Fremin and Benard especially) more or less behave as noblemen, and their hurdles parallel those of mid- to late-sixteenth-century *gentilshommes* in France. The damsel in distress (Restitue, named after a martyr and a Boccaccian character) can only wait for a shining knight to restore her honor, in accordance with the noble ethical ideal to which La Taille still adheres. Her fertility is to be celebrated regardless of the sin that taints it, which reflects the intense dynastic anxieties that plagued a mournful French aristocracy, caught in lasting civil wars. Likewise Jacqueline and Benard, a rich widow and widower, are destined to marry, thus reforming a perfect—since their respective children too will wind up married—and safe family unit, preserving the integrity and transmission of patrimony. Such dignified, "noble-like" social behaviors are accompanied by the constant display of noble sentiments and virtues. Here we recognize the humanist idea, extolled by Montaigne among others,[56] that a noble heart can grow independently from, and sometimes trump, noble blood.

Antagonistic difference inscribed in the dialogue and staged interactions also contribute to the dramatization of "strangeness" as an original aspect of *Les corrivaux* and La Taille's dramaturgy. The dialogue uses elegiac and tragic speech for comic effect, as found in Ariosto and other erudite comedies parodying the Petrarchan lover, but at times clearly to show how much a character is alienated from his own feelings or reality. This is the case for the old Benard, who claims he is nearing death while he is about to experience an Aristotelian recognition [*anagnoresis/agnitio*] and rebirth, having found his lost child again.[57] The crisscrossings, secrets, and numerous asides that support the double scheme to kidnap Fleurdelis, a young woman whom two rival lovers are courting (hence the title), additionally show that the two "parties" do not know each other, especially on the victims' side. Furthermore, the strategic "back door" of stage comedies and abduction plots appears as a symbolic locus of the boundary between an imposed life and clandestine estrangement, between domestic preservation and public exposure to damageable libel. In this respect, the unexpected central fight scene in 3.3 between two servants (Claude and Alizon) working for two different families reveals that surface familiarity based on social equality can turn into open antagonism out of a simple verbal altercation. Showing that quarrelling neighbors easily turn into strangers, the scene follows a dramatic crescendo, with the dispute escalating from separate soliloquies to insults, then physical threats, with hostile gesturing involving no less than a torch and a distaff.

In short, in *Les corrivaux*, unwarranted estrangement is effectively dramatized and resolved. It is meant to stimulate reflective and active emulation rather than to lampoon and passively deter. While inspired by Italian humanism (Boccaccio et al.), La Taille's original play is thus far less satirical than *Le négromant*, taken from Ariosto. Addressing those who can, the powers that be, is an uphill battle in a contentious climate, and yet the author tries. His willing voice is also geared toward those who know, like-minded thinkers with or without authority. He tries to strike an uneasy balance that may ultimately have robbed him of truly appreciative understanding and adequate reception.

Addressing Those Who Know: Christian Humanists and Moderate Protestants

Toward whom are the political undertones aimed, if not solely or chiefly the First Estate and the powers that be? Although the author's family and early allegiances point to Huguenot sympathies, the allusive mode of address that characterizes his comedies is neither definitely partisan nor neutral or apolitical, as some other *Pléiade*-era plays tended to be. Just as the Roman theater offered tiered seating to accommodate all walks of life, La Taille is attempting to reach a tiered audience of partially antagonistic forces, and partly failing to be heard for this very reason. His allegiances were not clear, for those hungry for partisan language; his detachment was lacking, for those seeking to stay above the fray; his boldness was off-putting—although we may only speculate—to the powers that be.

As cited above, Estienne insists on the difference between Old and New Comedy in terms of public appropriateness and political risk-taking, since for him, (barely) covertly critical plays upset too many dignitaries and thus were rightfully overthrown in favor of a more innocuous type of *comoedia* centered on amorous affairs.[58] In the preface to *Les abusez* addressed to the Dauphin of France, attacking notables [*taxer*] even allusively ("la couverture et le taxer des superieurs" ["the covert blaming of people higher up"]) is stigmatized as offensive ("impudence," "folies," "temeraires," ["impudence, foolish acts, reckless"]).[59] Jean de la Taille did not share such a—self-defensive, perhaps—view that comedy should be devoid of references to current affairs or political portent. Even though the parallels he draws and the critical allusions he makes remain cautiously covert, he does take a stance on current affairs, albeit obliquely. Among other humanist writers, the original author of *Le né-*

gromant, Ariosto, is known for his use of irony and allusive discourse. Double entendre can function at several levels in translation, due to the space-time transposition at play, thus further blurring the message. In the prologue to *Le négromant*, one may hear La Taille's voice, superimposed onto Ariosto's and echoing contemporary debates and struggles, through the ambivalence of marvel ("Ne pensez plus ouir chose impossible" ["Quit thinking you're hearing something impossible"]);[60] the Protestant-leaning Estes court of Ferrara "brought to Rome"; the protagonist coming all the way from Cremona to admire the pope (and later, being displaced by black magic);[61] and polysemic terms also pervasive in the discourse of religious polemics, such as "comedie toute nouvelle" [brand new comedy], "alliances," and "remedies" (a recurring word). All can alert us to the presence of covert content and cryptic intent not unrelated to contemporary polemics and ideological divides.

As both authorized and normally "flattened" by the framework of erudite comedy, historical parallels abound in La Taille's comedies: parallels between midcentury France and early-century Italy, and between past conflicts with the Hapsburgs (e.g., the Three Bishoprics in *Les corrivaux* and the Italian Wars in *Le négromant*) and contemporary civil wars. Broad parallels prevail, both as a matter of caution and to convey an above-the-fray ethical ideal; peace and unity are the desired order upset by wars, which destroy territorial integrity and political unity. La Taille selects as a backdrop a nation atomized by tensions, factions, and invasions: Italy at the time of *Il negromante* is like France at the time the translated play is composed and published.[62] According to *Les corrivaux*'s fable, long-contested border territories such as Lorraine and Picardie sent the characters into a lengthy exile; they all wind up converging in Paris, a city as central as 1520 Rome in the Ariosto comedy transposed.[63] Such converging also partly bears a meta-dramatic meaning, since the original setting of "stage plays" [*jeux sceniques*]—both on- and offstage, as regards comedy—is defined as an intersection, a heavy-traffic crossroads or *carrefour*.[64]

Among broad symbolic parallels, figurative impotence and problematic filiations (want of heirs and descendants, adopted or lost children) additionally underpin both published comedies. Bestiality and predatory behavior, on the other hand, pervade *Le négromant* (verbs such as *piller* [to ransack] and *becqueter* [to peck, like a bird] recur, especially regarding the title character). This goes beyond the decorum of comedy, since predatory imagery structures La Taille's tragedies;[65] the near-cannibalistic cruelty of civil war and corrupted, uncharitable relations are hereby denounced. The wise Nebbien's soliloquy in *Le négromant* 2.2 also features an oblique commentary on Erasmian/Paulinian folly, since the greedy charlatan knowingly exploits human folly: "Ainsi il jouit et me fait jouir des biens d'autrui, en aydant à la follie, de laquelle le monde a si grande abundance" ["And thus he enjoys and makes me enjoy what belongs to others, encouraging folly, with which the world is replete"].[66] He is shown as an alien, a false prophet, and "truly Jewish," as false Christians were polemically called.[67]

As for secrecy, a standard element of erudite New Comedy, it serves to bring forth clandestine alliances and hidden filiations; children and parents remain separated and seemingly unrelated due to deception, flight, and new ties contracted in the face of war. Accordingly, Aristotelian recognition can only happen *after* the times of invasions and war. As does *Les corrivaux*, *Le négromant* explains how the families' hurdles all take their source in the territorial instability and perpetual conquests of the times, invasions that caused a character (Maxime) to flee to Calabria and assume a false (Alexandrian) identity, start a new family, then run away again when the French invaded in turn, only to lose his wife and child, who thought he had returned to Alexandria.[68] Now that Maxime's twelve-year wandering exile is over, reunions can occur and a long-held secret can be lifted, based on multiple "signes manifestes" ["evident signs"].[69] *Le négromant* is more than a mere translation; the fact that matching tokens—"contresigne,"[70] a true *symbolon* that warrants recognition—were always destined to help the next of kin identify each other, for instance, can incidentally apply to the scattered Protestant brotherhood, without La Taille's words ever radically marking confessional fault lines.

So, is the goal to artfully revive erudite comedy a deceptive contraption for the most part, a trompe-l'œil effect? And why did La Taille deliberately opt for the blurred or tiered reception that hindered his success? What we are attempting to capture here is irreducible to hard evidence, as it is meant to remain partially cryptic and open to interpretation. Perhaps such ambiguous allusiveness—complex in that it betrays moral if not spiritual beliefs as well as pragmatic constraints— is to be situated closer to Isabelle Garnier-Mathez's findings surrounding the language shared by the evangelical community (connected to Marguerite de Navarre: Guillaume Farel, Marot, Lambert Meigret, Jacques Lefèvre d'Étaples, and so forth).[71] From the 1520s through the 1530s in France, in writings by and for evangelical-leaning circles, common adjectives (*vrai* [true], *seul* [sole, alone], *vif* [live, lively] and *spirituel* [spiritual] vs. *humain* [human]), among other forms, were ideologically polarized, and amplified notably via metaphors, emphasis, antithesis, and a play on commonplaces. Figurative intertextuality and allusive signifying was, let us remember as well, a practice common to all the liberal and fine arts in the Renaissance, as demonstrated by Kristin Phillips-Court in the case of Italian painting and drama, in particular.[72]

The uneasy address and purpose featured in *Les corrivaux* and *Le négromant* thus betray a tension between a nationalistic and (mildly) dissident impulse. La Taille's comedies' failure to reach an audience is partly due to conflicting strategies deployed to target and define a dual audience, "those who can" and "those who know" ideally converging in the theater as the symbolic body and mind of France trying to stay alive, as fellow subjects of the French Crown, and as Christian neighbors.

Not unlike the *drame*, a new theatrical genre theorized and exemplified by Denis Diderot in the eighteenth century, French erudite comedy thus never quite made its mark in the sixteenth century due to internal and external obstacles, not the least of which was the lack of royal interest, and pressure to favor apolitical content due to religious turmoil and a crisis of patronage as a corollary. In La Taille's plays, a perceptible pragmatic thrust and a prudent insistence on moral if not spiritual concerns such as kinship and care beyond frontiers and divisions appears partially at odds with some highly normative aspects of "regular" neoclassical comedy. Such tensions stand out in *Les corrivaux*, particularly regarding its character dynamics. What if the technical features of the newly restored genre of comedy were partly smoke and mirrors for our author—that is, a means to an end bearing relative prestige, but also a diversion, a protective shield in a highly inflammable context? Allusive language etymologically points to *something else* [*allia*]; it toys with oblique expression. Such a message, it can be argued, surpasses the medium, and ultimately could have been cast in any literary genre. Yet showing alternatives to violence through comedy and lending a voice to the *commoner*, albeit a humanist aristocrat in disguise, does buttress the author's conciliatory purpose. In the midst of serious empirical hazards and uncertainties, a clash of exigencies and a blurred horizon of expectations ultimately reveal in La Taille the compelling yet powerless clear-sightedness of a soldier-poet who painfully understood that his dramatic ambition, especially in the "comic" genre, blossomed at a time when politics and war were no laughing matter.

Notes

1. Madeleine Lazard, *La comédie humaniste au seizième siècle et ses personnages* (Paris: Presses Universitaires de France, 1978), 18, 78; Raymond Lebègue, *Le théâtre comique en France de Pathelin à Mélite* (Paris: Hatier, 1972), 167–68, conclusion.

Part of the research for this chapter was made possible by generous short-term fellowships from the Folger Shakespeare Library and the Harvard Houghton Library.

2. Jean de la Taille, *Les corrivaus*, in *Œuvres*, ed. R. de Maulde (Geneva: Slatkine Reprints, 1968), 4:i–cvi; *Le négromant, comedie de M. Lovis Arioste: Nouvellement mise en françois par Jehan de la Taille de Bondaroy*, in ibid., cvi–ccxxvii. I refer in this chapter to these original editions and cite the page numbers from these plays. *Les corrivaus* is modernized to *Les corrivaux*, *Corrivaux* for short. All translations are mine unless otherwise noted.

3. In a substantial overview article, Lazard does mention La Taille's plays. Madeleine Lazard, "Du théâtre médiéval à la comédie du XVIe siècle: Continuité et rupture," *Bulletin de l'Association d'Etude sur l'Humanisme, la Réforme et la Renaissance* 44 (1997): 65–78. Roger Guichemerre also marvels at how Renaissance and baroque comedy never took hold (although he mentions Turnèbe and Larivey), in *La comédie avant Molière: 1640–1660* (Paris: Armand Colin, 1972), 10–11.

4. Most of this first section's content is synthesized from past research and publications, especially Lebègue, *Le théâtre comique*; Lazard, *La comédie humaniste*; Marvin T. Herrick, *Comic Theory in the Sixteenth Century* (1950) (Urbana: University of Illinois Press, 1994); and Richard F. Hardin, "Encountering Plautus in the Renaissance: A Humanist Debate on Comedy," *Renaissance Quarterly* 60, no. 3 (Fall 2007): 789–818; "Menaechmi and the Renaissance of Comedy," *Comparative Drama* 37, nos. 3–4 (2003): 255–74.

5. Herrick, *Comic Theory*, 57–69.

6. Hardin, "Encountering Plautus," 811.

7. Hardin, "Menaechmi," 261.

8. Herrick, *Comic Theory*, 37–56; Hardin, "Encountering Plautus," 811–18.

9. Aelius Donatus, "On Comedy," trans. O. B. Hardison, in *Classical and Medieval Literary Criticism. Translations and Interpretations*, ed. Alexander Preminger et al. (New York: Frederick Ungar, 1974), 305–9, 305; Emmanuel Buron, "'Comique' et 'propriété' dans la préface de *L'amoureux repos* de Guillaume des Autels," in *Le lexique métalittéraire français. XIVe–XVIIe siècles*, ed. Michel Jourde and Jean-Charles Monferran (Geneva: Droz, 2006), 67–87, 81–85.

10. Donatus, "On Comedy," 306.

11. Charles Estienne, Preface to *Les abusez*, in *Critical Prefaces of the French Renaissance* (1950), by Bernard Weinberg (New York: AMS Press, 1970), 135–38, 138.

12. La Taille, *Corrivaux*, viii. See also Donatus: comedy imitates the private lives of "middle state" characters ("On Comedy," 305–6).

13. Donatus, "On Comedy," 305–6; Hardin, "Encountering Plautus," 791.

14. Buron, "'Comique,'" 68, 81; Harold W. Lawton, *Handbook of French Renaissance Dramatic Theory* (1949) (Westport, CT: Greenwood Press, 1972), 2; Corinne Noirot, *"Entre deux airs": Style simple et ethos poétique chez Clément Marot et Joachim Du Bellay (1515–1560)* (Laval, 2011; Paris: repr. Hermann Editeurs, 2013), 63.

15. Herrick, *Comic Theory*, 57–69.

16. Hardin, "Encountering Plautus," 811 (on Heinsius's position in the Plautus/Terence debate, in humanist discussions surrounding drama and comedy).

17. *Sotties*: short satirical plays common in France in the fifteenth and sixteenth centuries; *fatrasie*: a medieval poetic genre, often satirical; *fabliaux*: comic tales, often with bawdy or scatological obscenities.

18. See Lazard, "Du théâtre médiéval."

19. Daniel C. Boughner, *The Braggart in Renaissance Comedy. A Study in Comparative Drama from Aristophanes to Shakespeare* (Minneapolis: University of Minnesota Press, 1954), esp. ch. 10, "French Comedy from Grévin to Molière," 254–302, 257.

20. La Taille, *Corrivaux*, vii–viii. In his edition of *Les corrivaus* (1974), Giuseppe Macri cites as the main source for *Les corrivaux* Giovanni Boccaccio's *Decamerone* V.5, itself inspired by Plautus's *Edipicus*. Giuseppe Macri, ed., *Les corrivaus: Commedia del Rinascimento francese*, by Jean de la Taille (de Bondaroy) (Galatina: Editrice Salentina, 1974), 18. (Appears as Macri hereinafter.)

21. La Taille, *Corrivaux*, Prologue, v–viii.

22. Estienne, Preface to *Les abusez*, 138.

23. Hardin, "Menaechmi," 256; Weinberg, *Critical Prefaces*, 27.

24. Macri, *Les corrivaus*, 16–17.

25. Lebègue, *Le théâtre comique*, 127–46; Lazard, "Du théâtre médiéval."

26. Geoffrey Brereton, *French Comic Drama from the Sixteenth to the Eighteenth Century* (London: Methuen, 1977), 3.

27. Macri, *Les corrivaus*, 16–17.

28. Even Pierre de Ronsard, the *Prince des poètes* (prince of poets) favored by the crown before Philippe Desportes, had trouble receiving strong support for his projects, including the *Franciade* epic. See Phillip John Usher, *Epic Arts in Renaissance France* (Oxford: Oxford University Press, 2013), esp. ch. 3, "Ronsard's Franciade: From National Genealogy to Tragic Love Story."

29. La Taille, *Corrivaux*, Prologue, v.

30. La Taille, *Négromant*, Prologue, cix.

31. La Taille, *Négromant*, ccxxvii.

32. Herrick, *Comic Theory*, 106–28.

33. Jean de la Taille, *Tragédies: Saül le furieux; La famine ou Les gabéonites*, ed. Elliott Forsyth (Paris: STFM, 1998), 94; *Les corrivaux*, Prologue, vi–vii; Charles Estienne, Preface to Terence's *Andria*, 1542, in *Critical Prefaces of the French Renaissance* (1950), ed. by Bernard Weinberg (New York: AMS Press, 1970), 89–103, 97–98; Estienne, Preface to *Les Abusez*, 137.

34. Macri, *Les corrivaus*, 19.

35. La Taille, *Négromant*, cxxv, cxxviii.

36. Ibid., ccix, ccxxi, 3.5, clxxxvii.

37. *Négromant*, 2.2, cxlix.

38. Estienne, Preface to Terence's *Andria*, , 91.

39. Ibid., 93. On La Taille's echoing Estienne's paratextual considerations on drama, see Bernard Weinberg, "Charles Estienne and Jean de la Taille," *Modern Language Notes* 61 (1946): 262–65.

40. Estienne, Preface to Terence's *Andria*, , 98, 101–2.

41. Ibid., 103.

42. Estienne, Preface to *Les Abusez*, 137; cf. *Corrivaux*, Prologue, vii.

43. In a dedicatory epistle, La Taille tells Marguerite de France he aims to "prof-iter de quelque chose à [s]a Republique" ["to be of service to (his) state/nation"] (*Tragédies*, 94).

44. See Corinne Noirot, "French Humanist Comedy during the Wars of Religion: The Familiar and the Strange in Jean de la Taille's *The Rivals (Les corrivaux)*," in "French across Borders," ed. Anne-Hélène Miller, special issue, *Explorations in Renaissance Culture* 39, no. 2 (2014): 128–43.

45. Jacob discusses the fact that French Protestant thinkers (e.g., Guillaume Postel, a.k.a. Eusèbe Philadelphe) particularly valued transgressive cosmopolitans and dignified commoners. Margaret C. Jacob, Introduction to *The Rise of Cosmopolitanism in Early Modern Europe* (Philadelphia: University of Pennsylvania Press, 2006).

46. La Taille, *Corrivaux*, vii, cvi.

47. Ibid., iii.

48. La Taille, *Corrivaux*, Prologue, v, viii. The prologue in *Le négromant* announces "une comedie toute nouvelle, laquelle veut estre nommée LE NEGROMANT, et se jouera enhuy devant vous" ["a brand new comedy, which ought to be titled THE NECROMANCER and which shall be performed in front of you today"] (cix).

49. "A Dieu Messieurs: et faictes bruit des mains, en signe que nostre jeu vous a pleu" ["Farewell, Gentlemen; and make noise with your hands, to signify you were entertained by our play"] (La Taille, *Corrivaux*, 5.6, cvi, final words).

50. Ibid., viii; iii, l.10.

51. Ibid., viii.

52. The prologue in *Les corrivaux*: "Escoutez donc soigneusement tout ce qu'on y dira: car si vous faisiez autrement, vous perdriez à sçavoir l'histoire" ["Listen carefully, then, to all that shall be said; for if you did otherwise, you would lose track of the story"] (*Prologue*, viii); you would miss the point, the author also tells his audience—would fail to grasp the embedded message ["entendre le discours de ce qui est ici contenu"] (ibid.).

53. In short: showing the ravages of rebels and tyrants so no one is tempted to become one.

54. Felix in *Corrivaux*, 4.3, lxvii.

55. La Taille, *Corrivaux*, 3.1, xliv. The language of Erasmus's *Colloquia* and Clément Marot's French translations thereof comes to mind.

56. Montaigne composed his *Essais* right at the time when La Taille published his works and was influenced by the contemporary thinkers, from the *Pléiade* to Jacques Amyot and Turnebus.

57. La Taille, *Corrivaux*, 4.4, lxxvi–lxxvii.

58. Of the "*satyra*," Estienne writes that it "ne declaroit riens que par enigmes et circumlocutions" ["would only speak in enigmatic, circumlocutory ways"]. Estienne, Preface to Terence's *Andria*, , 91–92. Comedic political commentary was danger-

ous even though masks helped to avoid upsetting identifications ("parler reciter ou chanter sans fascherie" ["speak, recite, or sing with no axe to grind"]) (ibid., 97).

59. Estienne, Preface to *Les Abusez*, 136.

60. La Taille, *Négromant*, Prologue, cviii.

61. Ibid., cix.

62. Robert Griffin, *Ludovico Ariosto* (New York: Twayne Publishers, 1974), 13–15.

63. Ibid., 32–33.

64. Estienne, Preface to Terence's *Andria*, , 92; after Donatus, 306.

65. Corinne Noirot, "Conjurer le mal: Jean de la Taille et le paradoxe de la tragédie humaniste," in "Spectacle in Late Medieval and Early Modern France," ed. Jeff Persels and Russell Ganim, special issue, *EMF: Studies in Early Modern France* 13 (2010): 121–43, 123.

66. La Taille, *Négromant*, 2.2, cxlix.

67. Ibid.

68. La Taille, *Négromant*, ccxxii–ccxxiv. Hardin also contends that the "fascination of identity" (e.g., symmetrical plots, twins, lost siblings, quid pro quos and cross-dressing) accounts for the huge success of erudite comedy—based in part on Plautus's *Menaechmi* ("Menaechmi," 2).

69. La Taille, *Corrivaux*, ccxxv.

70. Ibid., ccxxiii.

71. Isabelle Garnier-Mathez, *L'épithète et la connivence. Écriture concertée chez les Évangéliques français (1523–1534)* (Geneva: Droz, 2005).

72. Kristin Phillips-Court, *The Perfect Genre: Drama and Painting in Renaissance Italy* (Burlington, VT: Ashgate, 2011).

〜

CHAPTER SIX

Rethinking the Politics of Court Spectacle

Performance and Diplomacy under the Valois

ELLEN R. WELCH

In a 1580 dispatch to Sir Francis Walsingham, principal secretary to Elizabeth I, English ambassador Henry Cobham described a masquerade prepared specially for a select group of diplomats at the French court.[1] Cobham reported that Catherine de' Medici summoned him along with the ambassadors from Portugal, Venice, Savoy, Ferrara, and the Vatican to an intimate soirée at the palace. Following a "private banquet" with Catherine and King Henri III, the guests were treated to a masquerade dance prepared by Guy de Lanssac.[2] Cobham recounts:

There entered a masque; the order of which was: First six musician maskers, playing on their lutes; then two young boys in apparel representing Cupids, having small bows and quivers full of shafts, with certain garlands on their arms and their eyes bound with thin veils. Then there followed one of the maskers habited *alla Portughese*, with a "cassack" and "gargasses" of "cramoyzin" satin, "laid on" with silver lace; his Portugal "capecloak" and cap both of russet cloth of silver; having in one hand a Portugal dart, blunt at both ends and in the other a timbrell with bells after their manner. There followed him five other maskers attired like him in all points. After they had passed once or twice about the hall they came up to where their Majesties sate and the two boys sang a French song to the lute; afterwards they returned down again, shaking their timbrells in measure; at the sound of which came forth six attired like women in long Spanish white satin gowns, "garded" with carnation and silver lace, dancing with their timbrells; and on passing each of them took an arrow out of the quivers of the Cupids, with which they threatened each other. The Portugueses likewise took arrows. Thereon the two boys having two scarfs of carnation and silver tinsel made a barrier by holding the scarfs at both ends, the Spanish women keeping on one side and the Portugal men on the other. They came to the barriers one to one still observing the measure in offering "their fight"; but the Portuguese when it came to striking the women threw down their darts, submitting themselves by their countenances as overcome, which act they passed one after another. On this a garland was put on the women's heads by the Cupids. Then the Portuguese by gestures requested the Spanish women to have compassion on them; whereon the Cupids went away with the barriers. Then the ladies after a while, with cheerful gestures, put the garlands on the Portugueses' heads, and so they entered into sundry dances together. Thus the greater part of the afternoon of that day was spent.[3]

As the dispatch goes on to explain, Cobham understood that the costumed performers were meant to comment on the recent crisis of Portuguese suc-cession. The mimed violent courtship between dancers dressed in Spanish and Portuguese styles unmistakably referenced that conflict. But how ex-actly did the masque comment on the political drama? On the one hand, the performance humiliated Spain through the use of male dancers dressed "like women" to represent that country. On the other hand, the dance had Portuguese figures "submitting" passively to the Spanish ladies' aggressive courtship. Cobham recounts in his letter that he assumed at first that the pantomime signaled France's approbation for Spain's annexation of their Iberian neighbor. A conversation with the king, however, soon corrected his interpretation. Henri greeted Cobham immediately after the performance and called to Lanssac to bring over the masquerade's written verses for his perusal, "whereon I said: 'This should present how your Majesty's will were to celebrate the unity of Portugal with Spain.' He said: 'No; it is to show what they "pass"[4] and our mislike'; for his mother pretended a right to that realm."[5]

Cobham's account of his own interpretive mistake raises a fundamental question about the legibility of court entertainments' political meanings. Modern scholarship has often portrayed these performances as quasi-propagandistic in their force and univocal in their meanings. Warburgian analyses of the mystical symbolism and ritualistic qualities of entertainments demonstrate how they served, in Roy Strong's words, as a "liturgy of the state" designed to exalt the crown.[6] More recent post-structuralist and New Historicist readings of court spectacles show how they operate as ideologi-cally driven displays of power.[7] These theories work well within the context of a domestic politics of kingship, when audience members share cultural and aesthetic codes that are further reinforced by real power relations. But they fail to account for the reactions of foreign diplomats, who made up a significant—indeed, privileged—portion of the courtly audience. Early modern writers frequently depicted foreigners as favored spectators at court entertainments. Brantôme, for example, justified Catherine de' Medici's extravagant outlays for festivals through reference to the international audience: "Je sçay que plusieurs en France blasmarent ceste despance par trop superflue; mais la Reyne disoit qu'elle le faisoit pour monstrer à l'Estrangier que la France n'estoit si totalement ruinée et pauvre, à cause des guerres passées, comme il estimoit" ["I know that many in France criticize this expense as unnecessary; but the Queen said that she did it to show foreigners that France was not as ruined and impoverished, on account of the past wars, as they judged"].[8] These remarks provide evidence that royal patrons considered court spectacles a tool not only for domestic politics but also for transmitting explicit or implicit messages to foreign powers. But how often did foreign observers, who were not subject to the monarchal patron's authority, "correctly" perceive the import of court entertainments? How might their perspectives challenge the conventional understanding of the way entertainments conveyed, or failed to convey, political messages?

Diplomats' own accounts of the court entertainments provide frustratingly little evidence to address these questions. In dispatches and memoirs, brief references to balls, masquerades, and other festivities suggest that small entertainments designed for an intimate group of spectators made up part of the day-to-day practice of diplomacy. Yet the diplomats rarely offer their own analysis of the spectacles' political import in their writings. In part, their reticence reflects the early modern diplomat's imperative to operate as the "ears and eyes" of his sovereign; only the monarch had the authority to decide meaning, although he depended on the vicarious spectatorship provided by the diplomat.[9] Memoirs and dispatches destined to be read by the ambassador's sovereign or his secretaries constitute a self-conscious performance of this diplomatic discretion. In addition, accounts of the ambassador's participation in court festivities often demonstrate his social standing in the host court.

Venetian ambassador Jerome Lippano, for example, noted in his *Relazione* how, in the early months of 1579, "il était invité par le roi et par la reine à toutes les joutes, à la chasse, aux tournois, aux fêtes publiques" ["he would be invited by the queen to all the jousts, hunting parties, tournaments, public festivals"].[10] Lippano's account of his privileged participation in court festivities is part of his "performance" as an excellent ambassador for the audience of Venetian senators.

Elsewhere, a diplomat criticizes the host court's management of entertainments as a way of reassuring his monarch of his own country's superiority. In his account of the October 1581 *Ballet comique de la Reine*, for example, Henry Cobham deplores his and the other ambassadors' treatment by their hosts: "We were brought on the stairs to be let into the place, but we stayed there from 5 till 8 in a very 'homely' place, without light. At last, with the press, in homely manner, we were brought in this rude sort, and thrust without respect into the great chamber, where we sat fasting till 12 at night. The other ambassadors have complained thereof."[11] Cobham uses the plural pronoun "we" to show that the whole diplomatic corps suffered the same mistreatment and to dispel any notion that it was meant as a particular slight against the English delegation. In the aftermath of the recently failed negotiation of a potential marriage between Elizabeth and the Duke of Anjou, this scene allows Cobham to reassure the English by depicting the French court as inferior to that of his much more hospitable queen. In these and similar accounts, the ambassador's self-representation as spectator transforms court entertainments into a kind of mise en abyme of the larger diplomatic "stage." Here, political and personal relationships are reflected in the theatricalized space of the audience rather than on the dance floor itself. Still, the scarcity of diplomats' own documented interpretations of the court spectacles they witnessed should not imply that the content of these entertainments had no significance for them. Rather, they demonstrate that the elaborate, carefully crafted displays on the courtly stage were not the sole focus of attention or the only site of the production of political meanings.

This is just one example of the ways in which the diplomatic context allows us to revise and broaden our understanding of the relationship between representation and politics in court entertainments. As Timothy Hampton has recently shown in *Fictions of Diplomacy*, a focus on diplomacy offers a substantially different model for understanding the relationship between art and politics, not least because within early modern diplomatic culture, representation itself was figured as duplicitous and fallible.[12] Language was a tool for manipulation as much as for communication. Diplomatic chains of mediation had the potential to distort sovereign will. Above all, in the diplomatic scene, power was not concentrated in one royal body but rather distributed among multiple powers in dynamic relation to one another. This power struggle shaped the form of literary and art works produced in the diplomatic context and, in turn, "the artifice of literary form . . . function[ed] as a space and tool of compromise."[13]

Multimedia court entertainments, I contend, served as an even more powerful "space and tool of compromise" than literary arts alone. They modeled diplomatic negotiation at the level of art by containing multiple, often conflicting aesthetics within one performance, and by distributing meaning throughout different artistic disciplines and forms. Moreover, through a combination of poetry along with the "languages" of visual display, music, and physical performance, court spectacle offered the viewer several points of entry for interpretation. The fractured, polysemous nature of the form might even be considered an advantage for diplomatic communication when obfuscation and vagueness was more appropriate than clarity. When examined through the critical lens offered by diplomacy, in other words, court entertainments appear as a complex space of politics in which creators, performers, and multiple types of spectators all played a role in negotiating meaning.

The remainder of this chapter explores how a focus on diplomacy might lead us to new ways of reading early modern court spectacle through the case study of one explicitly diplomatic court spectacle: the 1573 *Magnificentissimi spectaculi a regina regum matre*, better known as the *Ballet des Polonais*. The various textual traces and eyewitness accounts of this entertainment suggest how its creators attended to the privileged audience of Polish ambassadors in whose honor the ballet was staged by relying on verbal and artistic languages thought to be accessible to these outsiders. Previous scholarly work on the "legibility" of this famous ballet throws into relief the multiple, indeterminate valences of meaning produced by a diplomatic reading, showing how the form could accommodate different political agendas. Although there is not space here for an exhaustive analysis of this ballet or of the Valois culture of spectacle as a whole, this discussion is meant to suggest a range of more flexible approaches to theorizing the politics of court spectacle in early modern Europe.

In September 1573, an extraordinary embassy from Poland visited Paris in honor of the Duke of Anjou's election as the Polish king. In honor of the ambassadors' arrival, Catherine de' Medici organized the *Ballet des Polonais* as part of a larger celebration held in the Tuileries. Choreographed by Balthasar Beaujoyeulx and set to music by Orlando di Lasso, the *Ballet des Polonais* took place after supper in a torch-lit room "made to order" for the event.[14] Sixteen ladies in the queen mother's service were costumed as nymphs and appeared to the audience in a silvered structure meant to resemble a large rock. They descended onto the floor from their "niches" in the edifice and danced for about an hour, performing a complex series of steps first with masks and then with bare faces. At the end of their performance, they approached the royal family and foreign guests of honor to present them with small gold and enamel plaques, each decorated with an image representing a province of France.

At least, this is the display suggested by the textual remains of the *Ballet des Polonais*. As is often the case for early modern performances, the documentary evidence for the ballet is tantalizingly incomplete and somewhat contradictory. A slim pamphlet of Latin verses by Jean Dorat entitled "Magnificentissimi spectaculi a regina regum matre in hortis suburbanis editi" contains the libretto along with descriptive poems and woodcut images documenting the event.[15] Chroniclers' accounts supplement and complicate the mental image of the ballet the libretto allows us to re-create. Brantôme's life of Catherine de' Medici in his *Recueil des dames* gives a detailed description of the nymph ballet, but omits the allegorical dialogue signaled in Dorat's libretto.[16] Agrippa d'Aubigné's short descriptive passage in the seventh book of *L'Histoire universelle* claims that the libretto was written not by Dorat but by Amadis Jamyn (and "mal composez" ["badly written"] at that).[17]

The complex, multifaceted documentation of the texts, images, and movements that made up the *Ballet des Polonais* have inspired several scholars to offer their "visions" and interpretations of its meaning for its first spectators. Frances Yates, for example, focuses on the dance's evocations of celestial harmony to argue that the entertainment was designed to produce "conciliatory mingling" not only between the French and the Poles but also between the Catholic and Protestant individuals in both national groups.[18] Thomas Greene's careful reading of the ballet's intertextual relationship with the funeral games for Anchises recounted in book five of the *Aeneid* characterizes the dance as an instance of the French court communing with antiquity and as a "choreographic trope of the life cycle."[19] More overtly political readings include Mark Franko's interpretation of the ballet as an attempt to fashion Henri as an omniscient monarch.[20] Ewa Kocisweksa contends that the festivities aimed to present an image of an emergent, glorious "Valois empire," as well as to express Catherine's personal sadness over the imminent departure of her favorite son.[21] This examination of the ballet in its diplomatic context synthesizes the valuable insights of these previous works of scholarship while also resisting their tendency to foreclose rival meanings. It is the very indeterminacy of the political and spiritual import of the dance, I argue, that makes it so powerful for a diplomatic encounter.

The diverse accounts of the *Ballet des Polonais* vividly demonstrate that performance is always a fragile, fragmentary event even at the moment of its enactment. Any performance literally appears different to each observer. This is especially true in the case of the *Ballet des Polonais*, despite—or perhaps because of—its creators' efforts to mediate the ballet's symbolism and provide a ready-made explication of its meaning. Despite assertions by early modern theorists of music and dance that these art forms had universal significance and could communicate where language failed, the creators of this entertainment went out of their way to explain the spectacle to its view-ers and make it accessible to audiences within and beyond the ballroom.[22] Dorat's pamphlet distinguishes itself from most ballet libretti published in the period by its unusually large number of separate explanatory texts and images. His concern for rendering the entertainment legible to its audi-ence is reflected in his choice of language: Latin rather than the standard vernacular, in honor of the Polish guests, who were thought not to speak or understand French very well. It seems that the Latin text was useful to the ambassadors. In his diary entry recounting the spectacle, Polish ambassador Andrzej Górka notes that the opening songs were performed in French, but he quotes the Latin verses to convey their meaning.[23]

The pamphlet itself consists of several distinct pieces: a Latin dialogue between *Gallia* [France] and *Pax et Prosperitas* [Peace and Prosperity] that was sung at the beginning of the festivities to a motet composed previously by Orlando di Lasso;[24] an elegy praising the spectacle's patron, Catherine de' Medici, and her two kingly sons (which evidence suggests was not pronounced aloud at the performance); "Montis nympharum, descriptio," a poetic description and explanation of the theatrical edifice upon which the dancers first appeared on the dance floor; *Nympha Gallia* [Nymph of France] and *Nympha Andegavis* [Nymph of Anjou], Latin translations of poems by Ronsard and Jamyn, respectively, which were recited by two of the dancers in their original French;[25] an ode "Ad Galliam" [To France]; "Chorea nympharum" [Dance of the Nymphs], a poetic description of the ladies' dance; the "Catalogus nympharum" [Catalogue of the Nymphs], reproductions of the emblematic plaques carried by the dancers, with a poetic explication of their representation of particular provinces of France; and finally a summary "Scenae descriptio" [Description of the Stage] and address "ad lectorem" [To the Reader] that serve as prefaces to woodcuts representing scenes from the entertainment.[26]

Like a typical ballet libretto, the pamphlet transcribed texts performed as part of the spectacle and contained some description to commemorate the ephemeral event. It served both as an explanatory aid and a souvenir for guests present at the event and as a textual and visual reproduction of the display for a larger number of readers who did not have the privilege of attending in person. The final message to the reader announces the attempt to provide a vicarious experience of viewership: "Et iam spectator, nec modo lector eris" ["And now you are also a spectator, not just a reader"].[27] Through these diverse elements, the text mediates the entertainment in several ways and on multiple levels: translating French into Latin for the foreign guests, translating a restricted spectacle into print for a broader audience, and explaining and highlighting meaningful features for viewers present at the event. It transforms readers into spectators, but it also transforms spectators into readers and interpreters of the display.

The tension between readership and spectatorship extends to the way the text shapes the experience of those present at the event. In his suggestive analysis of Dorat's descriptive poem "Chorea nympharum," Mark Franko has argued that the text represents the danced spectacle itself as another text to be deciphered. In the middle of the dance, after making "a thousand passes and a thousand returns," after hovering like bees and dancing in a pointed formation like birds in flight, the dancers change configuration: "Nunc hanc, nunc illam, variant per plana figuram: / Descripsit plures nulla tabella notas" ["They make different clear shapes: now this one now that / no tablet describes more signs"].[28] Franko's somewhat free translation of the lines—"Now this one and now that switches to a flat figure / Which describes many letters without a tablet"—allows him to see the nymphs' dance as a close precursor to a tradition of figural choreography.[29] In later works such as *Le ballet de Monseigneur le duc de Vandosme* (1610), dancers traced letters onto the dance floor with their steps, transforming the audience into readers: "Viewing a group of dancers as a living alphabet, and dancing bodies as letters, the spectator would reassemble each sequence of letters as a word, and each sequence of words as a phrase."[30] That is not quite what the dancers were doing in 1573. As a reference to Euclid in the next line makes clear, these "shapes" were inspired by geometry rather than by alphabetic characters, and as such they resist efforts to decode them. Indeed, as Greene notes of the reference to the plentiful "signs" made by the dancers, Dorat "leaves it to us to try to guess their meaning."[31]

Still, Franko is persuasive when he points to the frequency of verbs for reading in Dorat's text, at least in association with the privileged spectator, Henri. Focusing on Dorat's line "Henrico lecto quae modò Rege, capit" ["Henri reading in the way of kings, grasped"],[32] he concludes that "the spectacle empowered the monarch as reader. Furthermore, the dancing subjects were his text."[33] For at least one audience member, the dance was meant to be deciphered and interpreted as a series of signs. Franko contends, however, that other spectators were denied this privilege: "Henry can read the true meaning of the action for himself, but the audience is destined to observe it crudely as an event of visual splendor."[34]

The apparent favoring of Henri as "reader" of the performance, however, creates something of a paradox when considered alongside the libretto's function as a hermeneutic aid. It might be more accurate to say that the libretto figures the newly elected Polish king as the best, most efficient interpreter of the performance, but not as the exclusive one. The section devoted to a reproduction of the plaques offered by the dancers to the honored spectators illustrates how the libretto facilitates interpretation for multiple kinds of readers and viewers. A full sixteen pages of the slim pamphlet are devoted to the presentation of the plaques. Each page contains a woodcut facsimile of the design borne on one plaque, labeled with the "identity" of the nymph who carries it (e.g., *Nympha acquitanica, Nympha belgica* [Nymph of Aquitaine, Nymph of Belgium]; see figures 6.1 and 6.2) and a quatrain in Latin playfully explaining the metonymic logic through which the warriors or the wheat stalk, to take the examples of Aquitaine and Belgium as cases in point, stand in for a province of France.

Although mimicking the form of emblems, these pages are not at all cryptic or obscure. Rather, their remarkably lucid explanations of the plaques' regional symbolism anticipate and accommodate a foreign readership, for whom the significance of the images would not be obvious. Moreover, the reproduction of the images makes their significance available to the spectators not given the gift of a physical plaque, as well as to those readers who

NYMPHA AQVI-
TANICA.

IIII.

Huic ab Aquitanis comes it pulcherrima terris,
Armatas acies per sua dona ferens.
Scilicet hoc quia sint duce Rege futura per orbem,
Cuncta secuturis peruia militibus.

N. Armoric.

NYMPHA BEL-
GICA.

X.

Belgica fert densas, aptum sibi munus, aristas;
Quáque tenet spicas fert & aratra manu.
Hac per signa monens, quò fructus vsque laborem
Excipiant, fructus vt labor excipiat.

N. Sequan.

Figures 6.1 and 6.2. Plaques for the Nymphs of Aquitaine (left) and Belgium (right), in Dorat, *Magnificentissimi spectaculi a regina regum matre* (1573).

did not witness the entertainment firsthand. The libretto thus offers a range of interpretive experiences and points of entry into the ballet's meaning.

A careful reading of the libretto, moreover, reveals that interpretation is not the only legitimate way to experience the spectacle. Indeed, Dorat often privileges appreciation of the "visual splendor" of the dance over the act of deciphering. Far from a "crude" experience, the pure spectator enjoys a quasi-divine experience of confused astonishment. Spectators are not so much confounded by the "signs" formed by the dancers as stunned by the force of their constant movement.[35] Thomas Greene observes that the poetic structure of the text, especially the "heavy use of anaphora," underlines the constant interruption and change of formation, "as though to dramatize the fragility of any one pattern."[36] For Margaret McGowan, the libretto reflects a poetic "imagination run riot" under the spell of the dizzying movements of the dance.[37]

French spectators confirm McGowan's impression. Brantôme, for example, describes the audience's marveling over the uncanny order and virtuosity underpinning the "ballet si bizarrement inventé" ["ballet so bizarrely/originally invented"]. Echoing Dorat's description of "Mille breves cursus iterants et mille recursus," Brantôme marvels that despite "tant de tours, contours et destours, d'entrelasseures et meslanges, affrontements et arretz, . . . aucune Dame jamais ne faillist de se trouver à son poinct ny à son rang" ["so many circular movements, turnings together and turnings away, interlacings and mixings, confrontations and hard stops . . . no lady ever failed to find herself on her mark and in her rank"].[38] He comments that the women danced "si bien que tout le monde s'esbahist que, parmy une telle confusion et ung tel desordre, jamais ne faillirent leur ordre, tant ces Dames avoient le jugement sollide et la retentive bonne, et s'estoient si bien apprises" ["so well that everyone was astonished that, among such confusion and disorder, they never broke their order, such the ladies had solid judgment and a good memory, and were so well taught"]. Brantôme here insists on the ballet's status as a literally extraordinary event, a fantastical display that provokes wonderment ["tout le monde s'esbahit"] rather than interpretation. While the spectacle created by the dancers—echoed in the entrancing rhythm of Brantôme's "tours, contours et destours," "entrelassures et meslanges"—is marvelous in itself, the ballet also amazes the audience through its revelation of the performers' virtuosity: Brantôme opposes the "desordre" experienced by the spectator to the mysterious yet rigorous "ordre" maintained by the dancers. The enjoyment Brantôme describes in this passage, in other words, depends on the dance's fundamental illegibility. It appears as a wonder to behold rather than as a text to be read.[39]

This kind of response was arguably available to all members of the audience, regardless of rank or national origin. The Polish ambassador repeatedly describes the dance as "beautiful," using the word a dozen times in his short diary account of the spectacle as though other descriptors eluded him.[40] In fact, Agrippa d'Aubigné ascribes a similar reaction of amazement to the foreign observers: "Les Polonnois admirerent les confusions bien desmeslees, les chiffres bien formez du ballet, les musiques differentes, et dirent que le bal de France estoit chose impossible à contrefaire à tous les Rois de la terre" ["The Poles admired the well untangled chaos, the well-formed figures of the ballet, the different sorts of music, and said that the French ball was a thing impossible for any king on earth to counterfeit"].[41]

Jacques-Auguste de Thou reported a similar reaction among French audience members, noting: "Le bel ordre de leurs mouvemens, leurs gestes pleins de graces, et les figures extraordinaires de ces danses pleines de tours et de retours qu'on n'avoit jamais vû, et qu'on avoit inventés en cette occasion pour donner plus de plaisir, amuserent agréablement les spectateurs" ["The beautiful order of their movements, their gestures full of grace, the extraordinary figures of the dances full of turns and returns that no one had ever seen before, and that had been created on this occasion to give more pleasure and pleasantly entertain the spectators"].[42] By resisting easy signification, the ballet united its diverse spectators in a shared experience of pleasure and admiration. This response could prove useful to the diplomatic aims of the encounter. Especially when considered in light of *Pléiade* theories of the harmonizing effects of music and dance, the seemingly purposeful impenetrability of the dance functions to encourage a sense of unity among the spectators. By juxtaposing a vocabulary of interpretation with one of astonishment, Dorat's pamphlet suggests that dance can be treated as "text," but not only as text. Its powers reach beyond the ability to transmit messages to astute spectators. The type of viewership that Dorat imagines takes the form of a process of negotiation between understanding and confusion, reasoning and wonder, order and chaos, penetration and impenetrability—a process that mirrors the dynamic of diplomacy itself.

The ballet's openness to multiple kinds of appreciation and interpretation is especially salient in its particular diplomatic context. While celebrating Henri's ascension to the throne of Poland, the French court continued to be ruled by his ailing brother, Charles IX. Two monarchs, therefore, presided over the festival room, and the audience members were divided in their political allegiance as well as in their cultures and languages. Rather than glorifying one sovereign over the other, the ballet's texts and images share praise among both kings as well as their mother, Catherine. The concluding encomiastic poem

Figure 6.3. Frontispiece, in Dorat, *Magnificentissimi spectaculi a regina regum matre* **(1573).**

lauds all three members of the royal family: "Plaudite vos Galli nunc Regibus atque Poloni / Fratribus: & Matri plaudite, quae peperit" ["Now you Gauls and Poles applaud the brother kings, and applaud the mother who gave birth to them"].[43] The even-handed allocation of plaudits in these verses echoes the image that appears as a frontispiece to Dorat's libretto (see figure 6.3).[44]

The woodcut depicts a seemingly pained Jupiter seated on a tree-shaped throne with a muscular breastplate positioned at the crux above his head. Pallas stands to his right and Apollo to his left. For once, the imagery is unmistakable, assimilating the royal family simultaneously to the classical pantheon and the Christian trinity.[45] Along with the verses that end the ballet, this initial image offers a compelling conceptual model for distributing political authority among the three figures and for acknowledging the coexistence of two kings and their subjects at this diplomatic gathering.

Although not as tendentious as other diplomatic encounters in sixteenth-century France, the visit of the Polish ambassadors required the Valois court to deploy the diplomatic arsenal of ceremony and spectacle to promote their own image and to extend hospitality to their foreign guests. These rival imperatives characterize all court entertainments staged for a diplomatic audience. Orchestrating several layers of signification at once, they forced their witnesses to engage in a constant negotiation of meaning. The process of viewing, reflecting on, and discussing the entertainments parallels the constant state of negotiation of early modern European diplomacy. In this sense, diplomatic court entertainments make a compelling case for the political value of art, not only because of its ability to signify, but also because of its power to elude or transcend singular meanings.

Notes

1. Margaret McGowan names it the *Ballet des portugaises et des espagnols*, but from Cobham's description it seems to be a less fleshed-out entertainment than a proper ballet. See *Dance in the Renaissance: European Fashion, French Obsession* (New Haven, CT: Yale University Press, 2008), 130. To my knowledge, no extant libretto has been discovered.

2. He was the son of Louis de Lanssac, a former French ambassador to Rome, the Council of Trent, and Spain, and Knight of Honor to the Queen Mother. See Nicolas Le Roux, "Guerre civile, entreprises maritimes et identité nobiliaire: Les imaginations de Guy de Lanssac (1544–1622)," *Bibliothèque d'Humanisme et Renaissance* 65, no. 3 (2003): 529–69, 544.

3. Cobham to the Secretaries, February 21, 1580, in *Calendar of State Papers Foreign, Elizabeth, Volume 14: 1579–1580* (1904), 160–176, 172. http://www.british -history.ac.uk/report.aspx?compid=73442 (accessed June 5, 2013).

4. *Oxford English Dictionary*'s third definition of the verb "pass" is "to exceed or overstep . . . to go beyond (one's province, knowledge, etc.)." This meaning of the word has been in use since 1390, and in premodern usage the clarifying object "limit" or "bounds" was often omitted.

5. For a lucid explanation of Catherine de' Medici's claim to Portugal, see R. J. Knecht, *Catherine de' Medici* (London: Longman, 1998), 207–12.

6. Roy Strong, *Splendor at Court: Renaissance Spectacle and the Theater of Power* (Boston: Houghton Mifflin, 1973), 22. See also Frances Yates, *The Valois Tapestries* (London: Warburg Institute, 1959).

7. The model for this approach is Stephen Orgel, *The Illusion of Power: Political Theater in the English Renaissance* (Berkeley: University of California Press, 1975). With respect to the French context in a later period, see Marie-Claude Canova-Green, *La politique-spectacle au grand siècle: Les rapports franco-anglais* (Paris: Papers on Seventeenth-Century French Literature, 1993).

8. Brantôme, *Recueil des dames, poésies et tombeaux*, ed. Etienne Vaucheret (Paris: Gallimard, 1991), 53. All translations are mine unless otherwise noted.

9. See, e.g., Alberico Gentili, *De legationibus libri tres (1594)*, trans. Gordon J. Laing, 2 vols. (New York: Oxford University Press, 1924), 2:169. Focusing on a slightly

later period, Ellen McClure eloquently observes that this imperative to "faithfully describe" reflects the diplomat's larger task of "making the sovereign 'seem' present" by allowing him to feel as though he has witnessed those events for himself. *Sunspots and the Sun King: Sovereignty and Mediation in Seventeenth-Century France* (Urbana: University of Illinois Press, 2006), 149.

10. Niccolo Tommaseo, ed., *Relations des ambassadeurs vénitiens sur les affaires de la France au XVIe siècle*, 2 vols. (Paris: Imprimerie Royale, 1838), 2:461.

11. Letter from Cobham to Walssingham, October 30, 1581. "Elizabeth: October 1581, 1–15," in *Calendar of State Papers Foreign, Elizabeth, Volume 15: 1581–1582* (1907), 325–41. http://www.british-history.ac.uk/report.aspx?compid=73525 (accessed June 22, 2013).

12. Timothy Hampton, *Fictions of Embassy: Literature and Diplomacy in Early Modern Europe* (Ithaca, NY: Cornell University Press, 2009), 5.

13. Ibid.

14. Brantôme notes that it took place in a "grand'salle faict à poste" ["a large room made to order"] (54). See also Margaret McGowan, *L'art du ballet de cour, 1581–1643* (Paris: Editions du CNRS, 1963), 41–42.

15. Jean Dorat, *Magnificentissimi spectaculi a regina regum matre in hortis suburbanis editi, in Henrici regis Poloniae invictissimi nuper renunciati gratulationem, descriptio* (Paris: F. Morel, 1573). The text and accompanying images can be consulted on the Bibliothèque nationale de France's and the British Library's Web sites, respectively: http://gallica.bnf.fr/ark:/12148/bpt6k715648.r=Magnificentissimi+spectaculi+a+regina+regum+matre.langEN and http://special-1.bl.uk/treasures/festivalbooks/BookDetails.aspx?strFest=0038.

16. Brantôme, *Recueil des dames*, 52–55.

17. Agrippa d'Aubigné, *Histoire universelle*, ed. André Thierry, 11 vols. (Geneva: Droz, 1987), 4:156.

18. Yates, *Valois Tapestries*, 105.

19. Thomas Greene, "Labyrinth Dances in the French and English Renaissance," *Renaissance Quarterly* 54, no. 4 (2001): 1403–66, 1413. He also analyzes the motif of the *recursus* or "turns and returns" and connects both of those described spectacles to a longer classical tradition of literary mazes and labyrinths as a reflection on the twists of fate and the struggle between human mastery and human weakness.

20. Mark Franko, *Dance as Text: Ideologies of the Baroque Body* (Cambridge, UK: Cambridge University Press, 1993), 21–31.

21. Ewa Kociszewska, "War and Seduction in Cybele's Garden: Contextualizing the *Ballet des Polonais*," *Renaissance Quarterly* 65, no. 3 (2012): 809–63, 812.

22. The question of the "universality" of music and dance is more complicated in the case of the Polish embassy's visit, because their home court had a somewhat different culture of music than that of most Western European courts. Polish court music was more closely rooted in the church. For a study of musical culture at the sixteenth-century Polish court, see Tomasz M. M. Czepiel, *Music at the Royal Court and Chapel in Poland, c. 1543–1600* (New York: Garland, 1996), esp. 133–52. For a discussion of

Henri's role in bringing a culture of court dancing to Poland following his election, see Margaret McGowan, "L'essor du ballet à la cour d'Henri III," in *Henri III, mécène des arts, des sciences et des lettres*, ed. Isabelle de Conihout, Jean-François Maillard, and Guy Poirier (Paris: Presses de l'Université Paris-Sorbonne, 2006), 81–89.

23. Kociszewska, "War and Seduction," 853.

24. Peter Bergquist has determined that the ballet creators redeployed a previously composed Lasso motet ("Unde revertimini"). See his introduction to Orlando di Lasso, *The Complete Motets 10: The Four-Language Print for Four and Eight Voices (Munich 1573)*, Recent Researches in the Music of the Renaissance, vol. 117 (Madison, WI: A-R Editions, 1995), xiv–xv. He reprints the original motet on pages 75–85 and provides a "hypothetical reconstruction" of the ballet dialogue "Unde recens reditus" on pages 111–21. Lasso knew the ballet's creators from his 1571 trip to Paris and his participation in the Académie de Baïf. Like the *Pléiade* artists, he believed that music and poetry were most powerful when melded together and has been considered by some critics the "most linguistically gifted" composer before Mozart. See Philip Weller, "Lasso, Man of Theater," in *Orlandus Lassus and His Time*, ed. Ignace Bossuyt, Eugeen Schreurs, and Annelies Wouters (Leuven: Alamire Foundation, 1995), 89–127, 121.

25. We know the poems were sung aloud and not just printed for spectators to read privately thanks to accounts by both Jacques-Auguste de Thou and the Polish ambassador Andrzej Górka. See de Thou, *Histoire universelle*, 16 vols. (London, 1734), 7:12; and the translation of Górka's diary published by Ewa Kociszewska as an appendix to her article "War and Seduction," 853. On the attribution of the French poems, see Paul Laumonier, "Deux cents vingt vers inédits de Ronsard: Un gala aux Tuileries (aout 1573)," *Revue de la Renaissance* 4 (1903): 201–20.

26. The pamphlet also contains three additional woodcuts: an image of the dance (http://special-1.bl.uk/treasures/festivalbooks/pageview.aspx?strFest=0038&strPage=049); an image of the "rock" on which the dancers first appeared (http://special-1.bl.uk/treasures/festivalbooks/pageview.aspx?strFest=0038&strPage=048); and an allegorical image of Catherine, Charles, and Henri depicted as Pallas, Jupiter and Apollo, arranged in a trinity, discussed below (http://special-1.bl.uk/treasures/festivalbooks/pageview.aspx?strFest=0038&strPage=002) (accessed July 4, 2014).

27. Dorat, *Magnificentissimi spectaculi*, sig. fiiʳ.

28. Ibid., sig. ciᵛ.

29. Franko, *Dance as Text*, 23.

30. Ibid., 16–17.

31. Greene, "Labyrinth Dances," 1406.

32. Dorat, *Magnificentissimi spectaculi*, sig. ciʳ.

33. Franko, *Dance as Text*, 23

34. Ibid.

35. As McGowan notes, "The principal focus in the ballet is on patterned movement; on its changes, its pauses and *reprises*." *Dance in the Renaissance*, 112.

36. Greene, "Labyrinth Dances," 1406.

37. McGowan, *Dance in the Renaissance*, 210.

38. Brantôme, *Recueil des dames*, 54. Françoise Lavocat notes that scholars disagree over the significance of "bizarre" in this context; the word has been glossed as "original" and "disarrayed." See "Ut Saltatio poiesis? Danse et ekphrasis à la fin de la Renaissance et à l'âge baroque," in *Ecrire la danse*, ed. Alain Montandon (Clermont-Ferrand: Presses Universitaires Blaise Pascal, 1999), 55–96.

39. In the late sixteenth century, the desire to unveil and explain wonders of nature was still considered a sin. See Lorraine Daston and Katherine Park, *Wonders and the Order of Nature, 1150–1750* (Cambridge, MA: MIT Press, 1998), ch. 8.

40. Kociszewska, "War and Seduction," 852–4.

41. d'Aubigné, *Histoire universelle*, 4:156.

42. De Thou, *Histoire universelle*, 7:11–12.

43. Dorat, *Magnificentissimi spectaculi*, sig. eiiᵛ.

44. See also the image provided on the British Library Web site of Renaissance Festival Books: http://special-1.bl.uk/treasures/festivalbooks/pageview.aspx?strFest=0038&strPage=002 (accessed July 3, 2014).

45. This tableau mirrors the one that courtiers observed during the formal reading of the ambassador's decree confirming Henri's election as the king of Poland. On a raised platform constructed specifically for the ceremony, Charles occupied the highest and leftmost position, with Catherine at his right, Henri at her right, and other members of the court further down. J. A. Taschereau, "Élection et règne de Henri d'Anjou (Henri III) en Pologne (1572–1576)," *Revue rétrospective ou Bibliothèque historique contenant des Mémoires et Document authentiques, inédits et originaux* 4 (1834): 68–71. See also Ewa Kociszewska, "La Pologne, un don maternel de Catherine de Médicis? La cérémonie de la remise du Decretum electionis à Henri de Valois," *Le Moyen Age* 117, no. 3 (2011): 561–75.

~

CHAPTER SEVEN

Our Future Barbarism

Sacrifice, the Body, and Performance in Robert Garnier's Greek Tragedies

Antónia Szabari

In Robert Garnier's *Hippolyte* (1572), the tragedy's eponymous hero has a presentiment of his own impending violent death when an animal sacrifice he tries to perform to gratify the gods goes awry. In Garnier's subsequent Greek tragedy, *La Troade* (1579), the widowed Trojan queen Hecube fears that the war's sole survivors, children and women, will be brutally sacrificed by the victorious Greek army.[1] This fear partially comes true in the fourth act, when Hecube's daughter Polyxene is carried away to be sacrificed on an altar erected over the tomb of the Greek hero Achille. In both plays, ritual sacrifice is described in concrete images that show Garnier's familiarity with classical rituals. The dramatist also continues the conversation on the significance and uses of symbolic violence with other sixteenth-century artists, poets, philosophers, and politicians. This chapter goes beyond analyzing Garnier's visceral and highly physical language of description, in which the fire of blood and sacrifice conjoin with the fire and blood of war and, metaphorically, of passion, and asks how sacrifice as a form of ritualized violence helps us understand the effects of performance, which is Garnier's concern in these plays. The strong ties he establishes between this ritual and tragedy certainly increase the pathos, but more importantly, they also suggest that Garnier was aware of the similarities between ritual and performance.

While description, rather than action, dominates Garnier's plays, they were intended for the stage and were frequently performed in the sixteenth century. Scholars have argued that studying performance on the Renaissance stage has to do with looking for intentions of mise-en-scène (staging) in the text rather than searching for documentation on actual productions.[2] Moreover, we are not locked into a historically limited time frame. Gillian Jondorf argues that modern readers can gain access to these plays, and in fact to the sensible experience they provide, because they are allowed to imagine the performance on the basis of the text. This kind of imaginative reconstruction opens these plays, otherwise stodgy and erudite, to the pleasure of reading.[3]

Jondorf's argument implies a critique of the view that sixteenth-century audiences had privileged access to the meaning of plays, and we have to reconstruct their experience in order to understand them. She points to circumstances that in fact prevented contemporary audiences from getting full access to the experiences intended by the author: plays were not always performed, and Horatian conventions sometimes prevented the performance of violence on stage even though many tragedies, including Garnier's, were about acts of violence.

Rebecca Zorach's work in art history reminds us that Renaissance visual culture was strange, demanding the effort of reading from both contemporaries and us. She cites as proof the *Pléiade* poet Étienne Jodelle, who explains in his *Recueil des inscriptions* the various circumstances that prevented the audience from understanding the meaning he intended to give to the victory celebration he choreographed for Henri II in the city hall of Paris in 1558. The Parisians did not read the carefully crafted Latin inscriptions, the workmen brought bells instead of the rocks he asked for, the model of the ship *Argo* was too big in the already crowded hall, the actors did not learn their lines well, and the Parisians did not want to lend their children to serve as naked *putti*.[4] The question of performance is then not just a matter of historical reconstruction but also engaged interpretation—and this is perhaps the most important predicament that is shared, despite differences in our interpretive horizons, by us now with the early moderns.

Zorach has also pointed to the interpretive difficulty provided by symbolic violence in general, and especially images of sacrifice in Renaissance art. She shows that the violent and sacrificial iconography of the gallery of Francis I in Fontainebleau troubles the expectations of modern viewers: in this display of violence, including mutilated or castrated bodies and blood that has been spilled, our assumptions about beauty and gender normativity are contradicted. The rediscovery of ancient sacrifice and the encounter with similar rituals in the newly "discovered" parts of the world presented an interpretive puzzle and a challenge to early modern Europeans. In Garnier's Greek plays, the gestural and material world of sacrifice strongly contributes to the tragic plot in ways that also mirror the violence that afflicted French society in the second half of the sixteenth century.

Sacrifice Comes to Renaissance France

In a period in which princes and kings were expected to be moral authorities and "philosophers," poets and writers, especially those who wrote tragedy, tried to justify their art by acting as moral guides to those in power by teaching them about humility and warning them about the error of arrogance. Yet it seems that those involved in writing tragedies were also aware of the proximity of tragic performance to mystery, the performative power with which Christian mythology and religious visual culture provided kings throughout the Middle Ages but was increasingly more dangerous to perform because of the divisive aspects of religion and especially of Christian sacraments in early modern France.

On November 17, 1548, the Paris *parlement* issued a decree banning the performance of religious dramas—a date conventionally considered the birth date of theater (although this claim has been increasingly challenged in more recent scholarship). According to this narrative, theater was "born" in a time when the monarchy promoted the "secular sacred" (Zorach's term) and sacrifice, as Zorach contends was a way of creating new mysteries without specifically referencing the crucifixion and the bread and wine of the Eucharist, which became a source of vehement theological disagreement between Catholics and Protestants. Zorach moreover argues that the blood of sacrifice was linked in the sixteenth century to ideas of violence, on the one hand, and abundance, life, fertility and mystery, on the other. She analyzes images of emasculation and self-castration, through the figures of Jupiter and Attis/ Adonis (often conflated in syncretic Renaissance thought), along with the resurgence of references to Cybele in the paintings decorating the gallery of Francis I in Fontainebleau. Castration, Zorach argues, was not linked to impotence, asexualization, or feminization, but on the contrary, to potency and masculinity.[5] Following the work of anthropologists, psychoanalysts, and historians of religion, she argues that the civilizatory process that renders sacrifice more symbolic and masculine—in a process in which women's bodies become transformed into symbols that support masculine genealogies— informs these images of sacrifice in Renaissance France. However, she also points to the fact that, paradoxically, the resurgence of sacrificial symbolism centers on images of matter and the materiality of the body such as blood and soil, both of which figure prominently, for example, in *chthonic* or earth sacrifice. Garnier's plays contribute to the symbolic return of images of sacrifice, and, like Zorach's examples, they reshape the ancient iconography of sacrifice into an ambivalent but ultimately productive ritual as performance.

Garnier follows a number of humanists who saw ancient sacrifice as particularly relevant to their age. In his *Discourses*, Machiavelli equates the magnificent and ferocious ritual of animal sacrifice in antiquity with a masculine ethos that valued honor and liberty and contrasts it with Christian ethos, more concerned with inward contemplation and humility, which he calls "effeminate."[6] So it is all the more surprising to see that the return to the iconography of sacrifice often brought about images of emasculation or that, as Zorach argues, potency was associated with the spilling of blood.

The uses of sacrificial imagery in art, printed books, and theater were multiple, often reflecting the artists' views. Renaissance humanists had an archeological interest in the material world of ancient sacrificial and religious rituals, as evinced by books such as Guillaume du Choul's *Discours de la religion des anciens romains* (1556), which made available the iconography of ancient rituals, including sacrifice.[7] Du Choul culled his images from several archeological sites, among them Trajan's column and a marble relief above the door of the Church of Beauvieu, and he described the material culture of sacrifice in some detail, including *holocausts* (sacrifices in which the entire sacrificial animal was burnt) and commensal sacrifice (in which the meat was consumed and the fat was burned and thus offered to the gods), *hecatombs* (see figures 7.1 and 7.2), the kinds of animals sacrificed, knives and other tools used, clothing worn, and rituals involved. Du Choul also emphasized the continuity between Catholic ceremonies and ancient sacrificial ritual, which he depicted as pious rather than savage. His images, later republished in a book about the Roman art of war and baths, also exhibit the ethos of masculinity, since all the individuals depicted in the book are men.

Before Garnier began writing plays, the first tragedies written in French in the mid-sixteenth century also included scenes of sacrifice. The erudite Calvinist Théodore de Bèze published *Abraham sacrifiant* (1550) (translated in 1577 into English as *A Tragedie of Abrahams Sacrifice*[8]) to counter the cult of pagan gods that Bèze saw as a rampant vice in French poetry. His play reintroduces the blood sacrifice as human sacrifice into religious imagery.[9] The *Pléiade* poet Étienne Jodelle's tragedy *Cléopatre captive* (1552) hints at the Egyptian queen's ability to partake in the mythical cycle of death and rebirth, which is likened to the sun's cyclic rise and setting. As Cleopatre dies from no visible cause at the end of the play, Jodelle leaves open the possibility that she has died by the power of her own magic and is capable of revival, at least in the symbolic realm of theater, that is, thanks to Jodelle's art.

Figures 7.1 and 7.2. The image of a *hecatomb*, in Guillaume du Choul's *Discorso della religione antica de Romani* (1569).
Getty Research Institute

Jodelle's *Cleopatre* possesses distinctly Bacchic and Dionysiac qualities. The *Pléiade* associated sacrifice with hedonism and idealized and celebrated it by linking it to the figure of Bacchus. Both Jodelle's play and the legendary *pompe du bouc* (ceremony of the goat), performed by members of the *Pléiade* (including Jodelle, whose dramatic success they were celebrating), suggests that for the *Pléiade* poets it was no longer fierceness, as for Machiavelli, but pleasure-loving excess (i.e., the feasting, pomp, and communal spirit in the ritual of sacrifice) that enabled a love of freedom and was thus socially and morally useful. In the poem commemorating the ceremony that allegedly took place in the forest of Arcueil in April 1553,[10] Ronsard praises Bacchus, and essentially wine and excess, as the source of courage in the face of tyranny: "La liberté qui ayme mieux s'ofrir / À la mort, qu'un Tyran souffrir, / Te doit . . ." ["Freedom, which prefers rather to offer herself to death than putting up with a tyrant, owes (her courage) to you . . ."].[11] When Ronsard's Calvinist adversaries accused him of being an "[a]thée . . . qui un bouc à Bacchus sacrifice" ["an atheist who sacrifices a goat to Bacchus"], he promptly denied that the animal was literally immolated during the ceremony in Arcueil.[12] This easy, playful slippage between actual and symbolic or pretend violence is put in question in Garnier's plays, in which the significance of sacrifice seems precisely comment on the closeness of the symbolic representation and the experience of physical violence in civil-war-torn France. Ronsard and Jodelle treat sacrificial acts as forms of arcane mysteries that are (whether actually performed or simply symbolically represented) for the small group of the initiated. Garnier, however, adapts the communal or public character of the ancient ritual to the stage and incorporates it into his concerns about the effects of performance.

From the Simulacra of Violence to the Real of Ethical Feeling

Garnier's *Hippolyte* is one of the very few Renaissance humanist tragedies that have repeatedly been staged in recent years. Its significance to us has to do with the fact that it serves as an earlier counterpoint to Racine's neoclassic play *Phèdre*, which is based on the same story but was written a hundred years later.[13] Modern performances of this play—such as *Hippolyte* by Antoine Vitez in 1982, *Phèdre* and *Hippolyte* by Didier-Georges Gabily in the 1990s (inspired by the plays of several authors, among them Euripides, Seneca, Garnier, and Racine), and most recently, in 2012, *Hyppolite* by Robert Cantarella—emphasize the commonality between Garnier's characters, Phedre and Hippolyte in their closeness to the physical and natural world. Antoine Vitez, who directed the 1982 production of *Hippolyte* at the Théâtre National de Chaillot, underscores that Garnier's Phedre, unlike Racine's Phèdre, does not feel guilty because of her passion for Hippolyte.[14] Gabily singles out Garnier's Phedre and Hippolyte as "outsiders" (one from Crete, the other born of an Amazon), who are excluded from the Athenian civilization and made to feel alienated by the normalizing force exerted by Athenian democracy over the organic world.[15] Cantarella points out that the milieu of Garnier's play is the natural world; it is staged "on the edge of the forest" and the ocean, in a place where wild animals prowl, not inside, as in Racine's play.[16] Vitez, Gabily, and Cantarella are in conversation with their audiences, whose experiences stem from living in modern, late capitalist democratic societies, thus updating and modernizing Garnier's sixteenth-century concerns about the ways in which embodiedness subjects human beings to socially performed violence. However, here I argue that we should consider these productions as time-specific interpretations that underscore the potentials for performance in the play, rather than simply as anachronistic interpretations.

Hippolyte (1572) was composed in the aftermath of the massacres, St. Bartholomew's Day, but there are no direct allusions to these events in the play.[17] At the outset, the play's eponymous hero, Thesee's son by an Amazon, is made anxious by dreams and premonitions, which prompt him to carry out several *hecatombs*.[18] However, these expiatory acts turn out to be even more frustrating:

Quelle sortes de vœux, quelles sainctes manieres
D'appaiser les hauts Dieux, en leur faisant prières,
N'ay-je encore esprouvé? à qui des Immortels
N'ay-je d'un sacrifice échauffé les autels?
. . . .
Mais quoy? rien ne se change, on a beau faire vœux,
On a beau immoler des centaines de bœufs,
C'est en vain, c'est en vain. . . .[19]

[What sort of vows, what sacred rituals, have I not yet tried to appease the gods, while praying to them? To which one of the immortals have I not yet ignited an altar with sacrifice? . . . But why, to no use! In vain did I make vows, in vain did I sacrifice hundreds of oxen. It's all in vain, in vain. . . .]

Although Hippolyte intends to obtain the gods' forgiveness, the outcome of his actions suggests that the communication with the divine presupposed in sacrifice is somehow broken. Hippolyte cites one more sign of this failure in detail, the sacrificial lamb, which breaks out of the fire and scatters its blood over the unsuspecting hero:

Hier sacrifiant à toy pere Jupin,
Une blanche brebis, pour t'avoir plus bénin:
Bien que mortellement elle fust entamée
Et qu'ardist autour d'elle une flambe allumee,
Bien qu'elle eust pieds et teste ensemblement liez
Je la vis par trois fois dessur les quatre pieds:
Puis secouant son sang de mainte et mainte goutte,
M'en arrosa la face et ensanglata toute.[20]

[Yesterday, sacrificing to You, father Jupiter, a white lamb to make you more kind, (the lamb,) although it had been mortally wounded, around it the fire was ablaze, and its head and feet were tied together, jumped up, I saw it, three times on its feet, then shaking its blood in many small drops, covered my face and my whole body with blood.]

Hippolyte describes the ritual of a *holocaust*, a whole burnt offering to Zeus (who is called by his Roman name in the text). In a *holocaust*, the entire animal was burned, and the blood was poured over the altar. The ritual he recounts resembles the one later described by modern historian of Greek religion Jane Ellen Harrison, who has analyzed the Athenian Diasia festival of Zeus. Harrison argues that this festival differed radically from the communal sacrificial feast offered to Zeus in Homer. In the Diasia festival, she claims, Zeus worship was probably grafted upon a more archaic ritual of elimination, implying fear:

> Zeus Meilichios will have all or nothing. His sacrifice is not a happy common feast, it is a dread renunciation to a dreadful power; hence the atmosphere of "chilly gloom." It will later be seen that these *un*-eaten sacrifices are character-istic of angry ghosts demanding placation and of a whole class of underworld divinities in general, divinities who belong to a stratum of thought more primi-tive than Homer.[21]

As opposed to a feast in which people symbolically shared the food with the gods (abundant in Homer), this sort of ritual presupposes an angry god. Harrison shows that Zeus was grafted upon more archaic rituals of the "Mei-lichians" gods of the underworld similar to the Erynes, avenger gods, and he acquired the epithet *meilichios* ["the gracious one" or "easy-to-be-entreated"]. The Greeks used the epithet *meilichios* as a euphemism for another epithet, *maimaktes*, "raging" or "thirsting for blood." Garnier could have known about Zeus *maimaktes-meilichios*, the god of Olympus and Hades at once, from au-thors such as Euripides, Xenophon, and Paunasias.

Hippolyte prays and makes offerings to a god called *pere Jupin*, who, like the Zeus of Hades, is capable of revenge. This sacrificial offering (along with the appearance of the ghost of Egee) reminds the spectators early on that they are viewing a tragedy. The image of a Zeus of the underworld, as a potentially vengeful Jupin who demands *holocausts* but fails to honor them, introduces a fearful aspect into the world of Greek religion; however, this fearfulness also brings pagan sacrifice closer to Christian religious sentiments, the humble god-fearing piety, and distances it from the spirit of fierceness and unflinching self-mastery that Machiavelli associated with masculine virtue. In Garnier's play, sacrifice remains a pagan ritual, but one that has Christian undertones. It is not surprising then that the fate of Hippolyte, who becomes literally marked with the animal's blood, resembles that of Christ. Christian symbolism mixes with the pagan images of sacrifice, which contemporary audiences could not have missed: the white lamb, the blood, and the word *hostie*, from the Greek *hostia*, "victim," but also the "host," the presence of Christ in the Eucharistic meal.

Hippolyte goes on to narrate—in an image that evinces Garnier's histori-cal interest in the concrete details of ancient rituals—that the priest per-forming the sacrifice could not find the animal's liver. The organ conceived of as a seat of life (as the organ of blood) in ancient cultures, the missing liver indicates that the lamb is in fact lifeless, a mere image or "phantom" that simply prefigures the actual physical sacrifice to follow, Hippolyte's.[22] Like

Christ, Hippolyte is figured as a flesh-and-blood offering, while the lamb is a mere image, a premonition, not unlike the relationship between Jesus and his allegorical representations in the Old Testament. The Nurse's words, pronounced after Hippolyte's death by the sea monster, make this link between Hippolyte and the lamb even stronger: "Hé! le pauvre jeune homme, il est par ma malice, / Comme le simple agneau qu'on meine au sacrifice ["Oh! The poor man, he has been [killed] by malice, like the innocent lamb that one leads to be sacrificed"].[23] Here the word "malice" introduces a moral and quasi-Christian perspective into the amoral practice of ancient Greek and Roman sacrifice. Animal sacrifice was not associated with malice and was not considered a form of violence in ancient Greece.

Du Choul specifies that words like "kill" and "knife" were avoided in the language of ritual in favor of euphemisms, and modern anthropologists and classicists understand this practice as a kind of quid pro quo deal with the gods or as "ceremonies of riddance," as in the case of the *Meilichians*.[24] However, by presenting the lamb as an emblem of Christ, the Nurse introduces the ideas of both innocence and malice, moral and religious good and evil, into the play. The introduction of the lamb as innocent (as opposed to evil) also marks Hippolyte as the innocent and docile victim of the unfurling tragic drama that has now been transformed into a moral situation. Just as du Choul oscillates between an archeological, historical view of ancient ritual and a syncretic one that emphasizes its similarity with Christianity, so does Garnier between portraying the heroes of his play as superstitious pagans and characters with sentiments that are reconcilable with Christian morality and ethos.

For those who are familiar with Racine's *Phèdre*, in which the heroine experiences guilt for her desire and takes responsibility for the tragic outcome, it is tempting to read this reference to "malice" as a reference to Phedre's sexual and "fleshy" passion as the primary cause of Hippolyte's violent death, to which the corruptions of the Nurse (who helps her plant the lie that Hippolyte has raped Phedre) and Thesee (who abandons his city and his responsibilities as both ruler and husband/father) are secondary. Is this slimy sea monster the grotesque symbol of Phedre's physical desire for Hippolyte, whose body she admires in a monologue? Or does it stand for something else? The monster has exotic qualities that would have fit into a Renaissance natural history book on monsters. It is blue, its neck is covered in green fur, it has two horns that bear motley-colored shapes, fire comes out of its nostrils and sparks from its eyes, its stomach is covered in moss, there are red spots on its flanks, a mane covers its neck, spikes cover its back, and scales cover its rear. It does not share the typology of the animals of bucolic nature that both Hippolyte and Phedre prefer to society. The monster evokes an elsewhere of much greater violence than common nature, and it perhaps recalled to the audience their distance from the world of the play.

When the sea monster kills Hippolyte, his maimed body dragged on the ground by his horse traces a line of blood, prompting the image of the snail: "La teste luy bondist et essaute sanglante, / De ses membres saignes la terre est rougissante, / Comme on voit un limas qui rampe advantureux / Le long d'un sep tortu laisser un trac glaireux" ["His bleeding head jerks and jumps, the earth is painted red by his gory limbs, like a snail that glides haphazardly, and leaves a glossy trace along a twisted furrow"].[25] Jurgis Baltrusaitis notes that in the Middle Ages, the snail (seen as a "worm" with a "house") symbolized death, and its house the tomb, though because of this it also symbolized resurrection, the tomb from which life recommences. Thought to be born of slime, the snail likewise represented the fertility of the earth.[26] Garnier resorts to this rich and ambivalent medieval religious symbol of the dead Hippolyte blood in order to render the image more familiar to the audience and adapt it to their moral sentiments. The Christian view of resurrection is, however, only evoked rather than treated as an actuality in the pagan setting of the play. No palpable increase of fertility or rebirth is to be expected. There is no indication of redemption, neither for Hippolyte nor for his community, except in and through the remorse shared by all three agents who contributed to his death: Phedre, the Nurse, and Thesee. This feeling of remorse comes to these characters after Hippolyte's death, and it does not simply concern their own sexual behavior.

Phedre accuses "men's tyranny over nature," which does not allow women to act upon the same natural passions that they allow themselves. Garnier was quite possibly idealizing nature as Phedre refers to it, and in doing so, he was able to draw on an image of natural freedom opposed to civilization that was promoted in early modern travel literature. Phedre is the exotic woman who hails from Crete, and early modern travelers depicted the women of Mediterranean islands as in possession of natural freedom, in opposition to women in more modern and civilized societies like France, who were bound by societal rules and expectations.[27] Phedre defends her passions by alleging that all animals in nature love and desire. Hippolyte and his stepmother Phedre are each other's opposites, but both refer to nature and materiality to defend their views: while Phedre takes her example from the world of wild animals, Hippolyte devotes himself to the woods and the hills, where he hunts, and holds sanguine passion in cool contempt. Compared to Phedre's "animal" passion, Hippolyte's vegetal and mineral coolness is expressed through his devotion to the chaste Diana. He also worships Saturn, the god of the peaceful, mythical golden age, while Phedre admits to being under the yoke of Venus's son, Cupid. However, both Hippolyte and Phedre criticize civilized society: Phedre for the tyranny of men over all others, Hippolyte for the "bourgeois" passions and luxury that he sees embodied in women. Hyppolyte's misogynistic assessment of bourgeois society does not provide the moral lesson of the play.

The tension between Phedre and Hyppolyte creates the most intense drama in the play: Phedre declares before she kills herself, "je veux / Amortir de mon sang mes impudiques feux" ["I want to quench with my blood my unchaste fire"], thus announcing the spilling of her own blood in an act that resembles sacrifice.[28] Bérangère Bonvoisin, who played Phedre in Vitez's production of Hippolyte, suggests that Garnier's Phedre is amoral rather than immoral, as her acts are prompted by physical desire alone, rather than by corrupt motives, and this interpretation does not appear to contradict Garnier's play.[29] Her spilled blood partakes in and completes the cycle of destruction set in motion by the "fire" of passion.

The play does not so much present Hippolyte's or Phedre's views as ethical models as their deaths, first Hippolyte's, then Phedre's, initiate a cascade of ethical responses in the form of the Nurse's and Thesee's remorse. As Michael Meere has shown, Renaissance tragedies that stage violence do so in order to encourage an ethical response in the audience. While Garnier does not stage sacrifice, the described acts of sacrifice create scenes of spectatorship and ethical response within these plays similar to the effects of staging described by Meere. In this sense, the important dramaturgical devices of "showing" and "seeing" work even when they are mediated by language of the play, wherein Phedre responds to Hippolyte's death, the Nurse to Phedre's, and Thesee to both Hippolyte's and Phedre's, with each death acting as a catalyst of other characters' ethical response.[30] Sacrifice lingers in Hippolyte—as it will later, too, in La Troade—as a commitment to the physical and material, or the barbarous, that is not revalorized for its own sake (as it was by Machiavelli). Nor is it redeemed as the basis of a new mythology promoting a pagan "lifestyle," as Jodelle and Ronsard attest, but rather as a form of spectacle that is both distant and close, distant and exotic in its brutal violence and amorality, yet close since it is conducive to ethical responsiveness that has familiar, Christian elements. The barbarity of these people is a spectacle for the French to contemplate, to recognize themselves in it as in a mirror.

Nourishment by Fire and Blood

If Hippolyte offers the sacrifice of a handsome and chaste (but also misogynistic) young man in order to inspire an ethical reaction in the audience (first those who witness it, then those who read or view the play), *La Troade* shows the helplessness of those who use compassionate wisdom amid social crisis caused by passion.[31] In this play, Garnier carries the visceral images of tragedy one step further. "De feu, de sang," says Hecube, the Trojan queen, "de cris, de larmes je me pais" ["I feed myself with fire, blood, cries, and tears"],[32] evoking the idea that human life in defeated and Troy is now paradoxically to be maintained by destruction. She makes this statement when she is about to listen to the messenger's report about the death of her grandson Astyanax, who was hurled off a cliff. Garnier's *La Troade* is set in a Troy that has been almost completely annihilated by the Greeks, and the dramatic action begins at the moment when the women who have survived are burning the dead and smearing ashes, "le demeurant / De nostre defuncte Troye" ["the rest of our destroyed Troy"], on their foreheads.[33] Fire and blood constitute the elements left behind by discord and war, just as cries indicate not so much a commemorative social ritual as the destruction of society: ashes and cries are almost all that is left in Troy, whose people have been slain, except for some women who are left to mourn and burn or bury the bleeding bodies. The tragedy develops out of this already desolate situation, when the women's desperate attempts to put to rest the past through rituals of mourning fail.

We have seen that Hippolyte is Christ-like in that he rejects passions, and especially because he is an innocent victim, but this insight, which is merely intimated in the play by the Nurse, can only be fully understood by the modern, Christian audience of the play. However, while Hippolyte's fate is to die in a manner that recalls *chthonic* sacrifice—Hippolyte's blood spills on the earth—and the possibility of ascension, a vertical movement, is merely intimated by Phedre, who surmises that the chaste Hippolyte after his death may become a "new star" in the sky, *La Troade* introduces upward movement into the ritual of sacrifice. Hecube stops the lament of Trojan women, telling them that Priam does not need their pity, for he has actually been blessed to see his kingdom perish with him and is now wandering in the Elysian Fields, under fragrant myrtle trees, looking for his beloved son Hector.[34] She suggests that the flesh is nothing but "encombres" ["obstacles"] and that happiness and salvation lie outside and above the material realm, in an ascent toward the immaterial, which is concretized in the image of a bucolic Elysian Fields. She even goes further and claims that Priam's luck is to have died without leaving behind heirs (his son Hector was slain by Achille) and without seeing all things annihilated ["avecques sa mort toute chose perir!"].[35] She thus rejects mourning and compassion as modes of coping with immense loss. In fact, the tragedy in the play derives from the necessity that the survivors continue to live in a material world that is *left* after the destruction: ruins, ashes, dead bodies, blood, and the survivors' own bodies. The problem, from Hecube's point of view, is that something always remains—ashes, the bodies of those who survive—and tragedy is comprised of the paroxysms of those who "remain" and who are encumbered by the remains of human things.

Fire and blood are the material elements of sacrifice, and sacrifice plays an even more central role in *La Troade* than in *Hippolyte*. Instead of animal sacrifice as an attempt to reconcile the vengeful gods and avert tragedy, it is Hecube's dark premonition that the Greeks will sacrifice the survivors of Troy that introduces this theme: "Veut-on sacrifier? Veut-on de nous captives / Faire couler le sang sur ses moiteuses rives? ["Do they want to sacrifice us prisoners of war? Do they want to spill our blood upon these humid shores?"].[36] This image resonates with the description of Hippolyte's death, in which his blood spills over the seashore and mixes with the monster's slime. Unlike Hippolyte's vague premonitions, Hecube's fear of sacrifice is quickly articulated as a moral question, as a critique of cruelty. Her presentiment that, as long as there is blood and living left there will also be cruelty and suffering, comes true as the Greek ships laden with booty stay anchored in the ports. *La Troade* dramatizes the fate of those who remain in Troy when Achille's ghost appears to demand Polyxene, Hecube's daughter, to be sacrificed and threatens that otherwise no wind will arrive to allow the Greeks to sail away. In the play, this violence unfurls over the remains of Troy: Agamemnon demands Cassandre as a booty wife; Achille demands that Polyxene be sacrificed; and the Greeks resolve to kill Astyanax, Andromache and Hector's son, to circumvent a future act of revenge. Technically only Polyxene is sacrificed in an explicit ritual, but the death of the young Astyanax, who is hurled from the top of a cliff, resembles Hippolyte's death and evokes the idea of sacrificing the innocent.

The envoy of the Greek camp, Ulysse, claims that killing Astyanax alone would bring peace to both the Greeks and the Trojans. He vows he would do the same with his own sons and argues by bringing up Agamemnon's example, he who sacrificed his daughter, Iphigenie. His arguments are countered by the arguments of Andromache and Hecube, for whom sacrifice is a terrible act of cruelty. The play's moral perspective on sacrifice as cruelty foreshadows Montaigne's later dismissal of sacrifice in general and, in particular, Agamemnon's sacrificing his daughter as a misguided attempt to expiate the Greek army's offenses with the death of a young woman.[37] Hecube and Andromache, women, voice this "gentler" outlook. When it comes to sacrificing Polyxene, Garnier makes no other than Agamemnon oppose Pyrrhe, set on executing his father Achille's will:

Quelle execrable horreur? Qui veit jamais cela
Qu'un homme trespassé dans sa tombe eust envie
D'un autre homme vivant, de son sang, de sa vie?
Vous rendriez vostre pere à chacun odieux,
Le voulant honorer d'actes injurieux.[38]

[What an abhorrent idea! Who has ever witnessed that a dead man in his grave needed the blood, the life, of a living man? If you want to honor your father through offensive acts, you will render him odious to everyone.]

Garnier, who was a lawyer, presents in his tragedies people who defend their positions, which are often irreconcilable.[39] As we have seen in *Hippolyte*, the ethical thought channeled by the play does not reside in any one of these particular viewpoints, but is to be put together by the viewer of the drama, and thus it implies performance or imagined performance. Agamemnon, who sacrifices his own daughter Iphigenia in Euripides's play, thinks that sacrifice demanded by "a dead man in his grave" is odious and terrifying. He argues from a moral position that he projects onto the community ("you will render him odious to everyone"). This argument does not convince Pyrrhe, who declares to Hecube that it is not for lack of compassion, but out of a sense of filial duty ["pieté vers mon pere"] that he wants to carry out the sacrifice of Polyxene. Compassion, the play suggests, may have limited efficacy in a society where having status implies strong demands placed on the individual by paternal or patriarchal authorities. Pyrrhe will not be deterred: "Ja de son tiede sang deust fumer le tombeau, / Ja dans sa gorge deust plonger le saint couteau" ["Her warm blood must burn on the tomb, the sacred knife must be plunged into (her) breast"].[40]

But can the spectacle of violence done to others, far away from the here and now of civil-war-torn France, inspire cooler and freer reflection in the viewer or reader? Sacrifice is a spectacle that provokes ethical questions in observers, and the play invites the viewers or readers to enter this specular-reflective structure—away from the pressures of their actual social bonds and loyalties—so they too can receive nourishment from the fire and blood.

While Hecube and Agamemnon plead with Pyrrhe, Polyxene quietly submits herself to his will. Pyrrhe envisions sacrificing Polyxene as an expiatory act, the kind Hippolyte also performs, a *holocaust*, in which the blood is spilled onto the ground, but her own acts introduce the element of a vertical ascent into the choreography of the *chthonic* ritual. In *Hippolyte*, the fact that the hero could not avoid a fate similar to that of the white lamb that he sacrificed revealed him as helpless and innocent, but Polyxene creates a different theatrical effect by actively taking on the role of the innocent, passive sacrifice. The details of the material and gestural world of ancient sacrifice, which are carefully rendered in Pyrrhe's act of offering of Polyxene to Achille, help Garnier to highlight the important theatricality of ritual.

"D'une franche allure": Ritual and Performance

Many humanist tragedies avoided the direct acting out of violent scenes, and Polyxene's death is similarly presented in the form of a *récit*, narrated to Hecube by Thaltybie, the messenger of the Greeks. The theatricality of the act is, however, shown in the way in which the *récit* opens up a gap between Pyrrhe's orders, which function like stage directions (Her warm blood must burn . . .) and Polyxene's acts. It is clear that Garnier thought of performance when writing the account of Polyxene's death or self-immolation, which is meta-theatrical. He closely follows Seneca's *Troades* in describing the place where she is to be sacrificed like a theater. Achille's tomb is built by the River Rhesus (mentioned by Homer and Seneca), and behind it rises a hill, creating an amphitheater-like space ["qui fait en theatre un grand contourna-ment"].[41] Nature conspires to make an amphitheater out of Achille's tomb in a pleasantly curved space that encloses the spectacle and the large crowd of spectators that gathered to watch the ritual. This pleasant place softens the cruelty of Pyrrhe's undertakings.

Garnier's depiction of Polyxene's sacrifice is very much based on the corresponding scene in Seneca's *Troades*, but Garnier further elaborates the bucolic setting by adding wreaths and garlands to offer some escape from the physical world of sacrifice and to allow Polyxene to transcend the physical violence of the act by her gently submissive act of self-sacrifice. It is possible that in writing these lines Garnier had in mind a painting on stage that would exhibit the gently ascending meadow, with the tomb that serves as an altar and the river.

The act, narrated by the messenger, is thus supposed to appear pleasant to the French audience. Thaltybie narrates, following Seneca, that only a small part of the spectators were spurred on by the desire for revenge, and the majority felt pity for Polyxene. The ritual is described in detail, with attention to gesture and ritual, with the messenger zooming in on Polyxene's acts:

Quelques jeunes enfans
. . . .
Marchoyent le front orné d'odoreuses guirlandes:
Pyrrhe suivait apres, de la main conduisant
La vierge coste à coste, au sepulchre nuisant.
. . . .

Elle d'honneste honte ayant les yeux baissez,
Traverse avecques luy les escadrons pressez.

. . . .

Elle devance Pyrrhe, et d'une franche allure
Monte au plus haut sommet de ceste sepulture:
Et alors le Pelean du tombeau s'approchant,
Et de sa main l'autel reveremment touchant,
Les deux genoux pliez va dire en ceste sorte. . . .[42]

[A few young children . . . walked wearing fragrant wreaths on their heads.
Pyrrhe followed them leading the virgin with his arms by her two sides to the
offensive sepulcher. . . . With sincere shame, her eyes lowered, she crosses
past the troops of cavaliers with Pyrrhe. . . . She overtakes Pyrrhe and, with a
decisive gait, ascends to the topmost point of the sepulcher. Then the Pelean
(Pyrrhe), walking up to the tomb, touching it with his hands full of reverence,
kneeling down, begins to say. . . .]

Garnier may have been inspired by the iconography of the *holocaust* present
in du Choul, who depicts a boy carrying a wreath as part of the ceremony
(see figure 7.3).

Polyxene's "franche allure" ["both decisive and free gait"] as she climbs to
the top of the sepulcher evokes the image of the "smoky air" that rises from
the burning trees: another vegetal image that the chorus evokes to speak
about immortality:

[C]omme d'un bois gommeux,
Sort en flambant un air fumeux,
Qui haut se guide,
Et volé bien avant és cieux
Se pert, eloigné de nos yeux,
Dedans le vuide.
Ainsi de nostre corps mourant
La belle ame se retirant,
Au ciel remonte,
Invisible aux humains regards,
Et là, franche des mortels dards,
La Parque dompte.[43]

[[L]ike a smoky air ascending that a moist tree exudes when it is burning, and
flying up is soon lost in the sky, disappearing from our eyes into the void, so
the soul leaving the body ascends to the sky, and there, free from lethal arrows,
conquers the Parcae.]

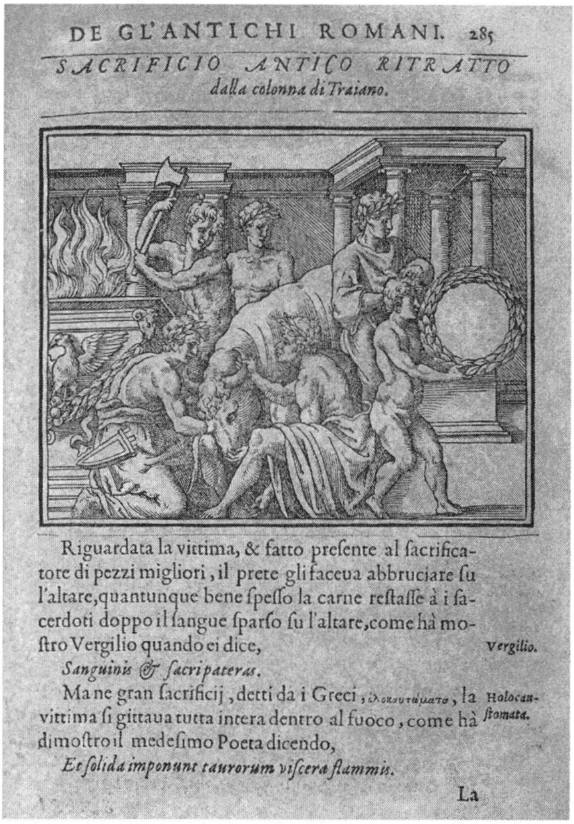
DE GL'ANTICHI ROMANI. 285

SACRIFICIO ANTICO RITRATTO
dalla colonna di Traiano.

Riguardata la vittima, & fatto preſente al ſacrificatore di pezzi migliori, il prete gli faceua abbruciare ſu l'altare, quantunque bene ſpeſſo la carne reſtaſſe à i ſacerdoti doppo il ſangue ſparſo ſu l'altare, come hà moſtro Vergilio quando ei dice, *Vergilio.*

Sanguinis & ſacri pateras.

Ma ne gran ſacrificij, detti da i Greci, ὁλοκαυτώματα, la vittima ſi gittaua tutta intera dentro al fuoco, come hà dimoſtro il medeſimo Poeta dicendo, *Holocauſtomata.*

Et ſolida imponunt taurorum viſcera flammis.

La

Figure 7.3. The image of a *holocaust* with the participants wearing wreaths, in Guillaume du Choul's *Discorso della religione antica de Romani* (1569).
Getty Research Institute

This image of the soul's ascent is transformed in these lines into a wish ("Puissé-je . . . / Franche de ces maux ennuyeux / A jamais vivre" ["May I live . . . forever free of worrisome tribulations!"]),[44] expressed by the chorus in order to mitigate the anachronism of putting Christian ideas of immortality into the mouth of a pagan. Yet the "bois gommeux" ["moist tree"] is also analogous to the human body and its humors, so the image of the burning wood helps to mediate between pagan and Christian worlds. The image of the burning wood moreover evokes the sacrificial altar, but this time it is the ascending smoke of Olympian sacrifice, the kind in which a banquet was offered to the gods and enjoyed by the human participants. Garnier carefully balances images of the materiality of the body with images that imply transcendence. In describing Pyrrhe's gestures, Garnier may be commenting on the deceptive outer appearance of piety. Pious rituals do not guarantee piety or redemption, as in this case Pyrrhe's respect for the altar erected over Achille's tomb. It is instead Polyxene's decisive and graceful gait that introduces the "secular sacred" into the ritual. Polyxene interrupts the ritual to declare that she wants to die freely and with dignity, like a princess. Her dignified self-immolation involves her opening her robe and exposing her chest, and breasts, down to her navel ["fendit sa robe avec sa blanche main, / Et jusques au nombril se decouvrit le sein"].[45] The play exposes the female body as far as it is turned into a symbol and balances carefully between showing and concealing the body.

In his history of French theater, Charles Mazouer derives tragic action from Stoic ethics, which recommends that one resort to courage in the face of adversity and choose suicide when no other option is available, and thus to act freely and with dignity. At the same time he suggests that this Stoic moral advice was at odds with the Christian sentiments of the French in the sixteenth century.[46] No doubt Polyxene resembles a Stoic heroine, but Garnier softens the Stoic ideal. Her willing submission resembles Stoic resolve, but without the fierceness and violence done to oneself. It also likens her to a martyr, but without the pathos attached to martyrdom. There is something graceful and appealing in Polyxene's gestures, which invite spectatorship. As we have seen, Montaigne thinks of sacrifice as barbarity that every society practiced at some point but can either leave behind or fall back into. Garnier's plays look at this "barbarous" ritual of the past in order to allude to the return of violence in France. But in these Greek plays, sacrifice as a ritual is newly invested with meaning and ethical significance as Garnier exploits the theatricality of sacrifice and its ability to inspire both cruelty and mercy, both tribal loyalty and an aversion to cruelty, both moral and immoral responses. Jean-Yves Dubois, who played the role of Hippolyte at the Théâtre de Chaillot, notes that he felt like dragging the carcass of a wild bore onto the stage and reading the future in the animal's guts.[47] This is precisely how Garnier forces the spectators to "read the future" or see themselves and their society in the acts of sacrifice described, verbally performed, on stage.

Notes

1. Throughout this chapter I use Garnier's gallicized forms of Greek proper names. All translations are mine unless otherwise indicated.

2. The first scholar to address the question of performance was Germain Bapst, who, in the late nineteenth century, argued that the question of mise-en-scène

[staging] was relevant even if the play in question was never performed, since many authors intended their plays to be represented on stage. Françoise Charpentier goes further to question the primacy of the printed text, arguing that it was usually the record of the memory of a performance. Germain Bapst, *Essai sur l'histoire du théâtre, orné de 85 gravures* (Paris: Librairie Hachette, 1893); Françoise Charpentier, "Les débuts de la tragedie heroique: Antoine de Montchrestien (1575–1621)" (PhD diss., Université de Lille, 1976 [pub. 1981]), 573.

3. "Nowadays, we are very unlikely to be spectators of humanist tragedy— attempts to try the plays out in the theatre in this century have been few and far between. Nevertheless, as readers, we always have the freedom to be spectators of an imagined performance. Even at the time of their composition, many of these plays had more readers than spectators." Gillian Jondorf, *French Renaissance Tragedy: The Dramatic Word* (Cambridge, UK: Cambridge University Press, 2006), 131.

4. Rebecca Zorach, *Blood, Milk, Ink, Gold: Abundance and Excess in the French Renaissance* (Chicago: University of Chicago Press, 2005), 48. On the problem of interpreting performance in the context of the court and international diplomacy, see Ellen R. Welch's chapter in this volume (6).

5. Ibid., 69.

6. Nicolò Machiavelli, "What Kinds of Peoples the Romans Had to Fight, and How Stubbornly These Peoples Defended Their Liberty," in *Discourses on Livy*, trans. Julia Conaway Bondanella and Peter Bondanella (Oxford: Oxford University Press, 1997), 156–61. Cited by Ann Hartle in *Montaigne: Accidental Philosopher* (Cambridge, UK: Cambridge University Press, 2003), 208–9.

7. Guillaume du Choul, *Discours de la religion* (Lyon: Guillaume Rouillé, 1556). A reprint edition has been issued in the series The Renaissance and the Gods, edited by Stephen Orgel (New York: Garland Publishing, 1976).

8. Théodore de Bèze, *A Tragedie of Abrahams Sacrifice*, trans. Arthur Golding (London: Thomas Vautroullier, 1577).

9. For more on sacrifice in Bèze's play, see John D. Lyons's chapter in this volume (2).

10. Ronsard celebrated the event in his *Livret de Folastries*, which he published anonymously because of the risqué nature of the activities described in the poems (sacrifice, erotic and sexual games, etc.). The poem that describes the "ceremony of the goat" is a wine-induced vision in which the poet sees the forest peopled with frenzied maenads, the female followers of Bacchus, clothing themselves with snakes; satyrs; Silenus; and other companions of Bacchus, along with the god himself. But the poet also sees members of the brigade leading and pushing the goat, with horns adorned with ivy, and Ronsard himself mounts the goat, which is led to Jodelle's "immortal feet," who sacrifices it after pulling out its beard hair. The poem plays on the similarities of the stamping movement of feet and the rhythm of poetry. We are in an imaginary forest, where the poetic rhythm and the poetic feet together evoke the rhythm of unbridled reveling of the communality of the inspired few, possibly including erotic games. On the latter, see Gary Ferguson, *Queer*

(Re)Readings in the French Renaissance: Homosexuality, Gender, Culture (Aldershot, UK: Ashgate, 2008), 113.

11. Ronsard, Œuvres complètes, ed. Jean Céard, Daniel Ménager, and Michel Simonin (Paris: Gallimard, 1994), 1:568, v. 321–22.

12. In Ronsard's poem the ambiguity is maintained through the representation of the ceremony as a vision and the ceremony as the effect of the symbolic intoxication induced by poetry. With the confusion between literal and poetic "feet," we do not know if we are in a real place or a poetic, imaginary one. See La Polémique protestante contre Ronsard, ed. Jacques Pineaux (Paris: Marcel Didier, 1973), 1:41, 81 and 2:265. Ronsard's response follows in "Discours des Misères de ce temps" in Ronsard, Œuvres complètes, 2:1054–55. He dismisses the ritual as a joke that was carried out for fun, with no intention of killing the goat.

13. For a modern edition of Jean Racine's play, see his Œuvres complètes, vol. 1, ed. Georges Forestier et al. (Paris: Gallimard, Bibliothèque de la Pléiade, 1999).

14. Antoine Vitez, "Notes en désordre sur Hippolyte et l'Orfeo," Écrits sur le théâtre, vol. 3 (Paris: P.O.L., 1996), 240–41.

15. Didier-Georges Gabily notes "Phèdre(s) and Hippolyte(s)," from "Notes traversières" (July 1990–May 1992), http://www.didiergeorgesgabily.net/miseensce-nephedresethippolytes-2.html (accessed July 3, 2014). The original copy can be found at the archives of l'Institut Mémoires de l'édition contemporaine (IMEC).

16. http://www.leforumbm.fr/uploads/d299631dfe6ebb38e04a939bab1b6f46.pdf (accessed July 3, 2014).

17. On Hippolyte's historical significance, see Phillip John Usher, "Tragedy in the Aftermath of the Saint Bartholomew's Day Massacre: France's First Phèdre and the Hope for Peace," Romance Notes 52, no. 3 (2012): 255–62.

18. Figures 7.1 and 7.2, along with the woodcut in figure 7.3, are taken from the Italian edition, Guillame du Choul's Discorso della religione antica de Romani (Lione: Appresso Gvglielmo Rovillio, 1569).

19. Robert Garnier, Hippolyte, in Théâtre complet, vol. 2, ed. Jean-Dominique Beaudin (Paris: Garnier, 2009), 1.253–61, 71. The citations from Hippolyte henceforth refer to this edition by act and verse number(s).

20. Ibid., 1.263–70.

21. Jane Ellen Harrison, Prolegomena to the Study of Greek Religion (Cambridge, UK: Cambridge University Press, 1922; repr. Forgotten Books, 2012), 15–17.

22. Poppy Siahaan, "Did He Break Your Heart or Your Liver?" in Culture, Body, and Language: Conceptualizations of Internal Body Organs across Cultures and Languages, ed. Farzad Sharifian, René Dirven, Jing Yu, and Susanne Niemeier (New York: Mouton de Gruyter, 2008), 45–74, esp. 52–54.

23. Garnier, Hippolyte, 4.1857–58.

24. The expression "ceremony of riddance" is borrowed from Harrison, Prolegomena.

25. Garnier, Hippolyte, 5.2119–22.

26. Jurgis Baltrusaitis, Le Moyen Âge fantastique (Paris: Colin, 1955).

27. I owe this insight to Michèle Longino, who in a talk at the Huntington Library in San Marino, California, in 2012 remarked on the topos in early modern travel literature of the difference between civilized women in France and "natural women" who live on the islands of the Mediterranean and have supposedly not been corrupted by shame.

28. Garnier, *Hippolyte*, 5.2229–30.

29. "Barbare et précieux: Entretien avec Bérangère Bonvoisin et Jean-Yves Dubois sur la mise en scène d'*Hippolyte* par Antoine Vitez," in *Lectures de Robert Garnier*, ed. Emmanuel Buron (Rennes: Presses universitaires de Rennes, 2000), 71–85.

30. Garnier explains in the dedicatory letter to Messire Regnaud (1579), which he prefaced to the play *La Troade*, that "seeing" that example of the Trojans who suffered "extreme calamities" should be of comfort to the audience. Meere, whose dissertation deals with direct representations of violence, has pointed to the ethical function of "showing and seeing" in Garnier's and other French tragedies. See Michael Meere, "Troubling Tragedies: Staging Violence in Early Modern France" (PhD diss., University of Virginia, 2009), 50.

31. On the topic of compassion in later, seventeenth-century French plays, see Katherine Ibbett, "Pity, Compassion, Commiseration: Theories of Theatrical Relatedness," *Seventeenth-Century French Studies* 30, no. 2 (2008): 196–208.

32. Robert Garnier, *La Troade, tragédie*, in *Théâtre complet*, vol. 5, ed. Jean-Dominique Beaudin (Paris: Honoré Champion, 1999), 4.1843, 124. As with *Hippolyte*, all citations to this play in the body of the text refer to this edition by act and verse number(s).

33. Ibid., 1.187–88.

34. Ibid., 1.263–68.

35. Ibid., 1.272.

36. Ibid., 1.281–82.

37. Montaigne:

[A] C'estoit une estrange fantasie de vouloir payer la bonté divine de nostre affliction, comme les Lacedemoniens qui mignardoient leur Diane par le bourrellement des jeunes garçons qu'ils faisoient foiter en sa faveur, souvent jusques à la mort. C'estoit une humeur farouche de vouloir gratifier l'architecte de la subversion de son bastiment, et de vouloir garentir la peine deue aux coulpables par la punition des non coulpables; et que la povre Iphigenia, au port d'Aulide, par sa mort et immolation, deschargeast envers Dieu l'armée des Grecs des offences qu'ils avoient commises. (Michel de Montaigne, "Apologie de Raimond Sebond," in *Les essais*, ed. Pierre Villey and V.-L. Saulnier [Paris: Presses universitaires de France, 1965], II.12.521–22)

Florio:

It was a strange conceit, with our owne affliction to goe about to please and appay divine goodnesse: As the Lacedemonians, who flattered and wantonized their Diana by torturing of young boys, whom often in favour of her they caused to be whipped to death. It was a savage kinde of humour to thinke to gratifie the Architect with the subversion of his Architecture, and to cancel the punishment due unto the guiltie by punishing the guiltles, and to imagine that poore Iphigenia, in the port of Aulis, should by her death and sacrifice discharge and expiate towards God, the Grecians armie of the offences which they had committed. ("An Apologie of Raymond Sebond," in *The Essayes or Morall, Politike and Millitarie Discourses of Lord Michaell de Montaigne*, trans. John Florio [London: Val. Sims,1603], http://www.luminarium.org/renascence-editions/montaigne/2xii.htm, [accessed May 15, 2014])

Frame:

[A] It is a strange fancy to try to pay for divine goodness with our affliction, like the Lacedaemonians who wheedled their Diana by the torture of young boys, whom they had whipped for her sake, often to death. It was a savage impulse to try to gratify the architect by the overthrow of his building, and to try to cover the penalty due to the guilty punishment of the guiltless; and to think that poor Iphigenia, at the port of Aulis, would by her death and sacrifice clear the army of the Greeks in the eyes of God of the offenses they had committed. ("Apology for Raymond Sebond," in *The Complete Essays of Montaigne*, trans. Donald Frame [London: Everyman's Library, 2003], II.12.471)

38. Garnier, *La Troade*, 3.1451–56.

39. For more on Garnier and the legal system, see Phillip John Usher's chapter in this volume (8).

40. Garnier, *La Troade*, 3.1531–32.

41. Ibid., 4.2074.

42. Ibid., 4.2083–2111.

43. Ibid., 3.1342–54.

44. Ibid., 3.1374–76.

45. Ibid., 4.2141–42.

46. Charles Mazouer, *Le théâtre français de la Renaissance* (Paris: Honoré Champion, 2002), 198.

47. "Barbare et précieux," 76–77.

~

CHAPTER EIGHT

Courtroom Drama during the Wars of Religion

Robert Garnier and the Paris Parlement

PHILLIP JOHN USHER

For Penelope Meyers Usher[1]

It is universally recognized that the tragedies of Robert Garnier—*Porcie* (1568), *Hippolyte* (1573), *Cornélie* (1574), *Marc Antoine* (1578), *La Troade* (1579), *Antigone* (1580), and *Les Juives* (1583)—depict and/or resonate with the French Wars of Religion that pitted Catholics and Protestants against each other, from the massacre of Vassy in 1562 through the proclamation of the Edict of Nantes in 1598.[2] The three Roman plays (*Porcie*, *Cornélie*, and *Marc Antoine*) are frequently cited in this respect, for they all make clear and easily recognizable parallels, in both the plays themselves and in the various liminary materials, between wars past and present.[3] The original title page of *Porcie* positions the play as a "tragedie françoise, representant la cruelle et sanglante saison des guerres Ciuiles de Rome" ["French tragedy, which represents the cruel and bloody season of Rome's civil wars"] deemed to be "propre et conuenable *pour y voir depeincte la calamité de ce temps*" ["proper and suitable *as depictions of our own time's calamities*"].[4] The first act thus gains immediate resonance: fraternal bloodshed is evoked via a vocabulary of internecine warfare (*s'entre-égorger* [to slit each other's throats]; *s'entre-ouvrir l'estomach* [to carve open each other's stomachs], etc.), depicting a destroyed Rome and its beleaguered citizens, whose situation could be easily transposed onto the French context.[5] *Cornélie* and *Marc Antoine* offer similar immediate historical interpretations, as does *Hippolyte* (albeit in a different way).[6] *Antigone*, too, is frequently read allegorically—George Steiner has opined definitively that "[the] desolate Argos lamented by Jocasta is France" and that "[the] House of Laius intimately parallels that of the Valois or of the Guises."[7] And *Les Juives*, finally, with its story of divine anger and Jewish exile ("Jusques à quand, Seigneur, épandras-tu ton ire?" ["Until when, oh Lord, will you continue to spread around your anger?"]), again tells of tyranny, clemency, and religious strife in ways that quickly find their historical counterparts.[8] As Garnier announces in the dedicatory letter to his final play, it is a tragedy about "les souspirables calamitez d'un peuple, qui a *comme nous* abandonné son Dieu" ["the sigh-inducing calamities of a nation that has, *like us*, abandoned its God"].[9]

Indeed, then, Garnier's tragedies call out to be—and generally are—read allegorically, as relating to the French *troubles* [civil wars]. Two problems, however, suggest themselves. First, while such allegorical readings are, in a general way, justified and important, it can be difficult to pin down their details. For sure, it is clear that Garnier's tragedies return again and again to certain key themes that are pertinent to the *troubles*, such as the opposition between clemency and rigor on the part of a leader. But how the plays resonate with contemporary politics, who (if anyone in particular) is "attacked" or "defended," and other similar questions are often hard to state with precision. It can be tempting to seek out clear judgments—and critics sometimes do just that: in his reading of *Les Juives*, Raymond Lebègue underscores the mention of "heresy" in the dedicatory epistle, suggesting that the play puts responsibility for the *troubles* squarely on the reformers.[10] In a similar way, it has been suggested, in readings of *Bradamante* (Garnier's only tragicomedy), that the Christian/Saracen conflict stands in for the Catholic/Protestant one, such that certain lines might be read as outright Protestant-bashing: "[il faut] rompre les Sarasins, / Ennemis de ton nom, pour l'Eglise defendre" ["(We must) break down the Saracens, / enemies to your name, so as to defend the Church"];[11] "Il nous faut rebastir nos Eglises rompues" ["We must rebuild our broken Churches"].[12]

But correlations are not always clear or provable. To what extent *Marc Antoine* (1578) "attacks" the new king Henri III is far from obvious, such that Jean-Claude Ternaux argues for a more subtle reading: "le but visé est donc de délivrer une leçon pour faire réfléchir, et non d'attaquer avec virulence un souverain dont l'originalité constitue une cible facile" ["the chosen goal is thus to deliver a lesson that engenders reflection, not violently to attack a sovereign whose originality is an easy target"]. If Garnier, argues Ternaux, "ne fait pas allusion à des faits précis, il n'empêche que la mise en garde existe" ["does not allude to precise facts, there is nonetheless a distinct warning"].[13] Ternaux's careful conclusion is that Garnier, faithful to his monarchical beliefs, is nevertheless "inquiet" ["worried"].[14] *Inquiétude* [worry, concern] indeed seems to be an appropriate term for what the plays express vis-à-vis the *troubles*. The second (related) problem is knowing to what extent these allegorical depictions of civil war, understood as warnings rather than attacks, enter into the public sphere.[15] Given just how little information there is concerning the existence and conditions of Renaissance performances of Garnier's tragedies, it cannot be taken for granted that their political resonances would have influenced or otherwise connected with public opinion within the context of actual performances—as we may assume for more modern incarnations of politically charged plays.[16]

To address these two problems and to suggest a new perspective on how Garnier's tragedies partook of public life in the sixteenth century, whether or not they were performed, I focus on the ways in which two of Garnier's plays (*Marc Antoine* and *Antigone*) specifically associate themselves with the *parlement*, an institution whose roles during the Wars of Religion have been the subject of much recent debate. Jean-Louis Bourgeon, Sarah Hanley, Sylvie Daubresse, Marie Houllemare, Nancy Lyman Roelker, and others urge us to go beyond some of the most celebrated moments of the Renaissance *parlement*[17]—for example the trial of Etienne de la Boétie's teacher Anne du Bourg, which resulted in his being executed as a heretic.[18]

As recent studies show, the *parlement* was not just a mouthpiece for the king (in Anne du Bourg's case, Henri II), as illustrated by one of its key roles: while this institution indeed had the charge of recording royal edicts and laws, it also—and increasingly throughout the sixteenth century—had the possibility to respond by issuing *remontrances*, a term that the first edition of the *Académie française* (1694) defines as "discours par lequel on represente à quelqu'un les inconveniens d'une chose qu'il a faite, ou qu'il est sur le point de faire" ["speech in which one represents to someone the inconveniences of a thing that he has done, or which he is about to do"]. Not everyone agrees on the exact meaning and *portée* [significance] of these *remontrances*, but we must acknowledge—as, for example, does Houllemare—that while the *parlement* renders justice in the name of the monarch, it also takes part in the debates of the time.[19] The *parlement* did not merely deliver the king's laws to the people. It also represented to the king in what ways certain laws or future laws might be deemed unjust or unwise. As Daubresse has phrased it, the various actors in the *parlements* were both the king's most ardent defenders and his firmest critics.[20] They occupied a position between the king and the *peuple* and their role was not only—to use terms borrowed from

Jürgen Habermas—that of representing the king *before* the people, but also of being a representative *for* the people[21]—with all the qualifiers, footnotes, and exceptions that such a statement obviously requires. The title of Sylvie Daubresse's study—*Le parlement de Paris, ou, La voix de la raison* [*The Parlement of Paris, or the Voice of Reason*]—seems to beckon for a *rapprochement* with Habermasian *öffentliches Räsonnement* [public use of reason], for there private citizens (magistrates, lawyers, etc.) frequently contributed to public debate about how France could survive and stop the warfare, rarely if ever opposing the king's authority, but frequently seeking to redirect it.

Borrowing terms from Habermas's description of media and the public sphere in his *Between Facts and Norms*, I suggest that Garnier's tragedies function as a "warning system" that "amplifies the pressure of problems," and also that—and the applicability of the language is uncanny—these plays not only "thematize" problems, but also "dramatize them in such a way that they are taken up and dealt with by parliamentary complexes."[22] On the horizon is thus the idea that—before the eighteenth-century bourgeois public sphere, with its coffeehouses and other specific *topoi*—a different kind of public sphere might have existed in Renaissance France, localized in the French *parlements* and with which the tragedies of Robert Garnier sought out connections.

To explore these associations, I turn first to Garnier's *Antigone*, a play that takes up and stitches together into a very long tableau Seneca's *Phoenician Women*, Statius's *Thebaid*, and Sophocles's *Antigone*.[23] As this stitching together suggests, Garnier's *Antigone* does not just replay the Sophoclean confrontation between Antigone and Creon, normally read through Hegel as a confrontation between two equally justified ethical claims.[24] Rather, it emphasizes how that conflict is part of a wider tragic situation originating in the fratricidal strife that opposes Polynice and Eteocle, a strife that leaves Antigone and Jocaste with split sympathies.

As numerous critics have noted (including Steiner, mentioned above), the play thus echoes France's situation, with families torn apart by religious turmoil, with brother killing brother. Jocaste embodies France. Just as the nation has been divided along religious lines, so Jocaste is the mother of warring sons: "Pour qui me banderay-je? Helas! Auquel des deux / Ma faveur donneray-je, estant la mere d'eux?" ["For whom will I stan up? Alas, to which will I lend my favor, for I am mother to both?"].[25] Following in the tradition of Greek female lament, about which classicists have for several decades been underlining the political nature, Antigone hopes that the tears of her mother will be able to stop the warring sons: "Allons, Madame, allons, vos maternelles larmes / De leurs guerrieres mains feront tomber les armes" ["Come on, mother, come on—your motherly tears will cause their weapons to fall from that bellicose hands"].[26] Jocaste seeks to intervene directly in the life of the *polis*. She quite literally offers up her maternal body as a sacrifice that might be able to stop the war. First her breast: "Dressez vers moy vos dards et vos glaives meurtriers, / Sacquez-les dans mon sein, dedans cette poitrine, / Qui coupable a porté la semence mutine" ["Aim at me your arrows and your murderous swords, punch them into my breast, into this chest, which is guilty for having carried the seed of mutiny"],[27] then her flank, womb, and entrails: "Que ne destrempez-vous vos armes en mon flanc, / Si vous n'avez horreur de les souiller au sang / Tiré de mesme ventre, au sang de mes entrailles, / Vous entremassacrant au pied de ces murailes?" ["Why do you not dip your weapons into my flank, if you are not horrified by sullying them in blood drawn from my belly, in the blood of my entrails, as you massacre each other at the foot of these walls?"].[28] Garnier's repeated use throughout of reflexive verbs to describe war underscore its civil nature: brothers *hack each other apart*, they *murder each other*, they *clash against each other*, they *confront each other*, expressed in French via verbs like *s'entre-déhacher* [to hack each other apart],[29] some of which (although immediately comprehensible) seem to occur *only* in Garnier. I need not, I think, belabor the point that the play offers up a private citizen's public opinion about matters concerning not his own interests, but those of the well-being of civil society.

I want to emphasize how the play, beginning with its dedicatory letter, seeks to enter into the public sphere—not by performance, not by discussion of the play in the aisles by spectators, but by the way it attaches itself to the parliamentary system. Published in 1580, the play appeared in the middle of the seventh religious war (1579–1580), which began when the Protestant Prince de Condé declared war on the town of La Fère in Picardie, and which ended with the Peace of Fleix (Poitou-Charentes) in November 1580, negotiated between representatives of the Catholic Henri III and the Protestant Henri de Navarre (future Henri IV). What interests me here is that the dedicatory letter that precedes the play is addressed to "Monseigneur Brisson, conseiller du Roy en son conseil privé, et President en sa Cour de Parlement" ["My Lord Brisson, advisor to the King in his private council, and President in his Parliament Court"], a double title that situates him as attached to the king *and* to the people. But who was Barnabé Brisson, and why is this dedication important?[30]

Brisson had begun his career as an *avocat* (roughly meaning "lawyer") in the *Cour du Parlement de Paris*, arguing various famous cases with success, including against Jacques-Auguste de Thou. Following in the footsteps of Guy du Faur, seigneur de Pibrac (to whom I return shortly), Barnabé then became *avocat du roi* in 1575. And in 1579, Barnabé played an important role in the *Grands Jours de Poitou*, an exceptional hearing that played a large role in bringing about peace during a period of anarchy—during those *grands jours*, many nobles (both Catholics and Protestants) were put to death for having committed violent acts during the recent *troubles*. In August 1580, Brisson became the "président de la Grande Chambre du parlement de Paris, président à mortier" ["president in the Grand Chamber of the Paris Parliament"], a function he purchased for something like 60,000 *livres* from Pomponne de Bellièvre, himself in turn selling his role as *avocat du roi* to Jacques Faye d'Espeisses. Eventually killed by the Catholic League, Brisson was then—at the moment when *Antigone* was published—the *president à mortier* (a special title carried by certain judges in reference to the mortar they wear) and had very recently played a key role, in Poitou, in bringing peace and restoring order, not along confessional lines, but to restore peace and punish those who were violent.

Contextually, then, Garnier's dedication of the play to Brisson seems to perform the necessary suturing between—to return to Habermas's turn of phrase—*amplifying and thematizing* and the *taking up by the parliamentary complex*. Garnier's dedicatory is praiseful: "qui est le François, chez lequel n'ait penetré la celebrité de vostre nom? Qui n'ait l'oreille repue et traversee du son de vos louanges?" ["What Frenchman has not heard of your name? Whose ear is not full and resounding with the sound of your praises?"].[31] Dedicating *Antigone* to such a man is not a small thing—nor is it a purely personal or encomiastic *thing*. It brings *Antigone* into the purview of the social and political history of the Wars of Religion in a direct manner.

The dedicatory epistle, read in more detail, yields a number of traces of this intention of intervention. One essential trace pertains to the way in which the dedication is enacted. Garnier does not just dedicate the play to Brisson, nor does he sketch some broad equivalency between Brisson's possible roles in the *parlement* and the Wars of Religion and the struggle over the Theban throne. Garnier states that he aims to "entretenir [Brisson] des infortunes de ceste pitoyable Antigone" ["tell (Brisson) about the misfortunes of this pitiful Antigone"], of whom he says that she is "revivant en nostre France" ["living in today's France"] and who "se vient, comme esperdue, jetter entre vos bras" ["comes, disheveled, throwing herself into your arms"] (i.e., into Brisson's arms) in the hope that the latter might provide as much "favorable support" ["help and support"] as did Antigone in supporting "son miserable pere" ["her pitiful father"] (Oedipus).

This moment of dedication is strikingly powerful and calls for a number of remarks. First, we notice here a breaking of boundaries between play and nonplay, between the dramatic and (because of Brisson's real-world position) the parliamentary public sphere. It is as if Antigone (the character and/or the play) leaves the play proper to enter into the arms of Brisson. The boundary crossing is reinforced by the comparison between Brisson's support of Antigone and the latter's guidance of her father.

Second, the image that breaks the boundary (of Antigone leaping into Brisson's arms) is a very specific one. It might, at first, be thought pure rhetoric (in the weak sense of the term). Yet it actually belongs to a very precise form of rhetoric, that of the *parlements*. As one can gather from the letters of Estienne Pasquier, or from somewhat laboriously turning the handwritten and difficult-to-read pages of the institution's records, available for anyone to consult until this day in the *série* X of France's Archives Nationales, the image occurs often in records of Renaissance court trials, of which I give just two (close-to-home) examples. In a trial between Bobie (the accuser) and Arconville (the accused), Brisson represented the former and Pasquier the latter. In his account of the trial, Pasquier describes Bobie's position vis-à-vis Brisson in a manner strikingly similar to how Garnier describes Antigone in that same posture. Pasquier writes of Bobie that he throws himself "aux pieds de Monsieur Brisson" ["at the feet of Mr. Brisson"] and as having many "larmes à ses yeux" ["tears in her eyes"] as he calls out for Brisson to take up his case in court.[32] Pasquier describes Arconville, his own client, in a very similar position: "[à mes] pieds estoit le Gentil-homme [Arconville] et avec luy sa femme larmoyante, comme aussi deux petits enfans" ["at my feet was Arconville and with him his crying wife, as well as two little children"]. Garnier's dedication to Brisson—in which a "pitoyable Antigone" ["pitiful Antigone"] seeks support in Brisson's arms—finds here a historical correlate in a documented trial.

The unpublished court records of another trial are of interest here and gesture in a similar direction. They relate to a trial in which Garnier himself stood accused of having put to death the man who supposedly provided poisons to his domestic staff when they wanted to kill him. The widow of the dead man (named Champion) brought a case against Garnier for abuse of justice, with support from the lawyer Louis Servin (1555–1626), who several years after the trial would become Henri III's *avocat général.*[33] Just as Garnier presents Antigone as leaping into Brisson's arms, and just as Pasquier describes both Bobie and Arconville at the feet of their respective *avocats*, so the official trial records in this case describe Champion's widow in the position of the supplicant: "Mainctenant vous voiez une pauvre veufve qui vous demande justice pour venger la mort de son mary et pour avoir en ceste court ce qu'elle ne pouvoict esperer ailleurs" ["Now you see a poor widow who asks for justice to avenge the death of her husband and to receive in this courtroom that which she could not hope for elsewhere"].[34] It is not impossible that Servin read Garnier's plays, for he certainly plays with irony throughout the trial: he accuses Garnier of having been more a tyrant than the tyrants he describes in his tragedies. Servin identifies his role as describing "les acts inhumains de celluy . . . qui fait estat de composer des tragedies, et, [qui] fait des actes aultant et plus tragiques que ceulx qu'il a tasché imiter par ses escriptz" ["the inhuman acts of he . . . who makes a living composing tragedies, and who commits acts as tragic—and more tragic—that those he has attempts to imitate in his writing"].[35] The posture (a victim calling out for justice and seeking the support of an intermediary) is shared by both tragedy and the Renaissance law court. By dedicating *Antigone* to Brisson—who had recently played a role in attempts to bring about peace and restore order during the Wars of Religion—and by securing this dedication via an image (a supplicant leaping into her lawyer's arms), also abundantly present in the records (letters and court archives) relating to the French *parlements*, Garnier seems to be calling for his play to be understood *as if* it were a real trial of contemporary significance.

A similar case can be made for Garnier's *Marc Antoine* (1578), the last of the three Roman plays—thus following on from, and closing, the cycle begun by *Porcie* and *Cornélie*. Taking up the story of Mark Anthony and Cleopatra already portrayed by Etienne Jodelle in his *Cléopâtre captive* (1553), Garnier (as did Jodelle) relies heavily on sources including Plutarch's *Life of Anthony*, recently translated into French by Jacques Amyot. As already noted, the tragedy is arguably not a direct attack on Henri III, but does constitute a warning: like Jean Bodin's *République* (1576), it argues that unchecked passion can bring down a leader and his country. Notable, too, are the comments made about how the populace suffers from war. For example, Caesar is reminded in act 4 that as leaders fight for power, "le peuple en porte seul la peine" ["the populace alone pays the price of it"].[36] The chorus of Caesar's soldiers, at the end of the fourth act, brings home the complaint: "Tousjours la geurre domestique / Rongera nostre Republique?" ["Will civil war always gnaw at our Republic?"].[37] As is not the case for *Antigone*, we know that *Marc Antoine* was actually performed in the sixteenth century: in Saint-Maixent (a commune in the Sarthe *département*) on May 11, 1578; then again in 1579 (for the Prince de la Roche-sur-Yon); and in 1594 or 1595 in Paris.[38] Yet the entrance of the play into the arena of public opinion is, as with *Antigone*, inherently tied up with the *parlement* system.

Marc Antoine is not dedicated to Brisson, but to the magistrate, diplomat (and occasional poet) Guy Du Faur de Pibrac (1529–1584), to whom he had already dedicated his "Hymne de la monarchie" ["Hymn to Monarchy"] (1567). Garnier's dedication to Pibrac is similar in that it is addressed to

"Monseigneur de Pibrac, conseiller du Roy en son privé Conseil, President en sa Cour de Parlement, et Chancelier de Monsieur frere de sa Majesté" ["His Lord Pibrac, advisor to the King in his private council, President in his Court Parliament"], again underlining his role *between* the king and the *peuple*. Garnier says that he dedicates these "representations Tragiques des guerres civiles à Rome" ["tragic representations of our civil wars in Rome"] specifically because Pibrac has "en telle horreur nos dissentions domestiques" ["in such horror our civil disagreements"]. The tragedy is dedicated to him because of the latter's dislike of "les malheureux troubles de ce Royaume" ["the pitiful troubles of this kingdom"].

It must be acknowledged that Pibrac's role in the Wars of Religion was, of course, quite complicated—he is remembered for, among other things, seemingly defending the St. Bartholomew's Day Massacre in his *Ornatissimi cujusdam viri, de rebus gallicis, ad Stanislaum Elvidium Epistola* [*Letter on Gallic Matters*] (1573), a position probably adopted to ensure that the future Henri III (then Duke of Anjou) would become king of Poland (as Charles IX wished)—the letter served "to exculpate Anjou from any guilt in the massacre and ensure its [Polish] readers that religious troubles would not be settled by the sword."[39] It is indeed difficult not to be struck by the off-handed nature of the apology, where we find lines like this one: "Animadversum in paucos scio, sed quid agas? In tanto tumultu aliter fieri non posse, nec expediere" ["I know that there were a few murders, but what of it? In such great tumult, it is impossible to act any other way"].[40] Still, as one modern scholar notes, this opinion was likely one he was told to put down on paper, for "his desire to avoid bloodshed is a matter of historical record."[41] In fact, it would seem that Pibrac (in the *lit de justice* of August 26, 1572) had stood up to Charles IX and asked that he put an end to the violence, while the king himself seemingly ordered massacres.[42] In addition, we can note that in 1578—the year of *Marc Antoine*'s publication—Pibrac accompanied Catherine de' Medici on her tour of the South of France, the goal of which was pacification.[43]

In reading these two tragedies for their connection to the parliamentary milieu, I have tried to hint at how they attach themselves to the very complicated position held by the *parlement*, representing to key actors therein the problems of France's civil war, by breaking down the barrier between tragedy and the courtroom, via these specific dedications to Brisson and Pibrac, and via the language employed. My point is not about allegory, but about how the texts seek entrance into, or create, a public sphere. There are many more parallels that could be drawn between the French *parlement* and theater—as Marie Houllemare has done recently—but I conclude here by recalling how such a perspective on Garnier's tragedies aligns itself with the growing realization, advanced by recent studies, that the Wars of Religion were a period defined not just by violence, but also by interruptions of, and negotiations aimed at reestablishing, peace. It is *this* that Garnier's plays arguably portray—not only the violence itself, and *this* is the level at which they call to enter into the space of the *parlement*. Arguably, via the *parlement* the plays enter into an even wider public sphere.

One direction forward is already suggested by recent work on the political, social, and religious history of Renaissance Europe, especially regarding the Wars of Religion. Scholars like Mario Turchetti, Thierry Wanegffelen, and Olivier Christin have made a huge contribution to our understanding of civil and religious strife in the Renaissance by excavating the efforts, successes, and sometimes failures of those early modern Europeans who, throughout the wars, fought not along confessional lines or to ensure the success of any one party, but in a more independent manner, and who sometimes were most interested in pacification, concord, and coexistence of one kind or another.[44] Building on and going beyond the work of Turchetti, Wanegffelen studies those—the *insatisfaits* [the unsatisfied ones]—who, during the Reformation, choose neither Roman Catholicism nor Genevan Protestantism. And for his part, Christin has shown that throughout the religious wars in Francophone and Germanophone Europe, many individuals sought religious peace outside of confessional boundaries, a process that participated in an autonomization of political thought. Such trends in research, and bringing them into dialogue with work on Renaissance theater, offer many promising possibilities along the lines I have been sketching out here.

To underscore the public nature of court trials in the sixteenth century, I should like to conclude my thoughts by returning to a point earlier in the period. I turn to chapter 24 of *Gargantua*, wherein Rabelais describes how the eponymous giant occupied his time on rainy days. There, we read how he and his master would visit workshops to see "comment on tiroit les metaulx ou comment on fondoit l'artillerye: ou alloient veoir les lapidaires, orfevres et tailleurs de pierreries, ou les Alchymistes et monoyeurs, ou les haultelissiers, les tissotiers, les velotiers, les horologiers, miralliers, imprimeurs, organistes, tinturiers et aultres telles sortes d'ouvriers" ["how metals were drawn or how artillery was cast; or they went to watch the lapidaries, goldsmiths, and cutters of precious stones; or the alchemists and the coin minters, or the makers of great tapestries, the weavers, the velvet makers, watchmakers, mirror makers, printers, organists, dyers, and other such kinds of workmen"], but also how he would go "ouir les leçons publicques, les actes solennelz, les repetitions, les declamations, les playdoiez des gentilz advocatz" ["hear public readings, solemn acts, rehearsals, declamations, the pleading of the nice lawyers"].[45] *Plaidoyers* [speeches for the defense] were, then, just as much a part of a generally accessible public life as were the sounds of hammers in workshops as one walked by in the street.

As the letters of Etienne Pasquier and the records in the Archives Nationale's *série* X tell us, Rabelais's account is not just fictional: in the Renaissance, the *parlements* were, on most occasions, open to the public. Pasquier's son, for one, would go and watch, then debate with his father about what he'd heard. *This*, I think, is what Garnier was trying to do: to make the story of Eteocle, Polynice, Antigone, and Jocaste, or the story of Marc Antoine and Cleopatre, appear as public trials worthy of the *parlement's* attention.

Notes

1. An earlier version of this chapter was presented at the MLA conference in Boston in 2013, on a panel about public space in Renaissance France. I should like to thank the panel's organizer, David P. Laguardia, as well as fellow presenters and audience members who offered feedback and encouragement.

2. For an introduction to Robert Garnier, see Phillip John Usher, "Robert Garnier," *Literary Encyclopedia*, August 2012, http://www.litencyc.com/php/speople .php?rec=true&UID=1691 (accessed June 5, 2013). Although of its time and in need of a successor, the fullest study of Garnier's life and works remains the three volumes by Marie-Madeleine Mouflard, *Robert Garnier (1545–90)* (La Roche-sur-Yon [Vendée]: Impr. Centrale de l'ouest, 1961–1964). The first volume deals with sources, the second analyzes Garnier's plays, and the third provides a biography.

3. See Margaret McGowan, *The Vision of Rome in Late Renaissance France* (New Haven, CT: Yale University Press, 2000), 272–82. For an earlier version of McGowan's study on Garnier, see "The Presence of Rome in some Plays of Robert Garnier," in *Myth and Its Making in the French Theatre*, ed. Edward Freeman et al. (Cambridge, UK: Cambridge University Press, 1988), 12–19. See also Raymond Lebègue, "Les guerres civiles de Rome et les tragédies de Robert Garnier," in *Actes du colloque Renaissance-Classicisme du Maine* (Paris: Nizet, 1975), 283–89.

4. Robert Garnier, *Porcie* (Paris: Robert Estienne, 1568) (emphasis added). All translations are mine unless otherwise noted.

5. Robert Garnier, *Porcie*, ed. Jean-Claude Ternaux (Paris: Champion, 1999), 1.24, 1.27. Rome is described as being nothing but a ruin and a tomb: "Rome, il faut qu'à l'entour de la ronde machine / Lon entende aujourd'huy le son de ta ruine" ["Rome, it is necessary that around the round machine be heard today the son of your ruin"] (1.129–30); "Rome n'est qu'un sepulchre à tant de funerailles / Qu'elle voit entasser en ses froides entrailles" ["Rome is nothing but a tomb for so many funerals that she sees piling up in her cold entrails"] (1.145–46). The citations for the plays indicate first the page number (when appropriate), followed by act and verse number(s).

6. On *Hippolyte's* historical significance, see Phillip John Usher, "Tragedy in the Aftermath of the Saint Bartholomew's Day Massacre: France's First *Phèdre* and the Hope for Peace," *Romance Notes* 52, no. 3 (2012): 255–262.

7. George Steiner, *Antigones* (Oxford: Clarendon Press, 1984), 139.

8. Robert Garnier, *Les Juifves, Hippolyte*, ed. Raymond Lebègue (Paris: Les Belles Lettres, 2000), 17, 1.1.

9. Ibid., 10. Moreover, Lebègue recalled many years ago, in contemporary political debates, the point of view of Protestants (that revolt against an unjust leader
was legitimate) was denied by Catholics, who asserted in support of their claim that
Israel was abandoned by God because of its revolt against Nabuchodonosor, the very
story taken up by Garnier in this, his last, play. See Lebègue, "Notice," in Garnier,
Les Juifves, 112. Lebègue draws on Georges Weill, *Les théories sur le pouvoir royal en
France pendant les guerres de religion* (Paris: Hachette 1891), 83.

10. The pertinent part of the letter reads as follows: "Or vous ay-je representé les
souspirables calamitez d'un peuple, qui a comme nous abdonné son Dieu. C'est un
sujet delectable, et de bonne et saincte edification. Vous y voyez le chastiment d'un
Prince issu de l'ancienne race de David, pour son infidelité et rebellion contre son
superieur" (Garnier, *Les Juifves*, 10) ["Now I have shown you the deplorable calamities of a people who has abandoned its god as we have. It is a delectable subject,
and of good and saintly edification. You see the punishment of a prince, borne of
the ancient lineage of David, who has been unfaithful and has rebelled against his
superior"]. See also Lebègue, "Les Guerres civiles," 559.

11. Robert Garnier, *Bradamante*, ed. Raymond Lebègue (Paris: Les Belles Lettres,
1949), 120, 1.32–34. See, e.g., Frank Lestringant, who writes: "*Bradamante* mêle les
tons les plus divers, du registre épique sur lequel s'exprime l'empereur Charlemagne
pour appeler la chrétienté à l'unité contre l'infidèle (entendez; les protestants) à celui
de la franche comédie" ["*Bradamante* mixes together the most diverse tones, from the
epic register on which Charlemagne expresses himself as he calls for Christian unity
against the infidel [i.e., the Protestants] to that of open comedy"] ("Garnier" in *Dictionnaire des littératures de langue française*, ed. Jean-Pierre de Beaumarchais, Daniel
Couty, and Alain Rey [Paris: Bordas, 1984], 870).

12. Garnier, *Bradamante*, 124, 1.153.

13. Jean-Claude Ternaux, introduction to *Marc Antoine*, by Robert Garnier
(Paris: Classiques Garnier, 2010), 12.

14. The term *worried* seems somehow banal compared to *inquiet*. Lestringant has
recently showed the poignancy of being not just *inquiet*, but an *inquiéteur*, in his
excellent biography of André Gide: Frank Lestringant, *André Gide l'inquiéteur. Le
ciel sur la terre ou l'inquiétude partagée, 1869–1918*, vol. 1 (Paris: Flammarion, 2011).

15. I herein borrow the term *public sphere* from Jürgen Habermas, *Structural
Transformation of the Public Sphere*, trans. Thomas Burger with Frederick Lawrence
(Cambridge, MA: MIT Press, 1989). The term, for Habermas, only applies to later
contexts. The applicability of the term to the case of Renaissance space is thus both
controversial and a topic I am currently investigating elsewhere.

16. One example among many would be the production of Bertolt Brecht's *Mother
Courage and Her Children* at the Delacorte Theater in New York City in 2006, which
gave rise both in the theater and in the press to reflection about the ongoing wars
under the presidency of George W. Bush.

17. Jean-Louis Bourgeon, "La Fronde parlementaire à la veille de la Saint-
Barthélemy," *Bibliothèque de l'Ecole des Chartes* 148, no. 1 (1990): 17–89; Sylvie

Daubresse, *Le parlement de Paris, ou, la voix de la raison (1559–1589)* (Geneva: Droz, 2005); Sarah Hanley, *The "Lit de Justice" of the Kings of France: Constitutional Ideology in Legend, Ritual, and Discourse* (Princeton, NJ: Princeton University Press, 1983); Marie Houllemare, *Politiques de la parole: Le parlement de Paris au XVIe siècle* (Geneva: Droz, 2011); Nancy Lyman Roelker, *One King, One Faith: The Parlement of Paris and the Religious Reformations of the Sixteenth Century* (Berkeley: University of California Press, 1996).

18. A recent reading of this trial is provided by Nikki Shepardson, *Burning Zeal. The Rhetoric of Martyrdom and the Protestant Community in Reformation France* (Bethlehem, PA: Lehigh University Press, 2007). See my review of Shepardson's work in *Sixteenth Century Journal* 39, no. 4 (Winter 2008): 1183–84.

19. Houllemare, *Politiques de la Parole*, 19.

20. Daubresse, *Le Parlement de Paris*, 110.

21. Habermas, *Structural Transformation of the Public Sphere*, 8.

22. Jürgen Habermas, *Between Facts and Norms: Contributions to a Discourse Theory of Law and Democracy*, trans. William Rehg (Cambridge, MA: MIT Press, 1996), 359.

23. All references are to Robert Garnier, *Antigone, ou La pieté*, ed. Jean-Dominique Beaudin (Paris: Champion, 1997). My English translation of this play is forthcoming.

24. "The original essence of tragedy consists then in the fact that within such a conflict each of the opposed sides, if taken by itself, has justification, while on the other hand each can establish the true and positive content of its own aim and character only by negating and damaging the equally justified power of the other" (Georg Wilhelm Friedrich Hegel, *Aesthetics*, trans. T. M. Knox [Oxford: Clarendon Press, 1998], 15:523).

25. Garnier, *Antigone*, 2.520–21.

26. Ibid., 2.502–3.

27. Ibid., 3.657–59.

28. Ibid., 3.672–75.

29. Ibid., 1.332.

30. Alfred Giraud, *La vie et la mort du président Brisson* (Nantes: Imprimerie de A. Guéraud, 1855); Ludovic Vallette, *Étude sur Barnabé Brisson, premier président au Parlement de Paris* (Fontenay-le-Comte: Imprimerie de C. Caurit, 1875); Paul Gambier, *Au temps des Guerres de Religion. Le Président Barnabé Brisson* (Paris: Perrin, 1957); Elie Barnavi, *La Sainte Ligue, le juge et la potence. L'assassinat du président Brisson* (Paris: Hachette, 1985).

31. Garnier, *Antigone* (Dedicatory Letter), 57.

32. Etienne Pasquier, *Les lettres* (Paris: Jean Petit-Pas, 1619), col. 312.

33. The Bibliothèque nationale de France (BnF) possesses many documents about Servin. See in particular Louis Servin, *Plaidoyez de Mre Loys Servin*, 4 vols. (Paris: J. de Heuquevill, 1603–1613) (BnF shelf numbers F-27603, F-44533, F-26799, F-27606) and Louis Servin, *Actions notables et plaidoyez de messire Louys Servin, . . . à la fin desquels sont les arrests intervenus sur iceux. Dernière édition . . . Ensemble les plaidoyers de M. A. Robert, Arnault et autres* (Paris: G. Alliot, 1631) (BnF shelf number F-13877).

34. Archives Nationales, X2a1394, January 25, 1586. See Houllemare, *Politiques de la parole*, 462.

35. Archives Nationales, X2a1394, January 25, 1586. See Houllemare, *Politiques de la parole*, 463.

36. Robert Garnier, *Marc Antoine*, ed. Jean-Claude Ternaux (Paris: Classiques Garnier, 2010), 4.1493.

37. Ibid., 4.1712–13.

38. See Ternaux, "Introduction," in Garnier, *Marc Antoine*, 23.

39. Robert J. Sealy, *The Palace Academy of Henri III* (Geneva: Droz, 1981), 30. In other words: "news of the massacres of Saint Bartholomew's Day . . . arrived in Poland. . . . To counter these reports and save Henri's candidacy [to become King of Poland], the diplomat wrote to Paris asking for a more detailed account of the [events]. In response, the government commissioned Guy du Faur de Pibrac to write a Latin pamphlet defending the official royal version of the massacres in Paris and exonerating Henri from the massacres. Pibrac's treatise, which portrayed Anjou as a 'heroic prince' who had even rescued a number of Protestants from angry Catholic crowds, was published in several editions and sent to Poland through diplomatic channels." Scott M. Manetsch, *Theodora Beza and the Quest for Peace in France, 1572–98* (Leiden: Brill, 2000), 80. See also René Redouant, "Pibrac et la Saint-Barthelémy," *Revue d'histoire littéraire de la France* 26 (1919): 11–35.

40. Guy du Faur de Pibrac, *Un essai de propagande à l'étranger au XVIe siècle; L'apologie de la Saint-Barthélemy*, ed. Alban Cabos (Paris: Edouard Champion, 1922), 10.

41. Katherine MacDonald, *Biography in Early Modern France 1540–1630* (Oxford: Legenda, 2007), 31.

42. Ibid. As MacDonald notes in his biography of Pibrac: "Paschal could not record Pibrac's earlier demand for a halt to the killings without besmirching Charles [IX]'s behaviour, something clearly not in the interests of one seeking a career in royal administration" (ibid.).

43. See Robert J. Knecht, *Catherine de' Medici* (London: Longman, 1998), 193–201.

44. See Thierry Wanegffelen, *Ni Rome ni Genève: Des fidèles entre deux chaires en France au XVIe siècle* (Paris: Champion, 1997); Mario Turchetti, *Concordia o tolleranza? François Bauduin (1520–1573) et i "Moyenneurs"* (Geneva: Droz, 1984); "Concorde ou tolerance: Les Moyenneurs à la veille des guerres de religion en France," *Revue de théologie et de philosophie* 118 (1986): 255–67; "Religious Concord and Political Tolerance in Sixteenth- and Seventeenth-Century France," *Sixteenth Century Journal* 22 (1991): 15–25; Olivier Christin, *La paix de religion. L'autonomisation de la raison politique au XVIe siècle* (Paris: Seuil, 1997).

45. Rabelais, *Œuvres complètes*, ed. Mireille Huchon (Paris: Gallimard, "Bibliothèque de la Pléiade," 1994), 71; *The Complete Works of François Rabelais*, trans. Donald M. Frame (Berkeley: University of California Press, 1991), 60. Rabelais ends this sentence with "les concions des prescheurs evangeliques" ["the sermons of the Evangelical preachers"], but that is another story.

~

CHAPTER NINE

From the Politics of Performance to the Anthropology of Festivals

Montaigne's "Of the Education of Children" (I.26) and "Of Coaches" (III.6)

FABIEN CAVAILLÉ

In its attempts to understand theatrical practices in the Renaissance, the French critical tradition has often sought out theoretical support in treatises on poetics and rhetoric, which are few in number and do not say much about the topic. In privileging these texts, this tradition has approached theater as a textual work of art, with visual and audible components, conceived by a poet. However, we must be cautious of the false obviousness of words, because their meanings have evolved since the Renaissance. By *théâtre*, sixteenth-century writers understood first and foremost an architectural structure (tiers or stage). To evoke the art of theater, they preferred the term *jeu* [play or game], a term with wide semantic extensions, including jousts, balls, ballets, and carnival; in short, all forms of spectacle. Placed in the category of "play/game," Renaissance publics thus perceived theater less as a textual product or as an art and more as an event: a collective practice of rejoicing and public festivities. Because it is a "game" and because it is collective, theater leads sixteenth-century thinkers to reflect on the governing of society—to the extent that one must think about the forms and finalities of leisure, its institution, or its censorship.[1] A theory of theater as a social practice, a theory of a political type, does exist in the French tradition, which in contrast to the poetic treatises, allows us to understand the place of "play" among the men and women of Renaissance France.

A trace of this political theory of theater can be found in a passage from Montaigne's essay "De l'institution des enfants" ["Of the Education of Children"]:

[B] Car j'ay tousjours accusé d'impertinence ceux qui condemnent ces esbatte-ments, et d'injustice ceux qui refusent l'entrée de nos bonnes villes aux come-diens qui le valent, et envient au peuple ces plaisirs publicques. Les bonnes polices prennent soing d'assembler les citoyens et les r'allier, comme aux offices serieux de la devotion, aussi aux exercices et jeux; la société et amitié s'en augmente. Et puis on ne leur sçauroit conceder des passetemps plus reglez que ceux qui se font en presence d'un chacun et et le prince, à ses despens, en gratifiast quelquefois la commune, d'une affection et bonté comme paternelle; [C] et qu'aux villes populeuses il y eust des lieux destinez et disposez pour ces spectacles: quelque divertissement de pires actions et occultes.[2]

[And I have ever accused them of impertinencie, that condemne and disalow such kindes of recreations, and blame those of injustice that refuse good and honest Comedians, or (as we call them) Players, to enter our good townes, and grudge the common people such publike sports. Politike and wel ordered commonwealths endevour rather carefully to unite and assemble their Citizens together; as in serious offices of devotion, so in honest exercises of recreation. Common societie and loving friendship is thereby cherished and increased. And besides, they cannot have more formal and regular pastimes allowed them, than such as are acted and represented in open view of all, and in the presence of the magistrates themselves: And if I might beare sway I would thinke it reasonable, that Princes should sometimes, at their proper charges, gratifie the common people with them as an argument of a fatherly affection, and loving goodness towards them: and that in populous and frequented cities, there should be Theatres and places appointed for such spectacles; as a divert-ing of worse inconveniences, and secret actions.][3]

This passage grants political benefit to "play," a motor of civil concord since it develops "common societie and loving friendship" among the spectators and citizens.[4]

We must, however, examine the originality of Montaigne's position by reading it in the light of political treatises of the second half of the sixteenth century. My hypothesis—which I am taking in part from Marie-Madeleine Fragonard and Daniel Ménager—is that a coherent theoretical model to discuss the practice of "play" exists. Montaigne is only one example of this tradition, and we can find other formulations before him.[5] Even so, as will be shown, Montaigne's and his predecessors' positions differ in various ways, precisely because the very idea of concord through "play" is problematic.

"[C]ommon societie and loving friendship" may very well increase through entertainment, but we do not know how or why. By which means could "play" work toward the well-being of the social body? And if it does have a political benefit, does it still belong to the order of leisure, since spare time is by definition outside of the usual business of politics? The question of the means of concord through play is closely linked to the social sphere— central or marginal—that one grants collective leisure, which Montaigne understood better than the others, and in different terms. The link between spectacle and social peace will bring us from what was not yet called cultural politics to the anthropology of festivals.

"Play": Cords or Chains of Concord?

What can be the civic virtue of "play"? Political thought of the sixteenth century underscores its capacity to link power to society. Spectacles, it was thought, always come from a man or an institution, addressed to other men and women. These spectacles are gifts that the sovereign and his subjects exchange freely, like tokens of love.

Such is the most widespread underpinning of a political theory of "play": a tangled set of relations that weave concord between sovereign and subjects. According to a false medieval etymology, *concordia* was thought to have derived from the word *cord* [*corde*]. For all political thinkers, in fact, the spectacle ties, connects, and attaches organizers and participants, patrons and receivers together—as if the spectacle itself were worth less than its capacity to be handed from one person to another, to be a transactional object. This transactional nature of "play" lends itself to two opposed analyses that mutually confirm one another. Thus, Etienne de la Boétie does not deny the mediating qualities of spectacles in his *Discours sur la servitude volontaire*, but they enchain the spectators in such a way that the political utility of "play" is to establish tyranny and render servitude voluntary:

Tous les peuples s'aleschent vistement à la servitude par la moindre plume qu'on leur passe, comme l'on dit, devant la bouche: et c'est chose merveilleuse qu'ils se laissent aller ainsi tost, mais seulement qu'on les chatouille. Les theatres, les jeus, les farces, les spectacles, les gladiateurs, les bestes estranges, les medailles, les tableaus et autres telles drogueries, c'estoient aus peuples anciens les apasts de la servitude, le pris de leur liberté, les outils de la tirannie; ce moien, ceste pratique, ces allechemens avoient les anciens tirans pour endormir leurs sujets sous le joug. Ainsi les peuples assottis, trouvans beaus ces passetemps, amusés d'un vain plaisir qui leur passoit devant les yeulx, s'accoustumoient à servir aussi niaisement, mais plus mal, que les petits enfans qui pour voir les luisans images des livres enluminés aprenent à lire.[6]

[All these poor fools (are) neatly tricked into servitude by the slightest feather passed, so to speak, before their mouths. Truly it is a marvelous thing that they let themselves be caught so quickly at the slightest tickling of their fancy. Plays, farces, spectacles, gladiators, strange beasts, medals, pictures, and other such opiates, these were for ancient people the bait toward slavery, the price of their liberty, the instrument of tyranny. By these practices and enticements the ancient dictators so successfully lulled their subjects under the yoke, that the stupefied people, fascinated by the pastimes and vain pleasures flashed before their eyes, learned subservience as naively, but not so creditably, as little children learn to read by looking at bright picture books.][7]

For La Boétie, spectacles transform themselves into a kind of fly-fishing, a soothing drug, or a seductive act. The gentleness of "play" and the false bonds it forges also facilitate this tyrannical domination.

Toward the end of the century, the reverse argument appears as a result of progressive disillusions of political thought. Despite all those who oppose spectacles, Giovanni Boterò, the theoretician of raison d'état, agrees with La Boétie: "play" establishes an authority, turns people away from violence, and retains them in the bonds of submission. Spectacle provides a means to govern:

Ma non giova la copia delle vettovaglie, se non si può godere, ò per violenza de' nemici, ò eper iniquità de' compagni; perciò bisogna accompagnarla con Pace, e con Giustitia. Appresso, perché il popolo è di natura sua instabile, e desideroso di novità, ne avviene, che s'egli non è trattenuto con varii mezi dal suo Prencipe, la cerca da se stesso anco con la mutatione di Stato, e di governo. Perciò tutti i Prencipi savii hanno introdotto alcuni trattenimenti popolari, ne' quali, quanto più si ecceiterà la virtù dell'animo, e del corpo.[8]

[An abundance of bread, however, is of no avail if the violence of enemies or the wickedness of one's fellow prevents its enjoyment: and it must therefore be accompanied by peace and justice. And then, because the common people are by nature unstable and long for novelty, they will seek it out for themselves, changing even their government and their rulers if their prince does not provide some kind of diversion of it. Knowing this, the wisest rulers have introduced various popular entertainments which exercise the power of the mind and body and which are the more effective the better they succeed in doing this.][9]

According to Boterò, one also governs through pleasure, and so much the better if this pleasure is serious and decent. Within the spectrum of spectacles to promote, Boterò, the former secretary of Cardinal Charles Borromeo, highly regards the "spectacles provided by the church."[10] Under the guidance of a Borromeo impresario, the churches of Milan were full of spectators and "no people was ever so happy, so contented and so tranquil as the Milanese in those days." Spectacles are no longer the expression but the mechanism of an agreement between the sovereigns and the subjects. For these spectacles create love and gratitude, they invent bonds that do not always exist, and they stabilize the balance of power. What is more, their institution within the church, through confusion with the liturgy, elevates them to the rank of ceremony. According to Boterò, in the realm of collective devotion, the sacred can be entertaining and the entertaining sacred. It is a manner, too, to ward off the demon of idleness, mother of all vices.

Which Kind of "Play" Can Temper Hearts?

Parallel to the political arguments, another set of reasons exists, founded on the affective experience that the spectacle allows. If "play" can have civic virtue, it is also because it speaks to hearts, not to minds. The crystallization of passions distinguishes spectacles from other manifestations of magnificence such as monuments or the protection of the arts. These demonstrations of "play" make up experiences; ephemeral as they may be, they are nonetheless collective and intense. They ensure to a lesser extent the durability of the glory of the sovereign or of an institution, but they create a social climate, as it were. This highly affective "play" works toward the pacification of the people. Con-cordia, according to its proper etymology, is the community of hearts.[11]

Before going any further, however, let us examine for a moment Jean Bodin's position, found in his sixth book of the Republique, dedicated to censorship. This theoretician of absolute sovereignty vehemently rejects theater:

Je tais aussi l'abus qui se commet en souffrant les Comiques, et Jongleurs, qui est une autre peste de la Republique des plus pernicieuses qu'on sçauroit imaginer: car il n'y a rien qui gaste plus les bonnes meurs, et la simplicité, et la bonté naturelle d'un peuple. Ce qui a d'autant plus d'effect, et de puissance, que les parolles, les accens, les gestes, les mouvements, et actions conduites avec tous les artifices qu'on peut imaginer, et d'un suget le plus ord, et le plus deshonneste qu'on peut choisir, laisse une impression vive en l'ame de ceux qui tendent là tous leurs sens. Brief on peut dire, que le theatre des joüeurs, est un apprentissage de toute impudicité, lubricité, paillardise, ruse, finesse, meschanceté.[12]

[I will not speak of the breach that one commits when tolerating players and entertainers, who are one of the most pernicious infections for the Republic that we can imagine. For nothing corrupts good mores, simplicity, and natural virtue of a people more than they do. That which has even more efficiency and power than the words, the voices, the gestures, the movements, and the actions conducted with all the artifice one can imagine, and of the vilest and the most indecent subject matter that one can find, leaves a vivid impression in the soul of those who lend all their senses to them. In short, we can say that the theater of players is an apprenticeship of impudicity, lubricity, debauchery, ruse, trickery, and impiety.]

The players are "an infection of the Republic," even more dangerous because they "leave a vivid impression in the soul of those who lend all their senses to them." However, it is not this affective dimension that poses a problem for Bodin. Indeed, he nuances his analysis by having recourse to his theory of national temperaments, which are defined by humors and passions. The real problem is balancing this temperament. It is not good to perform in front of "peuples tirant plus vers le Septentrion [qui sont] de leur naturel sanguins, legers, et volages" ["people leaning more toward the north [who are] naturally sanguine, fickle, and rash"].[13] If comical types of "play" were inserted into the sanguine realm, adding to the collective humor, then there would only be one step to go from popular rashness to general anarchy, which would be dangerous for the state. Social concord remains Bodin's reference point of argumentation, even if he posits that theater is politically useless.

Bodin could have stopped there, but he cannot neglect the institution of public pleasure, necessary for the right temperament of society. The "honnestes exercices de la musique" ["decent practice of music"] provides the model of harmonizing leisure because, in its Renaissance conception, terrestrial music makes us hear celestial music—and perhaps also because it has the advantage of being neither discourse nor a representation of this lower world and thus less suitable for satire or critique.[14] Concerts and dance temper society, as these forms of leisure are by nature founded on harmony.

Though Bodin is an opponent of theater, his thoughts revolve nonetheless around the same ideas: "play" is intended for the "affections . . . de l'âme" ["affections . . . of the soul"]; consequently, it must pacify.[15] For Bodin as for his enemy Boterò, "play" occupies an important place in society: for Boterò because it becomes the tool of the church, for Bodin because musical practice translates the harmony of the world. It is this harmony that must regulate the practice of the judge, the legislator, and the entire social organization. In both cases, these thoughts on the state place "play," if not at the center of society, at least next to the center, in relation to the transcendence or the power that represents it.

"Play": A Question of Space?

We can thus begin to appreciate how Montaigne falls within these political theories. On the whole, he aligns himself with them, as there is nothing very new in "Of the Education of Children." But he also disrupts them because he brings a third reason to the realization of concord through "play." In the first passage cited above, Montaigne establishes a comparison between liturgy ("serious offices of devotion") and that which is not serious at all (sport and culture). The comparison holds, for devotion and games are in effect opportunities to bring people together; however, during intense religious wars, it is difficult to maintain that the "serious offices of devotion" increase "common societie and loving friendship." What heightens concord among citizens is that they have another opportunity to get together—not a serious one—that Montaigne proposes as an alternative to confessional practices. Where others grant a central place to spectacles within the social organization, Montaigne privileges the marginal position: the *jeux* are there, "as in" but not identical to "serious offices of devotion." This position translates into the question of space, since in the "populous and frequented cities" the *jeux* must have a "theater and places appointed for such spectacles," specific spaces that are neither the church nor the public square. The originality of Montaigne here is distinguishing the forms of gatherings and proposing that concord is based on this distinction. He does not suggest a withdrawal into the private sphere, for it is a question of encountering others in a space that is open to everyone without being a space of collective destiny, of a political or eschatological order. If concord can emerge out of the leisure of "play," this is because it creates, within the "populous and frequented cit[y]," a space of sociability that is neither private nor public, but an intermediary or liminal space, to borrow a concept from the anthropologist Victor Turner. Leisure remains leisure, without getting lost in religious or princely ceremony.

Indeed, this passage from Montaigne can be understood in the light of Turner's theory of ritual and theatrical performances. Turner analyzes that which brings together and separates "liminal" rites in tribal societies from "liminoid" pastimes (that is to say, those activities that resemble liminal rites without being them) in industrial societies, among which he includes theater.[16] In a way, pastimes and rites are in opposition as regards the compulsory or optional participation in the event, just as they are different in terms of the collective or individual dimension of the experience.[17] And it is this type of distinction that Montaigne makes when he juxtaposes "serious offices of devotion," in other words ceremonies and rituals of the liminal type, and "honest exercises of recreation," which are "liminoid" leisure activities.

But Turner also underscores the profound relationship that unites the two concepts. In both cases, these activities take place in a distinct time and space of ordinary life. The separation is most often materialized by the different spaces and times; a special building—"des lieux destinez et disposez pour ces spectacles" ["theaters and places appointed for such spectacles"], as Montaigne writes. Societies need to construct, within themselves, spaces that are exterior, which in a sense, Michel Foucault calls "hétérotopies" ["heterotopias"],[18] "contre-espaces" ["counter-sites"],[19] spaces "qui sont absolument différents; des lieux qui s'opposent à tous les autres, qui sont destinés en quelque sorte à les effacer, à les neutraliser ou à les purifier" ["that are absolutely different; sites that are in opposition to all others, that are destined in some way to erase them, to neutralize them, or to purify them"].[20]

In Turner's anthropological perspective, these distinct spaces welcome performances that play with, criticize, and reinvent cultural codes. Turner sees these "liminal and liminoid situations as the settings in which new models, symbols, paradigms, and so forth, arise—as the seedbeds of cultural creativity in fact."[21] Far from being mere subversions of cultural norms, these other spaces allow for new modes of expression, engage in beneficial creativity for society.[22] Even in the most institutionalized forms of leisure, notably in the case of theater, "leisure is potentially capable of releasing creative powers, individual or communal, either to criticize or buttress the dominant social structural values."[23]

The positivity of liminal or liminoid situations also resides, according to Turner, in their capacity to produce a *communitas*, in other words, "an unmediated relationship between historical, idiosyncratic, concrete individuals":[24]

In tribal societies and other pre-industrial social formations, liminality provides a propitious setting for the development of these direct, immediate, and total confrontations of human identities. In industrial societies, it is within leisure, and sometimes aided by the projections of art that this way of experiencing one's fellows can be portrayed, grasped, and sometimes realized.[25]

Turner's analysis helps understand Montaigne's position because the utterances about *communitas* echo the idea according to which "societie and loving friendship" are increased by the leisure of theater. The liminality of "play" allows for an engagement with accepted cultural values and norms to reinforce or to subvert them, but this marginality also produces, in the spectators, an experience that they share with each other and that founds an ephemeral community, alongside (or against) the political sphere. In distinguishing leisure and ritual, "play" and ceremony, and in evoking the experience of *communitas* in this particular framework, Montaigne's reflection leaves the domain of political philosophy to propose an anthropology of social and cultural practices.

Admittedly, one could read the passage differently and highlight its political dimension. The memory of his time as a city officer does pervade the end of Montainge's essay, where he expresses a condescending tone toward the common people: Montaigne intimates that the magistrate or the prince are present to enjoy the "publike sports," to oversee what happens, and to collect testimonies of love produced by the gift of the spectacle. I wish, however, to corroborate my original hypothesis by considering the relations between politics and friendship and by reflecting on the kind of spectator that Montaigne can or hopes to be.

On the one hand, as Thomas Berns has shown, Montaignian friendship, from the most banal to the most admirable, founds a kind of sociability that ignores power relations but that, at the same time, is necessary to politics.[26] In this sense, "play" is in the same position in relation to politics as friendship: marginal, but necessary because marginal.

On the other hand, Montaigne himself provides an example of the exteriority of "play" in relation to the political sphere. The essay "Des coches" ["Of Coaches"] is presented as a political reflection on magnificence, condemning the princely "montre" ["display"] as too expensive and too futile.[27] From here, we might imagine that Montaigne would take up again and treat as his own La Boétie's critique of "play." This is not the case at all, however, as he rewrites his friend's passage only to contradict him:

[B] C'estoit pourtant une belle chose, d'aller faire apporter et planter en la place aus arenes une grande quantité de gros arbres, tous branchus et tous verts, representans une grande forest ombrageuse, despartie en belle symmetrie, et, le premier jour, jetter là dedans mille austruches, mille cerfs, mille sangliers et mille daims, . . . S'il y a quelque chose qui soit excusable en tels excez, c'est où l'invention et la noueauté fournit d'admiration, non pas la despence.[28]

[Yet was it a goodly thing to cause a great quantity of great trees, all branchie and greene, to bee far brought and planted in plots yeelding nothing but dry gravell, representing a wilde shady forrest, divided in due seemely proportion; And the first day to put into the same a thousand Estriges, a thousand Stagges, a thousand wilde Boares, and a thousand Buckes, . . . If any thing bee excusable in such lavish excesses it is where the invention and strangenesse breedeth admiration, and not the costlie charge.][29]

Montaigne attempts to see spectacles that he has not seen and describes them "malgré sa philosophie de la magnificence" ["despite his philosophy of magnificence"], as Ménager remarks.[30] We may ask ourselves: Why can Montaigne write this page *in spite of* his political reflection? It may be because the space of "play" is disconnected from political space, and thus the experiences and the expectations are different. A spectator through the imagination of Roman games, Montaigne does not pay attention to the prince who offers the spectacle but to the object given that captivates all his attention. The distinction between the spaces and the types of gazes that result from them emerges in the last sentence: the "costlie charge" is the doing of the prince and is not worthy of admiration. Only the "invention and strangeness" deserve it, and they are the responsibility of the artists. As in "Of the Education of Children," Montaigne distinguishes collective leisure from politics, and this distinction nourishes the pleasure and the freedom of the gaze, both of which have a role to play in the realization of civil concord.

The Model of the Arts versus the Model of Festival

In spite of these different explanations, and despite the fascination with ceremony that usefully recovers a leisure activity that is always somewhat suspicious, the civic utility of "play" is grasped from the vantage point of an anthropological model that is common to all the texts.

The idea of the political benefit of theater is rooted in the irenicism of the first humanists, such as Erasmus, who granted the arts a civilizing power: poetry, philosophy, and history work toward social harmony because they educate the sovereign and the subject. They teach them to speak to one another, to think about the world, and to act discerningly.[31] The arguments that support political benefit from the arts valorize the text, the meaning, and the content. But the thinkers studied here, and Montaigne more radically than the others, develop another system of argumentation. To the idea of civil concord through the arts, they respond with the model of the festival without truly dealing with what one performs or not. Boterò writes of festivals and places them under the sign of religion; Bodin deals with festivals by privileging music that channels collective excitement or agitation; Montaigne makes the "honest exercises of recreation" rather marginal yet necessary activities. Shall theater be interpreted as a type of otium literatum [literary leisure] in the Renaissance?[32] In this chapter, I have attempted to show that the Renaissance philosophers had a wider view than poetics, and were able to think about social and anthropological issues, thanks to the festive paradigm when we interpret Renaissance theater, we thus have in mind that it was still a festival.

Notes

1. On this question, see Virginia Krause, *Idle Pursuits. Literature and "Oisiveté" in the French Renaissance* (Newark: University of Delaware Press, 2003); and Marie-Madeleine Fragonard, "Oisiveté et hérésie," in *L'oisiveté au temps de la Renaissance*, ed. Marie-Thérèse Jones-Davies (Paris: Presses de l'Université Paris-Sorbonne, 2002), 29–50.

2. Michel de Montaigne, *Les essais*, ed. Pierre Villey and V.-L. Saulnier (Paris: Presses Universitaires de France, 1965), 1.26.177.

3. John Florio, *The Essayes or Morall, Politike and Millitarie Discourses of Lord Michaell de Montaigne* (London: Val. Sims, 1603), http://www.luminarium.org/renascence-editions/montaigne/ (accessed June 12, 2013). Florio translates this chapter "Of the Institution and Education of Children," and it appears as the twenty-fifth essay in book 1 instead of the twenty-sixth, for Florio placed Montaigne's fourteenth essay, "Que le goust des biens et des maux depend en bonne partie de l'opinion que nous en avons" [That the taste of good and evil depends in large part on the opinion we have of them], as the fortieth essay in his translation. Donald Frame renders the passage as follows:

> [B] I have always blamed as undiscerning those who condemn these recreations, and as unjust those who refuse entry into our good towns to the comedians [players] who deserve it, and begrudge the people these public amusements. Good governments take care to assemble the citizens and bring them together for sports and amusements as well as for the serious functions of piety; sociability and friendliness are thereby increased. And besides, they could not be granted more orderly pastimes than those that take place in the presence of everyone and right in the sight of the magistrate. And I should think it reasonable that the magistrate and the prince, at their own expense, should sometimes give the people this treat, out of a sort of paternal goodness and affection; [C] and that in populous cities there should be places intended and arranged for these spectacles—a diversion from worse and hidden doings. (*The Complete Essays of Montaigne* (London: Everyman's Library, 2003), I.26.160)

All other translations are mine unless otherwise noted.

4. In fact, the French seventeenth century will forget the civic ideals of theater, illustrated by the transformation of playwriting, in terms of its subjects as well as its forms. Fabien Cavaillé, "Applaudissement universel et ricanements importuns: représentations de l'assemblée théâtrale de la Querelle du *Cid* à la *Pratique du Théâtre*," in *Concordia discors*, ed. Benoît Bolduc and Henriette Goldwin, Biblio 17, no. 194 (Tübingen: Günter Narr Verlag, 2011), 211–21.

5. Marie-Madeleine Fragonard, "Du bon usage politique de la tragédie," in *Les tragédies de Jean de la Taille*, ed. Françoise Charpentier, *Cahiers Textuel* no. 18 (1998), 43–56; Daniel Ménager, "Montaigne et la magnificence," *Bulletin de la Société des Amis de Montaigne* 7, nos. 29–32 (July–December 1992/January–June 1993): 63–71.

6. Etienne de la Boétie, *Discours sur la servitude volontaire*, ed. Malcolm Smith (Geneva: Droz, 2001), 58.

7. Etienne de la Boétie, *Anti-Dictator: The "Discours sur la servitude volontaire"*, trans. Harry Kurz (New York: Columbia University Press, 1942), 33.

8. Giovanni Boterò, *Della Ragione di Stato* (Milano: Pacifico Pontio, 1596), 109.

9. Giovanni Boterò, *The Reason of State*, trans. P. J. and D. P. Waley (New Haven, CT: Yale University Press, 1956), 73–74.

10. Boterò:

Hanno anco più del grave, e del meraviglioso i trattenimenti Ecclesiastici, che i Secolari; perche partecipano del sacro, e del divino. Onde anco Aristotele consiglia il Prencipe a far sacrificii solenni. E noi habbiamo visto il Cardinal Borromeo haver tranttenuto l'infinito popolo di Milano con feste celebrate religiosamente, e con attioni ecclesiastiche, fatte da lui con cerimonia, e con gravità incomparabile; di tal maniera, che le Chiese erano dalla mattina fino alla sera sempre piene; ne fu mai popolo, ò più allegro, ò più contento, ò più quieto di quel ch'erano li Milanesi, in quei tempi. (Boterò, *Della Ragione*, 111)

[The spectacle provided by the church are more wonderful and dignified than secular entertainments because they contain sacred and divine elements. Aristotle advises a prince to offer solemn sacrifices; we ourselves have seen Cardinal Borromeo entertain the multitudes of Milan with celebrations of religious feasts and with church functions performed with elaborate ceremony and great dignity, so that the churches were filled with people from morning to evening and no people was ever so happy, so contented and so tranquil as the Milanese in those days.] (*Reason of State*, 75)

11. Jean Nagle, *La civilisation du cœur. Histoire du sentiment politique en France, du XIIe au XIXe siècle* (Paris: Fayard, 1998).

12. Jean Bodin, *Les six livres de la Republique de J. Bodin Angevin* (Paris: Jacques du Puys, 1576), 611.

13. Ibid., 611.

14. Ibid., 612.

15. Ibid.

16. Victor Turner, *From Ritual to Theatre: The Human Seriousness of Play* (New York: PAJ Publications, 1982). On a Turnerian interpretation of the Chiquanous episode in Rabelais's *Quart Livre*, see chapter 3, by Gates and Meere.

17. Turner, *From Ritual to Theatre*, 36, 42

18. Michel Foucault, "Les hétérotopies," in *Le corps utopique, les hétérotopies*, ed. Daniel Defert (Paris: Lignes, 2009).

19. Ibid., 24.

20. Ibid.

21. Turner, *From Ritual to Theatre*, 28.

22. Turner:

I see the "liminoid" as an independent and critical source . . . and here we observe how "liminoid" actions of industrial leisure genres can repossess the character of "work" though originating in a "free-time" arbitrarily separated by managerial fiat from the time of "labor"—how the liminoid can be an independent domain of creative activity, not simply a distorted mirror-image, mask, or cloak, for structural activity in the "centers" or "mainstreams" of "productive social labor" (ibid., 33)

23. Ibid., 37.
24. Ibid., 45.
25. Ibid., 46.
26. Thomas Berns, "'Ô mes conseillers, il n'y a nul conseiller': La politique de l'amitié chez Montaigne," in Montaigne politique, ed. Philippe Desan (Paris: Honoré Champion, 2006), 57–72.
27. Montainge, Essais, III.6.902; trans. Frame, Essays, III.6.836.
28. Montaigne, Essais, III.6.905, 907.
29. Florio, http://www.luminarium.org/renascence-editions/montaigne/#p1 (accessed June 12, 2013). Frame:

[B] It was, however, a fine thing to bring and plant in the amphitheater a great quantity of big trees, all branching and green, representing a great shady forest, arranged in beautiful symmetry, and on the first day to cast into it a thousand ostriches, a thousand stags, a thousand wild boars, and a thousand fallow deer, . . . If there is anything excusable in such extravagances, it is when the inventiveness and the novelty of them, not the expense, provide amazement. (III.6.838, 840)

30. Ménager, "Montaigne et la magnificence," 66.
31. On the relation between the arts and civil concord, see Bruno Petey-Girard, Le sceptre et la plume. Images du prince protecteur des lettres de la Renaissance au Grand Siècle (Geneva: Droz, 2010), in particular the first part, "Quelles théories pour une protection royale des Lettres?" and chapter 2, "Les Lettres et le royaume," 33–82.
32. Marc Fumaroli, "Loisirs et loisir," in Le loisir lettré à l'âge classique, ed. Marc Fumaroli, Philippe-Joseph Salazar, and Emmanuel Bury (Genève: Droz, 1996), 5–26.

CHAPTER TEN

Too Late?

The Drama of the Cannibals in Rouen

ELIZABETH GUILD

The "cannibal savages" encountered by Montaigne in Rouen in November 1562 had a long prehistory: before them came texts—Tacitus's *Germania*, Plutarch's *Moralia*, *On the Malice of Herodotus* [Περί της Ἡροδότου κακοηθείας], André Thevet's *Singularitez de la France Antarctique*, to name but a few—and ideologies. Whether the narratives in which the savage figured were historical, philosophical, proto-ethnographic, fictions, or horror stories, his place was predetermined: primarily that of the *barbaron*, the barbarian other from whom the civilized humanity of the writer and the community he addressed could be reassuringly distanced and confirmed—even if at the cost of this confirmation resting on an only fictional other. But along with this logic and rhetoric of antithesis that so reduced the savage, there had also been, at times, an alternative version: the idealized savage, a figure of goodness or heroism, playing his role in myths of origins or *parousia* [presence].[1] The various fates of the savage (horror, opposite, or ideal) seemed bound by preexisting logical and rhetorical models: likeness or difference, ideal or antithetical other,[2] as well as, materially, by processes of exchange calculated to exorbitantly benefit the European: the "human"? This seems an instance of the form of encounter posited by Jacques Lacan in "Le temps logique et l'assertion de certitude anticipée" ["*Logical Time and the Assertion of Anticipated Certainty*"]:

1. Un homme sait ce qui n'est pas un homme;
2. Les hommes se reconnaissent entre eux pour être des hommes;
3. Je m'affirme être un homme, de peur d'être convaincu par les hommes de n'être pas un homme.

Mouvement qui donne la forme logique de toute assimilation "humaine," en tant précisément qu'elle se pose comme assimilatrice d'une barbarie, et qui pourtant réserve la détermination essentielle du "*je*". . .[3]

[1. A human being knows what a human is not;
2. Human beings recognize each other as human beings;
3. I affirm myself to be human, for fear of being convinced by them that I am not human.

This movement provides the logical form of all "human" assimilation, precisely insofar as it posits itself as assimilative of a barbarism, but it nonetheless reserves the essential determination of the "*I*" . . .][4]

By the sixteenth century in France, the savage as an idealized figure was vanishing; but the cannibal savage was becoming more familiar. He had been "invented" by Christopher Columbus,[5] introduced to French readers in 1515 with Mathurin du Redouer's French translation of Francanzío da Montalboddo's 1507 *Mondo novo e paesi novamente ritrovati da Alberico Vespuzio fiorentino* [*Countries Recently Discovered and the View of the World of the Florentine Amerigo Vespucci*], and had already entered French fiction in the *Chroniques du grant Gargantua* by the time that further reports arrived in 1533 with the French translation of Peter Martyr's 1511 *De Orbe Novo Decades* [*On the New World*]. While the figure of the cannibal was primarily used to represent that which was not human, there was initially scope for rehabilitation in some of the accounts of Christian voyagers (so long as they supposed they had souls); the good (but not idealizable) cannibal, whose practice was construed as ritual vengeance, could be set against the bad, whose appetite for human flesh was cruel and unnatural.[6] However, by the time of the Rouen encounter, the cannibal savage was *all but* reduced to his function as negative other, a version of the *barbaron* that had become amplified from meaning the one who does not speak one's language (originally, Greek) into that which "resisting assimilation, cannot be handled and must be annihilated."[7] This description takes us in two converging directions: on the one hand, that of the religious conflict that, in the second half of the sixteenth century, would sunder France, and on the other, toward theories of trauma (i.e., that which is psychically inassimilable). Traumatic conflict of wars in which each side, French Roman Catholic and Huguenot, having ruled out the possibility of toleration, set about destroying the other, and in which for extremist Hugue-nots, the Roman Catholic Eucharist was a "cannibal" feast, an act of horror beyond assimilation; that is, an act the meaning of which fell too far beyond the bounds of their epistemological, theological, and rhetorical models to be conceivable or bearable.

Although it was too late to avert war or as yet broker peace, for Mon-taigne it was perhaps not too late to lend the cannibal some other meanings: neither ideal nor horror, but a more ambiguous and fluid array of possible interpretations, enabling a different relationship between cannibals and French counterparts, self and other, human being and not. Many commen-tators have already offered readings of "Des cannibales" ["Of Cannibals"] that illuminate the epistemological and ethical dimensions of Montaigne's reflections.[8] Still, there remains much to explore in the passage toward the end of the chapter—the apparently remembered encounter in Rouen, with three cannibals with whom a meeting with the king and court was orches-trated—as regards its inflection of the themes and logic of the chapter as a whole, and in particular, as regards what it reveals about the thinking Montaigne was using the relationship with the cannibal other to do.[9] As we shall discover, this was not the first presentation of the savage in Rouen, but the earlier performance (or even impersonation) for the monarch was designed to conform seamlessly to preexisting conceptions. Montaigne's use of this appearance of the cannibal, however, refuses such self-interested and appropriative aesthetics and instead uses the inherently dramatic encounter with the other to put such use into question and to return us to the theater of horror that was France at war in 1562—horrors from which the royal visit to Rouen was designed, at the least, to distract. From the difference between the scene in Rouen that Montaigne foregrounds and the significance of the political performance involving Charles IX in which it occurred; the differ-ences between the encounter historically in 1562 and its meanings at the time of writing, thought to be some seventeen years later; between different modes of understanding of the relationship between the present and the past that emerge through the grain of his writing; to the difference located in the other that will put in question the desire for full knowledge and con-clusion. All of these differences have also to do with the form of difference that is deferred understanding of psychic causality and temporality, Freud's *Nachträglichkeit* [*après-coup*, or afterwardness].

Details of the encounter with the cannibal trace the importance for Mon-taigne of both the suspension of judgment and of the understanding that the present reinscribes the past; both of these are symptomatic of his political conservatism and also of his unending rewriting of his own *Essais*. While it may indeed already have been in many ways too late for the aboriginals of parts of what would become Latin America, Montaigne's representation dramatizes the significance of waiting until later for understanding, rather than—whether through the illusion of knowing already, or driven by fear of being too late—rushing to have the last word and thereby excluding other possible pasts and futures.

These abstractions about the temporality of understanding, which resonate with aspects of skepticism that are also, as will be seen, relevant to the passage in question, belong to Freudian and Lacanian thinking about psychic causality and temporality, about the nature of what will have been, and the relationship between the time of understanding and the rush to conclude. While, as I show, they are directly related to the passage, their idiom is different, and it is on the passage's own details that I build what follows. My analysis has three parts, forming a kind of temporality: from questions of origins, to the *après-coup*, to possible futures; running through all three parts are questions relating to curiosity and accidents.

Of Others and Origins

That one's own origins might be found in the other was already, by Montaigne's time, a topos. Whether that of the French originating with Francus or the savage symbolizing a lost origin in nature, this is a dimension of the desire to locate an originary source of truth, authority, or identity that is written through many sixteenth-century texts, above and beyond those of humanist philologists, legists, and theologians. This project was fed by the recovery of ancient texts (an expanding "Old [textual] World") and by the discovery of "New Worlds" (the East, the Americas). Moreover, as humanist optimism faded in response to the religious and political disorders that beset France, the desire felt by some for the possible existence of a whole and uncorrupted society was fueled by the intractable dislocations of their own. A nostalgic, melancholy turn, therefore, which would accept the substitution of one myth (purity, untainted proximity to origins) for another (that of—now lost—wholeness).

But as Montaigne's chapter makes plain, the savage other as a possible source of truth or purity is always already beyond reach, being preceded as he was, and is in the chapter, by his textual representations. Ultimately, whether the function of this represented savage was to act as an ideal or an antithetical other was less significant than the overriding fact of his having already been assimilated to others' (Greek, Latin, French, Spanish, pagan, Judeo-Christian) languages and desires—his textual others. Insofar as these others could be precluded, Montaigne draws neither on overt fictions nor on the theatrics of Peter Martyr's version.[10] The chapter opens with existing recognitions of the ideological function of the term *barbare* [barbarian or barbarous]: to "other" the other, seen only as alien and lesser, that which is not like oneself. So, far from being a source of truth, the other is used to support self-deception. Even if earlier texts invoked are insightful correctives, the other is now within the circuit of desire and exchange that is linguistic representation—*both* speech and writing. The opening pages of the chapter worry away at problems of representation; even Montaigne's faithful eyewitness, "propre à rendre veritable tesmoignage" ["fit to yeeld a true testimonie"],[11] can only mediate, and his presence among the Tupinamba, during Villegaignon's time, was not "innocent," that is, free of the desires that propelled the French expedition to Brazil.

Others have already dexterously examined the extensive issues of witnessing, orality, and representation that crowd these pages. What matters for my argument here is less the specificity of the different textual representations drawn into Montaigne's reflections and their functions there than the issue of deixis. For while the first-person pronoun subject recurs frequently in the course of these reflections, the narrative perspective is fluid, and the time, place, and situation in which the chapter is written are not consistently identifiable. Indeed, one of the many questions raised by the ironic comment with which the chapter ends is: To whom can we ascribe it? The place of the "self" quite as much as the sources of its version of the "other" seems deliberately elusive, as if attempting to avoid the conventional dialectical function of the "self"/"other" model, whereby the one seeks to fix its identity through its use of the other. As if Montaigne could thus begin to relocate the other, not only to enable his version of an other that can be both ideal and source of anxiety, rather than either one (ideal) or its polarity (figure of horror, nonhuman, phobic object), but also to restore to this other some of the autonomy lost in its European assimilations.

There are two punctual moments in the chapter in which the position of the writer emerges with a greater clarity and force than at any other. The first is the comment on the comparative barbarity of the behavior of the French during the current wars. Cruelty, so dehumanizing a vice in Montaigne's eyes, is ascribed more to the French than to the (therefore, not "bad other") cannibal:

je ne suis pas marry que nous remerquons l'horreur barbaresque qu'il y a en une telle action, mais ouy bien dequoy, jugeans bien de leurs fautes, nous soyons si aveuglez aux nostres. Je pense qu'il y a plus de barbarie à manger un homme

vivant qu'à le manger mort, à deschirer, par tourmens et par geénes, un corps
encore plein de sentiment, le faire rostir par le menu, le faire mordre et meur-
trir aux chiens et aux pourceaux (comme nous l'avons, non seulement leu,
mais veu de fresche memoire, non entre des ennemis anciens, mais entre des
voisins et concitoyens, et, qui pis est, *sous pretexte de pieté et de religion*), que de
le rostir et manger apres qu'il est trespassé.[12]

[I am not sorie we note the barbarous horror of such an action, but grieved,
that prying so narrowly into their faults we are so blinded in ours. I thinke
there is more barbarisme in eating men alive, than to feed upon them being dead; to mangle by tortures and torments a body full of lively sense, to
roast him in peeces, and to make dogs and swine to gnaw and teare him in
mammocks (as we have not only read, but seene very lately, yea and in our
owne memorie, not amongst ancient enemies, but our neighbours and fellow-
citizens; and which is worse, *under pretence of pietie and religion*) than to roast
and eat him after he is dead.][13]

The "bad faith" and self-deception of the French who behave this way line
up with the self-deceptions that the uses of the (so-called barbaric) other had
traditionally served. The reemergence of the first-person subject at precisely
this point, simultaneously taking his distance from his fellow Frenchmen and
acknowledging his inclusion in their number, "nous," "nostres" ["we," "our
own"], underwrites the implied point that never again should it be possible
to make use of the other in this way.

The second moment arrives in the passage on which I now increasingly
focus; Montaigne's represented memory of his own experience in Rouen, his
encounter with cannibals:

Trois d'entre eux, ignorans combien coutera un jour à leur repos et à leur bon
heur la connoissance des corruptions de deçà, et que de ce commerce naistra leur
ruyne, comme je presuppose qu'elle soit desjà avancée, bien miserables de s'estre
laissez piper au desir de la nouvelleté, et avoir quitté la douceur de leur ciel pour
venir voir le nostre, furent à Rouan, du temps que le feu Roy Charles neufiesme y
estoit. Le Roy parla à eux long temps; on leur fit voir nostre façon, nostre pompe,
la forme d'une belle ville. Apres cela quelqu'un en demanda leur advis, et voulut
sçavoir d'eux ce qu'ils y avoient trouvé de plus admirable: ils respondirent trios
choses, d'où j'ay perdu la troisiesme, et en suis bien marry; mais j'en ay encore
deux en memoire. Ils dirent qu'ils trouvoient en premier lieu fort estrange que
tant de grands hommes, portans barbe, forts et armez, qui estoient autour du Roy
(il est vray-semblable que ils parloient des Suisses de sa garde), se soubsmissent
à obeyr à un enfant, et qu'on ne choisissoit plus tost quelqu'un d'entr'eux pour
commander; secondement (ils ont une façon de leur langage telle, qu'ils nomment les hommes moitié les uns des autres) qu'ils avoyent aperçeu qu'il y avoit

parmy nous des hommes pleins et gorgez de toutes sortes de commoditez, et que leurs moitiez estoient mendians à leurs portes, décharnez de faim et de pauvreté; et trouvoient estrange comme ces moitiez icy necessiteuses pouvoient souffrir une telle injustice, qu'ils ne prinsent les autres à la gorge, ou missent le feu à leurs maisons. Je parlay à l'un d'eux fort long temps; mais j'avois un truchement qui me suyvoit si mal, et qui estoit si empesché à recevoir mes imaginations par sa bestise, que je n'en peus tirer guiere de plaisir.[14]

[Three of that nation, ignorant how deare the knowledge of our corruptions will one day cost their repose, securitie, and happinesse, and how their ruine shall proceed from this commerce, which I imagine is already well advanced (miserable as they are to have suffered themselves to be so cosened by a desire of new-fangled novelties, and to have quit the calmnesse of their climate to come and see ours), were at Roane in the time of our late King Charles the ninth, who talked with them a great while. They were shewed our fashions, our pompe, and the forme of a faire citie; afterward some demanded their advice, and would needs know of them what things of note and admirable they had observed amongst us: they answered three things, the last of which I have forgotten, and am very sorie for it, the other two I yet remember. They said, "First they found it very strange that so many tall men with long beards, strong and well armed, as it were about the Kings person [it is very likely they meant the Switzers of his guard] would submit themselves to obey a beardlesse childe, and that we did not rather chuse one amongst them to command the rest." Secondly (they have a manner of phrase whereby they call men but a moytie [half] one of another.) "They had perceived there were men amongst us full gorged with all sorts of commodities, and others which, hunger-starved and bare with need and povertie, begged at their gates: and found it strange these moyties so needy could endure such an injustice, and that they tooke not the others by the throate, or set fire on their houses." I talked a good while with one of them, but I had so bad an interpreter, who did so ill apprehend my meaning, and who through his foolishnesse was so troubled to conceive my imaginations, that I could draw no great matter from him.][15]

Here the cannibal is displaced, removed from the symbolic geography of the logic and rhetorical structures in which he had been captured. From the timeless dimension of myth, symbolic, or allegorical function, he enters historical time. And from silent object of scrutiny and fantasy, he seems to be invited to speak for himself, as Montaigne recalls. As a preliminary to exploring in greater detail the questions that the other's new location seems to allow, let us return, briefly, to the question of origins. For it is by dramatizing the absence of origins that the cannibals in Rouen open up Montaigne's reorientation of the significance of the place of the other in his larger inquiries into the lures and problems of the desire for knowledge.[16]

For while this was Montaigne's first and only encounter with cannibals, it was not in fact the first time savages had come to Rouen. Already in 1550 a group of savages had been shown to a French king there, in that instance Henri II, the father of Charles IX and patron of the attempt to construct *France Antarctique* in Brazil.[17] Again, a question of performance: the exotic other was on show to the king and his court. However, as Blanchard observes, "to obviate the scarcity of real savages available, sailors of various South American expeditions had been used to impersonate them, i.e., to dress, behave and speak in a manner thought to befit savages."[18] Savages already seen through their French other's eyes: the first, original visit was already adrift in fiction, a performance of primitive savagery as befitted the civilized French.

Between the earlier event and that of 1562, the project in Brazil had failed, not least because it had become mired in conflict between its Roman Catholic and Huguenot members. Henri II had died, as had his first successor, Francis II. With the massacre of reformers at worship in Vassy in March 1562, the first of the religious and civil wars had broken out. Prompted by news of that massacre, Huguenots had taken control of Rouen, one of the first cities in France to change hands, and it had been restored to Roman Catholic, monarchic governance after a siege, as is marked by this visit to the city of Charles IX and his court. This places the cannibal firmly within the arena of the wars, beyond the immediate context of the political performance that was the visit of the king and court to the city.

None of these details are mentioned, but the allusion to the event is both so specific and so vague that the reader is drawn to supply such missing details. So, between the visits in 1550 and 1562 there had been a series of violent and connected crises, precursors to a series of traumatic events between the 1562 visit and the time of writing, nearly two decades later. Moreover, during that time knowledge of the vulnerability of the aboriginals of the Americas both to diseases brought by the conquistadors and to violent exploitation by them, as decried in "Des coches" ["Of Coaches"], had spread. I now turn to these traumatic events in both France and the Americas, to the forms of understanding of the relationship between self and other that Montaigne reconfigures in his account of the visit, and to the reflections on causality and the temporality of human understanding adumbrated in the account.

The *Après-Coup*

If the earlier visit was a demonstration of assimilation, the second has more to do with that which is unassimilable. However, where, on the first occasion, the *barbaron* was represented to the French ruler and his court as savage, barbaric other, Montaigne's representation questions both the assimilation of the *barbaron* to the logic, rhetoric, and needs of the affirmation of French identity and also the existing alternative, that the *barbaron* is the site of that which is unassimilable and must therefore be excluded or destroyed. He produces a different position, in which the unassimilability of the other is potentially (although not wholly) respected and nontraumatic.

The inclusion in the chapter of the 1562 encounter between Montaigne and three unidentified cannibals has a number of functions. Until this point, the cannibals had been primarily symbolic figures, existing in an ahistorical, geographically unspecified dimension—a "país infini" ["infinit and vast a countrie"].[19] Montaigne had drawn on a range of the existing textual sources, classical and contemporary (his attribution of his ideas to those sources markedly vague), and had engaged critically with the existing functions of the savage other. His cannibal, were it not for the unfortunate—traumatic?—appetite for human flesh, is a heroic ideal, and figures the desire for a lost origin, for harmonious, utopian community uncorrupted by human desires (and therefore, implicitly, not subject to lack) and for a locus of truthfulness, pure knowledge: "les paroles mesmes qui signifient le mensonge, la trahison, la dissimulation, l'avarice, l'envie, la detraction, le pardon, inouïes" ["the very words that import lying, falshood, treason, dissimulations, covetousnes, envie, detraction, and pardon, were never heard of amongst them"].[20]

Had Montaigne worked with the figure of the savage, it could have functioned as another version of earlier idealizations, opposing the contemporary tendency for the cannibal to represent that which is not human. However, his chapter prefers ambiguities to polarizations—albeit at the cost of a gesture of assimilation. For when he finally focuses on what makes the cannibal, cannibal, he is quick to *comprehend* the act by analogy with honorable European behavior. It is akin to the rituals of honorable vengeance, and moreover, as Lestringant notes, is virtuous in that this is a form of "sacrifice librement consenti" ["sacrifice that is freely consented to"].[21] A gesture of open-mindedness, a stance against the all-too-imaginary uses of the cannibal, or savage, other, as a figure of *either* love *or* hate (like me, or not like me), as what is not human? An acknowledgment of the cannibal's not being locatable in a pure dimension beyond or before language, desire, and exchange? Or an example of the tendency to understand in one's own (preferred) terms? All of these are possible readings; all of them support a principle of ambiguity; and all feed a notion of intersubjectivity, challenging the uses of the "other" by the "self" as if the latter (human) were primary and independent of the former (not human)—as Montaigne has a willing, about-to-be cannibalized, other remind the reader. The other, this man calmly observes, is already the self and vice versa: each so constituted by the process over time of cannibalistic incorporations of the other that their identities are interrelated. The challenge for the late sixteenth-century reader, living in a culture in which the barbaric other is the enemy to be annihilated, is—by a process of assimilation, let's be clear—to learn to tolerate that other, whether by acknowledging the ways in which the other's desires and his own in fact converge, or by allowing that the other's different desires arouse anxieties and ambivalence, without those anxieties precipitating polarization.

Such are the issues that formed the backdrop to the scene in Rouen in 1562, a year that had begun with the possibility still of toleration (in the form of the January Edict). The scene seems literally to manifest the presence of "the cannibal" inside France, at precisely a juncture when, historically, the other—Huguenot—had been bloodily put in his place, with the retaking of Rouen by royal forces. Such "historical fact," even the year of the visit, is missing from Montaigne's representation, as if to dissociate the encounter from the violent polarizations that were its context. However, given that Montaigne's representation will go on to call attention to the significance of what is missing, this seems too simple a reading. At the time of writing and publication, would readers have forgotten the date and the events of such a year? The absence of date seems, rather, an invitation to the reader to remember, and what is more, to reflect on the meaning of those events in the light of the present—whether the time of writing or of reading. The time of writing is not explicit; indeed, it is as unlocatable as the deictic position of the earlier parts of the chapter. However, the encounter (in 1562) is emphatically preceded by reflections on what will have happened to the cannibals between 1562 and the time of writing: "ignorans combien coutera un jour à leur repos et à leur bon heur la connoissance des corruptions de deçà, et que de ce commerce naistra leur ruyne, comme je presuppose qu'elle soit desjà avancée, bien miserables de s'estre laissez piper au desir de la nouvelleté, et avoir quitté la douceur de leur ciel pour venir voir le nostre" ["ignorant how deare the knowledge of our corruptions will one day cost their repose, securitie, and happinesse, and how their ruine shall proceed from this commerce, which I imagine is already well advanced, miserable as they are to have suffered themselves to be so cosened by a desire of new-fangled novelties, and to have quit the calmnesse of their climate to come and see ours"].[22] The representation is framed in such a way as to make it an inquiry into the nature of understanding as it unfolds over time.

This event, Montaigne signals, must be understood in terms of the significance it will have come to have, which will emerge only later; that is, in terms of the *après-coup*. The temporal perspective initially takes the form of future tenses—"coutera" ["will one day cost"], "naistra leur ruyne" ["their ruine shall proceed"]—followed by a hypothetical subjunctive future perfect tense, "comme je presuppose qu'elle soit desjà avancée" ["which I imagine is already well advanced"]: that which will happen, will have happened, is that which the visitors did not know but which must inform the reader's interpretation. The disjunction between actors (cannibals) and audience (king, court, Montaigne) at the time is one dimension of the encounter that is dramatized, but even more so is that between all of those agents and the writer and reader—to the extent that we could say that *this* is the site of the drama of the passage. While their comments on the state of France, which were so far from those invited, could be dismissed as evidence of barbaric ignorance, Montaigne's focus is on a very different form of not knowing. Let us now take this temporal drama step by step.

First, 1562: "le Roy parla à eux longtemps: on leur fit voir. . . ." ["King Charles the ninth who talked with them a great while. They were shewed. . . ."]. Only after the greatness of France had been extolled were the visitors asked what seemed most remarkable to them. Not an open or equitable dialogue, and strikingly in contrast to the curiosity about the other and the relation between self and other characteristic of the chapter so far. The French courtiers cast the other in the role of an echo; it is for Montaigne to restore some semblance of equitability to the exchange and to rescue the other, along with the self's curiosity, from foreclosure. For rather than speak of what was most wondrous, which would have been to respond to the demand implicit in the French question, they—true to their otherness (not the same as the other of the French fantasy)—responded as if they heard something different in the French words and preferred to give voice to what gave them most to wonder about. What most puzzled or troubled them? That a child ruled men, and the injustice, disproportion, and inequity they identified in the gap between haves and have-nots in France. Montaigne represents their views on the latter in quite some detail—even though he *seems* to have been less attentive to the third point they supposedly made: "j'ay perdu la troisieme" ["the last of which I have forgotten; I have forgotten the third"]. And he includes no record of the royal response to the cannibal perspective.

What is also not explicit is that 1562 was a remarkable year in the intellectual history of France, for it was the year of publication of the translation into Latin by Henri Estienne (a Huguenot) of Sextus Empiricus's *Hypotyposes*, which made the founding text of Pyrrhonist skepticism accessible for the first time to French readers, notably Montaigne. I return to possible connections between the "cannibal" perspective and the spirit of skepticism later in this chapter.

Second, 1579(?): given that the question of the relationship between what is known or knowable, and between present and past understanding, is written into the passage, let us consider what will have happened in the intervening years, between event and representation, to inflect the significance of the earlier encounter, as represented. Charles IX had died two years after another massacre, the St. Bartholomew's Day Massacre of 1572. Whether or not he, as king, was directly responsible for it remains perhaps unknowable, but at the time his association with it seemed irrefragable. It prompted other massacres, such as that of Huguenots in Rouen a month later, mostly of have-nots: "envyron de trois a quatre cens huguenotz . . . pauvres et de bas estage les autres se sauverent par fuittes par argent et par amys" ["some three or four hundred poor, low-born Huguenots; the others were saved by taking flight, by paying for safety, and by friends"].[23] Thus the child of 1562, the fitness and injustice of whose rule is questioned by the cannibals, for readers in 1579 or later already had a history of association with polarizations and injustices so intractable as to have led to decades of war as well as outbursts of traumatic collective violence: in Montaigne's idiom, the "desmambremens" ["dismemberings"] of the body politic.[24]

This points toward a reading of the passage in terms of the unrepresented being that was traumatic, and which may only have become representable later, while having in the meantime been the shaper if not the cause of subsequent events. This seems borne out by Montaigne's private trauma as well as the public traumas, in the form of the death of Etienne de la Boétie in 1563, and also Montaigne's failure—albeit for the "best" of reasons—to keep his promise to him to publish his *Discours de la servitude volontaire*.[25] As well as raising further questions for us relating to psychic causality and temporality as traceable in the passage, if we remember the views conveyed in his friend's (by now unpublishable) essay, we find remarkable resonances between them and the "cannibal" perspective. Lestringant notes that the cannibal view "rappelle" ["recalls"] those of La Boétie; this seems something of a short circuit.[26] By 1579 the view ascribed to the cannibal in 1562 will have become unutterable except in the form of this possibly fictitious anticipation, presented as if it did not yet mean what it would go on to mean. And yet for readers after 1579, who cannot unknow what they already know, it means all that and more, for it invites reflection simultaneously on what might have been different had the consequences been anticipated earlier and on why this had not yet been thinkable.

Moreover, it invites reflection on the unforeseeable and with that, on the limits of human knowledge, on accidents, and on the relation not only between past and present, but among past, present, and future. Montaigne's initial emphasis on the relationship between past (1562) and present (unspecified time of writing, time of knowing the cannibals' future) opens out onto the question of what remains to be known.

Whether through his own seeming to have forgotten the cannibals' third comment, or the limits to his interpreter's competence, or the famous last words of the chapter, which hold open the potential significance of the relationship between Montaigne, cannibals, and European readers, two features are clear: the ways in which the present (time of writing, time of reading) reinscribes the past and the preference for a time of intersubjective understanding, of continuing reflection and possibility, over the time of conclusion.

For what is at stake here exceeds the particular encounter. Lacan's three-step version (see above) casts it in terms of the logic and uses of the relationship between self and other, particularly when the other is vulnerable to being cast as the *barbaron*, rather than his truths being acknowledged. Montaigne's writing resists the tendency to rush to conclude with an assertion of the self's being human, at the expense of the other. Why? To avoid the risk of revelation of the ways in which the self may not, after all, be fully human (civilized, humane, open-minded, open to others)?

From the proleptic framing in Montaigne's and the reader's knowledge of the cannibals' future, through both the tenor of their observations of French society and politics and the missing observation, resulting from Montaigne's forgetting, to his other apparent flaw, his narcissistic frustration about his interpreter letting him down,[27] and the chapter's closing irony with its open-ended deixis—who addresses whom?—the chapter's closing paragraphs are saturated with problems of interpretation, of the desire for knowledge and its frustration, at the same time that they prolong the time of understanding, rather than precipitating the conclusion that the human is on the side of the self, and not the other.

To explore this further, let us return to the detail of Montaigne's representation. The encounter with the cannibal other is dramatic in structure and purpose: the other is presented as a spectacle to the king and his court and is given an audience with the king, in function of the drama that the king himself is playing out to the people of Rouen, making a show of the renewed presence of legitimate—divinely sanctioned—royal authority, as instanced by his attending the All Saints' Day service in the cathedral. But the drama that holds more of Montaigne's attention has to do with the dislocation between the expected script—cannibals marvel at French culture—and what they chose to say. Moreover, the absence of their third observation, which has been dramatically leveraged by the play with the rhetoric of three (three cannibals, the three features of Frenchness to which their attention was drawn, their three observations), leaves the reader with the drama both of an enigma and also of possible scandal. The other has already addressed the king in ways that a French subject would not have dared. But Montaigne does not represent the royal reaction, and the reader can infer that at this juncture, the other's role as *barbaron*, unassimilable, not human (like the French) comes into play: both protection and travesty. On the other hand, by allowing that the other may still represent an ideal rather than not-human other, a fantasy that the other figures are the locus of truth or pure knowledge untainted by desire, Montaigne lures the reader in that direction and then frustrates her. The logic of the rhetoric of three combines with anticipation of political danger to imply that the third comment would have been even more transgressive than the first two, but does forgetting also imply this? Yes, if forgetting is repression, but not necessarily so, unless our interpretation assumes that the cannibal would have said something dramatically difficult to hear. Forgetting is a form of remembering, and it draws attention to the question of whether it was the event or the remembering of it, or in fact both, that was traumatic.

Moreover, performatively it lures the reader into supplying meaning,[28] while simultaneously posing the absence of full knowledge as a test of the reader. Montaigne plays with the reader's desire for knowledge and the desire to interpret, which obstruct the acceptance of frustration. Through what is staged as forgetfulness, he presents himself already as a flawed interpreter, and goes on to mirror this with his comment about his own frustrated pleasure. But as Montaigne's presentation of the remembered encounter has hinted in so many ways, what is at stake are questions to do with the function of the cannibal other in relation to the desire for knowledge. Both the desire and the difficulty of accepting its nonsatisfaction are in play here, but can give way to an acceptance that the frustration of the fantasy of there being a site of truth, or pure or full knowledge (the other), together with recognition of the absence of fixed difference between self and supposed other, is the condition of creative, open interpretation.

Neither the other nor the self possesses truth or full, pure knowledge; let us not forget the fate of the aboriginal other by the time of writing, made vulnerable by what he did not know about his other, the conquistadors. Moreover, the realization that the pleasure of the encounter with the other is narcissistic is a moment of acknowledging the less than ideally human nature of the self; not the same as the narcissism of the French haves identified by the cannibals, but a reminder of the potential intractability of the tensions in any social order between one person's desire and another's.

What compensates for this is, first, the representation's insistence on the plurality of others in play, which enables new thoughtfulness about the use of the self-other structure, as does the prior reminder in the chapter of the lack of clear differentiation between self and other. Second, the dramas that play through the representation of the encounter between self and other seem grounded in Montaigne's locating the less than human on the side of the self, whether French, French Roman Catholic, or French Huguenot, conquistador, or himself, anyone who wittingly or unwittingly uses the other as less human than himself. Through the cannibal, typically the other, the reader is asked to reflect on the inhumanity of the "hommes pleins et gorgez de toutes sortes de commoditez" ["men amongst us full gorged with all sorts of commodities; men that were full and gorged with all sorts of good things"]. The cannibals identify the hungry and poor of France as human in their terms, by calling them "moitiez" ["halves"]: as a parenthetical comment explains, "ils ont une façon de leur langage telle, qu'ils nomment les hommes moitié les uns des autres" ["they have a manner of phrase whereby they call men but a moytie one of another; they have a way in their language of speaking of men as halves of one another"], which suggests a symmetrical relationship of mutual recognition. The "hommmes pleins" ["the 'haves'"] however, are not "moitiez" ["halves"] but merely "les autres" ["others"]. For the cannibals the unjust subject who refuses to acknowledge the other's humanity is the one whose unacknowledged inhumanity renders him other. Inhumanity may still be on the side of the other, but the logic that leads to this identification has changed, and this identification is not an act of foreclosure. The cannibals merely observe that they find so unjust a situation *estrange* (strange); they remain curious, but they do not rush to conclude.

Desire for New Things, a Matter for Curiosity?

This reading of the reorientation of the self-other logic offered by Montaigne aligns it with both skepticism and Lacan's distinction between the time of understanding and the rush to conclude, the second and third of the three stages laid out in my quotation from "Logical Time and the Assertion of Anticipated Certainty." What is at stake is the illusion of one's own humanity. The second stage is one in which intersubjectivity, mutual recognition, and uncertainty still prevail ("les hommes se reconnaissent entre eux pour être des hommes" ["human beings recognize each other as human beings"]); with the third, so great is the anxiety that it may already be too late to guarantee one's own humanity that it precipitates the conclusion in favor of this being the case, at the cost of the humanity of others. From intersubjectivity to a (falsely) polarized binary, in other words.

The Pyrrhonist skeptic's ideal may have been the tranquility that comes with suspension of judgment, but what both Lacan's schema and the issues dramatized by the encounter with the—unknowingly skeptical?—cannibals suggest is that to remain in the time of understanding and not conclude may be too anxiety-provoking to bear. For the notion of the time of understanding we might substitute that of curiosity, one monument to which is, of course, the *Essais*.[29] While the commitment to curiosity that sits with suspension of judgment can be seen as a trace of Montaigne's skeptical tendencies, they are not tranquil. At the time of writing, curiosity was a topic about which there was much disagreement, much of which was redolent of anxieties about its power.[30] In this chapter we find this in the "ruyne" of the aboriginals, not only through dealing with corrupt Europeans, the "corruptions du deçà" ["our corruptions"; "corruptions on this side of the ocean"] noted by Montaigne, but also through their "desir de la nouvelleté" ["desire of new-fangled novelties"; "desire for new things"], which in "Des coches" ["Of Coaches"] is explicitly termed curiosity: "[B] la curiosité de veoir des choses estrangeres et incogneues" ["the curiosity to see strange and unknowne things"].[31] The cost of their curiosity has been mortal,[32] but it is not too late for Montaigne to ask his readers to remain curious, to resist conclusion and the binaries that dehumanize both self and other. His chapter concludes with an ironic apparent dismissal, so dramatically disjunctive from all that has gone before as to seem rather a way of asking the reader: "So, who or what is the cannibal to you, and who or what does that make you to the cannibal? Who is the human here?" This renders the future of Montaigne's cannibals—as the great wealth of responses to them over the centuries attests—an open question and underlines that the encounter with them was, not least, about interpretation, and about the temporality of human understanding. Montaigne has used a contingent historical event, which conventionally belongs to a model of causation according to which the past produces the future, to explore ways in which what will be the future reinscribes the past, bringing new insights but not certain understanding, the cost of which may be anxiety, or frustration, but is far from ruinous.

Notes

1. See Jacques Derrida's reflections in *De la grammatologie* (Paris: Minuit, 1967), pt. 2, ch. 1, for further discussion of this aspect of ethnographic representations of the savage.

2. An illuminating point of entry into such issues is provided by Frank Lestringant, *Le cannibale: grandeur et décadence* (Paris: Librairie Académique Perrin, 1994).

3. Jacques Lacan, "Le temps logique et l'assertion de certitude anticipée," in *Ecrits* (Paris: Seuil, 1966), 197–214, 213.

4. Jacques Lacan, *Logical Time and the Assertion of Anticipated Certainty*, trans. Bruce Fink (New York: W.W. Norton, 2006), 161–75, 174 (translation modified). All other translations are mine unless otherwise noted.

5. Ibid., 228.

6. Ibid., ch. 5.

7. Jean-Marc Blanchard, "Of Cannibalism and Autobiography," *Modern Language Notes* 93, no. 4 (1978): 654–76, 663.

8. Notably among them, Gérad Defaux, "Un cannibale en haut de chausses: Montaigne, la différence et la logique de l'identité," *Modern Language Notes* 97, no. 4 (1982): 919–57; Tzvetan Todorov, "L'être et l'autre: Montaigne," in "Montaigne: Essays in Reading," special issue, *Yale French Studies* 64 (1983): 113–44; Michel de Certeau, "Montaigne's 'Of Cannibals': The Savage 'I'," in *Heterologies: Discourse on the Other*, trans. Brian Massumi (Minneapolis: University of Minnesota Press, 1986), 67–79; and Olivier Pot, *L'inquiétante étrangeté: Montaigne, la pierre, le cannibale, la mélancolie* (Paris: Honoré Champion, 1993).

9. This chapter was completed before the publication of Philippe Desan's *Montaigne: Une biographie politique* (Paris: Odile Jacob, 2014), and therefore does not take into account his precisely argued case for the encounter not actually having taken place in Rouen, but rather in Bordeaux, some years later. The interpretation presented here rests as much on questions of representation and on the force of the encounter being *represented as if* it took place in Rouen in 1562 as on its actually having happened then and there.

10. "Le tableau anthropophage de la Guadeloupe s'ordonne à la manière d'une scène imaginaire vide de tout acteur vivant" ["the representation of anthropophagy in Guadeloupe is organised like an imaginary scene, devoid of all living agents"] (Lestringant, *Le Cannibale*, 49).

11. All references are to the Villey-Saulnier edition of the *Essais* (Paris: Presses Universitaires de France, 2004), I.31.205; the English translations are taken from John Florio's text, *The Essayes or Morall, Politike and Millitarie Discourses of Lord Michaell de Montaigne* (London: Val. Sims, 1603), http://www.luminarium.org/renascence-editions/montaigne/ (accessed June 12, 2013). Florio titles the essay "Of the Caniballes". Donald Frame's modern English translations are provided in the notes. *The Complete Essays of Montaigne*, trans. Donald Frame (London: Everyman's Library, 2003). When both translations are cited in apposition, a semicolon separates them and Florio's translation is first, followed by Frame's. Frame translates "propre à rendre veritable tesmoignage" as "fit to bear true witness" (*The Complete Essays*, I.31.184).

12. Montaigne, *Essais*, I.31.209 (emphasis added).

13. Florio, *The Essayes*, I.30, http://www.luminarium.org/renascence-editions/montaigne/1xxx.htm (emphasis added). Frame:

I am not sorry that we notice the barbarous horror of such acts, but I am heartily sorry that, judging their faults rightly, we should be so blind to our own. I think there is more barbarity in eating a man alive than in eating him dead; and by tearing by tortures and the rack a body still full of feeling, in roasting a man bit by bit, in having him bitten and mangled by dogs and swine (as we have not only read but seen within fresh memory, not among the ancient enemies, but among neighbors and fellow citizens, and what is worse, *on the pretext of piety and religion*), than in roasting and eating him after he is dead. (*The Complete Essays*, I.31.189; emphasis added)

14. Montaigne, *Essais*, I.31.213–14.

15. Florio, *The Essayes*, I.30, http://www.luminarium.org/renascence-editions/montaigne/1xxx.htm. Frame:

Three of these men, ignorant of the price they will pay some day, in loss of repose and happiness, for gaining knowledge of the corruptions on this side of the ocean; ignorant also of the fact that of this intercourse will come their ruin (which I suppose is already well advanced: poor wretches, to let themselves be tricked by the desire for new things, and to have left the serenity of their own sky to come and see ours!)—three of these men were at Rouen, at the time the late King Charles IX was there. The king talked to them for a long time; they were shown our ways, our splendor, the aspect of a fine city. After that, someone asked their opinion, and wanted to know what they had found most amazing. They mentioned three things, of which I have forgotten the third, and I am very sorry for it; but I still remember two of them. They said that in the first place they thought it very strange that so many grown men, bearded, strong, and armed, who were around the king (it is likely that they were talking about the Swiss of his guard) should submit to obey a child, and that one of them was not chosen to command instead. Second (they have a way in their language of speaking of men as halves of one another), they had noticed that there were among us men that were full and gorged with all sorts of good things, and that their other halves were beggars at their doors, emaciated with hunger and poverty; and they thought it strange that these needy halves could endure such an injustice, and did not take the others by the throat, or set fire to their houses. I had a very long talk with one of them; but I had an interpreter who followed my meaning so badly, and who was so hindered by his stupidity in taking in my ideas, that I could hardly get any satisfaction from the man. (*The Complete Essays*, I.31.193)

16. I am not suggesting that Montaigne's move is without precedent; as Lestringant confirms, the "révolution sociologique" ["sociological revolution"] whereby "self" and "other" change places, had already been used by Guillaume Postel in relation to Christians and their Ottoman other (*Le Cannibale*, 101–2).

17. On this royal entry, see the excellent study by Michael Wintroub, *A Savage Mirror: Power, Identity, and Knowledge in Early Modern France* (Stanford, CA: Stanford University Press, 2006).

18. Blanchard, "Of Cannibalism and Autobiography," 670.

19. Montaigne, *Essais*, I.31.203 ; Florio, *The Essayes*, I.30, http://www.luminarium.org/renascence-editions/montaigne/1xxx.htm. Frame: "boundless country" (*The Complete Essays*, I.31.182).

20. Montaigne, *Essais*, I.31.206. Frame: "the very words that signify lying, treachery, dissimulation, avarice, envy, belittling, pardon—unheard of" (*The Complete Essays*, I.31.186).

21. Lestringant, *Le Cannibale*, 200.

22. Montaigne, *Essais*, I.31.213 ; Florio, *The Essayes*, I.30, http://www.luminarium .org/renascence-editions/montaigne/1xxx.htm. Frame:

> ignorant of the price they will pay some day, in loss of repose and happiness, for gaining knowledge of the corruptions on this side of the ocean; ignorant also of the fact that of this intercourse will come their ruin (which I suppose is already well advanced: poor wretches, to let themselves be tricked by the desire for new things, and to have left the serenity of their own sky to come and see ours!). (*The Complete Essays*, I.31.193)

23. Hand-written marginalia on a copy of a *Brief discours sur la mort de la Royne de Navarre* . . ., cited in Nathanaël Weiss, "Un témoin de la Saint-Barthélemy," *Bulletin de la Société de l'Histoire du Protestantisme Français* (1901): 445–48, 445.

24. "J'aperçois en ces desmambremens de la France et divisions où nous sommes tombez" ("De la vanité," III.9.993). Florio: "In these dismembrings or havocks of France and divisions whereinto we are miserably falne" (*The Essayes*, http://www .luminarium.org/renascence-editions/montaigne/3ix.htm; emphasis in original). Frame: "I perceive that in the strife that is tearing France to pieces and dividing us into factions" (*The Complete Essays*, III.9.924).

25. Namely, to forestall its being drawn on by Huguenots arguing the case for tyrannicide.

26. Lestringant, *Le Cannibale*, 182.

27. "J'avois un truchement qui me suyvoit si mal, et qui estoit si empesché à recevoir mes imaginations par sa bestise, *que je n'en peus tirer guiere de plaisir*" ["I had so bad an interpreter, who did so ill apprehend my meaning, and who through his foolishnesse was so troubled to conceive my imaginations, *that I could draw no great matter from him*; I had an interpreter who followed my meaning so badly, and who was so hindered by his stupidity in taking in my ideas, *that I could hardly get any satisfaction from the man*"] (emphasis added).

28. André Tournon, for instance, hypothesizes: "S'agirait-il d'autre chose que de la religion?" ["Would it be about anything other than religion?"] (*Montaigne: La glose et l'essai* [Lyon: Presses Universitaires de Lyon, 1983], 219), while others speculate it is extreme, even—in French eyes—treasonable, violence that is left out. On the religious aspects, see also George Hoffman, "Anatomy of the Mass: Montaigne's 'Cannibals,'" *PMLA* 117, no. 2 (March 2002): 207–21.

29. This is Frame's translation of two lines from two different essays (*The Complete Essays*, I.31.193; II.12.459). In French: "desir de la nouvelleté," "matiere à sa curiosité" (Montaigne, *Essais*, I.31.213; II.12.510). Florio: "desire of new-fangled novelties," "curiosity of matter to worke upon" (*The Complete Essayes*, http://www .luminarium.org/renascence-editions/montaigne/2xii.htm).

30. See Neil Kenny, *The Uses of Curiosity in Early Modern France and Germany* (Oxford: Oxford University Press, 2004).

31. Montaigne, *Essais*, III.6.910. Frame's rendering is the same as Florio's (Frame, *The Complete Essays*, III.6.843).

32. Arguably then this is precisely what humanizes—Europeanizes—the cannibal, in that it converts him from symbolic ideal into lapsarian figure.

CHAPTER ELEVEN

Red and Black, Pink and Green

Jacques de Fonteny's Gay Pastoral Play

CHRISTIAN BIET

Melancholy seems to grow its roots in the very soil of pastoral drama.[1] Shepherds in the groves of love show that it is possible to stay clear from the bloodshed that fills the fields of their present time of history—or they remain in a uchronic or achronic state of separation from the gore of historical reality—to consider it from the distance of their bucolic withdrawal, and to wallow in their own black bile.

In this respect, the experience of melancholy can be seen as offering a satirical viewpoint on the world, or at times a secluded retreat, a private meditation that "heals" the effects of poetic and political violence. However, experiencing this doleful withdrawal is not without its risks. It excludes the melancholics from the city and leaves them in the throes of the most "anti-civic" of passions, a self-passion that is distinct from self-love. It plunges them into a painful state of submissive dereliction, or worse, into a fevered delirium likely to end in lethargy or death, with or without bouts of frenzy. Arcadia thus becomes an alternative reality that protects them from the bad blood of history. It is a *place* of refuge for "black evil" and mourning, but one where melancholics can, if need be, accommodate their pathological melancholy, glorify it as a dreamlike vision, or even entertain it with poetic forms, storytelling, and drama. All this contributes to making the abode of melancholy both habitable and literary, but also undeniably complex. Whoever suffers from melancholy therefore survives thanks to literary diversions and by letting her drive for death and mourning be channeled through her aesthetic endeavors (which might in time allow her to return to her existence as a member of society). It is on these sometimes bewildering aesthetic detours that I focus in this chapter, using as a case in point Jacques de Fonteny, who in 1587 published *L'eumorphopémie*, or *Le beau pasteur*, which would be renamed *Le beau berger* [*The Fair Shepherd*] in later editions.[2]

The dramatic pastoral, a genre developing in France at the time, was free to explore, or bend, rules that were only emerging and malleable. The laws of the genre were always eminently plastic and relative. It originated in Italy, was already being practiced in England, and was progressively establishing itself in France. Nicolas de Montreux was publishing pastoral dramas at the same time as Fonteny, and other writers were following this burgeoning fashion, using the Italians as models, Torquato Tasso and Giovanni Battista Guarini in particular.[3] Still, their freedom was boundless, since even if there were some general conventions, no fixed rules seemed to have been set.

Accordingly, the first recorded edition of Fonteny's pastoral play was published in a collection of love sonnets and religious poetry in which it is considered above all as a poetical piece. In the context of *La première partie des ébats poétiques* [*The First Part of Poetic Pastimes*], *Le beau pasteur* is thus first and foremost a poetic dialogue. The dedications of each sonnet, systematically addressed to luminaries of the court of King Henri III, principally from the Sourdis family, point toward the fact that this collection is part of a budding writer's and a courtier's strategy to forward his career. Fonteny also gives every sign he can that he is writing in the wake of Renaissance authors. He saturates his text with Latin quotes and Italianisms and uses Greek both for the names of some of his characters and for his very title, since the French title is only a translation of *L'eumorphopémie* (the tale of the fair [*eumorphos*] shepherd [*poimèn*]), translated in French both by *pasteur* and *berger* [shepherd].[4] This pastoral play is first and foremost to be read in a late Renaissance poetic context, both Hellenic and Italianizing, relying on a conventional genre but also sufficiently free to play with forms, themes, and figures. Similarly, the last two identified editions of this text, under the general title *Le bocage d'amour* [*The Grove of Love*],[5] placed *Le beau berger* in a two-piece collection, in which de Fonteny's pastoral play was followed by S.-G. de la Roque's *La chaste bergère* [*The Chaste Shepherdess*].

We might wonder, without much hope of finding an answer, whether Fonteny's play, apparently written for performance at a time when the dramatist was a fellow [*confrère*] of the Hôtel de Bourgogne, was in fact ever performed. In the current state of research there is no absolute proof. Nonetheless, this play should be considered as a theatrical piece, for it certainly fulfills all of the formal requirements, and even if it was only published and never performed, it *presupposes* performance.

But what interests us here is not to draw a historical overview or give the circumstances of publication or performance—on this count, despite all efforts, very little is known—but rather to examine the complex transfers, the enigmatic treatment of the play, and the detours proposed by Fonteny. Exploring the genre as he does, cramming it with unrelated elements, transgressing the narrowness of conventions, turning them around and distancing himself from them, Fonteny seems to want to experiment with the possibility of opening the pastoral drama to other forms and themes. Yet as he returns to Arcadia and transforms it, the author of *Le beau berger* perverts its harmony as much as its readability. Through an accumulation of forms; the exclusion of shepherdesses; and the multiplications of traps, enigmas, and warlike motifs set in his plot, the dramatist shows his desire to go beyond the conventions of his chosen "genre." At the same time, since he does not adhere to Guarinian commonplaces, he ends up bringing the grassy retreat closer to human history and mysteriously questioning the harmony of the golden age.

Le beau berger is thus, strictly speaking, an enigma to be deciphered and presents itself like a rambling exploration of the constraints of the pastoral play. Just as in his tragedy, *Cléophon*, Fonteny is in full possession of both answers and questions, showing that in order to understand him one needs to be able to translate and transpose what is only just hidden by his use of Greek names. It is also crucial, as will be seen, to attempt to decipher enigmas that remain rather opaque, and in particular, to interpret his perplexing presentation of the "homosexual" transposition as entirely unremarkable.[6] As a consequence, the difficulty of seeing through the many mysteries of the texts threatens to reduce the rural world of the pastoral play to nothing more than an absurd proposition, a logical dead-end bound to failure.

In an article written for *Le Débat* in 1984 and reprinted with a new title in *La diplomatie de l'esprit* ("Nous serons guéris si nous le voulons" ["We shall be healed if we will it"]), Marc Fumaroli develops the idea that the rhetoric and poetic conversion of blood into discourse counts as the most defining shift proposed by French neoclassicism.[7] Through a refusal of frenzied and heroic melancholy, the classical mind-set would thus offer an aesthetic solution standing in stark contrast with the dark appeal of the gore and gloom of European melancholy. Patrick Dandrey, on the contrary, insists that neoclassicism, far from renouncing melancholy or turning away from the European canker, does not abolish morbid temptation or excise black passions, but rather incorporates melancholic signs in its own productions as metaphors, be they literary, discursive, or dramatic.[8] As these metaphors become operative, steeped as they are in the four humors of the body, they grow into an illness of the soul, before slowly detaching themselves from the humoral system, progressively and necessarily giving birth to modern psychopathology.

The question then is to understand how the seventeenth century first used melancholy as a way of introducing a reflexive distance from cruel (i.e., tragic) experiences, thus proposing a refuge, a world at odds with the cruelty of narrated or dramatized history, in order to reach a sort of harmony either ideally or in literary terms. Black bile would then be the antidote to the floods of scarlet humors that were bloodying actual stages, both narrative and theatrical. However, the cure itself is not without its risks and needs to be controlled and channeled to restore peace to bodies, souls, and communities.[9] Immoderate love of seclusion, all too likely to end in death, can thus be healed, on the one hand through the use of irony, which looks at this love from a distance and degrades it, casting doubt on it, and on the other hand through tragicomic heroism, as a way to reunite with reality, and amorous heroism, able to restrain the intense desire for solitude and retreat. In order to find an alternative to the horrifying world presented in tragedies, while trying to avoid representing the altogether different but just as radical and deadly world of absolute seclusion, theater produced a hybrid: the tragicomic pastoral play. Tragicomedy, which is essentially transformed into pastoral drama by its cast of shepherds, thus has the capacity to heal melancholy through theater—that is to say, through a blend of comic, pathetic, and tragic components. Its medium is also by definition the representation of an action. Through performance the action is embodied and may bring spectators back to reality, or at least to a referential system. Because of this, and because it eventually manages to balance contradictory humors and temperaments into good health, tragicomedy is able to prevent melancholy from becoming radically dangerous.[10]

The dangers come from seclusion and from the necessity to find protection from a tragic and bloody reference system in temporary or permanent retreat. These perils are warded off in a number of ways, ranging from the resources of ironic distance (sometimes borrowing comic or even farcical features), to those of the action performed on stage (with its manifestations of physical energy, acting directly on passivity and inertia), and last but not least to the resources of language, amplified to the point of parody, ornamental and full of energy, metaphors, hyperboles, and the brilliance of *concetti* [conceits]. These devices and techniques include and blend, once more, all styles and forms of discourse, from lyrical lament and threnody, to epic grandeur and balanced deliberation. It is as if the pastoral play first wished to present an alternative to violence and war, through the literary elaboration of a place of retreat, safely at a distance from bloodshed, and only afterward became aware of the dangers and risks of choosing black humor; it is as if it then tried to buy some time and fend off morbidity through an anatomy of melancholy in literature and on the stage, going through all the different forms (either together or in succession) and all the different modes through which melancholy can be defined.

First, the pastoral story—or rather, what formalists would call the *fabula*, the raw stuff that makes up a story—offers a kind of therapeutic space in which melancholy has an active role, observing the bloodshed from a distance and turning spectators' attention away from it. At the heart of this therapy lies the hope that one evil will cure the other, that the dangers of vermilion blood will be averted by the dangerous efficiency of black bile. To achieve this, writers try to divert melancholic dramaturgy from its own end (death) through a number of solutions (love, happiness, heroic actions, or literary and aesthetic suspension). Literature and theater explore these forms and stage the melancholic subject in all his characteristics (from the most comic to the most pathetic, the most frenetic to the most lyrical) as he is caught in the processes of a regulated dramatization, but at the same time they come to focus increasingly on the archetype of the doleful lover (shepherd or not), which the play's *fabula* isolates as the highlight of the performance. It becomes clear as a consequence that the pastoral *fabula* later limited its dramatizing of melancholy to a type, and increasingly marginalized it in the plot. The melancholy lover, the poet seized by black humor, was destined to perform a pathological phantasmagoria often regarded as ridiculous. He became an extravagant shepherd, forgetting even his own dejection and overdoing the ludicrous signs of theatrical melancholy. As a result, the pastoral and melancholic space, which in the seventeenth century presented itself as an emotionally charged alternative to the world of blood, came to be deserted later in the century.

In the meantime, it was effective, used by such tragic authors as Alexandre Hardy as an alternative to tragic bloodlust and a therapeutic antidote to cruelty. It certainly played a part in the fact that tragedies progressively turned away from representations of violent actions to the benefit of discursive and rhetorical transcriptions. However, just as the melancholic figure despairs, broods, and wallows in prostrate affliction, he is more than capable of having fits of frantic delirium. This is in line with the Senecan, Shakespearean, and violent type of tragedy written at the beginning of the century, which demonstrates how difficult this contradictory, problematic, and paradoxical melancholic therapy is to use. Thus, while its etiology and its ornate dissection are effected, and it has been assigned a space that is finally too narrow for it, black bile eventually comes full circle to its rival and antidote, sanguine red. This is why authors also know how to take stock of the essential link that exists between the red and black humors in order to articulate and inscribe both within their *fabulae*, their language, and even at times their dramatic action. Hence, red and black, in some places still visible and paradoxically linked, are firmly joined together.

The Inescapable Fight between Harmony and War

Since the very origins of pastoral drama, then, we can see the link between the melancholic and sanguine humors, between the idyllic, forest world and the world that is, in principle, outside: the world of war. For, contrary to a canonical vision of the pastoral play, the shepherds' realm is problematic from its origin. Even when it stands as an answer to tragedy, there are many cases when the pastoral cannot really break away from the tragic.

Sadness, fear, hopeless affliction, fever, and delirium are the well-known marks of melancholy in pastoral plays, and they are sure to appear in the late sixteenth-century *pastorelles* dealing with the complex loves of shepherds and shepherdesses. They follow a dramatic pattern according to which one shepherd loves a shepherdess who loves another shepherd, himself in love with another shepherdess. Everything ends well after the many obstacles and plot twists favored by sylvan *fabulae*. The pastoral play would then be a kind of retreat and refuge, out of the reach of history, for both melancholic characters and lovers, a way of proposing harmony to the world, of representing the idealized restoration of a golden age, in spite of the bloodshed without and the protagonists' black bile within. However, it is undeniable that this schematic and idealizing depiction of the pastoral play is regularly defeated in a series of texts that refer to the convention only to pervert it. In one of the *pastorelles* or *bergeries* of the sixteenth century, one can see an instance of this impossibility to break away from history, and observe that the question arises from an unusual exploration of the genre that consists in excluding women from the grove. It would seem that when men are together, even if they are bound by love and friendship, they necessarily have to come to terms with violence; as if, when the rural genre stopped being the kind of utopia found in Guarini in order to avoid being wrecked by morbid melancholy, it was doomed to fight violence with violence in the name of past or ideal harmony.

Pink and Green: A Tale of Two Shepherds

In the course of one day, from sunrise to sunset, in a number of closely situated places all set in the same grove, a vaguely linear plot brings shepherds together in Fonteny's *Le beau berger*. Two peasants/shepherds wake up, make conversation, tell each other stories, read and recite poetry, and are eventually attacked by satyrs. Two other shepherds/heroes join them, and one of them enters the fight while the other remains on his own. The band of shepherds gets bigger, and the satyrs are on the brink of defeat when suddenly a penitent *Ombre* [Ghost] appears. It wistfully evokes the peace of the golden age and begs them to stop fighting. This could be the end of the story, but Chrisophile, the fighting shepherd, tells the others that he has received an enigma from a mysterious bloodstained hand and now needs to decipher it. To do so, the shepherds all go to a strange wizard, who claims that he will give them the solution the next day. Eventually, despite Chrisophile's frustration, the shepherds leave to celebrate their victory together. The hero shepherd is reunited with his lover, Chrisalde—the nonfighting shepherd—and the play ends.

Beyond a conventionally linear story line, relying only on an eventful day filled with obstacles, the play is essentially a succession of discontinuous dramatic events taking place one after the other, while monologues rhythmically punctuate the scenes. This *fabula* is therefore not a harmonious organic whole, but a sequence of more or less commonplace scenes. There is no real continuous logic link between such spectacular scenes (the fight against the satyrs, the appearance of the Ghost, the wizard in his den) and other situations (the conversations, the visit to the wizard), except for the two hero-shepherds who, together in the morning and separated at noon by various actions (the battle, the quest for understanding the enigma), are reunited in the evening.

This being said, just going through the list of characters, we immediately notice that the whole play is a very male affair. In stark contrast with the Italian model and the beginning of the French tradition, not one female role has made it into this pastoral play. No shepherd will love his shepherdess, which means that, since these plays are always about love, the shepherds will have to love one another. This first surprising feature puzzled and even scandalized Raymond Lebègue, while Henry C. Lancaster wrote that the matter was "rather equivocal."[11] The main dynamic of the genre, its principal convention, is deflected. Canonical "heterosexual" love is replaced by "homosexual" love, which apparently has exactly the same driving function for the unfolding of the plot. Here, homosexuality is not the result of a mistake, of an ambiguous travesty; it is neither an inflammatory element nor a malfunction that the plot is supposed to fix in the end. It is the valued core of the story, without any satirical intent, as if it was in all respects straightforward to replace couples of shepherds and shepherdesses by couples of shepherds.

In doing this, Fonteny shows that he knows ancient literature well, and he recycles the bucolic and idyllic sources of pastoral drama. Indeed, just as Stephen Guy-Bray and Bruce R. Smith have demonstrated in the case of English pastoral's homoerotic aspects, Fonteny knows perfectly well that Theocrites and Virgil, among other major writers, also place their heroes in the rural context of Greek love.[12] Through the course of this story line, oriented toward the definition of the shepherd's beauty, the hero Chrisophile (in Greek, the lover of gold) will be able to love Chrisalde (he who shines like gold) with the literary blessing of antiquity, and without any trace of moral judgment or condemnation. As if to strengthen this ancient authority, the play is saturated with direct or indirect intertextual references, echoes of Theocritus's *Idylls* and Virgil's *Eclogues*, all the while ensuring a certain updating of convention. These ancient literary shepherds thus also show that they are contemporaneous literary peasant-shepherds: they talk about Janot and Thoinet, try to outdo one another with their short country tales, cheerfully sprinkle their speeches with various *effets de réel* [effects of reality] such as lard-rubbed bread and barking dogs, and curse the stinginess of their landowner.

We only progressively notice the arguably homosexual turn given to the plot. At the beginning of the text nothing really unusual stands out. We are in Arcadia watching two typical shepherds (whose names, Firmot and Montin, show them to be peasant-shepherds). They are waking up rather late and languidly—conversely to women who are supposed to have extreme "vitesse de corps" ["quickness of bodies"] in the morning.[13] One even has a limp and a swollen foot;[14] the other tells him to walk "tout bellement" ["very gently"] and to be patient, promising him that the pain will fade.[15] As the sun is rising, they make ablutions and address their prayers to God and Pan the protector of herds. Being good actors, they dress up and do not forget to take with them the props they will need to play their part. We are waiting for the story to begin, and starting to wonder why no shepherdesses have been introduced yet.

Firmot, going to his ewes, then tells "le conte / De la vraye amitié, qui toute chose domte: / Et comment deux bergers de ces proches endrois / S'enlacerent le cueur dans le nœud de ses loix" ["the tale of a true all-subduing friendship and how two shepherds from these regions intertwined their hearts in the knots of its laws"].[16] Montin, immediately captivated by this story of deep friendship, wants them both to sit down and Firmot to go on with his tale, "proche de moy, ains que je gouste mieus / Ton discours de l'oreille, et ta grâce des yeus" ["close by me that I might better savor your words with my ears and your grace with my eyes"].[17] It is at this point that the theme of shepherds loving shepherds is introduced, thanks to Firmot's tale, in a conventionally bucolic setting and in keeping with discussions about ideal harmony, as instantiated here by same-sex male love and friendship. Firmot's story is interrupted by pauses between each scene, to take a rest or have dinner (they eat bacon-rubbed bread, cake, and a leg of gosling), but Montin also asks questions and makes observations, so that long monologues are avoided and conversation prevails.

Firmot relates that, in a village called Leucodecte (in Greek, pleasingly white), two shepherds, "presque de pareil aage" ["nearly the same age"],[18] love each other so dearly that they cannot bear to be apart. Chrisalde is, an eighteen-year-old shepherd, whose eyes, "munis d'arcs et de flesche / aux simples regardants décochaient maintes brêches" ["furnished with bows and arrow shot many holes into mere onlookers"];[19] nose "longuettement panché" ["longishly bent"], resembling that of Leda;[20] rosy complexion; teeth; and mouth all show that he is chosen by the gods and as fair as Love: "Qui n'aura veu cela qu'il pense que les dieus / Ont desployé sur luy le plus beau de leur mieus / Et que le Paradis des beautez est en terre, / Et que l'enclos du Ciel, rien que de laid n'enserre" ["May he who has not seen this imagine that the Gods lavished on him the fairest of their best and that the paradise of beauty is on earth, and that the enclosure of the heavens contains nothing foul"].[21] The other shepherd, Chrisophile, is twenty years old. He is an "ennemi du vulgaire, et de toute ignorance, / Indomté du travail" ["enemy of baseness, and every kind of ignorance un-tamed by craft"],[22] and "ayant en la pensee, / Les graces de Chrisalde empreintes vivement, / Fut forcé de l'aymer sur tous uniquement" ["having in his mind the graces of Chrisalde vividly etched, [he] was forced to love him above all else"].[23] The text makes the following comment: Is it not a common saying that "L'homme qui est bien né, ayme une belle chose. / L'odeur et l'incarnat font qu'on ayme la rose" ["a man well born loves a beautiful thing. Its fragrance and pinkness make us love the rose"]?[24] Chrisophile, the gold lover, predictably loves Chrisalde, the shining gold. The fact that they are both male does not seem to be problematic in the least, since they both have beauty and love beauty, and that the fragrant and flesh-colored rose of the one appeals to the other.

However, the other side of the pastoral world is jealous of "ceste alliance [qui] / Prenoit de jour en jour une telle accroissance" ["this alliance [that] grew stronger every day"]: Mélampe, the young satyr with hoofed feet, Toribo, just as hirsute, and "le gris Androgo [qui] se parforça souvent / De rompre cest amour" ["the gray Androgo (who) oft by force attempted to break their love"], all fought against it in vain: "plus qu'auparavant / Chrisalde et Chrisophile embrassez davantage / N'eurent qu'un mesme cueur, et un même courage" ["more narrowly entwined than ever Chrisalde and Chrisophile had but one heart and one courage"].[25]

> L'un n'estoit rien sans l'autre ainsi comme l'on voit
> Qu'un pippeau se tairoit si le vent ne l'enfloit.
> Lors que le maréchal moüille d'eau sa fournaise
> Les charbons les plus ardens, rendent plus grande braize.
> Ainsi ceus qui pensoient esteindre leur amour,
> Au lieu de l'assoupir l'ont mise en son plein jour.[26]

> [The one was never without the other as we see that the flute would be mute if wind did not blow through it. When the blacksmith throws water in the furnace, the hottest coals make the brightest embers. Likewise, those who thought to quell their love, instead of dulling it, brought it in full light.]

They both blow their flutes, sprinkle their furnaces with water, roast themselves at the embers, and in short never cease to give each other open proofs of their reciprocal love, through sexual metaphors, literary feats, and other exploits, Chrisophile writing verse and Chrisalde hunting fearsome boars. However, Chrisophile does not only write to and for Chrisalde, since Firmot proudly produces a sonnet that Chrisophile gave him "lautre jour" ["the other day"].[27] The sonnet, a charming poem written on bark, is addressed to Manin, "qui est un pastoureau / Sur tous les pastoureaus d'un visage très beau: / Gentil, leste, mignon" ["who is a shepherd boy, with fairness of visage above all shepherd boys: noble, handsome, and sweet"].[28] Montin greatly enjoys the beautiful love sonnet, and he adds a "little ode," an "odelette," addressed to him by the same Chrisophile, and that Firmot wants to hear as well: "Montre-là je te prie et tu m'obligeras / À faire une autre fois tout ce qu tu voudras" ["show it to me I pray and you will oblige me some other time to do anything you want"].[29] Montin obeys and reads a long ode ending with an invocation to love: "Rompon rompon le jour, / Et laisson à l'amour / Quelqueffois nos pensees ["Let us oh let us break the day and give our thoughts sometimes to love"].[30]

But this exchange of tales and commonplace poetry, which shows off Chrisophile's brilliance and his betrayals, does not provide enough subject matter for the *pastourelle*. More action is necessary, which is set in motion by a hint of jealousy. Not the jealousy that should have been sparked by Chrisophiles's unfaithfulness, since nothing seems to indicate that Chrisalde was in any way shocked by his lover's treacherous poems, but the jealousy felt by Chrisophile, who wants to protect Chrisalde from the culpable violence of an unnamed satyr. This feeling's only function is to kick-start the action, since it does not last more than two lines. It seems that, in this bucolic setting, the natural couple formed by Chrisophile and Chrisalde cannot really be subjected to the vagaries of the heart or the body. Their love does not depend on the conduct of the one who is drawn to everything that shines, or the potential infidelity of the other. In other words, there is no verisimilitude or amorous justification to be found in the intrusion of the satyrs. They simply invade a place of peace and loving harmony.

The Blood of Indecent Goats

The action therefore comes from outside, from the bloodthirsty and threatening part of the shepherds' world. It is just as mythological and traditional as the conversation that precedes it. Frontin and Montin are soon surrounded by misshapen sylvans (including Mélampe, the fiercest of cannibals), who threaten them and scare Firmot so much out of his wits that he scurries away like a "cocodrille."[31] Montin is outraged by the cowardice of his friend who, he recalls, used to show off a lot in front of younger shepherds. The brave shepherd then takes two slings out of his bag, exhorts Frontin to fight, and fully intends to stand his ground.

At this moment Chrisalde and Chrisophile appear with their dog, Louvet, so that the four shepherds can at last stand up to the "impudiques boucs" ["indecent goats"].[32] Chrisophile fights, but Chrisalde (who, as Montin says, gives "place et lieu à la melencolie" ["'way gives way entirely to melancholy"]), explains that Mélampe, Androgo, Toribo, and the other sylvans are jealous, that they "sans cesse nous moleste[nt]" ["keep harassing us"], and use foul means to try to put an end to their reciprocal love.[33] Montin wants to reassure him, declaring that, as long as he is not unfaithful, their love will conquer all, and Firmot tells melancholy Chrisalde to stand aside and wait. While Firmot, suddenly transformed into a fierce soldier, sounds the call to arms, Chrisophile, agreeing with the peasant shepherd's advice and fearing that his friend should fall prey to a lewd satyr, leaves for battle and delivers a vibrant farewell to his "petit œil" ["little eye"]:[34]

> Chrisalde en attendant que je sois en ce lieu
> Te presentant mon cueur je te prononce à Dieu,
> A dieu mon petit œil Pan veuille que la gloire
> D'un si juste combat nous donne la victoire:
> . . . .

Or je baize tes mains, à dieu ma chere vie
Ne verse de tes yeux ce deluge de pluie!
Rasseraine ton front ouvre moy ces dous ris
Aux liesses desquels heureus je me nourris.
Ne crains gentil berger, je croiy que la memoire
De tes perfections me donra la victoire . . .[35]

[Chrisalde while you wait for my return, I offer you my heart and give you my farewell. Farewell my little eye. May Pan be with us. May the glory of such a righteous war bring us victory. . . . Now I kiss your hands. Farewell dear life. Let not your eyes shed such a flood of rain drops! Smooth your brow, let laughter part these sweet lips on whose joy I feast so happily. Fear not, gentle shepherd. I believe that memory of your perfections will grant me victory.]

The fight then begins. Toribo, one of the satyrs, is felled and wounded by one of Firmot's big stones. Chrisophile kills the faun Mélampe, whose body is then tied to a chariot, to show villagers. The band of shepherds—including Rogé, who will be mentioned later—goes in pursuit of the rest of the fauns, and in particular of Elencho (Echo), who has run away. Firmot then goes back to Toribo. He wants to pluck his eyes "affin que les fillettes / Viennent se pourmener sans peur toutes seullettes" ["so that little girls may walk on their own without fear"], before skinning him: "Escorchons ce villain, et corroions sa peau / J'en veus dessus mon corps detailler un juppeau, / Pour resister au temps" ["let us skin the villain and tan his hide. I want to cut myself a small shepherd's pelt that will last a long time"].[36] Toribo begs for mercy and pity, but Firmot does not waver, until the ghost of Echo/Elencho appears and stuns them all.

In the course of a long embedded narration, the Ghost says that it had wanted to fight against the youth of shepherds, that it was killed by one stroke of Licastin's crook and is now wandering, full of remorse, in the underworld.[37] Expressing regrets for a golden age that it describes at length, and of which it says, just as extensively, that it has been replaced by a century of violence, war, and iniquity, it encourages shepherds to drop their weapons and temper their anger. Being a good commonplace ghost, it judiciously goes on to recall the past, regret its errors, both finding its place in the present and offering a glimpse of the future.[38] Stunned by this marvel, Firmot and Montin stop fighting and try to find Chrisophile, who got lost in the grassy country lanes. Now would be the time to go back to love and poetry:

CHRISOPHILE. Je me suis retrouvé, grace à Pan et à vous,
Et bien comment va il du combat de nos boucs?

FIRMOT.   Ce soir je t'en diray beaucoup d'estranges choses
               Cueille pour ton Chrisalde un chappelet de roses
               Il t'en saura bon gré.
CHRISOPHILE.   Je suis par trop lassé.
               Je ne peu sans douleur estre si peu baissé
               Quil ne me semble à voir que j'ay sur les espaules
               Ainsi que le bon Pan, tout le fardeau des Gaules.
MONTIN.   Chrisophile, tu scais souspirer de dous vers!
               . . . .
CHRISOPHILE.   Certes, je le feray . . .³⁹

[CHRISOPHILE. I am found again. Praise be to Pan and you. Now,
               how did the fight against our satyrs go?
FIRMOT.   Tonight I will tell you many a strange tale.
               Pluck for your Chrisalde a rosary of roses.
               He will thank you for it.
CHRISOPHILE.   I am far too tired.
               I cannot bend even a little without pain.
               Methinks I see on my shoulders not only our
               good Pan but all the burden of Gaul.
MONTIN.   Chrisophile, you know how to sigh sweet verse.
               . . . .
CHRISOPHILE.   Indeed I shall do so . . .]

A Mysterious Enigma

But, more urgent still than composing love verse, there are enigmas to deci-
pher.⁴⁰ This is the third part of the shepherds' world, caught between the bril-
liant world of bucolic idyll and the violent world of the fauns against whom the
shepherds have just fought. A new universe comes center stage, where meaning is uncertain, mysterious, and impossible to force open. Indeed, between
war and peace, somewhere on the way of his meanderings, the shepherd has
stumbled upon the deep mysteries of language. Chrisophile tells them that, as
he was trying to find his way, a blood-covered hand wrapped in mist gave him
a written message, and that a voice spoke the following words to him three
times: "Berger, Berger, Berger, les doits de ta main droite / Ne soient jamais
estraints par une bague estroite" ["Shepherd, shepherd, shepherd, may the fingers of your right hand never be clasped in a narrow ring"].⁴¹ As for the enigma,
Chrisophile shows the paper to all present and reads it aloud:

CHRISOPHILE.   AENIGME
               L'animal qui porte son toit,
               Voyant le temps chargé de pluye,

	Se retire où il aperçoit
	Que l'herbe ses humeurs essuye.
FIRMOT.	Que veut dire cecy?
CHRISOPHILE.	Ne disoi-je pas bien
	Que tu voyois trop court pour y cognoistre rien!
FIRMOT.	Considrons le reste, oy quelle estrange chose.
	MONTIN vien voir cecy quelque chose est enclose
	Sous ces figures cy, regarde ce Lyon
	Qui a le ventre ouvert et ce Chameleon
	Qui prent la couleur blanche encontre sa nature,
	Il y a quelque sens sous ceste couverture.[42]

[CHRISOPHILE.	Enigma.
	The roof carrying animal, when the sky is heavy
	with rain, retires to where he perceives
	where grass can wipe his humors.
FIRMOT.	What does this mean?
CHRISOPHILE.	Did I not tell you that you would be too shortsighted to understand any of it?
FIRMOT.	Let us look at the text, hark how strange this is.
	Montin, come here and look at this, this thing
	enclosed in these here figures. Look at this lion with
	his belly split, and this chameleon colored in white
	against its nature. There is meaning under this
	covering.]

Here our heroes are faced with three mysteries: an undecipherable commandment, a conventional enigma, and puzzling emblematic figures. How are they to understand what they mean? Perplexed, the shepherds decide to go and see Urchio, a ninety-year-old wizard, who, after describing his immense powers at length to the audience and invoking the relevant deities (Hecate and Venus), eventually receives Chrisophile and his companions. After hearing Chrisophile and taking both "le papier et toute la figure" ["the paper and the whole emblem"], Urchio asks to be left alone with demons and shadows and asks Chrisophile to come back on the morrow.[43] In the end, despite Chrisophile's impatience to know the answer, not to mention the reader's, who will never get to know the solution, the shepherds retrace their steps as the sun sets.

The French *Bergerie* and Its Laws

The homosexual idyll then regains its rights. The only remaining task is to find Chrisalde, who opportunely appears holding Rogé's hands. Chrisophile seems to find this mildly surprising ("où se sont il [*sic*] trouvez?" ["where have they found each other?"]),[44] but as we have seen, jealousy has no place in the natural world of peace. The end is at hand: Chrisalde asks the other shepherds to look after the sheep and prepare dinner so that he can lag behind with his companion ("Or allon donc mon cueur" ["So let us go my heart"]).[45]

CHRISALDE.	Di moy ores le tout.
CHRISOPHILE.	Attend je te supplie.
CHRISALDE.	Join toy proche de moy que ma levre s'allie
	Sur ton double corail pour suçger un baiser,
CHRISOPHILE.	Suivon nos compaignons, c'est trop nous amuser,
	Ce soir nous parlerons plus privement me semble
	Si l'opportunité et le temps nous assemble.
LE CUEUR DES BERGERS.	Il ne fault qu'on accuse
	Ceste nouvelle muse,
	De n'avoir observé
	Les loix de bergerie . . .[46]

[CHRISALDE.	So now tell me all of it.
CHRISOPHILE.	Wait, I beg you.
CHRISALDE.	Press yourself close to me, that my lips may join
	your twofold coral to smooch a kiss.
CHRISOPHILE.	Let us follow our companions. This is too much
	merrymaking. Methinks we shall tonight speak with
	more privacy if opportunity and time do us unite.
CHORUS OF SHEPHERDS.	Let no one accuse this new muse of not having
	followed the laws of *bergerie*.]

We leave our fair shepherds still waiting for an answer, in an all-male kissing scene. The night may reunite them and give them counsel. But what conclusion can be drawn? A new shepherd muse is born, and that it is more than able to follow the rules of the *bergerie*. It has all the commonplace features: the odes and the love sonnets, the conversations, the setting, jealousies and betrayals, fights against fauns, brave postures and melancholic withdrawals, wizards, enigmas, happy suspended ending, inconsistencies, and discontinuities. This new muse resembles the traditional pastoral play exactly, and in the 1587 dedication to Isabeau Babou, Fonteny states that he writes in the wake of Francesco Petrarch, Joachim du Bellay, Etienne Jodelle, and Philippe Desportes. There are only two exceptions. The first is that his play is not an Italian Tuscan *pastorelle*, but corresponds to the laws of French *bergerie*; the other is its all-male cast.

Heterosexual love was the main dramatic principle of Italian and Spanish pastoral drama, which had only recently been taken as models of the

French pastoral play. Here the pattern is deviated, completed, and replaced by French poetry and by the centrality of homosexual loves shown as positive and natural. What is more, it seems that when Fonteny puts only handsome men at the head of his bucolic theater, he provides legitimate new instances of ancient love (a Greek love in particular if we take into account the title, *L'eumorphopémie*), which was first described by Theocritus and Virgil, and relied on physical beauty on a backdrop of beautiful nature. France thus takes up an Italian model and liberates itself from it in three different ways: founding a new French genre, the *bergerie*, reclaiming an even stronger link with antiquity than the Tuscan pastoral play, and finally, representing homosexual love.

Fonteny depicts in his text and on stage an ideal community, both utopian and idyllic, where Gallic men are linked by love practices, aesthetic models, and fundamental moral and political values. The *bergerie* thus represents a homosexual civilization where beauty (the aesthetic dimension), goodness (ethic), and love [*eros*] meet in friendship [*amitié*] and harmony. This community is literally Neoplatonic, defined by intertwined love bonds [*entrelaces d'amour*]. There, natural and social harmony, driving out discord [*chassant le discord*], is realized both in peace (in a concord where jealousy has no place, in acts of love, poetry, and lyric songs) and in war (through collective resistance against the satyrs' violence). Interestingly, at the same time, England moves away from Italian models to establish its own genre: Edmund Spenser, in *The Shepheardes Calendar and Other Poems*, third eclogue, praises the love shared by young shepherds: "in this œglogue, two shepher's boys, taking occasion of the season, begin to make purpose of love, and other pleasance which to springtime is most agreeable."[47]

In this setting, all heroes have to face the quandaries of the world and of meaning. This is true both of the good singers, the two golden shepherds (Chrisophile and Chrisalde), but also of the storytelling churls, the two peasant-shepherds (Montin and Firmot).

At the top of the hierarchy, both active and passive shepherds, both the creative hero and the melancholic hero, each has his role. Fair Chrisophile acts, writes poems, is a tireless seducer, is both faithful and unfaithful, fights, meets "une brune nue" ["a dark cloud"] that gives him an enigma, and asks a sorcerer help him with an interpretation.[48] The fair Chrisalde is objectified: he remains in an entirely melancholic position, wanting Chrisophile to tell him the tale and almost stealing a kiss from him, for lack of anything better. Similarly, when Chrisophile stands out through his poetic, warlike, and amorous exploits, thus embodying Honoré d'Urfé's ideal of the aristocratic shepherd, Chrisalde braids laurel crowns for his lover in the fold and waits for the time when he will be able to kiss his coral-colored lips.[49]

The fair footmen-shepherds, Firmot and Montin, make garrulous comments and help at every stage in the process: they watch, converse, and sometimes even act as secondary characters in pastoral fashion. In doing so, they are above all part of the setting. They are commonplace shepherds, with their barking and gamboling dogs, always ready to tell peasants' anecdotes and rub their bread with bacon. But they too have had lovers, just as the splendid heroes (Montin himself might even have been loved by Chrisophile) and so fit easily in this male pastoral play. The two are difficult to tell apart. In the morning, Montin complains more and is more timorous, whereas Firmot is more magnanimous and brave, but at noon, the contrary is true. And, since they need to be given a touch of intertextual peasantry, in a reference to Virgil's *Eclogues*, they complain about the stinginess of the owner of their herds.

Foreign Blood and Uncertain Signs

What we have here are commonplace characters speaking with each other [*s'entreparlant*], in a canonical setting caught between the pacific world of bucolic nature and the violent mythological world apparently bordering it. Sometimes, realist streaks, often drawn from ancient texts, appear as in passing. But most of all, what Fonteny shows here is that an ideal is endangered. It is confronted with the invasion of a monstrous herd of lewd man-eating satyrs, in thrall to their brute destructive passions, who come to threaten peace. The issue now is to understand what they represent.

I suggested above that this herd points to a reverse side to this world, to an enemy erupting both from the inside and outside. First, the satyrs' names reveal a kind of violence that is at the same time brutal (Mélampe), cowardly (Toribo), and repetitive (Elencho/Echo), which may, under mythological disguise, refer to civil wars and the brutes who took part in them. Yet this violence also comes from the outside: Fonteny's satyrs are parodies of Italian ballets, Tuscan gardens, and both Neapolitan and Spanish masquerades. So much so that when Montin generously defends his country against foreign troops and particularly Spanish ones, the community in the name of which he fights is no longer a utopian Arcadia. In 1587, it is impossible not to see political references in the representing of a pacific, harmonious, and rural land, ravaged by bloody enemies and defended by good and handsome heroes. When we see that the *bergerie* bravely promotes itself as a representation of French aesthetics, breaking with its Italian and Spanish models, we come to understand that the play is defending not only France but also its literary identity. The French are good, sing well, and can also be great fighters, to the point where, like a new pair of Hercules, Montin and Firmot discard their shepherds' outfits and don a Herculean costume (with lion heads and hairy hides [toison pelue]). If some of them suffer from melancholia and wait, others, the greater number, fight back, defeat, and punish the enemy, and even give them the occasion to redeem themselves. Rogé makes the Faun disappear; Chrisophile, Montin, and eventually Firmot (who becomes firm again) are met by other shepherds who all want to preserve the harmony both of their own physical bodies and of the body politic. The inside and outside foreign elements are rejected and the hideous and bloodstained face of the world is (miraculously) abolished. In a word, the France of shepherds seems to be saved.

However, internal or external satyrs are not the only dangers threatening the Arcadia of fair shepherds. In this bergerie there are evils far more difficult to ward off, because they are at the very heart of this world. The figure of the faun, feverishly driven by his passions, is one embodiment of this evil, inasmuch as he is not only a personification of the foreign barbarian but also the inverted image of what a harmonious world could be. Other emblems of this inversion are the melancholic characters. Chrisalde is threatened, fearful, and complaining; infinitely attractive in his beautiful sadness; and all in all passive and despondent as he waits for his Chrisophile. The French bergerie might perhaps heal him, through a lover who will give him his dynamism and his energy, if opportunity and time unite them. Urchio the wizard, presented as a decipherer of all signs, great among magi, is in fact an unwashed old man. He is unable to act according to the desire that consumes him, eaten away by love-sickness, and incapable of solving the enigmas with which Chrisophile presents him. In the end, he even confesses in a monologue that he is the victim of morbid delirium. The shadow of Elencho/Echo, at the heart of the play, reveals the dark side of the bucolic landscape. He denounces the violence that has taken hold of Firmot and disappears in an abyss of nostalgic melancholia: "Où es tu aage d'or, ô beau siecle doré, / Siecle de nos ayeus sainctement adoré?" ["Where are you gone golden age, oh beautiful golden time, centuries of our revered ancestors?"].[50]

Worse still, as night falls, the signs cease to be legible: the fight against satyrs only leads to their disappearance, without any real victory or indication that things will be harmonious again, as they were before the battle. Chrisophile keeps his lover Chrisalde at a distance, none of the mysterious elements have been deciphered, and there can be legitimate doubts about

Urchio's ability to throw any light on the material the next morning. It is as if the "sanguine main" ["bloody hand"] emerging from the "brune nue" ["dark cloud"] has muddled meaning as well as unsettled Chrisophile, who as an accomplished poet should possess a good knowledge of signs.[51] On the contrary, the singer-poet-shepherd Chrisophile, unable to find a competent wizard to help him, falls in his turn in the throes of melancholy, hoping to die, and regretting ever having been born: "Il m'eut bien mieus valu au ventre de ma mere / Avorter que me voir reduict en la misere / Où je suis empiegé" ["It would have been better, in my mother's womb, to have been aborted than now live the misery in which I am trapped"].[52] Melancholy, which goes hand in hand with an inability to decipher the meaning of things and words, gets hold of everyone, including the spectators, themselves unable to interpret the signs and enigmas. As a result, hope of recovering a state of ideal harmony is all but lost.

This play thus proposes to the audience-reader both a situation and a story of suffering. At the beginning, this delightful rural morning could make the audience think that this charming, harmonious, homosexual order was timeless, but as early as noon the audience comes to doubt this harmony when violence disrupts this ideal world, followed by fever, delirium, failure to interpret the signs, and morbid depression. Spectators are then given the chance to witness what they really are in the actual world. The "case" of the spectator is once more defined as that of someone who, in 1587, sees every kind of crime on the stage or the scaffold in front of him and does nothing. The fiction confronts him with the same emotions as the ones he faced during real crimes of civil war: sadness, despondency, bewilderment, apathy, and doubt. In a way, the spectator is made to pay, in a kind of deceptive exchange, for the passivity with which he has endured (and suffered) troubles without doing anything, without understanding or wanting to understand anything. The melancholy spectator is the same person who once was a social spectator of the world's violence, who remained then and still is in a state of submissive affliction. He is at once Chrisalde, Chrisophile, Urchio, Firmot, and even the Ghost itself. He is fearful, afflicted, and passive; he has read, seen, and imagined all kind of things and horrors, all kinds of potential deliriums; he laments the disappearance of an ideal world that, for all he knows, might not even have existed before the troubles; and he is now incapable of solving the mystery of signs. The spectator then watches, thinks, and remembers, evoking memories of the recent chaos and actualizing them in his delirium, in order to fear again, and again to be unable to intervene. The melancholy spectator, summoned by the violence of the actions and the melancholy of the characters, now witnesses his own guilt.

Pink and Green Retreat

However, if sadness, despondency, and affliction are indeed contemporary responses to the disorders and to the inability to read the signs of the world, it seems that there are, both simultaneously and successively, other answers. They go beyond melancholy, and one could say that they present an escape from material humanity, from blood, black bile, and the feverish soul. What is left of the golden age, of harmony and the community of men, after all the disorder, all this melancholic killing game? There are the pleasures of love, the pleasures of art, a game, and ambiguous answers.

The pleasure of love is what Chrisalde asks for and what he takes, the pleasure of joining physically, of pressing his lips to the lips of Chrisophile, in spite of disorder and the opacity of words. The pleasure of art is that of reading and hearing varied dramatic poems, from the ode to the sonnet, from elegiac complaint to political discourse, from *sententiae* [brief moral sayings] to tales, as well as the pleasure of letting oneself follow the complex, layered structure of a new art: the French *bergerie*. The game is proposed by the enigma.

The fair shepherd is first Chrisophile, who writes and acts, who absolutely wants to understand the signs, to the point of falling into despair when he does not. Conversely, he could also be Chrisalde, who despite his fearful character accepts a universe in which meaning is lost, all the while taking into account that one still has to live and to love. The spectator, who is, as we have seen, alternately the one and the other, has a right to wonder who the fair shepherd is, and he has all the necessary cards to follow and to play an open game, knowing that he can examine all possibilities and find all the answers that suit him, since none is validated by the text. He will be able to refuse the limiting ring of meaning, of the univocal, and practice heterodoxy, heteronomy, heterogeneity, open diversity. Neither totally red nor entirely black, he will have the leisure to become one with the green grove, interact with it, and play with all its meanings. The game will not leave any trace since the reader/spectator does not appear in print or on stage, and as a good chameleon, he becomes one with the whiteness of the page.

Another solution to the enigmas could be to consider that the new shepherd muse points out to the fair homosexual shepherd that no *dextrarum conjunctio* [wedding, in Roman law], no union with the church (a ring on the right hand symbolizes a mystical union with Christ), no narrow ring, and thus no constraint, no wedding of any kind should mar his life ("Berger, Berger, Berger, les doigts de ta main droite / Ne soient jamais étreints par une bague étroite" ["Shepherd, shepherd, shepherd, may the fingers of your right hand never be clasped in a narrow ring"]).[53] The shepherd would thus have to remain infinitely free, both in his thinking and in his conduct in life. We then see that the snail leaves—this sexually curious animal who carries his own roof—when he sees that the rain is about to fall and that his saliva marks the grass. In other words, snails, tortoises, and men (and a fortiori homosexual men) have to know how to retreat into their shells if they become too visible, not to show too much of themselves, and to retreat when they do not want to be noticed. In this world, proud lions end with their bellies open, whereas prudent and calculating chameleons, knowing how to disguise themselves for their own good, can, when they go against nature, take the color of absolute neutrality. This series of enigmas would thus hide and reveal a hidden, private, homosexual way of life, strategically avoiding danger. Consequently, the whole of this new *bergerie* could read like an illustration of the homosexual dissimulation in the outside world, a representation of what homosexuality would be in a pastoral ideal, and a figuration both of the obstacles surrounding it (hostile satyrs) and of the evils inherent to it (the threat of melancholy). This makes of L'*eumorphopémie* a *bergerie* of a new kind, French and original. It pronounces itself in many different ways, both clearly and indirectly, explicitly or not, for beauty as it is represented, and in favor of the beauty of men and their reciprocal love.

These are only hypotheses whose purpose is to play with what Fonteny proposes: a complex enigma that others than myself will have the pleasure and the competence to explore in depth.[54] In any case, the game is there, and it states plainly that the quest for meaning is arduous, rendered even more so by the details of the enigmas included in the text, as well as by the overall dramatic structure itself. However, even if one does not come to understand all the nuances that Fonteny has built in his text, it seems possible to recapitulate the whole play through the colors running through it.

The pastoral world of this new *bergerie* is battled by vermilion violence, that of blood, and by black melancholy. It is caught between the necessary war of the world as it is—with its array of references to contemporary civil wars—and the many marks of submissive affliction, delirium, feverish action, and the inability to hold one's place in the world and to understand its signs. Fonteny includes the reader-spectator in this black and red process, but it remains true that in the green grove, men, that is to say males, can love each other without sin, and play.

There, perhaps, for one moment in this ideal retreat, freedom appears. It bears the marks of its time, of all its red and black components, but it is freedom still, reversing the heterosexual code of traditional pastoral drama. Fonteny takes his ancient sources literally, be they Theocritus or Virgil, and proposes an alternative imaginary world, surprising, without rules, parodic at times, often idyllic, encouraging one to think that it is possible for two men (characters and actors) to exchange a kiss in public without shocking the audience. This *bergerie*, which underwent three editions, is thus more than an exception. It is in all respects a proposition made to the spectator, a way of surprising, intriguing, and seducing him and setting his mind to work, bringing him to think what is conventionally beyond the confines of representation, letting him suppose that another order can be glimpsed, experienced even, and that it is both historically and literarily legitimate to perform it. Somewhere between the horrors of warring satyrs, the old sorcerer's frantic delirium, and the affliction of one utterly in despair, there would thus be room for another position, that of a friendship binding men morally, physically, and sexually; room for physical and aesthetic pleasure, for the games of the mind, the heart, and the loins.

But one must act quickly: time is so fragile, the world is so threatening, so much that one must hide, preserve oneself, and be sure not to leave any trace behind when it rains. The fair shepherds will not wait for the morrow, nor for the likely raving answer of the powerless old wizard. They might, just might, trust chance, opportunity, and time to meet in private. They have played with enigmas and forgotten them. They will strive to overcome the endless deceptive quest for meaning and find happiness, within the spectacle itself, by kissing coral-colored lips.

With all the freedom that this theater gives him, the *beau berger* may be truly able to enter the *bocage amoureux*, the grove of love.

Notes

1. This chapter is a modified translation by Cécile Dudouyt of an essay that originally appeared in French in a festschrift for Madeleine Alcover, titled "Le Rouge et le noir, le rose et le vert, ou la pastorale homosexuelle de Jacques de Fonteny (1587)," in *Dissidents, excentriques et marginaux de l'Age classique: Autour de Cyrano de Bergerac*, ed. Patricia Harry, Alain Mothu, and Philippe Sellier (Paris: Honoré Champion, 2006), 265–88. All translations are Dudouyt's unless otherwise noted.

2. Fonteny's pastoral play was printed in *La première partie des ébats poétiques de Jacques de Fonteny contenant une pastorelle du beau pasteur, églogues, amours, sonets spirituels et autres poésies* (Mont Saint Hilaire: Guillaume Linocier, 1587). Citations refer to page numbers from this edition.

In the early 1600s, Jacques de Fonteny would become an important figure in Parisian theater landscape. A member of the Confrérie de la Passion [Confraternity of the Passion], he became the financial auditor at the Hôtel de Bourgogne, the owner of a theater box that he could rent for his own profit, and a tragic playwright. *Cléo-*

phon, one of his tragedies, was written in 1600 (Paris: F. Jacquin). A modern edition exists in *Théâtre de la cruauté et récits sanglants en France (XVIe–XVIIe siècle)*, ed. Christian Biet et al. (Paris: Robert Laffont, 2006).

3. *Galathée divinement délivrée* [*Galathea Divinely Freed*], inspired by an episode from Tasso's *L'Aminta* (translated in 1593), is also attributed to Fonteny.

4. He also used Greek onomastics in the tragedy *Cléophon*.

5. (Paris: Jean Corrozet, 1615 and 1624).

6. The terms "homosexual" and "gay" are certainly problematic when discussing the early modern period, especially since some critics would argue that the terms are anachronistic and, following Foucault, that the modern concept of "homosexuality" did not come into existence until the nineteenth century. Still, I have chosen to employ these terms to designate the ambivalently erotic(ized) relationship between the male characters in Fonteny's pastoral. For more on the debates surrounding "queer" studies and the Renaissance, see, just to cite a few examples, Jonathan Goldberg, ed., *Queering the Renaissance* (Durham, NC: Duke University Press, 1994); Carla Freccero and Louise Fradenburg, eds., *Premodern Sexualities* (New York: Routledge, 1996); and David Halperin, *How to Do the History of Homosexuality* (Chicago: University of Chicago Press, 2002; repr. 2004). For the French context specifically, see Gary Ferguson, *Queer (Re)Readings in the Renaissance* (Aldershot, UK: Ashgate, 2008); Carla Freccero, *Queer/Early/Modern* (Durham, NC: Duke University Press, 2006); and Guy Poirier, *L'homosexualité dans l'imaginaire de la Renaissance* (Paris: Honoré Champion, 1996).

7. Marc Fumaroli, *La diplomatie de l'esprit* (Paris: Hermann, 1994).

8. Patrick Dandrey, *Les tréteaux de Saturne* (Paris: Klincksieck, 2003).

9. According to Fumaroli, the seventeenth century would then have had the duty to heal melancholia, to the point of eradicating, weakening, or changing it into a something else that would be classicism. But it would rather seem that melancholia strenuously adapted and transformed itself in tune with new aesthetic and discursive forms corresponding to as many social and aesthetic positions.

10. As demonstrated by Laurence Giavarini in "Représentation pastorale et guérison mélancolique au tournant de la Renaissance: questions de poétique," *Études Épistémè* 3 (2003): 1–27.

11. Lebègue seems to deplore the fact that this play contradicts the rule that French theater is reluctant to put on stage "les amours contre nature: l'homosexualité n'apparut pas sur notre théâtre; on ne peut citer que la pastorale du *Beau Pasteur*, où J. de Fonteny a exprimé l'amitié d'une façon équivoque" ["unnatural loves: homosexuality has had no place on our stages, one can only quote the pastoral of *The Fair Shepherd*, in which J. De Fonteny has shown friendship in an equivocal way"]. Raymond Lebègue, *Études sur le théâtre français* (Paris: Nizet, 1977), 1:356. H. C. Lancaster, *A History of French Dramatic Literature in the Seventeenth Century* (Baltimore, MD; Paris: Johns Hopkins University Press; Presses Universitaires de France, 1929–1942), pt. 3:793.

12. Stephen Guy-Bray, *Homoerotic Space: The Poetics of Loss in Renaissance Literature* (Toronto: University of Toronto Press, 2002); and Bruce R. Smith, *Homosexual*

Desire in Shakespeare's England: A Cultural Poetics (Chicago: University of Chicago Press, 1991; repr. 1994), esp. ch. 3 ("The Passionate Shepherd") and ch. 4 ("The Shipwrecked Youth").

13. Fonteny, *Le beau berger*, 7r.

14. We know through his friend Pierre de l'Estoile that Fonteny himself limped. Quoted in Lachèvre, *Les recueils collectifs de poésies libres et satiriques publiés depuis 1600 jusqu'à la mort de Théophile (1626)* (Paris: Champion, 1914), 212–13. I am grateful to Cécile Petit for pointing this out to me.

15. Fonteny, *Le beau berger*, 7v.

16. Ibid., 8v.

17. Ibid., 9r.

18. Ibid.

19. Ibid., 9v.

20. Ibid.

21. Ibid., 10r.

22. Ibid., 10v.

23. Ibid., 11v.

24. Ibid. These two lines are introduced with backward *guillemets*, which, in the typography of the early seventeenth century, indicates commonplace expressions, proverbs, and the like. On the term *incarnat*: Randle Cotgrave defines it as "carnation; and more particularly, light or pale carnation; flesh-coloured, or the colour of our damaske Rose" A *Distionarie of the French and English Tongues.* (London: Adam Islip, 1611), entry "incarnat."

25. Fonteny, *Le beau berger*, 11v.

26. Ibid.

27. Ibid., 12v.

28. Ibid., 13r.

29. Ibid., 13v.

30. Ibid., 15r.

31. Ibid., 16r.

32. Ibid., 16v.

33. Ibid., 17v.

34. One should point out that the eye [*œil*] and the carnation (*œillet*, which sounds in French like an affectionate diminutive name for eye) often find their way into these declarations. These could very well be a conventional ways of referring to anal sexuality.

35. Ibid., 18v.

36. Ibid., 21v.

37. Ibid., 23r.

38. Ibid., 23r.–25v.

39. Ibid., 26r.

40. Incidentally, according to his friend Pierre de L'Estoile, Fonteny loved this genre. See Lachèvre, *Les recueils collectifs*, 212–13.

41. Fonteny, *Le beau berger*, 26v.

42. Ibid., 27r.

43. Ibid., 27v.–33r.

44. Ibid., 33v.

45. Ibid., 34r.

46. Ibid., 34r.–34v.

47. Edmund Spenser, *The Shepherd's Calendar and Other Poems*, ed. Philip Henderson (London: Everyman's Library, 1965), 26. I am grateful to Cécile Petit for pointing this out to me.

48. Fonteny, *Le beau berger*, 26r.

49. Ibid., 34v.

50. Ibid., 23v.

51. Ibid., 26r.

52. Ibid., 32v.

53. Ibid., 26v.

54. In a seminar held at Paris Ouest-Nanterre-La Défense, Fabien Cavaillé proposed another, more politically oriented, solution by reading the disemboweled lion as a reference to Henri III's famous dream (told by Pierre de l'Estoile), in which the last Valois king saw himself surrounded by wild beasts, heralding his death. The paradoxical whiteness of the courtier-chameleon (the pure white garb symbolizing the courtier's hypocrisy) could designate the Guise family (in 1587, white was the rallying color of the *Archi-Congrégation* founded by Henri III, but really owned by the Leaguers, and the Guise in particular), so that one could see represented in these two emblems (the slaughtered lion and the white chameleon) an expression of the Guise threat against the crown. In this interpretation, refusing to wear a narrow ring on the right hand means refusing the restraining mystical alliance and so any kind of alliance with the League. Ideally one should imitate the tortoise and go back under one's roof deep into one's French countryside, the land of one's fathers (the tortoise being the emblem of the patriot), without alliances with foreign forces (such as the papacy and Spain, with which the Guise have made a pact). All these well-meaning pointers toward moderation would thus be sent to a Chrisophile who resembles Henri III quite well, since he is a handsome and brave leader (shepherd), and he practices a princely homosexuality with nothing to degrade him. This interpretation of the enigmas makes them a sequence of coded advice for a king of France caught in civil wars, who hesitates, remains passive and even melancholic, and does not know how to read the signs anymore.

CHAPTER TWELVE

⌒

Stage Designs of Cruelty

Theater in Rouen at the Turn of the Seventeenth Century

Sybile Chevallier-Micki

Criticism has long thought that the supposed irregularity, licentiousness, or "baroqueness" of French plays printed at the turn of the seventeenth century made them unperformable.[1] However, in order to outline the effectiveness of the stage designs of the Rouen stage and their significance for spectators who attended the performances of these plays, we must challenge this long-standing critical commonplace.

While information on the modalities of dramatic performance in France during Henri IV's and the beginning of Louis XIII's reigns (ca. 1589–1625)—an overwhelming majority of which exist in the provincial repertoires—has been limited to the drawings and annotations contained in Laurent Mahelot's Mémoire and the decorators at Paris's Hôtel de Bourgogne, the data are patchy on theatrical life in the provinces.[2] Still, after reading the forty-five tragedies that make up the Rouen corpus, we begin to notice patterns of stage settings that were regularly reused by numerous local playwrights who had their works performed in the Norman capital. Out of these forty-five plays, thirty-one stand out thanks to their use of stage directions and scenographic indications that allow us to expound upon the Rouen stage designs. Furthermore, these indications are often identical; in turn, I suggest that we think about the meanings and implications that their systematic usages have for the establishment of a collective memory for the playwrights, players, and spectators.

Among these set designs, I have chosen two of the most significant and the most common: first, the curtain or door that hides a private space and then reveals this space to the audience after a crime of some sort has been committed; and second, the elevated stage, either a fixed structure above the main stage or a temporary structure such as a scaffold, brought on and off the stage as needed. By examining just a few samples of the toponymy of theatrical space, we can attempt to reconstruct the Norman stage and propose connections between the spectators' and authors' memories of the time, still very regular attendees of the performances of mystery plays in the first few decades of the seventeenth century.[3] To begin to reflect more widely on the stage designs of performed works across the French-speaking territories, I compare various scenographic elements, information we have on medieval performance in Normandy, and Mahelot's designs from the *Mémoire*, in order to consider a common fertile ground of memory and symbols that a door, a room, a castle, or a scaffold might represent, all of which are recurring elements in the play texts, when they are used on the stage and when they are performed.

Rouen: A Center of Professional Theater

Modern theater—that is to say a theater that no longer relies solely on medieval craftsmanship—was taking place in Normandy well before Pierre Corneille's birth (Rouen, 1606), and this theater continued to develop during Corneille's adolescence. Several findings in the archives and rare anecdotes allow for such a supposition. First, as early as 1530, the Saint-Antoine *jeu de paume*,[4] in Sotteville, was used for the performance of a *Vie* [*Life*] of Judas.[5] In 1556, we find in the city a player named Le Pardonneur and his troupe, whose members all resided in Rouen ["demeurant en cette ville de Rouen"].[6] The troupe leader, after requesting authorization from the *parlement* to play within the walls of the city, set up in the Port du Salut *jeu de paume*. If the actors in Rouen wanted to establish their troupe in a closed space, it seems that there was a demand in the city for this type of entertainment, and above all that a professionalization of actors was possible. And since the actors settled into a closed space, the entrance to which would be charged for, entrance fees would have been more easily and effectively collected.[7]

Second, at the turn of the seventeenth century, François le Métel de Boisrobert related a comical anecdote to Gédéon Tallemant des Réaux about a performance in Rouen; the latter recorded it with delight to reveal the archaism of provincial theater:

Il [Boisrobert] raconte que de ce temps-là on s'avisa de jouer dans un quartier de Rouen une tragédie de *La mort d'Abel*. Une femme vint prier que son fils en fût, et qu'elle fournirait ce qu'on voudrait. Tous les personnages étaient donnés, cependant les offres étaient grandes; on s'avisa de lui donner le personnage du sang d'Abel. On le mit dans un porte-manteau de satin rouge cramoisi, on le roulait de derrière le théâtre, et il criait: *Vengeance, vengeance*.[8]

[Boisrobert says that during that time it was decided to play a tragedy titled *The Death of Abel* in a neighborhood in Rouen. A lady came to pray that her son be a part of it, and that she would provide whatever was wanted. All the roles were distributed, but the offers were not great; it was decided to give him the character of Abel's blood. He was put in a cloak bag made of crimson-colored satin, he was rolled around in the back of the stage, and he cried out "Revenge, revenge."]

Boisrobert was born in 1592 and left Rouen for Paris in 1622: we can trust his recollections and his Parisian habits. A play—at least one—was thus played in his place of residence while he was a young man. This anecdote inevitably evokes the play by Thomas le Coq, vicar of Falaise: *Tragedie représentant l'odieus et sanglant meurtre commis par le maudit Cain* (1580) [*Tragedy Depicting the Odious and Bloody Murder Committed by the Wretched Cain*]. The play, a work of a Norman, was still being performed in Rouen at the turn of the seventeenth century, which was the most fertile period for Norman tragedy that I am discussing here.[9]

Moreover, many dramatic works from this time were printed in Rouen, the capital of Normandy.[10] The editorial importance of Rouen at the turn of the seventeenth century thus leads us to believe that it was also a place where these plays, poets, and actors circulated. The fact that these plays were printed might mean that they were successful on stage and that, again, a demand for this type of product—both commercial and literary—existed at the time, which the printers knew how to exploit.

Finally, and above all, the predominance of tragedies is significant. These plays, moreover, which derived from what we might call a "theater of cruelty," generally display scenes of exacerbated violence; indeed, they show torture, murders, rapes, battles, falls, famines, and so forth, on stage. At the end of the religious wars, after the most violent and bloodiest conflicts that France had ever known, and all the more shocking since they were fratricidal, this was post-catastrophic theater for the dramatists and their audiences. What other form than tragedy, a *form-genre*, allows for a questioning, by transposition, of the misfortunes still fresh in the minds of authors, readers, and spectators? I attempt to answer this question in this chapter by examining two scenographic elements: first the tent, then the elevated stage.

The Tent, or the Technique of the Curtain

In her essay "Logis, portes et fenêtres" ["Houses, Doors, and Windows"], Anne Surgers proposes a "lecture du langage silencieux des images de mémoire" ["a reading of the silent language of images of memory"].[11] She focuses on emblems and their meanings in fashion until the last third of the seventeenth century, contending that the door represented in images is a motif for the emblem of love—physical as well as spiritual and divine love. On stage, the house, and more particularly its openings such as the door and the window, highlights the symbolism of love: in comedy, earthly; in tragedy, divine. The door or window frames, whether open or closed, make up the symbolic barrier to be surmounted to enter into the house and obtain the favors of the (female) lover, but are also the sign of divine accession.

The door, a dominant element of Rouen dramatic action, is present in a few texts, but it seems to have the particularity of belonging to a principal element that I call the tent, by assimilation with the Greek term *skèné* or *tabernacle*. In our case, it is a house of vice where a saint may be brought to be dishonored, but where a vengeful angel appears; this is the case in Pierre Troterel's *Tragédie de sainte Agnès*.[12] It is also the door to a room, where sits a bed, which seems to be, perhaps, a canopy that can be moved to reveal or mask a particular action, as in Nicolas Chrestien's *Rosemonde*.[13] Finally, it can be a structure that includes one or more private tents of a nomad population, where the closing of the door is recounted while its opening is performed in front of the spectators, to cast scorn more effectively on the raped and henceforth loathed woman; this is the case in Chrestien's *Amnon et Thamar*.[14]

By examining these three examples, I underscore the scenographic particularity of the "tent," whose doors open or close—lift up? or are pulled back?—to place the spectator, subjected to a spectacle of besmirched honor, in the position of witness, then of judge.

In *Sainte Agnès*, most spectators probably knew the story of the saint and knew that in the room, where armed men and prostitutes have brought Agnès, the Roman governor's son Martian would try to rape her, and Agnès's guardian angel would strike him down. In Troterel's adaptation of the legend, outside the tent, while this action is taking place inside the brothel, the men who are waiting for their turn to rape the saint bawdily comment on what they think is going on inside the structure.[15] It is unclear which action is hidden from view, for in any earlier scene we do see Agnès who, "enfermée seule au cabinet, se met à genoux et prie Dieu" ["locked up alone in her chamber, prays on her knees to God"].[16] Whatever the case, we observe three distinct spaces in the rape scene: Martian's attempted rape occurs "dedans un cabinet" ["within a small chamber"],[17] which is located inside another edifice, where the *Trompette* (the character who leads Agnès to the brothel) "frappe à la porte du bordeau" ["knocks on the brothel door"] to enter.[18] When Agnès first arrives at the brothel, the *Maquerelles* [prostitutes] welcome her and the *Trompette*:

> Entrez entrez monsieur, *voila la porte ouverte,*
> . . . .
> Entrez mignonne entrez en ce lieu de delice.
> . . . .
> Nous vous allons mener *dedans un cabinet,*
> Lequel est fort gentil, bien agreable et net,
> Il est fort bien meublé *de lict, et de couchette,*
> L'on vous y monstrera, comme vous fustes faitte.[19]

> [Come, come in, Monsieur, *the door is open,* . . . Come in, my sweet, come in this place of delight. . . . We will bring you *inside a chamber,* which is very nice, pleasant, and clean.
> It is very well furnished *with a bed and a little couch.* There, you'll see how you were made.]

We see here, clearly designated, a front door, made out of fabric or wood, which opens to show the decorated chamber where Agnès is taken. This same door closes and later reopens to let the rapist in the room, then to reveal Martian's inert body. When Simphronie learns of his son's (temporary) death—for Martian will be resuscitated by Agnès—he declares, "Mais ne retardons plus, *allons à la demeure,* / Où gist ce pauvre corps, pour le faire emporter" ["But let us not waste any more time, let us *go to the dwelling,* where this poor body lies, to take it back with us"], to which Censorin, Martian's confidant, replies, "*La porte est bien fermée* il nous la faut *heurter,* / Ho, ho, du premier coup elle s'est décroüillée" ["*The door is closed firmly,* we must *break it down.* Ho, ho, it has opened on the first attempt"].[20]

In *Rosemonde,* the eponymous heroine uses the same device when, helped by her companion Barcée, she tricks Barcée's lover Pérédée to force him to participate in the conspiracy against her husband, King Albouin. Barcée sets up a romantic rendezvous with Pérédée in the royal bedchamber to have "tout loisir de passer [leur] tems / Dedans [l'] antichambre [de Rosemonde], et [se] rendre contens" ["all the time in the world in Rosemonde's anteroom to make each other happy"].[21] Rosemonde takes Barcée's place in this love scene, performed offstage, for which a closed bedchamber is used, and the actors play with the darkness generated by the closed curtains. Barcée: "Je veux à ton vouloir aussi tost satisfaire. / Premier de cette place il nous convient distraire, / Et nous mettre en un lieu de tout bruit écarté / Qui soit durant ce tems veuf de toute clarté" ["I want to satisfy your desire straightaway. First from this place we must withdraw, and put ourselves in a place far from any noise that will be during this time void of all light"].[22] Pérédée is tricked into sleeping with Rosemonde, after which Rosemonde insults the confused lover: "Que tu ayes honni de mon mari la couche / Et de sales baisers méme polu ma bouche?" ["That you have held my husband's bed in contempt and with sluttish kisses even tainted my lips?"].[23]

After the hidden adultery, the bedroom is used for Albouin's assassination in the same act, yet this time the nuptial bed is shown in plain sight. The plan is hatched, and the conspirators attack Albouin while he is sleeping in his bed:

ALMACHIE.	Où est-il?
PEREDEE.	Que fait-il?
ROSEMONDE.	Dessus son lict il dort.

> . . . .
> Ayant *ouvert la porte*
> J'ay tout fait retirer
> . . . .

ALBOUIN.   Ce sont là de tes traits, ô louve d'Arcardie![24]

[ALAMCHIE.   Where is he?
PEREDEE.   What is he doing?
ROSEMONDE.   *In his bed* he is sleeping.

. . . .
Having *opened the door*
I've had everyone withdraw from the room.
. . . .

ALBOUIN.   So these are your tricks, you Arcadian whore!]

If the adultery is hidden, the murder that occurs in the same place is performed onstage. The assassins open the door to enter the room; the nuptial bed loses its private character and it has been opened, now, for the spectators to see.

The third and final example of a rape scene, still not shown on stage, takes place in another tragedy by Chrestien, titled *Amnon et Thamar*. In this play, the author stages a well-known biblical episode about the passion of David's eldest son Amnon for his half-sister Thamar, which leads him to rape her.

David sends Thamar to Amnon's house to nurse him in his supposed illness, which allows for Thamar to express a good dose of tragic irony, referring to her helping Amnon as a "charitable ouvrage" ["charitable work"].[25] While the rape takes place between acts 3 and 4, the fourth act opens with the Amnon's repudiation of Thamar and, scenographically, by the revelation of the crime scene. Amnon:

Oste toy, *sors d'ici*, puisque j'ay fait de toy,
Je ne veux plus te voir gisante aupres de moy,
Retire toy d'ici malheureuse insensee,
Apres avoir jouy, mon amour est passee
. . . .
Jonatas *ferme l'huis*, et laisse lamenter,
Cette folle qui vient mon repos agiter.[26]

[Get you hence, *leave this place*, since I have had you, I no longer want to see you lying next to me. Withdraw yourself from here, you raging wretch. After having possessed you, my love has vanished. . . . Jonatas, *close the door*, and let that madwoman weep who has disturbed my rest.]

A few scenes later, Absalon orders the death of his older brother Amnon, but this scene takes place at Absalon's residence, not Amnon's. Yet the similarity of the sojourns of this nomad people allows for an identical space that is nominally designated as Absalon's dwelling. Further, Chrestien carefully describes the space for the assassination, which takes place on stage, in Absalon's *house*, where he invites his brothers to eat:

ABSALON.	. . . Je le tiens, il est pris, le Traistre, le Perfide,
	. . . .
	Si l'on dit qu'Amnon sçeut Absalon outrager,
	On dira qu'Absalon sçeut d'Amnon se vanger
	. . . .
	Voicy qu'il est chez moi attendant un festin,
	. . . .
	Je m'en vais achever plein de sang, de courage;
	De haine, et de fureur, mon hazardeux ouvrage.
AMNON.	Hola, et qui vous fait contre la sainte Foy
	Ô Traistres, massacrer un fils aisné de Roi?
ABASLON.	Tuez, tuez, Soldats, et n'ayez point de doute,
	» Car l'Ennemy tué jamais on ne redoute.
AMNON.	*Je meurs*, et Dieu le void, mais son bras juste et fort
	Vengera quelque jour mon inhumaine mort.[27]

[ABSALON.   I've got him, he is caught, the perfidious traitor. . . .
                          If it was said that Amnon knew how to wrong Absalon,
                          it will be said that Absalon knew how to get revenge on
                          Amnon. . . . *Here he is at my house*, waiting for a feast,
                          . . . I'm going to carry out my risky enterprise, full of
                          blood, courage, hatred, and fury.

AMNON.   Hoe there, and who has made you, against sacred law, o
                          traitors, massacre a king's eldest son?

ABSALON.   Kill, kill, soldiers, and have no doubt, for one never fears
                          a killed enemy.

AMNON.   *I am dying*, and God sees it, but his just and mighty arm
                          will avenge one day my inhuman and cruel death.]

Absalon enters his house and offers to the spectators, by opening the door or by lifting the curtain, the spectacle of his brother's death. But the details concerning the stage setting of this place are contained within the text, when Éthay tells David about the circumstances of the death of his eldest son. Éthay:

Vos fils s'en vont alors avecques Absalon,

. . . .

Les meine *en son logis*, et d'un visage affable,
Qui deçoit tout défi, leur présente sa Table,
Le lieu pour la porter d'Absalon destiné,
De feuillages tortus estoit environné,
Qui paroissoient cousus sur la Tapisserie,
Qui cache le derriere à la veuë esjouye.

. . . .

Absalon avoit lors aux siens donné le Signe,

. . . .

Aux siens cachez és coins du *Palais tapissé,*
Où pour tuer Amnon le festin est dressé.[28]

[Your sons thus go with Absalon, . . . (who) takes them into his house, and with a friendly countenance, which beguiled all hostile defiance, presented his table to them. The place where Absalom intended to take it [the table] was surrounded with winding foliage, which appeared sewn onto a tapestry that hides the back side from the gleeful eye. . . . Absalon then gave the sign to his men . . . hidden in the corners of the palace furnished with tapestries, where to kill Amnon the banquet table was dressed.]

If the palace was furnished with tapestries, then either a tent was the frame reference for this place, or Chrestien was so used to Rouen's theater decors of his time that he was writing for these spaces, which he knew to be framed, painted backdrops. For the first hypothesis, the realism of the scenic space is shown: the palaces represented are *tapissés* [furnished with tapestries] and decorated, like the dwellings of David's people, and opening them suggests that the curtains were lifted, or pulled, to unveil the interior where the crime scenes were played out. But if Amnon's murder was perpetrated on stage, in a similar décor to the one in which he raped his sister, then it is because the first crime opened up and disclosed the place where it was committed.

By gesturing toward the principle of Norman law according to which anyone can go to court [*ester en justice*], witness, and call for the overlord's judgment, the staging of the crime confronts the spectators not only with the act itself, but also with the memory of things that they had seen perpetrated during the Wars of Religion, which were extremely violent in Rouen.[29] The authors place their spectators in the position of witness, and, because they know the principles of this theater design, in the role of inactive and nearly benevolent accomplice of the crime(s) committed. The authors remind the spectators of their role as witness, but also perhaps that of criminal or victim of the past abuse, all the while offering them a spectacle that provides them with (guilty) pleasure.

The Elevated Stage

Several texts highlight the mechanism of the raised stage, which intimates that an action was played above the main stage. Not only did actors play on top of the fortifications, but they also moved in front of them, and the stage setting is thus designed like a palace. This practice punctuates the texts many times, and we can find it in the illustrations and the frontispieces of works, notably the well-known ones from the *Tragédie française d'un more cruel* [*French Tragedy of a Cruel Moor*],[30] though we must be cautious when studying this type of image, for we cannot know for sure how realistic these engravings are.[31]

Nonetheless, before delving into these texts to examine the use of these scenographic, isolated, juxtaposed, and layered spaces, we should first question what might have been the very site where these elevated scenes were performed. It is in relation to this space, in turn, that the sets *below* can be envisaged and, in most of the works, described and used in relation to the structure *above*. Indeed, superposition and verticality would become the trademarks of early seventeenth-century theater in Rouen, and it is this aspect of its scenography to which we now turn.

In two studies from 1954 and 1968 on the functioning and the staging practices of the Hôtel de Bourgogne and the Théâtre du Marais,[32] S. Wilma

Deierkauf-Holsboer established that the contracts drawn up in 1644 for the Marais between Mondory's troupe and the carpenters clearly indicate the order and construction of "another *theater*" ["autre *théâtre*"] situated above the *théâtre* [the stage].[33] These findings have led recent historians of performance to consider this space as one for performance, reserved for elevated scenes, such as divine interventions. I attempt to support this thesis in the context of the Rouen stage, *pace* Anne Surgers, who refutes, in a 2007 essay, many of these claims.

Using two sources—a signed lease from 1631 between Lenoir's troupe and Mondory containing the adjustment of a *jeu de paume* and an order contract to a carpenter titled the *Mémoire de ce qu'il faut faire au jeu de paume des Marais* [Memorandum of What Needs to Be Done in the "Jeu de Paume" of the Marais], written for the reconstruction of this site in 1644[34]—Surgers suggests that this *théâtre* on top probably existed as a technical railing and walkway rather than a space for acting. The 1631 text indeed specifies that "sera fait au-dessus du ciel dudit théâtre un petit plancher de la grandeur dudit théâtre, de bon bois, pour servir à faire descendre les machines" ["above the said theater will be made a small floor, made of solid wood, which will serve to lower and raise the machines"]. The 1644 *Memorandum* evokes the construction of a staircase "pour monter depuis les fonds des deux théâtres jusqu'au haut" ["to climb from the bottom of the two theaters to the top"], as well as a second small staircase allowing for access underneath the "premier théâtre" ["main stage"]. Surgers maintains that this smaller staircase allowed for access from one floor to another and facilitated the moving around of stagehands in between the different levels of the theater structure.

Surgers also reminds us that the baroque spectator's vision is not a fixed one, but rather is led by the performativity of theatrical speech. The spectator places herself from the point of view of the character who is speaking, thus from the actor's viewpoint, and her vision is guided by the spoken word.[35] Since speech is performative, the evocation of the action that one is carrying out—climbing or entering a window, for instance—would suffice to abolish the necessity to represent it on stage.

But if, indeed, *speaking* avoids *doing*, we can argue *a contrario* the dual purpose of action and of performative speech, which would direct the spectator's gaze to what will happen. This would make the action all the more significant if it were performed, because it would be perceived twice, and the audience's attention would be directed toward it.

The elevated set's significance is double. First, it highlights, in the case of *Les amours de Dalcméon et de Flore* by Étienne Bellone (1610), *Guillaumde d'Aquitaine* by Pierre Troterel (printed 1632), and *La Rhodienne* by Pierre

Mainfray (1621), the paraclausithyron trope: a sad lover comes to conquer his mistress, who is locked inside or above the device, and then he attempts a consented kidnapping (*Dalcméon*), a hoped-for rescue (*Guillaume d'Aquitaine*), or an impossible conquest (*La Rhodienne*).[36] But the resulting stage design, according to the texts, also proposes a scenography of attack, which plays with the foundation of the spectators' common memory in Rouen about these scenic actions. In Jacques Du Hamel's *Acoubar* (1603), the eponymous character attacks his Canadian enemy Castio's land, arriving by sea and climbing up a cliff that blocks his men's route.[37] In *La Rhodienne*, Solyman attacks Rhodes to satisfy both his *libido dominandi* [desire to dominate] by conquering Rhodes and his *libido sentiendi* [lust of sensual pleasures], for, by conquering Rhodes, he also conquers his mistress Perside. In *Guillaume d'Aquitaine*, we first see an assault attempt on Guillaume's brother, who tries to take back by force his spouse, whom Guillaume has kidnapped and raped; then, later, Guillaume, on his way to redemption, attempts to join in on an attack—against Pisa, perhaps—with the Republic of Lucca's army, but he is struck with blindness and must abandon the campaign.

The attack and the conquest on the elevated stage recall political eminence and eventually refer to political and wartime episodes that took hold of Normandy during the previous century. Just as the *Mistere du siège d'Orléans* [*Mystery of the Siege of Orleans*] reenacted the siege that lasted six months, six years after the events that took place (i.e., ca. 1435),[38] the representation of siege or attack in Normandy plays on the same system of construction of memories by reminding the inhabitants of the grief and deprivation that they endured. By confronting the spectators with an attack in this way, in front of an admittedly decorated political scaffold but nonetheless an irrevocable referential system, the tragic playwrights remind them of this more or less faraway past in Rouen, of the aftereffects on their buildings and in their memories, despite the obligation to forget contained within the edicts of pacification.

A third elevated set can be found in *La magicienne estrangere* [*The Foreign Witch*]. After her condemnation, Galligay is led onto an *échaffaud* [scaffold], where she is executed, *onstage*.[39] If indeed we contest the modalities of performance on the *petit théâtre supérieur* [small upper stage], it is possible that it is not a matter, in Rouen at least, of a fixed raised platform on the very structure of the building, but rather of a scaffold placed on the stage, transformed *ad infinitum*, by means of painted backdrops, into castles, fortresses, palaces, or cliffs, or, in the case of *La magicienne estrangere*, left bare. This solution would answer, as it were, the questions of construction of this small theater, stockroom, technical room, secondary stage, by introducing the device *ad* hoc rather than having a systematic presence during each performance, which would explain, moreover, why the authors do not always refer to it and do not always use it.

La magicienne estrangere, which shows the accusation, the trial, and the execution of Léonora Galigaï, named Galligay in the play, highlights the convenience of a scaffold onstage: whereas few sites are evoked in the text, Galligay's execution occurs on this elevated stage. The action begins in medias res: Galligay has been taken to her torture site—is a curtain raised to reveal this scene?—and she must confess and commend her soul to God before being decapitated:

GALLIGAY.	C'est assez discouru amy fay ton office
	Puis que j'ay merité cent fois ce doux supplice.
II DOCTEUR.	Elevez votre esprit devers le firmament.
L'EXECUTEUR.	Recevez de vos maux doncques le payement,
	Sus sus montez en haut, et venez ce corps prendre
	Pour le jettant au feu le consommer en cendre.
II DOCTEUR.	Retirons nous Monsieur puis qu'avec gravité
	Nous voyons de la Court l'arrest executé.[40]
[GALLIGAY.	That is enough talking. Friend, do your duty
	since I have deserved a hundred times over this sweet punishment.
SECOND DOCTOR.	Lift up your spirit toward the firmament.
THE EXECUTIONER.	Receive thus payment for your evils.
	Quickly, quickly, climb up there, and come take this body
	to consume it to ash by throwing it into the fire.
SECOND DOCTOR.	Let us withdraw, Monsieur, since we see the court's sentence carried out with gravity.]

The elevated scaffold metonymically symbolizes public execution and judicial punishment. If a scaffold were used on the main stage, it would shed light on the performance of violent scenes and put into perspective those that necessitate the public carrying out of a judiciary sentence. The stage on the stage becomes, by its installation, the place of theater in the theater, not only by an emphasis on the scene played out on stage, but also by the reference to this judiciary, political, and religious prop, a reflection on life in general. If the whole world is a theater, the questioning of the state's actions and the future of humankind are condensed into, or onto, the bloody, theatrical, and sinister scaffold.

For, on the one hand, capital punishment in France has a prophylactic function that serves, in the first instance by the severity of the sentence, to keep those in attendance on the right track by frightening them with the cruelty of death and the publicity of the crime. On the other hand, capital punishment offers the criminal compensation, commensurate with the crime's severity, all the while offering a reinstatement by punishment in the social and spiritual community, by the way of confession and contrition. The Norman tragedies, by this scenographic technique of the scaffold on the "scaffold" (i.e., stage), which underscores the characters' deaths, establishes this parallel with the bloody urban spectacle.[41] Paradoxically, if the execution seems to allow for the criminal's return into the fold of the Christian community, when order is restored by his confession to God, society, and the king, his death and his suffering that pertain to his body (burnt remains and scattered ashes) definitively exclude the possibility of resurrection. This is the judicial, ontological, and religious paradox of French capital punishment. It is thus not so much a question of politics and judgment, but rather the importance of the spectacle that makes up capital punishment in the eyes of the crowd that gathers to attend the execution. Capital punishment may not be a solution of religious reintegration, but instead an affirmation of royal justice, which despite religious participation in the unraveling of the ceremony, does not offer the church the opportunity to help the criminal's redemption.

La magicienne estrangere and other plays highlight this paradox: whereas Galligay has recommended her soul to God, she ends up in hell, where she finds her dead husband, Concini, in a rather humorous scene. For the anonymous dramatist, the prophylactic system of probation by killing the criminal does not operate. Indeed, if the aim of punishment is the redemption of the community by the destruction of the criminal, the playwright condemns the character to a century of wandering on the banks of the Acheron, without offering her the redemption she has deserved during her torture.

This play affirms the political nature of capital punishment. The king and his agents have pronounced her sentence, which is then carried out. Despite Galligay's contrition and torture, however, she cannot attain salvation. What is more, this highly political play does not end with this infernal promise of a wandering fate, but with an act in which the character *Grand Pan français* (i.e., Louis XIII) and his noblemen celebrate the death of their enemies by going in search of pleasure in a hunting party.

On the sinister scaffold, just before the execution, a court clerk rushes onto the stage to reread the criminal's sentence, which leads the spectator to focus on the crime. Afterward, the criminal's attitude takes precedence.

The execution itself banalizes the criminal act by identically resolving all the crimes of the same type in the same way. The banalization participates in the process of legitimization of the institution that orders the resolution. In turn, death, in the Norman tragedies, is nothing but commonplace; it is thus expected, even if it is spectacularly carried out. It reestablishes *an* order.

The elevated stage, therefore, introduces disorder. Because the spectator-character of the raised set is put in the position of the spectator of capital punishment, the mise en abyme on the stage justifies the real necessity to execute and legitimizes death. The elevated stage underscores an exceptional and rare action, because it is this unexpected character of the action that disrupts and that, in turn, raises questions. Indeed, Arlette Farge has shown that the exceptional nature of an execution does not come from the ritual itself, which the society in attendance might assimilate as an unconditional unleashing of secular power, but rather from the exceptional events that take place within it, and that suddenly highlight, in some unique cases, a poor functioning of the ritual.[42]

If the goal of theater is to fascinate through performance, it must make the audience believe,[43] which is to say that the spectacle of the bloody, theatrical, or punitive scaffold has a duty to put in place a rhetoric of persuasion. Performing on the elevated stage showcases a scene whose narrative alone does not suffice. The presence of the actors' and characters' tortured bodies—for instance, the *Damoiselle* [Lady] from the *More cruel* or Dorotée from *Guillaume d'Aquitaine*, both raped, or Riviery's children from the *More cruel*, who are stabbed in the citadel and abandoned in a ditch, in front of the spectators—leads to a questioning of this strangeness and this extraordinary character.

Theatrical Genetics

In Normandy, especially Rouen, drama has a long history: the liturgical play *Les pèlerins d'Emmaüs* [*The Pilgrims of Emmaus*], for example, has been recorded as early as the twelfth century in Notre Dame cathedral. Mystery plays were regularly performed in Rouen and in the large Norman cities.[44] As in all the regions of Western Europe, royal entries were the occasion for many spectacles, while the brotherhood of the Conards ran about the city during Lent and Easter festivals, representing farce-like works commenting on the city's current events—though the extent to which these performances were public remains uncertain.[45] The Guibray Fair in Falaise was known both as a nerve center of northern commerce and as a site of spectacle where itinerant actors, jugglers, showmen, and charlatans came together.[46] Many witness accounts thus recall the spectacular past of the province, but they also attest to a form of affiliation or heredity, and suppose, by reading and analyzing the texts, a propensity for recycling the forms and the places, which the authors of the pre-Cornelian generations knew how to master.

These sites, however, are not original in the drama and in the stage designs of the early seventeenth century. Our findings, when compared to the set designs and prop lists from the *Mémoire de Mahelot*, confirm that the same stage settings and the same juxtapositions of scenic spaces were being used in Paris at this time. Their recurrence indicates, though, that they are not simple props for the carrying out of plots, but rather that, by their symbolic significance, they help put into place a common base of memory and a referential system shared by authors, actors, and spectators alike. The realization of crimes within these settings thus plays on this system and offers the dramatists a large range of scenographic situations to create necessary symbolic links for the understanding of the works and of their significance.

Above all, they raise the question of theatrical genetics. Their evocation, from the earliest texts published in Normandy, suggests that they were used, even created, for performance. But their systematicity raises a chicken-and-egg problem, which is difficult to answer satisfactorily: Were the works performed in these settings because they already existed, and so the authors got in the habit of writing texts to be performed in them, or were the settings designed in these ways because the authors had commonly and synchronically decided to have their plots played out in these places, playing on vertical and horizontal levels and putting forward the possibility of showing or hiding certain events of the plot in order to underscore them more effectively? This question gestures toward the establishment of a poetics of theater design: a meaningful scenography that is based either on texts that evoke some sort of stage design, or on scenic drama; that is to say, a kind of playwriting that is dictated by the stage settings that already exist. Theatrical genetics and theater design at the turn of the seventeenth century are thus at stake.

However, it is impossible to answer this question in a satisfactory way, except, perhaps, by a theory of (Darwinian?) evolution of theater stage settings through the centuries, which would propose that modern theater sets were only the rereading and reusing of scenic elements that existed before the theatrical genre that would be called "irregular" tragedy: medieval plays that were performed not only in Normandy but in the rest of the French-speaking territories at the turn of the seventeenth century. The multiplicity of spaces *in, within,* or *in front* of which actors played shows that the dramatists are not aware of the simple stage setting, the *palais à volonté*. The *Mémoire de Mahelot* cites this type of setting starting in the 1660s, and it would become the dominant tragic stage design from the end of the seventeenth and into the nineteenth centuries.

We must also question the disappearance of the multiplicity of performance spaces to reach, progressively, the simple stage setting. The small
stage above the main stage, still mentioned in 1644 at the Marais Theater,
is progressively removed and likely used for the performance of nonstandard-
ized genres such as tragicomedy. But this tragic element disappears with the
advent of "neoclassical" drama.

The multiplicity of stage settings and their juxtaposition, inherited from
medieval spectacles and stages, fade at the same time as the spectacular
practices that aimed, for the performance of mystery plays, to celebrate the
union of believers, for capital punishment, to commemorate and bolster the
predominance of royal justice. Royal power, spread throughout France as a
result of the policies of Louis XIII and his primary minister, the Cardinal of
Richelieu, presents itself as horizontal linearity of stage settings. The *palais à
volonté*, like the rules of neoclassical composition, ratifies absolutist politics
by its usage in the performance of tragic works. Verticality gives way to hori-
zontality, multiplicity to linearity. The disappearance of the elevated stage
reflects the translation of absolutist politics on stage: the scaffold remains,
but it is the urban scaffold on the street, which confirms the power of royal
justice by capital punishment and the torture of criminals.

Notes

1. For instance, Émile Faguet writes:

J'appelle drame irrégulier non pas tant celui qui s'affranchit de quelqu'une des règles que
nos théoriciens du XVIe siècle ont édictées, que celui qui, par sa composition générale
et par son esprit, se révèle comme étranger et à la tradition antique et à la tradition du
Moyen Age. . . . [D]'ordinaire tout y est inventé, sujet, intrigue, personnages. Le fond de
sa méthode consiste à ne rien demander à l'histoire: par suite, selon la complexion ou la
fantaisie de l'auteur, elle penche du côté de l'imagination pure, et devient le roman en
dialogue, le drame romanesque; ou elle va puiser son inspiration dans la réalité vulgaire,
et se fait d'une anecdote mise sur la scène, et c'est la tragédie bourgeoise. (*La tragédie
française au XVIe siècle* [Paris: Fontemoing, 1912], 395)

[I call irregular drama not so much one that frees itself from one of the rules that our
sixteenth-century theoreticians decreed, than one that, by its general composition and
its overall conception, turns out to be foreign both to ancient and medieval traditions.
. . . Normally, everything is made up: the subject, the plot, the characters. The basis of
its method consists in borrowing nothing from history. In turn, according to the nature
or the fantasy of the author, it tends toward pure imagination, and becomes a novel in
dialogue, a fictional drama; or it draws its inspiration from common, tasteless reality, and
becomes and anecdote performed on stage, and this is bourgeois tragedy.]

All translations are mine unless otherwise noted.

2. See the recent edition of the original manuscript by Pierre Pasquier, *Le mémoire de Mahelot: Mémoire pour la décoration des pièces qui se représentent par les Comédiens du Roi* (Paris: Honoré Champion, 2005).

3. A mystery play continued to be played in Rouen each year between 1598 and 1607.

4. A rough translation of *jeu de paume* would be royal tennis, though the *jeu de paume* here refers to the structure in which the game was played: a long, rectangular building divided by a low net and lined with a spectator's gallery. These structures were often transformed into makeshift, temporary theaters, while others, such as was the case for the Marais Theater, were converted into permanent theaters with all the machinery necessary for complex stage productions.

5. Edouard Gosselin, "Recherches sur les origines et l'histoire du théâtre à Rouen avant Pierre Corneille," *Revue de la Normandie* 8 (1868): 242–54, 253.

6. Judgment of the Rouen *parlement*, October 24, 1556, authorizing the troupe of Pierre Carpentier (called Le Pardonneur) the right to play in the Port du Salut *jeu de paume*, cited in Michel Rousse, "Une représentation théâtrale à Rouen en 1556," *European Medieval Drama* 7 (2003): 87–115, 87.

7. Despite these two anecdotes, the use of the city's most famous *jeux de paume* as theaters, the Deux-Maures and the Braques, is not attested before 1640.

8. *Les historiettes de Tallemant des Réaux* (Paris: Alphonse Levavasseur, 1834), 2:146.

9. Thomas le Coq, *Tragedie représentant l'odieus et sanglant meurtre commis par le maudit Cain, à l'encontre de son frere Abel, extraicte du 4. chap. de Genese* (Paris: Nicolas Bonfons, 1580).

10. I have found 172 editions of works that contain at least one play of any genre between 1594 and 1640.

11. Anne Surgers, "Logis, portes et fenêtres: le jeu des lieux de mémoire dans le décor du théâtre baroque, une 'caresse pour l'âme et le corps,'" in *La ville en scène en France et en Europe (1552–1709)*, ed. Jan Clarke, Pierre Pasquier, and Henry Phillips (Oxford: Peter Lang, 2011), 31–46, 45.

12. Pierre Troterel, sieur d'Aves, *Tragédie de sainte Agnès* (Rouen: David du Petit-Val, 1615). As no modern critical edition of *Saint Agnès* exists, the citations refer to act and page number(s) of the 1615 edition.

13. Nicolas Chrestien des Croix, *Rosemonde ou la vengeance* (Rouen: Théodore Reinsart, 1603). A slightly modified version of this tragedy appeared in 1608 from the same printer under the title *Alboüin ou la vengeance*. I cite the 1603 version, giving act page number(s).

14. Nicolas Chrestien des Croix, *Amnon et Thamar* (Rouen: Théodore Reinsart, 1608). I cite this edition, giving act and page number(s).

15. One could easily make a comparison with the drama of Judith and Holophernes in the *Mistére du Viel Testament* [Mystery of the Old Testament], vol. 5, ed. James de Rothschild (Paris: Firmin Didot et cie, 1885). See also Jean Molinet (?), *Le mystère de Judith et Holofernés: une édition critique de l'une des parties du "Mistére du Viel Testament"*, ed. Graham A. Runnalls (Geneva: Droz, 1995).

16. Troterel, *Sainte Agnès*, 4, 68.

17. Ibid., 4, 67.

18. Ibid. For more on these scenes of physical and sexual violence, see Michael Meere, "Staging Sanctity: Moral Confusion in Pierre Troterel's *La tragédie de sainte Agnès* (1615)," *L'esprit créateur* 50, no.1 (Spring 2010): 49–61.

19. Ibid. (emphasis added).

20. Ibid., 5, 80 (emphasis added).

21. Chrestien, *Rosemonde*, 4, 87.

22. Ibid.

23. Ibid., 4, 89.

24. Ibid., 4, 96–97 (emphasis added).

25. Chrestien, *Amnon et Thamar*, 3, 67.

26. Ibid., 4, 68 (emphasis added).

27. Ibid., 5, 91–93 (emphasis added). The *guillemet* (») is in the original text; in the theater of this time, the extra *guillemets* indicate the pronouncement of a moral commonplace, proverb, or the like.

28. Ibid., 5, 101 (emphasis added).

29. Many sieges took place, the city was attacked many times by the royal armies, and it was not until 1594 that Henri IV finally managed to walk through the doors of the city to be acclaimed the new king, five years after his accession to the throne, and well after Paris.

30. Anonymous, *Tragédie française d'un more cruel envers son seigneur nommé Riviery, gentilhomme espagnol, sa damoiselle et ses enfants* (Rouen: Abraham Cousturier, [ca. 1608]). A modern edition can be found in *Théâtre de la cruauté et récits sanglants en France fin XVIe–début XVIIe siècle*, ed. Christian Biet et al. (Paris: Robert Laffont, 2006).

31. Indeed, no contemporaneous eyewitness account of its performance in Rouen can attest to the veracity of this device. Furthermore, we must take into account the subjective nature of the engraver, for we are faced with what Surgers and Fabien Cavaillé have called the "regard baroque" ["baroque gaze"]. That is to say, a gaze that is not focused and does not favor the perception of one single, ideally positioned spectator facing the proposed spectacle, but rather corresponds to a layout on stage that includes several structures, several referential spaces, in which the actions are performed. Fabien Cavaillé and Anne Surgers, "La scénographie du théâtre baroque en France: quand le comédien n'était pas fermé dans une cage," *Cahiers du Dix-septième* XIII (2010): 92–123, 93n.

32. S. Wilma Deierkauf-Holsboer, *Le théâtre du Marais*, vol. 1 (Paris: Nizet, 1954) and *Le théâtre de l'Hôtel de Bourgogne, 1548–1635*, vol. 1 (Paris: Nizet, 1968).

33. Deierkauf-Holsboer, *Le théâtre du Marais*, 194.

34. *Mémoire de ce qu'il faut faire au jeu de paume des Marais*, cited in Deierkauf-Holsboer, *Le théâtre du Marais*, 194.

35. See Anne Surgers, "'Estants imitateurs de toute Nature': Analyse des outils de la fiction spatiale du théâtre baroque, à partir des *Galanteries du duc d'Ossonne*

de Mairet (1633)," in *L'âge de la représentation: L'art du spectacle au XVIIe siècle*, ed. Rainer Zaiser (Tübingen: Gunter Narr Verlag, 2007), 243–70, 263.

36. Étienne Bellone, *Les amours de Dalcméon et de Flore, tragédie* [1610] (Rouen: Raphaël du Petit-Val, 1621); Pierre Troterel, *La vie et sainte conversion de Guillaume duc d'Aquitaine escrite en vers, et disposée en actes pour representer sur le theatre* (Rouen: David du Petit-Val, 1632); Pierre Mainfray, *La Rhodienne ou la cruauté de Solyman* (Rouen: David du Petit-Val, 1621).

37. Jacques Du Hamel, *Acoubar ou la loyauté trahie* (Rouen: Raphaël du Petit-Val, 1603). At the top of the cliff, however, without Acoubar's knowledge, is Fortunie, whom he loves but who will betray him, which establishes a parallel with the para-clausithyron trope.

38. *Le mistere du siege d'Orleans* [ca. 1435], ed. François Guessard and Eugène de Certain (Paris: Imprimerie impériale, 1862). This medieval play represented the siege in front of the inhabitants of Orleans who had seen the tragic events, at the same sites where the actual battles took place.

39. Anonymous, *La magicienne estrangère, tragédie: En laquelle on voit les tirannicques comportemens, origine, entreprises, desseings, sortilleges, arrest, mort et supplice, tant du marquis d'Ancre que de Leonor Galligay sa femme, avec l'advantureuse rencontre de leurs funestes ombres* (Rouen: David Geuffroy et Jacques Besongne, 1617). I cite this edition.

40. 3.1, 27 (emphasis added). As *La magicienne estrangere* is divided into acts and scenes, I cite the act and scene numbers, followed by the page number in the original edition.

41. Pascal Bastien reinforces the spectacularity of capital punishment—contrary to Foucault, who highlights its religiosity. Pascal Bastien, *L'exécution publique à Paris au XVIIe siècle: Une histoire des rituels judiciaires* (Seyssel: Champ Vallon, 2006); Michel Foucault, *Surveiller et punir: Naissance de la prison* (Paris: Gallimard, 1975).

42. Arlette Farge, *La vie fragile: Violence, pouvoirs et solidarités à Paris au XVIIIe siècle* (Paris: Hachette, 1986); Arlette Farge and J. Revel, *Logiques de la foule: l'affaire des enlèvements d'enfants, Paris 1750* (Paris: Hachette, 1988).

43. Louis Marin, *Le récit est un piège* (Paris: Éditions de Minuit, 1978).

44. Besides the numerous witness accounts from the seventeenth century, see, for example, Louis Petit de Julleville, *Les mystères* (Paris: Hachette, 1880), 2:1–185; and Edouard Gosselin, *Recherchés sur les origines et l'histoire du théâtre à Rouen avant Pierre Corneille* (Rouen: Cagnard, 1868). We also find evidence in Dieppe, for instance, with a ceremonial performance that Anne of Austria and the young Louis XIV attended in 1647. See Charles Magnin, *Histoire des marionnettes en Europe depuis l'Antiquité jusqu'à nos jours* (Paris; Leipzig: Lévy frères; Michelsen, 1882), 117.

45. On the drama of royal entrances, see Elizabeth Guild's chapter in this volume (10); on the Conards and farce, see Sara Beam's chapter (4) on Calvinist comedies.

46. See Michael Desprez, "Les premiers profesionnels, ou du comédien à l'acteur: Constitution d'un métier, constitution d'une image, Italie-France, c. 1500–c. 1630" (PhD diss., Université Paris Ouest Nanterre, 2005).

~

CHAPTER THIRTEEN

The Court Turned Inside Out

The Collapse of Dignity in
Louis XIII's Burlesque Ballets

Alison Calhoun

On dit qu'un Président, qu'un Grand Seigneur parle avec dignité, qu'il agit avec dignité, qu'il marche avec dignité, pour dire, qu'il soustient bien son rang, qu'il ne dement point son caractere, qu'il parle, qu'il agit bien, qu'il a grand train. C'est un homme constitué en dignité. De tout temps il y a eu des marques de dignité par des habits, des ornements, des symboles.[1]

[We say that a president, that a great lord speaks with dignity, that he acts with dignity, that he walks with dignity, to say that he represents his rank well, that he does not alter his outward appearance, that he speaks and acts well, that he has a great entourage. He is a man made up of dignity. Dignity has always had its signs in clothes, ornaments, symbols.]

We most often associate the word "dignity" in our time with "merit" or "worth," and "dignified" with "worthy," based on the Latin meanings for *dignitatem* and *dignus*. But today, as in the early modern period, dignity is also related more concretely to a position of high rank, or title, as in a "dignitary." The entry from Antoine Furetière's 1690 dictionary above underlines that the person of a certain status has dignity when he maintains his rank by leaving its outward appearance [*caractere*] unaltered: "il ne dement point son caractere." This detail reinforces the fact that an important aspect of being dignified in early modern France, and possibly still today, is that one is a public persona, perhaps best understood in terms of the metaphorical mask.[2] During Louis XIII's reign dignity, not only as a quality and title, but also as a controllable attribute that was supposed to be maintained in public, was problematized by its very absence in royal burlesque ballet. The status of dignity in this art form is particularly interesting to study in context, because it falls at a time in the construction of the great edifice of absolutism when the building blocks are merely being laid. The result, if we look carefully, is a performance in which an absolutist hierarchy begins to emerge, notably in terms of the subordination of the nobility, and yet the majestic leader has yet to be generated. Although many burlesque entertainments were part of the topsy-turvy world of carnival, in which rank was traditionally and purposefully inverted, the ritual of carnival alone does not explain the intricacies of these ballets' role reversals, especially their emotional makeup and their potential for exposing some of the king's personal, private traits. As I argue in this chapter, burlesque ballets under Louis XIII depict and perform the critical tension between dignity (essentially public) and emotions (arguably both private and public) during Louis's dramatic rise to power after 1617.[3]

Under the reign of Louis XIII, royal court ballet took a decisive (though brief) turn, both in its outreach to public venues (the Hôtel de Ville, for example, instead of exclusive performances in the *salles* [rooms] of the Louvre) and in the basic subject matter of its diverse dance scenes [*entrées*]. Georgie Durosoir estimates that after about 1619, there was a marked decline in gallant, heroic, martial, and what we might simply assume to be "appropriate" topics for state building and for promoting the king's authority.[4] In its place, we find a ballet based on a maximum of disparate dance scenes in the burlesque mode. Louis XIII's "burlesque moment" was, as Mark Franko has more recently pointed out, short-lived, since by "the time of Louis XIV's productions, there were no longer any obvious burlesque ballets, only scattered burlesque roles."[5] This brief stylistic excursus dissuades us from assuming these were simply *carnavalesque* customs, striking us instead as a "moment" that was historically and politically driven.

The first reason these ballets challenged royal and courtly dignity is that they seem to promote instability and disorder, particularly, as we shall see, emotional breakdowns, at a time so near the personal and political crisis of the coup d'état in 1617. After the assassination of Concino Concini, cultural production around Louis, especially theater, tended to intone propagandistic messages that would help reinforce his position as the legitimate leader of the state.[6] As Orest Ranum explains, "the early years of the reign of Louis XIII were rife with plots, sieges, murders, and pillage, even in Paris. A more stable style of life was essential, lest the nobility destroy itself. Richelieu knew this; poets and artists may have sensed it."[7] Despite a clear need for stability, many of the burlesque ballets were performed concurrently with presumably regicidal uprisings, many if not most of them organized by Louis's own family members. For example, in 1626, the year in which the *Ballet du grand bal de la douairière de Billebahaut* [*The Royal Ballet of the Dowager of Bilbao's Grand Ball*] was performed, there was a conspiracy to assassinate Louis in which his own wife, Anne of Austria, took part. Just a year after this incident came the productions of the *Ballet du sérieux et du grotesque* [*Ballet of the Serious One and the Grotesque One*] as well as the *Ballet des quolibets* [*Ballet of Mockeries*]. Finally, in 1632, the year of the performance of the *Ballet du Château de Bicêtre*, Louis's brother Gaston d'Orléans was twice exiled for conspiring to undermine both the queen mother and Richelieu.

The second reason these ballets problematize dignity is that in context, in addition to their burlesque subject matter, the royal ballet's exposure extended from the walls of the Louvre to the city of Paris, where they were performed before an invited bourgeois public, usually after a premiere at the Louvre. They were, in other words, particularly public performances that demonstrated the increased openness of the aristocratic rank at the beginning of Louis XIII's reign, when nobility was for sale, and "extended to a much larger segment of the population."[8] Furthermore, these bodies in motion, few if any of them belonging to trained dancers, would have been replete with human error and rendered even more fallible and vulnerable the more complicated the choreography and staging were. These performances thus appear to be symptomatic of a period in which the dignity and privacy of the noble, courtly sphere collapsed, at least in the world of dance, into something that was its opposite.

The most common reasons given for these performances' accessibility to a public beyond the court is that they were propagandistic. This would indeed make sense for public ballets and balls that were clearly majestic, like the royal dance scenes that celebrated the presence of the monarch in the city or some of the later ballets commissioned by Richelieu, in which France and its Christian monarchy were allegorized with exemplary choreography. But as several specialists have studied,[9] the public performances of burlesque ballet confound the idea of propaganda, since they do not celebrate a monarchical festivity and their subject matter is base and comical.[10] This is especially the case in the psychological geography of the lengthiest burlesque ballet under Louis XIII, the *Ballet de la douairière de Billebauhaut*, in which each *entrée* exposes a leader who bares his soul and his vulnerability to the audience.

The ballet's poetry, mostly by René Bordier, though also by Théophile de Viau, Seigneur de Racan, Charles Sorel, and Claude de l'Estoile, along with its costume designs by Daniel Rabelin, suggest a performance in which continents and their climates served as a pretext for the discussion of emotional sterility, and sometimes, literal impotence. On the one hand, the tyrannical protagonists (a variety of world leaders) control their kingdoms with ease, while on the other hand, when it comes to controlling their hearts, they are powerless slaves to Cupid and to the circumstances of the weather. These examples of weakness and subordination (to Cupid) in foreign leaders, all of them symbolic subjects to the French crown, had, as we discuss here, the potential of making Louis appear powerful by contrast.

However, with their insistence on sentimental power, the power to feel, over martial or geographic control, the outcome is less a model of absolutism than it is a reflection of how Richelieu's ultimate hierarchical plan had not yet taken root. In the Bilbao ballet, the political climate is painted through geographical and sexual metaphors that effectively turned the court inside out in order to reveal a world in which private and public are confusingly fused; the emotional breakdowns were a constant reminder that the dangers in Louis's political world were often directly related to intimate, familial relationships. As the ballet presents a multitude of dignitaries on stage in the process of changing their public character into more frank, often grotesque expressions of their inner feelings of discomfort, as well as their longing and desire for love, the performance reveals a period in Louis's reign when the problem of his enemies may have been identified and generally felt at court, but during which the solution of the absolute monarch was still under construction.

Le ballet du grand bal de la douairière de Billebahaut

The royal *Ballet du grand bal de la douairière de Billebahaut* was first performed at the Louvre on February 24, 1626. Later that same night, a second performance was undertaken before a selected bourgeois public at the Hôtel de Ville. Its basic plot depicts a dowager from Bilbao who gives a ball in honor of her arduous admirer and now fiancé, Fanfan de Sotteville.[11] Each dance scene represents the arrival at the ball of distinguished guests, hailing from the four corners of the earth, spectacularly dressed and accompanied by their entourages. The dance scenes of the ballet are ordered according to the following appearances: Americans, Asians, Northerners from Greenland and the mythical place "Frisland," Africans, and finally the locals at the ball in Spain. A plaintive tyrant-lover leads each group, declaiming his military prowess, followed directly by his sentimental depravation, often suggesting that because of his surroundings, he is unable to feel or find love. While suspiciously powerful, the leaders all hope that by leaving their homelands and attending the dowager's ball they will somehow improve their romantic existence. They each introduce themselves as terrifying, virile chiefs, and then suddenly transform into pathetic, emotionally, and sexually unsatisfied nomads. The political allegory—that infidelity to France will result in an unsuccessful state, similar to the impotence of these tyrants—is further enhanced by the later link between Louis and Cupid, which will help develop the idea of subordination to the crown. In both readings, the dignity of the nobility is removed by a performance of sentimental vulnerability. Each tyrant's frank avowals display an alteration of the public persona, putting in its place the depiction of a more naked and private register that would normally be masked by world leaders, and the nobility dancing the roles.

In the first scene, one of the Americans following the leader of Cusco, played by a certain Monsieur le Comte, confesses "à cœur ouvert" ["with an open heart"] that even though he is covered in avian feathers, his love unfortunately "n'a point d'aisles" ["has no wings"].[12] On the level of performance, it is important to note here that the costumes for the Americans were almost exclusively made of feathers, leaving these dancers scantily clothed in comparison to other invited guests. The nakedness of their dress made them already more open to the public, perhaps heightening a sense of vulnerability that would accompany such declarations as we see from Monsieur le Comte. Bordier's poetry tends to play on the antithesis between outside and inside: the Americans' appearance, which is light like feathers, contrasts with their heavy, burdened hearts and sentiments.

Moreover, in Bordier's verse, the vast land of the New World serves as a geographical metaphor—we might be better off calling it a geographical psychology—for the highs and lows of love, representing both its secret treasures to be discovered and the difficulty, even impossibility, of their discovery. The New World's challenging navigation, thanks to its size, is compared to the long and arduous path to find love. As one American explains: "J'ai par terre et par mer cheminé nuit et jour, / Et n'ay voulu qu'Amour, / Tout aveugle qu'il est, pour pilote et pour guide" ["Night and day I have traveled by land and by sea, and wanted only Love, blind as he is, for pilot and guide"].[13] The American leader is not exempt from this struggle, either. Atabalipa, in his opening words, describes himself as "l'effroy des puissans Roys" ["the terror of powerful kings"], but, he continues, "Quand j'ay terre et mer surmonté / Invincible je suis domté / Par un enfant aveugle qui ne voit goutte" ["Although I have surmounted both land and sea, invincible, I am subdued by a blind child who cannot see a thing"].[14] Thus, the Americans are powerful, but are rendered lovesick by the geography of their continent and the difficulty of navigating it to find their beloved. They may have wings, but because of the weight of their hearts and the uncertainty of their route, their power of flight is useless. As for their leader, despite being terrifying to his peers, he is nevertheless subject to Cupid.

In the *Ballets de l'Asie* [*Asian Ballets*], we meet a Muslim, Turkish doctors, Persian gentlemen of letters (one played by the king), and the Grand Turk, all eager to reach the ball in Spain. After offering some Italian-styled *lazzi* involving the Muslim's fear that his young lover will be unfaithful to him[15] and some unfavorable verse suggesting that all doctors are quacks, the Grand Turk speaks. His part is one of the only overtly propagandistic moments in the ballet, since although he paints himself as a power "au dessus des Roys" ["above kings"], a master of the four elements who makes the entire world "tremble," he is not exempt from "la crainte d'accoistre un jour les palmes de LOUIS" ["the fear of one day increasing Louis's accolades"].[16] In other words, whereas the American leader feared Cupid, here the Turk declares that the only power that intimidates him is not a god, but Louis XIII. To be certain, the choice of having the Turk make this declaration significantly reinforces the French view of their dominance over the Ottoman Empire, while more generally reminding the public that foreign or local social climbers were not to feel overly comfortable at court. As the only reference to Louis's power as a monarch,[17] this passage nevertheless forges a link between the crown and Cupid, both powerful guides who possess the qualities these world leaders respect and fear. This parallel in turn suggests that Louis-as-Cupid has control over the romantic fates of the world's great powers that, though more trivial than the idea of political control over people and lands, sends a message about his superiority.

In the next scene, the *Ballets du Nort* [*Northern Ballet*], distance from court again proves to have a negative effect on lovers. The greatest challenge the Northerners experience is the cold climate, a disadvantage that the librettists underline by focusing on the bodily impotence that results from freezing temperatures. These impediments were humorously enhanced by the Northerners' costumes, which were voluminous, layered, fur robes, covering everything but the dancer's eyes and nose. The Northerners need Cupid, who "du vent de ses aisles / Evente deux Soleils" ["fans two suns with the wind from his wings"], warming the lover and, presumably, his parts.[18] The eyes of one's lover might also act as sunbeams, melting chilled bones: "Bien que transi de frois l'exercice m'appelle, / Mon Cœur ambitieux / Ne consent, ô Beautez, que ma glace dégele / Qu'aux rayons de vos yeux" ["Numbed with cold, although exercise calls me, my ambitious heart will only consent, o Beauty, to be melted by the sunbeams of your eyes"].[19] However, not all Northerners are so faithful. The anesthesia of the cold weather consequently provokes significant amounts of infidelity, allegedly for the naive purpose of trying, however in vain, to find warmth. One young gentleman of the North uses the freezing temperatures to defend his manhood:

> Beautés, chefs d'œuvres de nature,
> Qui riez voyant la froidure
> De nos membres transis que de glace a perdus,
> Songeant aux outrages passes,
> Nous n'osons nous nommer des amants glacés,
> De peur d'estre nommés des amans morfondus.[20]

[Beauties, masterpieces of nature, who laugh at the sight of our untreatable, frostbitten limbs, thinking about past wrongs, we do not dare name ourselves frozen lovers, for fear of being named cold and sick lovers.]

Northern men, thus, are emasculated by the weather; their bodies have no feeling and no effect thanks to the glacial temperatures. In addition, Northern women are fickle, and willing to forfeit steadfast love for practical reasons of warmth.

Two other burlesque figures appear at this point in the ballet, one wearing only pants and the other wearing only a doublet. In the case of the bottoms-only dancer, his performance is limited to his legs, since the rest of his body is imprisoned within the oversized trouser costume, the waist of which ends at his throat, leaving only his head peaking out from the top. As for his poor friend, we only see his feet peering out of the bottom of an enormous doublet, leaving him blind at his arrival at the ball. Margaret McGowan has argued that this was part of an inside joke directed at the king, who once paid his servants so little, they did not have enough income to pay for a complete wardrobe.[21] Whether or not this is the case, what is clear is that in this ballet, outward appearances, not only in the costumes that the dancers are wearing, but also in the consequent difficulty of movement those very costumes create, is meant to be read as an expression of inferiority and impotence. These dancers' fragmented presence in the ballet helps to reinforce the question of what Furetière defined as "marques de dignité" ["signs of dignity," quoted in the epigraph], such as a person's clothes. When these symbols of coded dress are deconstructed in the ballet, the result is actually twofold: the first outcome is comic, thanks to its inversion of the norm; but these costumes are also disconcerting, since in the context of the ball, they once again underline the character's inner depravation, leaving the dancers senseless and crippled, both physically and, as we saw with Bordier's verse, emotionally, in matters of love. This exterior and interior crippling continues in the next scene, which takes us to the opposite end of the climate spectrum, the weather in Africa, where we meet an elephant-mounted leader.

The African leader starts out emotionally dominant, exclaiming: "Je fais pleuvoir partout la honte et le Malheur, / Quand mon ambition fait tourner ma valeur" ["I make shame and misery shower down everywhere, when my ambition sours my worth"].[22] He loses credit, though, when all of his followers complain about the heat and its impediment to feeling the effects of love. Even an unknown Turkish leader, named the Grand Cam (played by the Duke of Liancourt), adds his opinion by comparing the problems with his empire to those in Africa: "Je ne m'esloigne pas des fins de mon empire / Pour trouver son pareil, / Mais, c'est que je desire / Brusler d'un plus beau feu que celuy du soleil" ["I do not have to go far from the ends of my empire to find its match, but, it is that I long to burn from a more beautiful fire than the sun"].[23] Whereas most cosmic political allegory starting in the late sixteenth century would have the sun represent the majesty of the sovereign, [24] this ballet uses it to continue to compare Louis and Cupid. Like Cupid, the sun (and by extension, the sovereign leader of France) has the power to produce the warmth of carnal love, reviving the frozen parts of Northern dwellers, or, as we saw in Africa, to burn and handicap lovers and their parts. If the king is associated with the sun according to this logic, he is indeed an all-powerful leader. The tone remains light, however, by concentrating on the sun's power over sexuality instead of grander, cosmic subjects. This causes the message about the sovereign to continue to operate on a more intimate, psychological level instead of a dignified, public one.

When we finally reach Europe, the dance scene introduces us to a world of Grenadian musicians and artists, the king the first musician who enters. Although he is not grotesque, unlike his musician's costume in the *Ballet du sérieux et du grotesque*,[25] his costume is simple and forgettable: he wears a black cloak striped with white lining and a matching hat with an ostrich feather, and he holds a guitar. On the one hand, his entrance is less than stately, especially in comparison to all the other great leaders, who had their entries with their animals and entourage. However, even more significant than taking a secondary role, Louis XIII appears here to reveal a more private and perhaps less dignified pastime. Indeed, less known for his love of books and learning, Louis nevertheless enjoyed spending time both composing and playing music, often with the lute.[26] His compositions were often part of the music for the ballets in which he danced. As a royal role, the musician had the potential, therefore, to alter his outward appearance as king by divulging to the public information about his tastes beyond state building. It is in this moment, therefore, that the king willingly acts against every aspect of dignity as we have defined it thus far: he has abandoned his mask, both in his manners and his dress; his rank has been all but erased; and he appears to be revealing part of his private sphere in a very public venue. In fact, the only way the casting seems to work politically is that unlike all the other leaders coming from the four corners of the earth, the Grenadians (the king among them) have no problem with love, though even that aspect seems to move from an impotent extreme to its bawdy opposite. As we shall see, the construction of power that is at the center of Louis's performance in this ballet is based on feeling, that is, the feeling of love and sexuality.

The king and his fellow Grenadians are equally uninhibited about their amorous adventures, which are numerous, since the European weather conditions are presumably optimal for lovemaking. They each take turns boasting about their abilities and comparing them (sometimes in opposition, sometimes as complementary proof) to their dancing and courtly persona. As the Count of Harcourt, one of the Grenadian dancers of the *sarabande*, claims: "Mais ne vous trompez pas, si je suis à la Cour / Damoiseau pour la danse, / Je suis Mars pour l'Amour" ["But do not be mistaken: if I am an effeminate young man for dance at court, I am Mars [a soldier/warrior] for Love"].[27] Another dancer, played by Gilles de Souvray, similarly underlines his sexual virility: "Si j'ai le pied friand, le reste va de mesme" ["If I have a pleasing foot, the rest is also the case"].[28] In this verse, the possible insinuation is that his talents in ballet, his foot referring to dance steps, extend to talents using other unspeakable, most likely sexual, parts of his body. In the same register, a musician from Grenada "Représenté par Monsieur le Marquis de Mortemar" ["performed by the Marquis of Mortemart"] cleverly states: "Mais sçachez que ma voix qui charme les oreilles / N'est pas ce que j'ay de plus doux" ["But know that my voice that enchants the ears is not the sweetest thing I have"].[29] As bawdy as the tone may be, there is a significant difference here between the Grenadians, where we find the king, and all other members of this ballet: they have feelings, both physical and emotional, and they are able to express those feelings in their dance, their song, and declaimed verses. It is likely that this kind of openness was, at this time, only possible to express in the burlesque mode, where it might be taken less seriously than in other public displays. While safe under the guise of a world turned upside-down, however, the dance scene with the king represents a certain climax in the uneasiness we witness as a series of emotional breakdowns and outbursts unfold. As these moments portray a lack of clear differentiation in hierarchy, and in public and private modes of existence, the king does not emerge as a dignified sovereign. The resulting discomfort is partially resolved in the explosion of grotesque and ridiculous characters that mark the end of the ballet.

The last characters to parade before the Parisian public are the dowager herself and her lover, both played by male members of Louis's closest entourage. The gentle, courtly vocabulary the lover uses contrasts with the overtly sexual desires of the musicians, until we find he is not at all favorable to the dowager: "Mais celle que je sers a bien d'autres appas, / Et je luy ferois tort de ne vous tracer pas / Quelques traits de sa gloire" ["But the woman I serve has many other lures, and I would do her wrong if I were not to outline some of the shapes of her glory"].[30] As for her "glory," he describes her as having eyes like dried up prunes and all other sorts of bodily irregularities. Her dignity is further tainted by her ridiculous physical nature (as seen in her costume),[31] her awkwardness on the dance floor, as well as at the very end of the ballet when she, ignorant of the fact, is unrelentingly mocked by her fiancé, the Fanfan de Sotteville. Since the emotions at the ballet's close are between an ignorant, delusional dowager and her future husband, an insincere trickster, there are therefore no reciprocal unions in the entire performance except for the ones the Grenadians claim to have, thanks to the optimal climate of their homeland. While McGowan has argued that the Bilbao ballet was satirizing the late Queen Marguerite de Valois and her style, I propose that it is more likely that this burlesque figure was meant to have some impact on the dowager whom Louis currently needed to keep in check, Marie de' Medici. This reading is supported by the degree to which the ballet emphasizes relationships, love, and—given the number of times Louis had to exile his family members for his own safety, his mother among them (exiled from 1617 to 1619)—the serious consequences of being distant from court.

The Court Turned Inside Out

Sullying or contaminating the dignified public sphere was the equivalent of two almost synonymous notions. On the one hand, it meant revealing an outward appearance or conduct that was unfit for one's rank. On the other hand, it could more simply mean representing *ce qui est sans dignité* [that which has no dignity], referring to a quality that is not public, but private, and so displaying in public that which was only destined for the private sphere (a distinction that was still under construction during the early modern period).

As the notion of public dignity developed in seventeenth-century France, comedians like Molière contributed to its disintegration. Hélène Merlin-Kajman suggests that "il faut comprendre que ce qui a commencé à scandaliser lors de la querelle du *Cid* continue à faire l'objet de la représentation théâtrale, et ceci de façon en quelque sorte aggravée avec Molière: le théâtre *montre* comment du particulier autonome s'est mis à souiller—du point de vue des adversaires—le public en tant que sphere des dignités" ["we must understand that what started to scandalize during the quarrel of the *Cid* (referring to the "indignity" of Chimène according to Georges de Scudéry) continues to be the subject of theatrical performance, and in some ways this was exacerbated with Molière, where theater *shows* how from an autonomous private sphere the public sphere of dignities began—from the point of view of some opponents—to be sullied"].[32] According to Merlin-Kajman's analysis of Molière, the writing, performance, and reception of comedy might have had a direct link with the disappearance of an outmoded social order in which rank and dignity were the supreme ordering factors. In its place was a world in which the lack of dignity, now public, was both troubling and grotesque, and yet where a receptive and reactive audience began to emerge and form more and more solid opinions.[33]

In the case of the Bilbao ballet, which figures at the period of absolutism's birth, we see a brief confusion about dignity and hierarchy, as foreign powers are subordinate to Cupid and romantic love, and the cosmic power of a sun king is nowhere to be found. This subject matter appears, moreover, to generate a performance of the curiously undignified nature of the beginning of Louis's ascendance to power, in which private and public were yet to be distinct spheres.

Burlesque ballet during the reign of Louis "the Just" should therefore be read as a key chapter in the early years of Louis's reign when the kingdom did not yet differentiate between the king's two bodies,[34] and when the growing distinction between public and private spheres that, according to Reinhart Koselleck, characterized the development of absolutism, was still very much underdeveloped. Under Louis XIII, royal ballet had the unique power to expose not only an emotional world that was supposed to remain suppressed, but also a private, "naked" side of the king. Indeed, court ballet, both inside and outside of the court, had an unprecedented ability for making visible what was normally hidden, which was perhaps most evident in the ballets danced by noble and aspiring-to-be-noble women put on display to please the queen or to show themselves to potential suitors.[35]

Although the public nature of court ballet tended to serve as a social ladder one was meant to climb, Louis XIII's ladder in the burlesque ballets worked in the reverse. He preferred to come down from his proverbial pedestal, literally down from his divine throne, in order to dance—playfully—roles related to his personal, sometimes undignified, and therefore private, tastes. This move was often accompanied by glimpses of his personality, since it meant casting him in marginal roles that related to his favorite pastimes.

Though never advised by Richelieu, Louis nevertheless chose to play these comic, grotesque characters and expose himself, inasmuch as he was not trying to dress, talk, or act in a manner that might be judged superior to his actual status. Sure, through subordination, as we have seen, he might have been punishing and correcting his potential enemies,[36] but by willingly taking part in the collapse of courtly codes, he proved to not yet incarnate the state as Richelieu would guide him to do in the later years of his reign.

Notes

1. Antoine Furetière, *Dictionnaire universelle contenant généralement tous les mots françois tant vieux que modernes, et les termes de toutes les sciences et des arts* (Rotterdam, 1690), article "dignité." All translations are mine unless otherwise noted.

2. I was first led to think about "dignity" and its relationship to "public" in Hélène Merlin-Kajman's work, especially "Indignité comique et public en débat," in *Les querelles dramatiques à l'âge classique*, ed. Emmanuelle Hénin (Leuven: Peeters, 2010), 97–111. Robert A. Schneider is currently working on a new study on the notion of dignity in the public and private sphere in a book project titled *Dignified Retreat: Writers and Intellectuals in the Age of Richelieu*.

3. Without reiterating their monumental work on the subject, the following essay aims to build on the theory of the king's two bodies, presented by Kantorowicz and the political structure of absolutism, described by Koselleck, both of which more recently have influenced Hélène Merlin-Kajman's research on public emotions in French studies. See Reinhart Koselleck, *Critique and Crisis: Enlightenment and the Pathogenesis of Modern Society* (Cambridge, MA: MIT Press, 1988); Ernst H. Kantorowicz, *The King's Two Bodies: A Study in Medieval Political Theology* (Princeton, NJ: Princeton University Press, 1957); and Hélène Merlin, *Public et littérature en France au XVIIe siècle* (Paris: Belles Lettres, 1994).

4. Georgie Durosoir, "Visages contrastés de l'Italie dans les ballets de la cour de France dans la première moitié du XVIIe siècle," *Revue De Musicologie* 77, no. 2 (1991): 169–78.

5. Mark Franko, "The King Cross-Dressed," in *From the Royal to the Republican Body: Incorporating the Political in Seventeenth- and Eighteenth-Century France*, ed. Sara E. Melzer and Kathryn Norberg (Berkeley: University of California Press, 1998), 64–84, 67. This is a reprint of his "Double Bodies: Androgyny and Power in the Performances of Louis XIV," *The Dance Review* 38, no. 4 (Winter 1994): 71–82.

6. For more on this subject matter and a helpful breakdown of these events, see Bernard Teyssandier et al., eds., *"Le roi hors de page" et autres textes: Une anthologie* (Reims: Épure. 2012); Hélène Duccini, *Faire voir, faire croire: L'opinion publique sous Louis XIII* (Seyssel: Champ Vallon, 2003); Michael Meere, "Social Drama, Cultural Pragmatics, and Louis XIII's Performativity: *La victoire du Phébus* (1617)," *The French Review* 85, no. 4 (March 2012): 672–83; and Jean-Vincent Blanchard,

"Dies Irae: Le coup d'État de Louis XIII, les pamphlets et l'institution du public," *Littératures classiques* 68 (2009): 31–42.

7. Orest Ranum, *Paris in the Age of Absolutism* (Bloomington: Indiana University Press, 1968), 134.

8. Ibid., 139.

9. Fabien Cavaillé, "Spectacle public, munificence royale et politique de la joie: Le cas du ballet de cour à la ville dans la première moitié su XVIIe siècle (*Le grand bal de la douairière de Billebahaut*, 1626)," *Biblio 17* 193 (2011): 29–42 ; Mark Franko, "Majestic Drag: Monarchical Performativity and the King's Body Theatrical," *The Drama Review* 47, no. 2 (Summer 2003): 71–87, esp. 77; Margaret McGowan, *L'art du ballet de cour en France, 1581–1643* (Paris: Editions du C.N.R.S., 1963), 102, 108.

10. In McGowan's reading, the reason for the burlesque nature of Louis's ballets was social and aesthetic: an effort to include the tastes of the bourgeoisie, which were not as refined as the tastes of the nobility (though we know this was not the case for the questionable tastes of Louis XIII, who preferred music and hunting to learning and refinement); a testament to the spread of the balletic art proper; and perhaps an effort to forge a separate identity from tragicomedy and pastoral. In Franko's view, McGowan ignores the evident battle in these ballets between nobles and royals, a subject he thinks would have secondarily entertained the bourgeoisie, but which, in the end, was a matter of higher power struggles. Cavaillé alerts us to yet another important facet of the public burlesque ballet, one that could indeed be read as a *carnavalesque* sense of political ballet: the union between the monarch and his city, a harmonious collaboration between royal and civic powers of a topsy-turvy spectacle. All three of these studies are essential to our understanding of burlesque ballet and, especially in Cavaillé's example, offer an understanding of why the king, in a festive attempt to harmonize with his city, would be part of a production that risked appearing undignified and ridiculous, perhaps even keeping a higher surveillance over the city during the frenzy of carnival.

11. McGowan has suggested that this ballet was "satirizing the old-fashioned style of Queen Marguerite de Valois, who had given a ball in 1612." *The Court Ballet of Louis XIII: A Collection of Working Designs for Costumes, 1615–33* (London: Victoria and Albert Museum, 1990), plates 63–89.

12. René Bordier, "Grand Bal de la douairière de Billebahaut : Ballet dansé par le Roy au mois de Fevrier 1626," in *Ballets et mascarades de cour de Henri III à Louis XIV (1581–1652)*, ed. M. Paul Lacroix (Geneva: Slatkine Reprints, 1968), 3:156. I hereafter cite page numbers from this edition.

13. Bordier, "Grand Bal," 158.

14. Ibid., 155–56.

15. *Lazzi* can be defined as improvised comic dialogue or action.

16. Ibid., 163.

17. In fact, without Louis himself appearing as this martial figure to be feared, there is little reason to think that this was more than an afterthought, perhaps even highlighted (or simply invented) in the abridged, printed libretto, in order to leave a more dignified trace of this royal event.

18. Ibid., 175.
19. Ibid.
20. Ibid., 178.
21. McGowan, *The Court Ballet*, plate 72.
22. Bordier, "Grand Bal," 180.
23. Ibid., 182.
24. One of the first examples I am aware of is in Ronsard's *Mascarades* for Charles IX during the Royal Tour that began in 1564.
25. This image is available in many sources. See, for example, McGowan, *The Court Ballet*, plate 9 in color, or plate 110.
26. For Louis's veritable obsession with music, see A. Lloyd Moote, *Louis the Just* (Berkeley: University of California Press, 1989), 268.
27. Bordier, "Grand Bal," 190.
28. Ibid., 191.
29. Ibid.
30. Ibid., 192.
31. See, for example, McGowan, *The Court Ballet*, plate 88.
32. Merlin-Kajman, "Indignité comique," 100.
33. Ibid., 106.
34. I do not focus on the Kantorowiczian reading of the burlesque ballet, since Franko already does this in his work. See, for example, "Majestic Drag."
35. For more on this gendered aspect, see Sharon Kettering, "Favour and Patronage: Dancers in the Court Ballets of Early Seventeenth-Century France," *Canadian Journal of History* 43 (Winter 2008): 391–415.
36. He cast his traitorous brother, for example, in the roles of a prostitute (McGowan, *The Court Ballet*, plate 80) and a "small, grotesque old man" (ibid., plate 108).

~

CHAPTER FOURTEEN

Poison in French Tragedy and Tragic Stories, 1600–1636

Stephanie O'Hara

The received narrative of French literary history sees the 1630s as a period when tragedy experienced a rebirth and laid the groundwork for the genre's subsequent flowering in the work of Pierre Corneille and Jean Racine.[1] This narrative tends to overlook or devalue French Renaissance tragedy in favor of the high neoclassical tragedy of the seventeenth century. However, for Charles Mazouer, the originality of French Renaissance theater lies in the way it looks both backward and forward, Janus-like, at the same time medieval and modern.[2] Inspired by this image of Janus, looking forward and looking back, I focus on the staging of poison in five plays from this period of rebirth—*Alcméon*, *Sophonisbe*, *Hercule mourant* [*Hercules Dying*], *Médée*, and *La mort de Mithridate* [*The Death of Mithridates*][3]—in order to ask two interrelated questions. First, what does an analysis of the dramaturgy of poison during this pivotal period tell us about the shift from humanist tragedy to neoclassical tragedy? Second, how does popular pamphlet literature from the same period contextualize these theatrical depictions of poison?

In Alexandre Hardy's *Alcméon, ou la vengeance féminine* (1628) [*Alcmaeon, or Female Vengence*],[4] the titular character seeks to seduce the young Callirhoé. To do so, he asks wife Alphesibée to return a jeweled choker that he had given her on their wedding day. After a bitter confrontation, Alphesibée appears to accede to her husband's wishes after he admits the truth and claims his is just a passing whim. She returns the choker to him after poisoning it. During a fit of poison-induced madness, Alcméon kills his children, so Alphesibée begs her brothers to avenge their deaths. In the ensuing fight, Alcméon and his brothers-in-law all die.[5] The poisoned necklace produces an impressive body count.

After the confrontation between husband and wife, the third act opens with a sixty-three-line monologue for Alphesibée, the longest one in the play. Implicit stage directions have Alphesibée brandish the necklace that she will poison in order to rein in her husband's "lascives chaleurs" ["lascivious heat"] and "luxure brutale" ["brutal concupiscence"].[6] She also draws an explicit parallel between herself and Dejanira, between her husband and the faithless Hercules. Instead of the poisoned blood of Nessus, however, she uses "sang . . . d'un enfant de la nue / Doué de certain charme à la force inconnue" ["blood . . . of a child of the clouds, endowed with a certain charm of unknown power"].[7] The editors of Alcméon in Théâtre de la cruauté propose "oiseau" ["bird"] for "enfant de la nue" ["child of the clouds"], but I suggest instead reading here the blood of a stillborn or aborted child.[8] Poison made from the blood of a fetus would be more cruel than that obtained from a bird. Indeed, the editors of Théâtre de la cruauté observe that the theater of very late sixteenth- and early seventeenth-century France is "bien proche des théâtres élisabéthain et espagnol" ["quite close to Elizabethan and Spanish theater"].[9] One thinks, for example, of Macbeth, when the Third Witch calls for a "[f]inger of birth-strangled babe" to be added to the potion she and her sisters are brewing.[10]

Hardy's staging of the poison/jealous woman topos stands out both for this bloody poison and for Alphesibée's pointed descriptions of her husband's raging libido. (Another example of her directness can be found in the confrontation scene, when she calls Callirhoé a "putain" ["whore"].[11]) Women as a whole have long been perceived as metaphorically poisonous; in addition, the female body itself has been thought to contain a poisonous substance, in the form of menstrual blood.[12] Not until the 1600s did academic physicians begin to think otherwise.[13] Thus, the poisonous nature of sexual jealousy perhaps finds its most baroque expression in Hardy; in the work of later dramatists, it will only be hinted at as poison.

Jean Mairet's Sophonisbe (1634–1635 season) concludes with the eponymous heroine committing suicide by poison, turning it into a remedy or pharmakon to escape a life no longer worth living.[14] Although suicide was forbidden by Christian morality, staging suicide was not forbidden by the rules of bienséance [seemliness].[15] However, throughout the play, before suicide by poison enters the picture, poison consistently figures in criticism of Sophonisbe, painting her as guilty by association with a poisoner, her first husband Syphax, or as metaphorically poisonous due to her beauty. For example, the jealous Syphax rages at her: "Tu l'as toujours aimé [Massinisse], depuis le jour fatal / Qu'il te fut accordé par ton père Asdrubal, / Et que de tes regards l'atteinte empoisonnée / Me fit prendre pour moi ce funeste hyménée" ["You have always loved Massinisse, since the fatal day that he was given to you by your father Asdrubal, and that the poisonous attack of your gaze made me take this ill-fated wedding upon myself"].[16] The reference to poisonous beauty is a well-known poetic trope and resurfaces in Racine's *Britannicus* and *Mithridate*.[17] Then Syphax switches from metaphorical poison to actual poison, telling Sophonisbe that were he to act within his rights, he could either kill her or force her to take poison. Instead, he prefers to leave things in the hands of Fate. After Syphax's death, the suspicious Romans remind Massinisse, who has just married Sophonisbe, that his new wife is the widow of that crafty poisoner, Syphax, and therefore cannot be trusted. Thus we see how Mairet links poison to Sophonisbe throughout the play, in preparation for her death by poison.

When it becomes clear that the Romans intend to treat her as a captive, Sophonisbe sends a messenger to Massinisse asking for the "présent" ["gift"] he had promised her. Two scenes later, the same messenger returns to Sophonisbe and her ladies bearing a cup of poison. Sophonisbe impatiently tells the messenger, "Avancez hardiment; / Montrez-moi ce papier, donnez-moi ce breuvage / Par où j'éviterai la honte du servage" ["Come boldly forth. Show me that paper. Give me that drink by which I will avoid the shame of servitude"].[18] Poison is thus framed as a gift enabling a triumphant death for the heroine, free of ignominy. Death by poison also allows Sophonisbe a clean death, like Racine's Phèdre, and like her, a last speech even as she draws her final breath. She asks her attendants to carry her to her bed: "et que je meure au moins dessus le même lit / Où mon funeste hymen hier au soir s'accomplit" ["and may I die, at least, on the same bed where my ill-fated wedding was consummated last night"].[19] When used as an instrument of suicide, poison allows for a nonviolent, noble, even sensual way of staging death. This *eros-thanatos* drive stands in direct contrast to the one at work in Hardy's *Alcméon*; it also resurfaces, of course, in *Phèdre*.

Jean de Rotrou's *Hercule mourant* (1634), considered fundamental to the rebirth of the tragic genre in French theater, contains similarly poisonous associations between love and death.[20] Indeed, the dramaturgy of poison in this play builds in subtle stages, from the credulous Déjanire's description of what she thinks is a love potion, which is really a poison, to her use of the Neoplatonic topos of poisonous beauty, in reference to her rival, to the stage device of Hercule's poisoned tunic, concluding with Hercule's references to the pain and death induced by the literal and metaphorical poison of jealousy. In act 2 Rotrou, following Seneca, has Déjanire recount the circumstances under which she came by her remedy, namely, her near-rape by Nessus, her rescue by Hercule, and Nessus's parting gift:

> . . . tiens (me dit-il) et tache
> Un de ses vêtements de ce sang précieux
> S'il est jamais blessé d'autres que de tes yeux,
> Il aura la vertu de te rendre son âme,
> Et le fera brûler de sa première flame.[21]

[. . . behold (he said to me) and endue some of his clothes with this precious blood. If ever he be wounded by the gaze of a woman other than you it will have the power to return his soul to you and will make him burn with the flame of his first love.]

Nessus's final words, as repeated by Déjanire, are heavy with dramatic irony. Hercule will indeed give up his soul, by dying, and Nessus's poisoned blood will cause Hercule's own blood to burn within him. A literal and metaphorical link connects jealousy, poison, and death.[22]

As he lies dying on a funeral pyre he himself prepared, Hercule at last understands the meaning of the oracle that had said he would be killed by one of his own victims. Yet Nessus's poison continues to act on a metaphorical level as well as a physical one. Burning with jealousy over Iole's love for Arcas, Hercule orders that once he himself has died, Arcas should be slain on his tomb, in front of Iole. Just as Iole prepares to stab herself rather than witness her lover be put to death, Hercule reappears as a deus ex machina, speaking in *stances* (lyric stanzas in octosyllables, as opposed to alexandrines): "Admis dans le céleste rang, / Je fais à la pitié céder la jalousie, / Ma soif éteinte d'ambroisie, / Ne vous demande plus de sang" ["Admitted to the heavenly ranks, I make jealousy give way to pity. My thirst now quenched with ambrosia requires no more blood from you"].[23] Celestial ambrosia and pity prove to be the antidote to Nessus's poisoned blood, putting an end to the vicious cycle of sexual jealousy and bloodshed that now exhausts itself, only just in time to spare Iole and Arcas.

This complex web of metaphorical poison doubled by poison as a stage device also underlines Corneille's *Médée*, which dates to 1634 as well. Act 4 opens with Médée alone in her magic grotto, a site of black magic and of dramatic revelation. Médée summons her confidante Nérine and shows her the poisoned robe she intends to give Créuse, explaining at length, in twenty-six lines, which ingredients went into the robe.[24] Some of Médée's poisons are unique mythological substances, such as the Hydra's blood, or fire that fell from the heavens along with Phaeton. The nonmythological substances, on the other hand, are threateningly plural: the venom of unnumbered African serpents, "mille autres venins" ["a thousand other venoms"], "ces herbes" ["these herbs"] that "ne sont pas d'une vertu commune" ["have no ordinary virtue"].[25] Médée, with her extensive pharmacy, makes *Macbeth's* witches look like amateurs. She has mixed up and displayed just about every poison-ous animal, vegetable, and mineral substance available: venom, herbs, two kinds of blood, diverse fires, harpy feathers, serpent's tongue, powders, roots, and waters. Médée advertises not just her store of ingredients, but also her skill at selecting them and mixing them into drugs. By *her* command, African serpents came to her; *she* forced them to provide her with their venom; she herself picked the herbs; she controls and handles the Hydra's blood and Phaeton's fire. Indeed, the scene ends with her imperiously reassuring Nérine that even though she is to deliver the robe to Créuse, the poisons are targeted specifically for the princess and her father. Of all the seventeenth-century French plays involving poison, this appears to be the only one containing a detailed recipe, even if this recipe is hardly practical but filled with magic, mythology, and hyperbole.

Yet Médée's knowledge appears to be not only pharmaceutical but also psychological in nature. She explains the benefits of her drugs to Nérine: "Mes maux dans ces poisons trouvent leur médecine" ["My sufferings find their remedy in these poisons"];[26] "L'amour à tous mes sens ne fut jamais si doux / Que ce triste appareil à mon esprit jaloux" ["Love was never as sweet to all my senses as this sad array to my jealous spirit"].[27] Médée links her jealousy to the preparation of her poisons, and here Corneille plays on the ambiguity of the *pharmakon*, a drug that can be either a healing medicine or a mortal poison.[28] In *Médée*, poison also acts simultaneously, in both harmful and salutary ways, since Médée's jealous rage will be healed by poisoning Créuse. This dual power of the *pharmakon* will have two different consequences for the staging of poison in this play: a concrete and visible effect in the death of Créuse and Créon, and also a psychological effect in the appeasement of Médée's wrath. The second effect stems symbolically from the first. In other words, the poison's doubly elemental nature, liquid and fire, allows for its twofold use: it is at once harmful for Créuse (fatal burns) and beneficial for Médée (soothing the burns of jealousy). Any one of the ingredients listed in Médée's pharmacy would have been sufficient for a typical poison, hidden in food or drink, but Médée wants to exact a total revenge. On one level, then, her knowledge of the poisons available in the natural world gives her enormous power, which serves as the basis for theatrical display.[29] On another level, the metaphorical poison originates within Médée, heroic and venomous, the literal and figurative source of poison and destruction. In this way, Corneille both echoes and transforms the jealous woman topos in *Médée*, giving his character a complexity and power unlike anything in *Alcméon* and *Hercule mourant.*

Like *Sophonisbe*, La Calprenède's *La mort de Mithridate* (1636) also features a main character who chooses suicide over being displayed in a Roman triumphal procession. Unlike Sophonisbe, however, Mithridate has a wife, daughters, and daughter-in-law who join him in death. In no other play of the era do we find so many dead bodies onstage, preceded by such a long agony over a hopeless situation. In this sense, the play is closer to French Renaissance tragedy than to classical tragedy. No member of Mithridate's family appears onstage without being accompanied by one or several members of that family (the notable exception is the traitor Pharnace). The characters hide nothing; they take pleasure in sharing their pains and fears with other characters. This transparency of emotion is most unusual for a play featuring poison, because poison is typically used by characters who prize secrecy and stealth.

This transparent circulation of emotion reaches its highest point with the group suicide of the last act. As if to highlight an additional degree of emotional intensity, Mithridate declaims *stances* in front of his wife and daughters. At the same time, according to the stage directions, the stage is supposed to contain a table with a chalice on it; spectators familiar with the story of Mithridates would metonymically associate the chalice with poison. Like Socrates reproaching his followers for crying like women after he has drunk poison, Mithridate reproaches his daughters for their tears and orders them to put on a happy face.[30] The act of suicide, although undertaken for political reasons, remains grounded in a domestic context. Poison is a gift, shared by family members, instantly claimed, offered and received as such.[31]

The sharing of poison thus symbolizes the ultimate act of family devotion, as is underlined by the fact that the drinking of the poison is accomplished hierarchically, beginning with the spouse's supplication, then that of the children (older daughter, then younger daughter). It should be pointed out that the poison does not work on Mithridate, since he has made himself immune to poison, and he takes the manly route and uses his sword to commit suicide. This unusual association of family love and poison is all the more striking inasmuch as poison typically figures into stories of dysfunctional families. Although the use of poison as a metaphor for erotic love in French poetry is well known, *La mort de Mithridate* demonstrates a perhaps unique use of poison to represent familial love and unity, as well as a late example of what has been called the stasis of Renaissance tragedy. During the pivotal period of the early seventeenth century, the staging of poison as a metaphor and plot device applied to tragedies featuring either suicide (*Sophonisbe, La mort de Mithridate*) or the figure of the jealous woman (*Alcméon, Hercule mourant, Médée*). In all but one of these plays, poison features as a woman's weapon, and an effective one at that. If we view the plays in chronological order, the first of the group, *Alcméon*, is also the most baroque in its use of poison, whereas the last, *La mort de Mithridate*, harks back to Renaissance theater. The other three plays lack the crude (but exciting) excess of Hardy or the inaction of La Calprenède; instead, Mairet, Rotrou, and Corneille explore the literal and metaphorical implications of poison as a stage device in ways that echo what Racine will later do in *Mithridate, Britannicus*, and *Phèdre*. The dramaturgy of poison thus represents an important thread in the transition from humanist to neoclassical tragedy.

I now turn to my second line of inquiry and ask how these onstage poison stories compare to offstage ones from the same time period, focusing on two pamphlets from the early seventeenth century. The first is a six-page octavo pamphlet entitled *Discours pitoyable de la cruauté et tyrannie d'un jeune garçon serviteur* [*Pitiable Story of the Cruelty and Tyranny of a Young Servant*].[32] At least two editions were printed, one in Rouen and one in Dinan. Judging from the nature of the story and its tone, this is the kind of ephemeral writing also known as a *canard*. These were printed hastily, on cheap paper, and sold by *colporteurs* or peddlers.[33] The Bibliothèque nationale de France's catalog notes that this pamphlet is "unknown to bibliographers," which might explain why it does not figure in Jean-Pierre Seguin's bibliographical study of 517 *canards* published between 1529 and 1631.[34] Seguin organizes his corpus thus: criminal affairs, natural disasters, celestial phenomena (such as comets), and strange or supernatural phenomena (devilry, two-headed cows, Siamese twins, and the like). Thus, this pamphlet belongs to a genre that could be considered an ancestor of the supermarket tabloid.

The *Garçon serviteur* pamphlet opens with a preface that to modern readers may sound melodramatic and moralizing. An anonymous narrator intones, "*Ami lecteur, quand sera-ce que nos yeux doivent être effrayés de ces étranges et horribles augures lesquels se commettent ce jourd'hui? (hélas non) car nous nous laissons emporter aux délices et voluptés du monde. . . . Mais Catholiques, quittez ces délices et mondanités Disons comme le Prophète royal David, Seigneur, mes iniquités surpassent mon chef*" ["Good reader, when will our eyes take fright at the sight of these strange and horrible signs that are observed today? (Alas, no) for we let ourselves be carried off by the delights and pleasures of the world. . . . But Catholics, quit these delights and worldly things Let us say like the royal Prophet David, Lord, my iniquities surpass my head"].[35] The tale of the servant poisoner, following this mini-sermon on man's depravity and on the importance of renouncing worldly pleasures, thus serves to illustrate a broader theme of waywardness and repentance.[36]

The tale, in brief, is that a servant in a bourgeois household in Ginguant, Brittany, seeks revenge on the family that fired him; he poisons their luncheon soup. Master, mistress, children, and female servant all die, except for one little girl, whose cries bring the neighbors running. Once captured, the culprit confesses and is sentenced to die as follows: "d'être pincé par les cuisses, bras, et mamelles avec des tenailles rouges sortants du feu, trainé sur une claie rompu tout vif, et [à] languir sur une roue tant que mort fût ensuivie" ["to have red-hot pincers applied to his thighs, arms, and nipples, dragged on a hurdle, broken alive on the wheel and left there until death follows"].[37] The pamphlet concludes with the criminal's last words and a rhyme about the danger of false appearances in servants.

The document lacks any identifying details about the criminal and his victims: no names, ages, or physical descriptions are given. Indeed, the only proper name in the story is that of the town where the events are supposed to have taken place, "Ginguant en Bretagne" (modern-day Guingamp, Brittany). Thus the story is told with a strict economy of detail and vocabulary; what description there is consists of moral qualifications. The adjective *cruel*, in its different forms, is used nine times, and is echoed by the noun *cruauté* [cruelty], used five times, for a total of fourteen times over six pages, making this the most frequently used descriptor in the text. *Cruel* is used by the criminal to describe himself, and the word also modifies *vengeance*, *meurtre* [murder], *violence*, and *poison*. The next most common descriptive word is *misérable*, which occurs nine times and is frequently used in reference to the servant. The master, on the other hand, is described by the narrator as "ce bon maître" ["this good master"] and "un honorable maître." The events of the poisoning unfurl with breathtaking, theatrical rapidity and efficiency. The poison takes effect "tout aussitôt" ["right at once"], "tant la violence du poison était cruelle" ["so cruel was the poison's violence"]; everyone except the little girl dies "à même instant" ["at the same moment"]; the neighbors arrive "promptement" ["quickly"] and alert the authorities "soudainement" ["suddenly"]; pursuit of the criminal, identified by the little girl, is effected "aussitôt" ["at once"]; once captured, he confesses "incontinent" ["immediately"]. It is also worth noting that we never learn exactly what kind of poison the servant used, and although we might guess that it was arsenic or some other easily obtained poisonous substance, the poison nevertheless remains generic and unidentifiable. The lack of description, counterbalanced by focus on moral descriptors and the remarkably swift course of justice, help frame the story as morally true. What matters most is that a lesson can be drawn from the behavior of the wicked servant.

The servant's last words deserve closer attention. After all, this title of the pamphlet promises the story of the regrets expressed by the criminal before dying, and it delivers on that promise:

Etant sur la roue [il] disait: "Assistance ouvrez maintenant vos yeux pour en-tendre les plus étranges et exécrables cruautés que moi misérable ai commis en la personne de mon maître, même à sa femme et enfants, ouvre-toi maintenant terre qui m'a porté. . . . venez serpents, dragons et tous engeances de vipère, venez déchirer et dévorer ce misérable corps, las que me servent ces regrets ni ces complaintes? je ne peux dire autre chose, sinon que je prie l'assistance de prier Dieu pour ma pauvre âme, et prendre exemple à mon horrible forfait".[38]

[Once on the wheel, [he] said: "You who witness this, open now your eyes in order to hear the strangest and most execrable cruelties that I, a miserable man, committed against the person of my master, even against his wife and children, open now, earth that bore me. . . . come serpents, dragons, and all kinds of vipers, come tear and devour this miserable body, alas what use to me are these regrets and laments? I can say nothing else, other than that I pray those who witness this to pray to God for my poor soul, and to learn from the example of my horrible crime".]

These edifying last words are extraordinarily eloquent coming from a provin-cial domestic in early seventeenth-century France, one who has just had sen-sitive areas of his flesh torn with red-hot pincers, been dragged on a hurdle, and been broken on the wheel. The tragic theatricality of this speech might not have disgraced Alexandre Hardy. There are several literary flourishes, such as the plea "ouvre-toi maintenant terre qui m'a porté" ["open now, earth that bore me"] and the alliteration in "tous engeances de vipère, venez déchirer et dévorer." The tone of these final words contrasts with the other sorts of language earlier attributed to the servant in the pamphlet, namely, insults, blasphemy, and scandalous and indecent speech.[39] The servant's new eloquence, coming as it does immediately after the description of the punishments visited upon his suffering body, points to the theatrical nature of his public execution. Indeed, the servant appeals to serpents and vipers to break an already broken body, which makes the pamphlet's depiction of his torments even more graphic. His suffering overpowers and displaces that of his victims in the final cathartic movement of this drama. But how does this apparently real-life poison drama differ from onstage dramas? First, it is noteworthy that the poisoner is not a jealous or suicidal woman. He is not of high birth, nor does he possess special knowledge (Médée, Alphesibée). Instead, he is petty, in every sense of the word.

I now turn from the poisoner to poison itself, by examining a 1611 pamphlet about a mercenary poisoner. The pamphlet is titled *Discours au vrai de l'étrange cruauté d'un soldat appelé la Planche, par lui exercée sur une jeune fille pour avoir de son lait empoisonné, et du cruel empoisonnement par lui attenté en la personne d'un grand Seigneur de Provence. Avec le récit de la punition qui s'en ensuivit* [True story of the strange cruelty of a soldier named La Planche, perpetrated by him on a young girl in order to have some of her poisoned milk, and of the cruel poisoning attempted by him on the person of a great Lord of Provence: With the tale of the punishment that followed].⁴⁰ As in the story of the wicked servant, the narrator frequently uses the words *cruel* and *cruauté*, in this case, twenty times over twelve pages. What is especially striking here, however, is the strange link between cruelty and poisoned breast milk. The story is horrific, and was probably meant to be so, given the lurid nature of other types of pamphlets. Indeed, this pamphlet calls to mind the genre of *histoires tragiques* [tragic stories].

The bitter enmity subsisting between two rival lords, whose real names will not be given for honor's sake, has led one of them to hire an assassin, described as "Un la Planche, mauvais garçon, et sorti des excréments de nos dernières guerres civiles, assez pervers pour une telle exécution, et assez nécessiteux pour se laisser gagner à ce leurre de ces mille écus, en prend la charge. . . . Etrange lâcheté d'une âme contrenaturée, de se laisser embeguiner à si peu de chose pour entreprendre sur la vie de l'innocent!" ["One La Planche, a wicked youth, sprung from the excrement of our late civil wars, perverted enough for such a deed, and needy enough to let himself be won over by the lure of these thousand *écus*, takes up the task. . . . Strange cruelty of an unnatural soul, to become enamored of so little in order to attack the life of an innocent!"].⁴¹ Not content with adjectives such as "wicked" and "perverted," the narrator uses a vivid scatological metaphor to drive home his point: the excrement of the atrocities stemming from the Wars of Religion has provided a breeding ground for criminals like La Planche. Of the pamphlets I have read, few make any use of figurative language. What distinguishes this pamphleteer is the way he combines metaphor with a brief historical allusion to the Wars of Religion. The pamphlet was published in 1611; Henri IV had been assassinated on May 14, 1610, after a twelve-year reign that had brought some measure of stability to the kingdom after the wars. Yet those wars were clearly still fresh in the mind of this writer, assuming there was little lag time between the writing of the pamphlet and its publication. The reference to the excrements of the civil wars is vague enough that we do not really know what role La Planche played in the conflict, either as a Huguenot soldier or as a Catholic one (recalling that in the pamphlet title his occupation is given as soldier). The bitter violence of the troubles suffices to highlight the brutality and perversity of the criminal. Financial greed is also a motivating factor here, but it is presented in second place, almost as a corollary of La Planche's perverse and cruel nature. The title of the pamphlet described La Planche's cruelty as "strange," and now here his cowardliness in carrying out a hit via poisoning is also described as "strange." But at this point we still do not know exactly what is so strange about the assassin's actions.

As the story continues, we learn the intended victim is particularly fond of *brousse*, a Provençal cottage cheese made from goat's milk, to the extent that he pays a woman to make this dish for him daily. All that remains, then, is for La Planche to befriend this woman and poison the goat's milk at the right moment. But La Planche does not go to the apothecary and mix up his own concoction, nor does he go to a *devin* or a *devineresse* [male or female fortune-teller] or to any other vaguely shady character who might fairly be said to know something about poison. Instead, he finds himself a nursing mother, a redhead of easy virtue, whom he flatters and wheedles to come with him to an out-of-the way cave on the promise of ten *écus* [crowns]. The poor girl (as the narrator calls her) is quite used to this sort of thing and agrees to La Planche's proposition. They go to the cave and have sex, after which La Planche ties her up and whips her,

> et la tourmente en mille sortes pour la faire entrer en colère [i.e., pour provoquer un flux d'humeur colérique], et la provoque en telle sorte que de colère le lait qu'elle avait aux mamelles se changea en sang comme violet, et fort enflammé, ce qu'ayant aperçu il prend un crapaud qu'il avait apporté à ce dessein en un vase, l'applique aux mamelles de cette misérable, les lui fait sucer par force, et prendre ce lait colérique, puis il la laisse là et s'en va. O cruauté plus que cruelle, et que jamais les plus cruels [lectigans] n'avaient pu imaginer! Il s'en va avec sa bête bien remplie, prend un alambic et à force de feu il tire le venin pestiféré de cet infect animal, le provoquant aussi tant qu'il pouvait à le rendre encore plus mortel.[42]

> [and torments her in a thousand ways in order to provoke a flow of choleric humor in her, and does so in such a way that the milk in her breasts turns to purple blood, quite enflamed; having noticed this he took a toad that he had brought in a vase for this purpose, applies it to the breasts of this poor

woman, forces the toad to suck them and ingest this choleric milk, then he leaves her there and goes away. O cruelty more than cruel, which the cruelest (criminals) could never have imagined! He goes off with his animal well filled, takes an alembic and by dint of flame he draws the pestiferous venom from this infected animal, torturing it as well as much as he could in order to make [its poison] more fatal.]

The full force of the narrator's implication that La Planche was like a maggot sprung from the excrement of the Wars of Religion now becomes clear. This is no ordinary poisoner, who could have easily obtained arsenic for killing rats at an apothecary's, or who could have used poisonous plants. Instead, he dreams up a peculiar combination of a poisonous toad, "choleric" human milk, and torture. La Planche not only beats the woman in order to make her milk bloodier and thus more choleric, he does the same thing to the toad in order to make its venom more venomous.

Human milk and blood are of course not inherently poisonous in and of themselves. In fact, they are life-giving substances that here become poisonous by dint of physical violence. The poison is cruel because it was cruelly obtained. While this may seem like a kind of perverse magical thinking, it is entirely logical in the light of early modern medical thought. For example, in her *Observations diverses* (first edition, 1609), the royal midwife Louise Bourgeois warns against redheads as wet nurses: "il faut regarder qu'elle ne soit rousse, d'autant que le lait en est extremement chaud: Je dirai en passant que j'ai vu une rousse nourrir aucunement bien ses enfants, mais tous ceux qu'elle a nourri d'autrui sont tombés en chartre et sont morts" ["take care that she is not a redhead, because their milk is very hot. In passing, I would add that I have seen a redhead nurse her own children successfully, but all those whom she nursed that were not her own withered away and died"].[43]

Once the poisoned *brousse* is brought to the victim, its effects are as follows:

Voilà soudain, un grand tremblement à ce pauvre patient, avec une difficulté d'haleine extrême, le battement de pouls, le suffoquement des artères, la convulsion de tous ses membres, et une enflure étrange, accompagnée de douleurs si cruelles qu'on le pourrait comparer à celle de l'enfer, enfin chacun juge Monsieur des Baquets mort. On court, on va, on vient, on tourne, les Médecins, les Apothicaires, les Chirurgiens, les contrepoisons, les antidotes, tout y est.[44]

[Behold, suddenly there was a great trembling seen in this poor patient, with extreme difficulty breathing; there was a [fast] pulse, suffocation of the arteries, the convulsion of all his limbs, and a strange swelling that was accompanied by pains so cruel that they could be compared to the torments of hell, finally, everyone judges Monsieur des Baquets to be dead. People run hither and thither, come and go, turn in all directions, Physicians, Apothecaries, Surgeons, counter-poisons, antidotes, everything is done that can be done.]

Just as in the *Garçon serviteur* pamphlet and in onstage poisonings, the effect is almost instantaneous. However, here the poison's effects on the victim are described in greater detail. No less than seven different symptoms are listed: trembling, difficulty breathing, elevated pulse, blocked circulation, convulsions, swelling, and general pain. This poison has attacked the circulatory system, the respiratory system, and the nervous system. By way of comparison, a 1626 poisoning victim named Étienne L'Hoste was described in a *factum* or *mémoire judiciaire* [legal brief] as having the following set of eight symptoms: "les évacuations par le haut et par le bas redoublèrent encore plus violemment avec syncopes, défaillances de cœur, hocquets, éternuements, agitations, et convulsions générales de tous ses membres" ["the vomiting and diarrhea redoubled more violently, with syncope, weak heartbeats, hiccups, sneezing, agitation, and general convulsions of all his limbs"].[45] In the context of early modern toxicology, then, the effects of this poison are not out of the ordinary.

From this point on, the pamphlet moves briskly toward its conclusion. The woman who provided the *brousse* swears her innocence and mentions that La Planche happened to be around as she was making the *brousse*. In the meantime, shepherds pass by the cave to which La Planche lured the redheaded woman, now "toute enflée" ["all swollen"], "bleue et défigurée" ["blue and disfigured"].[46] They hear her cries, see what has been done to her, and hear her story before she dies on the spot. This, in conjunction with the other woman's story, is enough to cause La Planche to be seized. Under torture, he readily confesses and implicates the man who hired him. Both are condemned to death, with the nobleman who paid for the killing being broken on the wheel, and La Planche

condamné d'être brûlé à petit feu, où il endurait les plus grands tourments que la rigueur des bourreaux saurait jamais enfanter, et par ce supplice infâme et malheureux il envoya son âme hors de son infâme conscience avec milles cris, mille lamentations, mille complaintes, et mille regrets, qu'il proféra encore avec une telle constance, que les cœurs les plus endurcis à la cruauté se fussent encore laissé toucher à la pitié, voyant un misérable en telle misère combattre si courageusement les rigueurs de la mort.[47]

[condemned to burn in a slow fire, where he would endure the greatest torments that the rigor of the executioners could ever devise, and by this infamous and unhappy torture he sent his soul out of his foul conscience with a

thousand cries, laments, moans, and regrets, which he yet uttered with such
constancy that hearts the most hardened to cruelty would have been touched
by pity, in seeing a miserable man in such misery so courageously fight the
rigors of death.]

Although both men are punished, La Planche, as the actual poisoner, is
subjected to a harsher punishment. The narrator, who was remarkably precise in his descriptions of the torment suffered by La Planche's victims, here
is remarkably vague in his description of the criminal's sufferings. He leaves
La Planche's final agony to the discretion of the individual reader or listener's imagination and goes so far as to say that even those hearts were most
hardened to cruelty would have pitied La Planche's *courageous* sufferings.

Like the servant poisoner, La Planche is base and petty. Like the servant
poisoner, his repentance and suffering offer readers and onlookers the dramatic spectacle of a good death. Unlike the servant, however, he creates a
bizarre and baroque poison, the likes of which I have yet to encounter in the
course of my research into early modern poison stories, and the likes of which
would certainly not be found onstage.[48] Thus, Hardy's *Alcméon*, although
drawn from ancient Greek mythology, ultimately has more in common with
popular print culture, in the form of tragic stories hawked in pamphlets, than
it does with the *épuration* ["refining"] of the emerging classical theater, as
represented by *Sophonisbe*, *Hercule mourant*, *Médée*, and *La Mort de Mithridate*.
If the dramaturgy of poison represents an important thread in the transition
from humanist to classical tragedy, the pamphlet literature shows that along
with this transition there is a disconnect between stylized representations of
violence onstage and gruesome violence and suffering offstage.

The reality of offstage poison crimes was much more complicated than
what plays and melodramatic pamphlet literature could provide, as the "Affair of the Poisons" (1679–1682) demonstrated. This scandal of epic propor-
tions implicated Parisians of every class, men and women, in the buying and
selling of poison. Louis XIV instituted a special tribunal to investigate and
judge the affair. Known as the *chambre ardente* or burning chamber because
of the burning tapers that lined its walls, the tribunal was made up of Paris's
top magistrates. Over a four-year period, a total of 442 people were accused
in the affair. Of those 442, 36 were sentenced to death, 5 were sent to the
galleys, and 23 were banished.[49] In other words, 14 percent of those accused met with some form of punishment; the other 86 percent were either
cleared of wrongdoing or released because of insufficient evidence. These
statistics give a sense of both the size and difficulty of the affair: the number
of people charged with the crime of poison was six times greater than the

number of people actually punished. In reality, it was much more difficult to convict someone of poisoning than it was to simply accuse him or her of the crime.[50] However unrealistic they may be, the poison stories found in early seventeenth-century tragedy and pamphlet literature suggest that the "Affair of the Poisons" was not an aberration. Poison crimes were an intractable political and social problem in early modern France, and they were more easily resolved onstage and in pamphlet stories than by the authorities.

Notes

1. For more on this "death" and "rebirth" of French tragedy in the early seventeenth century, see Georges Forestier, *La tragédie française. Passions tragiques et règles classiques* (Paris: Armand Colin. 2010). For a synthetic overview in English of the subsequent codifcation of neoclassical tragedy, see John D. Lyons, *Kingdom of Disorder: Theory of Tragedy in Classical France* (West Lafayette, IN: Purdue University Press, 1999).

2. Charles Mazouer, *Le théâtre français de la Renaissance* (Paris: Champion, 2002), 409–10.

3. Monléon's *Thyeste* (1638), although fascinating, was not integral to the development of French tragedy in the way that the plays discussed here are. For a discussion of poison in this play, see Stephanie O'Hara, "Family Ties: Death by Poison in *La Mort de Mithridate* and *Thyeste*," in *Relations and Relationships in Seventeenth-Century French Literature: Actes du 36e congrès annuel de la North American Society for Seventeenth-Century French Literature*, ed. Jennifer Perlmutter (Tübingen: Narr Biblio 17 166, 2006), 331–41.

4. Alexandre Hardy, *Alcméon, ou la vengeance féminine*, in *Théâtre de la cruauté et récits sanglants en France (XVIe–XVIIe siècle)*, ed. Christian Biet et al. (Paris: Robert Laffont, 2006), 391–451. Citations from all the plays in this chapter include act, scene, and verse number(s). All translations are mine unless otherwise noted.

5. On the poetic and affective implications of the violence in this tragedy, see Fabien Cavaillé, "Alexandre Hardy et le rêve perdu de la Renaissance: Spectacles violents, émotions, concorde civile au début du XVIIe siècle" (PhD diss., Université Paris III-Sorbonne Nouvelle, 2009).

6. Hardy, *Alcméon*, 3.1.641; 644.

7. Ibid., 3.1.655–56.

8. Biet, *Théâtre de la cruauté*, 420n1.

9. Ibid., XI.

10. William Shakespeare, *Macbeth*, in *The Norton Shakespeare*, 2nd ed., ed. Jean E. Howard et al. (Boston: W. W. Norton, 2008), 3.1.30.

11. Hardy, *Alcméon*, 2.2.565.

12. See Margaret Hallissy, *Venomous Woman: Fear of the Female in Literature* (Westport, CT: Greenwood Press, 1987); and Lynn Wood Mollenauer, *Strange Rev-*

262 ~ Stephanie O'Hara

elations: Magic, Poison, and Sacrilege in Louis XIV's France (University Park: Pennsylvania State University Press, 2007), 56–57.

13. See Michael Stolberg, "A Woman Down to Her Bones: The Anatomy of Sexual Difference in the Sixteenth and Early Seventeenth Centuries," *Isis* 94, no. 2 (2003): 294.

14. Mairet was not the only dramatist to treat this story, which was also popular during the Renaissance.

15. The word *suicide* did not exist in the seventeenth century, as Georges Couton points out. Instead, phrases such as *se précipiter* [to cast oneself down] were used. See Pierre Corneille, *Œuvres complètes*, ed. Georges Couton (Paris: Gallimard, 1980), 1:1392–93. See also Tom Bruyer, Introduction to *Le sang et les larmes: Le suicide dans les tragédies profanes de Jean Racine* (Amsterdam: Rodopi, 2012).

16. Jean Mairet, *Sophonisbe*, in *Théâtre du XVIIe siècle*, vol. 1, ed. Jacques Scherer (Paris: Gallimard, Bibliothèque de la Pléiade, 1975), 1.1.41–44.

17. See, for example, Marc Carnel, "Amour et poison dans l'œuvre de Ronsard," in *Poison et antidote dans l'Europe des XVIe et XVIIe siècles*, ed. Sarah Voinier and Guillaume Winter (Arras: Artois Presses Université, 2011), 185–99. For modern editions of Jean Racine's plays, see his *Œuvres complètes*, vol. 1, ed. Georges Forestier et al. (Paris: Gallimard, Bibliothèque de la Pléiade, 1999).

18. Mairet, *Sophonisbe*, 5.5.1618–20.

19. Ibid., 5.5.1687–88.

20. See Dominique Moncond'huy, "Introduction" to *Hercule mourant*, by Jean de Rotrou, in *Théâtre complet 2*, ed. Bénédicte Louvat et al. (Paris: S.T.F.M., 1999), 60–61. See also Ronald W. Tobin, "*Médée* and the Hercules Tradition of the Early Seventeenth Century," *Romance Notes* 8, no. 1 (1966): 65–69; André Stegmann, *L'héroïsme cornélien, genèse et signification* (Paris: Armand Colin, 1968), 1:40, 66; and Jacques Morel, *Agréables mensonges* (Paris: Klinksieck, 1991), 353.

21. Routrou, *Hercule mourant*, 2.2.474–78.

22. When water does not work, Hercule tries using the blood of the servant Lychas to put out the flames (Routrou, *Hercule mourant*, 3.2.709–10). After realizing that Déjanire is responsible for his suffering, he tells himself to eat her heart: "Mange son cœur jaloux, bois son perfide sang, / Et qu'entre tes vaincus elle ait le premier rang" ["Eat her jealous heart, drink her perfidious blood, and among those whom you have vanquished, let her have pride of place"] (ibid., 3.2.765–66). But the poison is too strong, and Hercule loses consciousness. In a later scene, he wonders aloud about the nature of the poison wracking him:

> D'où me naît cette peste? et quel est ce poison?
> Cerbère l'a versé, jadis ce monstre esclave
> Fit écumer ici sa venimeuse bave,
> Ou c'est du sang mortel qui de l'Hydre jaillit
> Et que ce traître esprit peut-être recueillit;
> De mes nerfs les plus forts cette peste dispose,
> Et presque à mes regards mes entrailles expose;

Moi-même je m'ignore en ce triste accident,
Et ce qui fut Alcide est un bûcher ardent. (Ibid., 4.1.932–40)

[Whence comes this pestilence? What is this poison? Cerberus poured it; formerly that enslaved monster made his venomous drool foam. Or it is the mortal blood that poured from the Hydra, which that traitor perhaps collected. This pestilence weakens my strongest nerves and almost shows my entrails to my sight. I do not recognize myself in this sad accident. And he who was once Alcides is now a burning funeral pyre.]

The reference to the monstrous Hydra is more accurate than Hercule yet knows. When he killed Nessus to save Déjanire, Hercule used arrows poisoned with the blood of the Hydra, which he had previously slain.

23. Ibid., 5.4.1451–54.

24. Pierre Corneille, *Médée*, in *Théâtre complet*, vol. 1, ed. Georges Couton (Paris: Garnier, Bibliothèque de la Pléiade, 1971), 4.1.985–1011

25. Ibid., 4.1.985, 981.

26. Ibid., 4.1.986.

27. Ibid., 4.1.991–92.

28. In the Platonic dialogues, for example, the poison or *pharmakon* that kills Socrates helps him to die in a way consistent with his philosophy, insofar as it leads him to that longed-for state in which the soul leaves the body. Monique Dixsaut recalls that, in Greek, *phármakon*

désigne aussi bien le remède qui guérit, le philtre magique, que le poison. Platon emploie ce terme sans jamais préciser la nature du *phármakon* en question, laissant ainsi jouer une ambiguïté qui se justifie par l'ensemble du dialogue: le poison est aussi remède et instrument de délivrance. On a posé la question de savoir si les effets décrits à la fin correspondaient bien à ceux de la ciguë. . . . Mais Platon aurait, dans la scène finale, passé sous silence tous les effets déplaisants: nausées, vomissements, spasmes,—la description pseudo-clinique ne servant qu'à attester une mort conçue comme libération progressive et comme séparation. (Introduction to Plato's *Phédon*, ed. Monique Dixsaut [Paris: GF-Flammarion, 1991], 314n.2)

[designates the remedy that heals, the magic philter, as well as poison. Plato uses this term without ever specifying the nature of the *phármakon* in question, playing on an ambiguity that is justified by the dialogue as a whole: the poison is also a remedy and an instrument of deliverance. The question has been raised as to whether the effects described at the end in fact correspond to those of hemlock. . . . But Plato seems to have glossed over, in the final scene, all the unpleasant effects of hemlock poisoning: nausea, vomiting, spasms— the pseudo-clinical description he gives only serving to attest to death conceived of as a progressive liberation and as a separation.]

On depictions of Medea's magical healing powers in early modern France, see Amy Wygant, *Medea, Magic, and Modernity in France. Stages and Histories, 1553–1797* (Aldershot, UK: Ashgate, 2007); and Zoe Schweitzer, "Une 'héroïne exécrable aux yeux des spectateurs'. Poétique de la violence: *Médée* de la Renaissance aux Lumières (Angleterre, France, Italie)" (PhD diss., Université Paris IV-Sorbonne, 2006).

29. The power of the theater, according to Marc Fumaroli; the power of the coup d'état, according to Louis Marin; power itself, according to Hélène Merlin. See Marc Fumaroli, "De Médée à Phèdre: Naissance et mise à mort de la tragédie 'cornélienne,'" in Héros et orateurs: Rhétorique et dramaturgie cornéliennes (Geneva: Droz, 1996), 493–518; Louis Marin, "Théâtralité et pouvoir : Magie, machination, machine ; Médée de Corneille," in Le pouvoir de la raison d'état, ed. Christian Lazzeri and Dominique Reynié (Paris: PUF, 1992), 231–59; and Hélène Merlin, Public et littérature en France au XVIIe siècle (Paris: Les Belles Lettres, 1994), 257.

30. "[Montrez] des signes sur ces fronts d'une parfaite joie / Ne me travaillez point de nouvelles douleurs, / C'est envier mon bien que d'en verser des pleurs. / C'est rendre à votre père un très mauvais office" ["(Show) signs of perfect joy on your face. Do not wrack me with new pain. To cry is to envy my good fortune and to lack in duty toward your father"] Gathier de la Costes de la Calprenéde, La mort de Mithridate, in Le Théâtre du XVIIIe Siècle, vol. 2, ed. Jacques Scherer and Jacques Truchet (Paris: Gallimard, Bibliothèque de la Pléiade, 1986).

31. "Ah! que votre amitié m'oblige en ce présent! / . . . Ce poison agréable est la fin de nos peines" ["Ah! How your friendship obliges me with this present! . . . This pleasing poison is the end of our pains"] (ibid., 5.1.1466, 1471); "Je reçois de bon cœur cet agréable don" ["I receive this pleasing gift with a glad heart"] (ibid., 5.1.1490).

32. The full title reads: Discours pitoyable de la cruauté et tirannie d'un jeune garçon serviteur, lequel a fait par poison mourir son maistre, maistresse et leurs enfants: Avec plusieurs regrets par luy faits avant son exécution [Pitiable story of the cruelty and tyranny of a young servant, who caused his Master, mistress, and their children to die by poison: With several regrets of his expressed before his execution] (Rouen: André Chalmenil; Dignent [Dinan]: Robert Recine, [1600]). The Bibliothèque nationale's online catalog dates this pamphlet ca. 1600.

33.

En fait, à côté des colporteurs autorisés et sévèrement contrôlés, souvent d'anciens ouvriers d'imprimerie devenus invalides, il y avait de nombreux colporteurs clandesti.., plus ou moins occasionnels. Les uns et les autres criaient dans les rues des nouvelles de toutes sortes: ils vendaient des feuilles d'informations (dont la parution n'avait aucune régularité, d'où le nom d'"occasionnels' donné par les bibliographes), des textes de chansons, des pamphlets politiques, des almananchs, des poèmes, des livrets de pronostications. (Robert Decsimon and Christian Jouhaud, La France du premier XVIIe siècle: 1594–1661 [Paris: Belin, 1996], 133)

[In fact, along with authorized peddlers, who were strictly regulated, and who were often former print shop workers that had become invalids, there were many clandestine peddlers, more or less temporary or occasional workers. Both kinds of peddlers shouted news of all kinds in the streets: they sold news sheets (which were not regularly published, hence the term used by bibliographers, occasionnels), song lyrics, political pamphlets, almanacs, booklets of predictions.]

34. Jean-Pierre Seguin, L'information en France avant le périodique: 517 canards imprimés entre 1529 et 1631 (Paris: G.-P. Maisonneuve et Larose, 1964).

35. *Garçon serviteur*, 1 (emphasis in original; original document not paginated).

36. Seguin, after reviewing his corpus of *canards* on news items, sums up their general lesson as "pénitence et humilité" ["penitence and humility"]. He notes that "[q]uoi qu'il en soit de la sincérité de ces informateurs moralistes ou de leur force de conviction, il faut bien admettre, avec Pierre de l'Estoile, que tant de leçons ne servaient guère: 'Le bruit, en ce temps, de beaucoup de prodiges avenus depuis peu en diverses contrées et endroits de la France et de l'Europe estonne prou le peuple, mais ne l'amende point, qui est pis,' écrit-il en octobre 1605" ["whatever may be the sincerity of these moralizing informers or the strength of their convictions, it must be said, along with Pierre de l'Estoile, that so many lessons had hardly any impact: 'In these times, the news of many prodigious things that recently happened in various countries and places in France and Europe greatly astonishes the people, but does not make them change their ways, which is worse,' he wrote in October 1605"] (Seguin, *L'information*, 62–63).

37. *Garçon serviteur*, 5.

38. Ibid., 5–6. Note the plea to the audience to open their *eyes* in order to *hear*. At the least, it seems that this pamphlet was written rather hastily.

39. "toutes imprécations, injures et blasphèmes contre Dieu le Créateur" ["all imprecations, insults, and blasphemy against God the Creator"] (ibid., 3); "opprobres et affronts" ["opprobrium and provocation"], "paroles scandaleuses et déshonnêtes" ["scandalous and indecent speech"] (ibid., 4).

40. Anonymous, *Discours au vrai de l'étrange cruauté d'un soldat* (Lyon: Antoine Bessy, 1611).

41. Ibid., 7.

42. Ibid., 9–10.

43. Louise Bourgeois, *Observations diverses sur la stérilité, perte de fruict, foecondité, accouchements et maladies des femmes et enfants nouveaux naiz* [*Diverse Observations on Sterility, Miscarriage, Fertility, Childbirth, and Women's and Newborns' Illnesses*] (Paris: Saugrain, 1626), 1:161–62.

44. Anonymous, *Discours au vrai de l'étrange*, 11.

45. *Factum du procez pendant en la cour entre Pierre et autre Pierre l'Hoste freres demandeurs en reparation de crime d'empoisonnement, suppositions, voleries, faussetés, et subornement de tesmoings* (n.p., [1626?]), 2.

46. Anonymous, *Discours au vrai*, 12.

47. Ibid., 13.

48. With the exception, perhaps, of Monléon's *Thyeste*.

49. Marcel Marion, *Dictionnaire des institutions de la France* (Paris: Picard, 1989), 80.

50. Also attested by the L'Hoste *factum* of 1626. No less a person than Louis's mistress Madame de Montespan was thought to have used dubious potions to win back his affections and to have had black masses said to that effect. See Mollenauer, *Strange Revelations*, 53–69 passim. Mollenauer's is one of the few scholarly works on the affair. Most books on the subject tend toward the sensationalistic.

~

CHAPTER FIFTEEN

Et in Arcadia alter egos

Playing Politics with Pastoral
in Two French Baroque Dramas

RICHARD HILLMAN

Criticism is (un)decidedly of two minds about the production and operation of political meanings in French baroque drama. For most of the period—at least from his entry into the king's council in April 1624 to his death in December 1642—the key figure to be reckoned with is, inevitably, Richelieu, and there is widespread agreement that the cardinal not only appreciated the theater for its literary qualities but promoted it as an instrument of power, a propaganda mechanism in at least the broadest sense. Still, in general, commentators have concentrated their attention on aesthetic history and practices, about which it is possible to speak more amply and with greater assurance.

There are notable exceptions: no one can ignore the frank allegorizing of *Europe*, the "comédie héroïque" attributed with near-certainty to Jean Desmarets de Saint-Sorlin, perhaps not merely instructed but aided by Richelieu himself, whom Desmarets loyally served;[1] likewise, the tragicomedy *Mirame*, also by Desmarets (composed 1639, staged 1641), has been widely accepted, on the basis of contemporary accounts, as pointing a finger at the romantic entanglement of Anne of Austria with Charles, Duke of Buckingham.[2] (It is relevant to my argument here that the politically subversive consequences of the queen's passion are implicitly highlighted—and that she seemingly could not avoid attending the performance, which inaugurated, with great pomp, the theater that Richelieu had incorporated into the Palais-

Cardinal.[3]) Certain historians, too, have called attention to the imitation of life by theatrical art—and indeed vice versa: particularly germane to this essay are the remarks of Jean-Marie Constant concerning Gaston d'Orléans and the respective pastoral dramas of Théophile de Viau (*Les amours tragiques de Pyrame et Thisbé*) and Jean Mairet (*La Sylvie*).[4] Finally, there are signs that some literary scholars, at least, may be moving in historical directions. The fact remains that critics of the French theater of the period have traditionally been chary about topical allusion-hunting.

Such caution has a salutary side. No doubt the contrasting vogue for self-styled "historicism" in criticism of early modern English drama has tended to proliferate speculative applications to persons and events. But there is an obvious risk of ignoring, with the historical context, an entire dimension of the original dramatic experience. One might suppose that recovering that experience as fully as possible would universally be considered the critic's business. Yet the recent editors of *Mirame* discount even that play's allusiveness on the grounds, not that such meaning may not have been present for contemporary spectators, but that it is of little interest today.[5] Such responses may finally be taken as a tribute to Richelieu's own representation of his literary preoccupations as disinterested and self-contained; they underrate the evidence that, in all his artistic activities, from the collecting of antiquities to the founding of the French Academy, the cardinal's guiding impulse was the consolidation and implementation of power in the nonfictive world around him.[6]

Arguably, moreover, topical allusiveness and aesthetic impact were mutually imbricated for contemporary spectators by way of the perceptual codes linking spectacle and audience. Georges Couton makes this point effectively with respect to the distinctive milieu of French dramatic production in the period:

Il faut se dire que cette génération nourrie de l'*Astrée* d'abord, et de bien d'autres romanciers, se mouvait à l'aise dans le romanesque. Il faut se dire aussi que les structures politiques, qui personnalisent à l'extrême le pouvoir et le "crédit," rendent possibles des démarches que nous ne pouvons que malaisément concevoir. La politique est le jeu tragique, comique, tragi-comique d'un petit nombre de privilégiés, pris dans un réseau d'intrigues souvent obscures.[7]

[One must acknowledge that this generation, nourished on the *Astrée* primarily, and on many other novelists, moved easily within the romance mode. One must acknowledge as well that the political structures, which personalized power and "credit" to an extreme, rendered possible procedures that we can only imagine with difficulty. Politics is the game—tragic, comic, tragicomic—of a small number of the privileged, caught in a network of intrigues that are often obscure.]

Necessarily, then, political intentions and the resonances they produce are especially difficult to recuperate with confidence at such a historical and cultural distance—especially because "deniability" is integral to their method. This is clear from Couton's conclusion about *Mirame*, which he terms "une pièce où se combinent les miroitements de la fiction théâtrale et les allusions à la réalité: assez d'allusions pour que l'avertissement soit entendu, assez de modifications—et surtout une fin heureuse—pour que les allusions puissent être niées" ["a play in which are combined the shimmering visions of the theatrical fiction and allusions to reality: sufficient allusions for the admonitory message to be heard, sufficient modifications—and especially a happy ending—to make it possible to deny the allusions"].[8]

Such an elusive double functioning may be detected, I believe, in the two plays, at once separated and linked by opposing political agendas, on which this chapter focuses: works generally considered as minor instances of dramatic pastoral, when they are considered at all. These are the prose tragedy *Pandoste, ou La princesse malheureuse* [*Pandosto, or the Unfortunate Princess*], by Jean Puget de la Serre (pub. 1631), who had a long career as a producer of texts in a wide range of genres, and the verse tragicomedy *La cour bergère ou l'Arcadie* [*The Pastoral Court, or The Arcadia*], by André Mareschal (pub. 1640).[9] The latter play at least enjoys some literary standing and has received a modern edition. Both are works that have never, to my knowledge, been approached in political terms. Yet in both cases, for a combination of exceptional reasons, it seems more possible than usual to gauge the political application of the theatrical product. The reasons are at once cultural, historical, and textual—or, more properly, intertextual. Both cases involve notably free adaptations of Elizabethan pastoral romances—respectively, Robert Greene's *Pandosto* (also the principal source for Shakespeare's *The Winter's Tale*) and Philip Sidney's *Arcadia*. This is a rare direction for literary influence to take in the period, and the effect is arguably twofold: to strengthen the disclaimer of topical allusiveness made by pastoral in general, even while opening up a new field of political meanings extending across the channel. Despite some uncertainties regarding their dates, both plays were presumably composed, performed, and published in circumstances involving fraught relations between France and England and turbulent domestic politics on both sides. Finally, in both cases, the fact of adaptation calls attention to a significant skewing of the originals, skewing that the public was in a better position to register because—again exceptionally—they were available in French translations.

I

The earlier text in question, that of Puget, opens a further window, and from an especially revealing angle, on the propagandistic operations of French theater in the period. For, if I am right, this is a rare instance of an anti-Richelieu dramatic vehicle. Such a proposal may seem at odds with Puget's production, in 1641, of an obvious work of flattery, *Le portrait de Scipion l'Africain, ou l'image de la gloire et de la vertu représentée au naturel dans celle de monseigneur le cardinal duc de Richelieu* [*The Portrait of Scipio Africanus, or the Image of Glory and Truth Naturally Represented in That the Lord Cardinal Duke of Richelieu*], in which the author aspires, as he informs the cardinal in the dedicatory epistle, "estre l'Echo de l'Oracle qui vous presche par tout l'Univers" ["to be the echo of the oracle that utters you forth through all the universe"].[10] Oracles are a staple of pastoral, of course, and I suggest that the image used here is particularly resonant—not least because it is liable to oblique and ironic application. But the immediate point is that the situation of the author had changed radically since *Pandoste*, whose publication dates from 1631, immediately after Marie de' Medici's decisive expulsion from power by Richelieu (on the so-called Day of the Dupes in November 1630) and subsequent detention in Compiègne.[11]

When the queen mother escaped from Compiègne to Brussels in July 1631, Puget was among her substantial train as her "homme de lettres" ["man of letters"].[12] He duly produced records of her ceremonial entries in the Low Countries, and eventually in England; panegyrics on the beauty of her waiting-women; and inevitably, ballets, which (together with visits to churches) constituted Marie de' Medici's favorite recreation.[13] The poet's allegiance dates from some years before. Near the beginning of the notably long and diverse (if not particularly distinguished) paper trail of Puget's productions comes a mythologized celebration (necessarily under the influence of propagandistic wishful thinking) of the loving relationship between Louis XIII and Anne of Austria.[14] This work's conclusion, in keeping with its date (pub. 1625), points to its true raison d'être when it refers to Henrietta Maria's English marriage—and remarkably, as Karen Britland has pointed out, in doing so it uses imagery from Ben Jonson's masque, *The Fortunate Isles, and Their Union* (also 1625).[15] Puget's apparent knowledge of such an English text at this period has implications for *Pandoste*, I suggest, but more immediately revealing is his discursive association with this key project of the queen mother. The English marriage also received the support of Richelieu, at a time when the latter, originally her *créature*, was still playing second fiddle to her.[16] The cardinal can thus figure in the *Amours*—already, perhaps, with a touch of irony—as the *Dieu des Oracles*

[God of Oracles], charged with eloquently transmitting to mankind the Destinies' "souverains decres" ["sovereign decrees"].[17]

The Puget paper trail thus intersects at an early stage with the politically and religiously charged court entertainments associated with Henrietta Maria in London, where Puget would accompany the queen mother in 1638 during the latter phase of her exile.[18] But eventually it winds back to Richelieu—and simultaneously, it would seem, to Gaston d'Orléans, whose librarian Puget may have become at the point when the king's unruly brother, too, whose various political interests and intrigues ran generally parallel to his mother's, had been brought uneasily to heel, so to speak, under the cardinal's watchful eye—or eyes.[19] What part, if any, Puget may have played in such operations can only be surmised, but the tragedy *Thomas Morus, ou Le triomphe de la foy, et de la constance* [*Thomas Morus, or the Triumph of Faith and Constancy*], the last play of his to be composed within Richelieu's lifetime (pub. 1642), was issued, as the title page states, by the "Libraire et Imprimeur du Monsieur Frere du Roy" ["bookseller and printer of Monsieur the king's brother"] yet apparently was staged for Richelieu in the Palais-Cardinal.[20] It was dedicated to the Duchess of Aiguillon, the cardinal's niece, who was nevertheless a favorite of Marie de' Medici and who was involved at the time in negotiating, in exchange for a cash settlement, the queen mother's return from England. Marie was supposed to settle finally in Italy, but she was evidently counting on the success of the conspiracy of Cinq-Mars with Gaston to rid her of Richelieu and enable her to come back to France.[21] (In the event, she died in Cologne about six months before the death of Richelieu.)

Puget's tragedy of More's martyrdom for religion's sake, featuring a nobly virtuous Catherine of Aragon, would naturally have struck a chord with French Catholics, even if few could foresee that England's Puritan Revolution would drive Henrietta Maria back to France and make a martyr of Charles. But the terms of the dedicatory epistle to the duchess intriguingly recall *Pandoste*, and in a way not without ambiguity. Puget allows her, predictably, superabundant gifts of fortune and nature, but chief among her virtues is a humility that wins hearts, where "la Puissance et la Tyrannie n'ont jamais pú [*sic*] establir leur Empire" ["power and tyranny have never been able to set up their empire"]; he welcomes the occasion, he says, to show the public "que je sçay subir avec toute sorte de respect la Loy de ses Oracles" ["that I know how to submit with every kind of respect to the law of its oracles"] when the latter proclaim her preeminence.[22] This might well suggest a command performance mandated by the *Dieu des Oracles* himself, with the image of a ruthless tyrant persecuting an innocent queen given a suitably pious and outward orientation.

Pandoste was composed under very different auspices. On the reason-able presumption that the 1631 date of publication is close to that of its composition—as for performance, significantly, there appears to be no evidence[23]—its production would coincide with Richelieu's coup, which sent Marie de' Medici first to house arrest, then into exile.[24] The play thereby entered a field of intense propaganda interventions involving pam-phlets and letters authored by supporters and detractors of both Marie and Gaston.[25] The cardinal had not yet consolidated the extensive networks, managed by his own *créatures*, that would afford him effective control over the production of political and literary—including theatrical—texts.[26] All in all, the known circumstances leave little doubt as to the resonances that Puget would have expected his subtitle to produce—*La princesse mal-heureuse*—and the application that would have accrued to his evocation of absolute power imposing rank injustice and riding roughshod over the pleas of honest but subservient counselors: "Nos vies et nos biens ne relev-ent que de vostre authorité, et vostre bouche rend tous les oracles de notre destinée" ["Our lives and our property depend wholly on your authority, and your mouth delivers all the oracles of our destiny"].[27] Prominent in the play, after all, is a countermanding Oracle who delivers the truth, and discloses its consequences, with truly divine authority.

The subtitle is not Greene's, nor that of the obscure L. Regnault, who pro-duced a quite faithful French translation of the novel in 1615—in unknown circumstances, although these obviously included the vogue for pastoral fic-tion sparked by Honoré d'Urfé's *Astrée*. Indeed, Regnault, seemingly to ad-vertise the variety of romance matter on offer (and to capitalize on the con-tinuing popularity of the "histoire tragique" [tragic story] as a form), chose a title effectively subordinating the story of Bellaria and giving tragic priority to her persecutor: *Histoire tragique de Pandosto, roy de Bohême et de Bellaria, sa femme: Ensemble les amours de Dorastus et de Faunia* [*The Tragic Story of Pand-osto, King of Bohemia, and His Wife Bellaria Together with the Loves of Dorastus and Faunia*].[28] As for the more recent French version demonstrably used by Puget for certain details—by the equally obscure but prolific producer of ro-mances, Louis Moreau Du Bail (1626)—it eschews all description in its title (as well as any acknowledgment that it is not an original novel).[29]

Puget's title, by contrast, is the first sign of his broad skewing of the romance to focus intensively on the sufferings of the innocent queen under the blatant tyranny of the king. (Richelieu always functioned, of course, as the mediator of a power presumed to emanate from Louis.) In a radical displacement of focus, even Puget's Oracle—in a way that throws down the gauntlet, perhaps, to the *Dieu des Oracles* himself—gives exclusive attention to the queen's successive miseries. Régnault's translation of Greene renders it thus: "Le soupçon n'est pas deüe preuve: la Jalousie est un Juge inesgal: Bellaria est chaste, Egistus est blasmé à tort: Franion est un tresloyal subject: Pandosto est blasmable: l'enfant qu'il a abandonné aux flots de la mer, est sien: et il mourra sans hoirs si celuy qui est perdu n'est retrouvé" ["Suspicion is not proper proof; Jealousy is not an impartial judge; Ballaria is chaste; Egistus is wrongly accused. Franion is a most loyal subject; Pandosto is at fault. The child he has abandoned to the waves of the sea is his, and he will die without heirs if the one[30] who is lost is not found"].[31] In Puget's version, the jealous tyrant and his fate are effaced; what matters is the queen's vindicated innocence and honor, which, however, cannot prevent her dying from her accumulated sorrows, which here, without oracular ambiguity, explicitly climax in her son's death: "Ceste Princesse aussi chaste qu'infortunée doibt perdre la vie, apres avoir recouvré l'honneur, mourant dans son innocence de la derniere attainte de ses mal-heurs, limitez du trespas de son fils unique" ["This princess, as chaste as unfortunate, must lose her life, after recovering her honor, dying in her innocence from the final blow of her miseries, which reach a limit with the death of her only son"].[32] Of course, the death of the queen's son is also the fatal blow in Greene's original. Arguably, however, to foreground it at this historical moment would have evoked the danger also posed by the royal tyranny to Marie's favored son, Gaston, who was likewise still the heir to the throne.

In keeping with the Oracle's shift of emphasis, the version of Puget restricts Pandoste's own participation in the *histoire tragique*, reserving full tragedy for the queen and her son. True, the king laments his actions fulsomely at the end of day 1, invoking the usual divine punishments upon himself (although he does not, as in the source, attempt suicide). The renewal of his tyranny in the final sequence of day 2, however, through his attempts to force himself incestuously (though unknowingly) on his daughter (here Favvye—one suspects inversion of the "n", such as also transforms Franion into Puget's Fravion), does not lead to an overwhelming access of remorse, followed by a successful suicide, as in Greene. There Pandosto's accusing conscience adds this offense to his other destructive deeds, most crucially his queen's death. Puget's protagonist briefly asks forgiveness of the young couple, but then announces the ending note of general joy and festivity. This is a king whose tyranny, while it is formally triggered in both cases by "deniable" nonpolitical forms of errance—jealousy, then illicit lust—goes on with impunity, as if having a life of its own and no memory, only victims. Puget's self-proclaimed tragedy, then, actually reverses Greene's decision to have his protagonist "close up the comedy with a tragical stratagem"[33] and opts, like *Mirame*, for a *fin heureuse* [happy ending] that sends mixed messages.

II

This is a reversal that, rather more famously, Shakespeare also managed in *The Winter's Tale*, although by making the queen's death a false one—a mitigation of her tragedy that would hardly have suited Puget, if he had known about it. Is there a chance he did? This is perhaps the appropriate moment to adduce some suggestive (if not conclusive) evidence that Puget's adaptation of Greene was inflected by some degree of familiarity with Shakespeare's— indeed, that several of the moments at which *Pandoste* rises in eloquence and dramatic effect above its habitual banality may owe something to the Shakespearean model.[34] This is, I realize, a doubtful proposition, and some of the parallels may stem simply from the common imperatives of dramatization. Still, what little we know of Puget's connection with the household of Marie de' Medici, at least from the point where Henrietta Maria became the wife of then Prince Charles, leaves room for possible English exchanges. After all, in 1622 Marie de' Medici furnished Jean Beaudoin, her *lecteur* [reader], with funds to travel to England and learn the language specifically in order to translate Sidney's *Arcadia*. (The translation appeared, with a dedication to her, in 1624–1625; Beaudoin, incidentally, whose translation served as the basis of Mareschal's dramatization, was destined, like Puget, to become Richelieu's man, taking a place as one of the first members of his academy.[35])

Acquaintance with *The Winter's Tale* as a printed text was possible (given knowledge of English) from its publication in the First Folio in 1623. And it is conceivable that Puget, like Beaudoin, visited England; if so, this would probably have been in the ample train of the Duke of Chevreuse, who was present there throughout 1624 to promote Marie de' Medici's marriage project.[36] There may have been public performances during this period; there was certainly one at court, at Whitehall, on January 18, given under the auspices of the Duchess of Richmond (the king himself being absent).[37] And if Puget's visit was a similarly extended one, he might have seen Jonson's *The Fortunate Isles* performed on January 9, 1625, although he might equally have consulted its text in the quarto published soon after.[38]

In any case, *The Winter's Tale* anticipates Puget in developing, well beyond Greene's original, the loving loyalty and devotion to honor of the slandered queen, on the one hand, and the tyranny of her obsessive persecutor, on the other. To take up the latter first, Pandosto is characterized as a tyrant only once in Greene's original, and only indirectly, at the point where his cupbearer (Franion, Shakespeare's Camillo) briefly considers resistance.[39] The term is absent from the translated versions. Nor does it figure in the equivalent speeches in either play. It is, however, firmly applied elsewhere in both: in Shakespeare, most resoundingly, by the Oracle ("Leontes a jealous tyrant"),[40] by Leontes himself in rejecting the epithet,[41] by Hermione at her trial,[42] then, insistently, by Paulina;[43] in Puget, by the imprisoned queen,[44] by the king at the moment of repentance,[45] and by his daughter.[46] Very much to the point here is the accusation of tyranny leveled at Richelieu in the 1631 manifesto of Gaston d'Orléans, in which the cardinal's ungrateful betrayal of Marie de' Medici is singled out for blame.[47]

The tyrant's violent and twisted thinking, which in Puget issues in Senecan bluster surprisingly redolent of psychotic aberration ("Je me baigne de joye dans l'eau de tes larmes, et le vent de tes sanglots me sert de Zephir" ["I bathe with joy in the water of your tears, and the wind of your sighs is as a zephyr to me"]),[48] also produces specific parallels absent from the novel. In both plays, the tyrant's idea of having both the queen and the newborn child burnt to death (an element from the source) is additionally applied to the queen alone, so as to illustrate his obsession; in both, the king—tormented to the point where he can no longer pronounce her name—imagines that he can thereby ease his mind. Leontes begins act 2, scene 3, by supposing that "a moiety of my rest / Might come to me again" if "[t]he cause," "[s]he, th'adultress," were "given to the fire";[49] Puget's Pandoste opens act 5 of day 1 by harping on the same theme: "Je ne suis qu'à demy satisfait, ma vengeance n'est point assouvie, elle ne peut terminer que par l'embrasement de ceste impudique, dont j'ay desja oublié le nom" ["I am only half-satisfied; my thirst for vengeance is by no means slaked; it can end only with the burning of that shameless women, whose name I have already forgotten"].[50]

There is no precedent at all in the source for a further distinctive measure of royal delusion. The kings in both plays are so sure of the queen's guilt that they consider their consultation of the Oracle merely a way of confirming the truth for the less perceptive. As Leontes explains,

> Though I am satisfied and need no more
> Than what I know, yet shall the oracle
> Give rest to th' minds of others, such as he
> Whose ignorant credulity will not
> Come up to th' truth.[51]

Puget has Pandoste retort, when his courtiers urge him to take this step, with a hint of the blasphemy that Leontes blatantly commits—and that might well have evoked Richelieu as a usurper of divine prerogative: "Les Dieux m'inspirent tout ce que je fais, je ne suis que l'instrument de la justice qu'ils veulent exercer contre les coulpables. Il n'est pas besoin d'informer l'oracle sur un crime, où mes propres yeux ont esté tesmoings" ["The gods inspire in me everything that I do; I am merely the instrument of the justice that they wish to exercise against the guilty. There is no need to inform the oracle about a crime when my own eyes have been witnesses"].[52] Finally, when a nobleman insists that the Oracle's pronouncement must be known before he can proceed with the punishment, Pandoste makes the point again in a way that confirms his delusion: "je n'ay fait consulter l'Oracle que pour vostre satisfaction. Car comme la verité ne change point de nature, elle paroistra à vos yeux telle qu'elle a paru devant moy" ["I caused the oracle to be consulted only for your satisfaction. For, since the truth does not at all change its na-ture, it will appear to your eyes such as it appears before me"].[53]

As for the queen's response to the accusations, Shakespeare and Puget add considerably to the source, and along the same lines. Both show her meeting the king's threats with a defiant acceptance of death, given the injuries he has inflicted on her, the chief of which, she poignantly states, is the with-drawal of his love. In *The Winter's Tale*, the confrontation occurs in the trial scene, which is far less developed in the novel. Puget dispenses with the trial as such—which is hardly surprising if his real "Princesse malheureuse" is cur-rently in prison or in exile—but he adapts the confrontation in terms similar to Shakespeare's. Hermione affirms,

> Sir, spare your threats.
> The bug that you would fright me with I seek.
> To me can life be no commodity;
> The crown and comfort of my life, your favour,
> I do give lost, for I do feel it gone,
> But know not how it went.[54]

Puget's heroine would agree: "si vous en voulez à ma vie je n'y ay plus d'interest, puis que je ne vis que pour vous" ["if you are aiming at my life, I have no more interest in it, since I live only for you"].[55] And after several further exchanges, she reiterates: "Vous me menacez de la mort, et je vous deffie de m'oster la vie. Car ce m'est un fardeau si pesant, que je cherche de tous costez un tombeau, pour y ensevelir ses miseres" ["You threaten me with death, and I challenge you to take away my life. For it is to me a burden so heavy that I seek at all costs a tomb in which to enclose its miseries"].[56] Finally, in prison, she laments, "Celuy que j'ayme mille fois plus que ma vie en est le Tiran, et le Bourreau" ["He whom I love a thousand times more than my life is its tyrant and torturer"].[57] The persistence of the queen's loyal devotion is essential, of course, to Shakespeare's ending; it would be equally germane to Puget's political purpose.

The two queens' defense of their chaste relations with the visiting king also introduces a common detail. Going beyond the source, Hermione affirms that this was "a love even such, / So, and no other, as yourself commanded."[58] Puget's queen similarly insists that she entertained the visitor as freely as she did because "vostre Majesté me l'a commandé" ["your majesty commanded this of me"].[59] This is an intriguing case in which the version of Du Bail also coincides closely: "J'avoüe avoir affectionné Agatocle, mais cest par vostre commandement, et pource qu'il estoit votre amy" ["I admit having had warm feelings for Agatocle, but this was at your command, and because he was your friend"].[60] If Puget was picking up the second translator's language at this point, might he have been doing so because of a reminiscence of *The Winter's Tale*? The possibility that Du Bail also knew the latter seems far-fetched, although it cannot, of course, be excluded.

Indeed, there is one further similarity of the same order, this one attached to a larger issue. The two dramatic queens share as a central preoccupation, and as a source of eloquence and dignity unmatched in the source, the vindication of their honor, which naturally depends on their innocence. Greene uses the word in this context only once and incidentally, when Bellaria expresses confidence in her exoneration, despite the fact that "lying report hath sought to appeach mine honour"—a speech faithfully rendered by both translators.[61] Without precedent, however, Hermione resoundingly declares of her honor, "'Tis a derivative from me to mine, and only that I stand for"; it is, she insists, what "I would free."[62] Puget makes his heroine's honor an explicit issue not only through the oracle itself, as has been seen, but also in her defiance of the king, who accuses her in these terms: "Ah! que tu as mauvaise grace à prescher ton innocence, n'ayant plus d'honneur, tu n'as plus de honte" ["Ah, it ill becomes you to preach your innocence: no longer having any honor, you have no more shame"].[63] Her retort is equally focused: "Si mon visage paslit, c'est de la crainte de perdre mon honneur, et non pas du regret de l'avoir perdu, vous voyant determiné à conjurer sa ruine" ["If my face turns pale, it is from fear of losing my honor, and not from regret at having lost it, since I see you are determined to bring about its ruin"].[64] And as with Hermione, Bellaire's concern with honor is the key to her royal self-possession. A fearful and sorrowful display, she adds, could not "eterniser le renom de [s]a mémoire" ["eternalize the fame of (her) memory"];[65] that she will entrust to her virtue.

As for her body, she states, "je ne pense qu'à mourir dans l'innocence que j'ay vescu" ["I think only of dying in the innocence in which I have lived"]. So does Hermione count on her "innocence" to "make / False accusation blush and tyranny / Tremble at patience":[66] her imagery and language here are modeled on Greene's original, in which, however, neither "tyranny" nor "innocence" figures: "I hope my patience shall make Fortune blush, and my unspotted life shall stain spiteful discredit."[67] It becomes remarkable, therefore, that, while Regnault translates faithfully ("j'espère que ma patience fera rougir la fortune: et que ma vie non entachee d'aucun vice, despitera la mescroyance"),[68] Du Bail introduces Hermione's key term: "j'espere que mon innocence fera rougir mes accusateurs de honte, et mourir de rage mes ennemis" ["I hope that my innocence will make my accusers blush with shame, and my enemies die with fury"].[69] (He also, however, lends Bellaire a vindictive aggressiveness and a sense of multiple enemies that are quite alien to Hermione.[70])

If Puget did have knowledge of Shakespeare's dramatization, it is not surprising that he would have drawn on it to embellish the stark outline given in the novel and enhance his portrait of a noble princess suffering at a tyrant's hands. It is more remarkable to find similarity in the handling of the pastoral element, which in both plays is not merely, as in the novel, a conventional, even drab, backdrop to the love of the prince and supposed shepherdess, but is thoroughly integrated into their relation. In particular, Favvye's association with nature is developed in Puget's tragedy to a degree that recalls Perdita, whereas the novel is far more sparing in both the imagery and the language used to represent her, with nature as such scarcely mentioned or evoked.[71] As in Shakespeare (and doubtless as a matter of practical dramaturgy), Puget's pastoral sequence, which here begins the "Deuxième Journée" ["Second Day"], skips over the meeting and initial courtship, to which Greene devotes the bulk of his attention, and presents the prince (here Doraste) and Favvye as already in love. Doraste first speaks of her (to his conveniently provided confidant) as a "chef-d'œuvre de la nature" ["masterpiece of nature"],[72] and the theme is richly sustained throughout their tender exchanges. The latter culminate in a sensual encounter recalling the flower-giving scene in act 4, scene 4 of The Winter's Tale.

There Perdita, at first associating Florizel with the young virgins present at the feast, then singling him out, wishes that she "had some flowers o' th' spring, that might / Become your time of day."[73] Some lines later, she reiterates that wish in terms that shift from the virgins' innocence to her own desire, enfolding her love for the prince into a seasonal cycle of death and rebirth:

PERDITA.   O, these I lack
To make you garlands of, and my sweet friend,
To strew him o'er and o'er.
FLORIZEL.   What, like a corpse?
PERDITA.   No, like a bank for love to lie and play on,

Not like a corpse; or if, not to be buried,
But quick, and in my arms. Come, take your flowers.[74]

In *Pandoste*, Doraste proposes to Favvye that they lie together in a secluded, pleasant spot and enjoy the pleasures of love (presumably within the
bounds, somehow, of chaste virtue). The shepherdess agrees, stating that
she has "resolu de vous faire present d'un bouquet de fleurs; n'ayant rien de
plus digne à vous offrir" ["resolved to give you a bouquet of flowers, having
nothing more worthy to offer you"].[75] The prince replies that he would rather
pluck a bouquet of flowery kisses at her lips:

DORASTE.   O Dieux! qu'elles sentent bon, les appas de leur odeur me
            font pasmer de joye. Mais le trespas en est trop delicieux
            pour le craindre, je veux mourir tout à faict.
FAVVYE.   Ne parlez point de mort, quand vous mourriez de joye, ie
            ne laisserois pas de mourir de tristesse.
DORASTE.   Mourons donc tous deux d'amour. Mais il me semble que
            vostre sein souspire de cholere, ou de jalousie, de ce que je
            ne cueille pas des fleurs de son jardin, j'en veux faire un
            nouveau bouquet.[76]

[DORASTE.   O gods, how good they smell! The attraction of their odor
            makes me faint with joy. But to die this way is too
            delicious to fear it. I want to die entirely.
FAVVYE.   Do not speak of death at all. When you should die of joy, I
            would not fail to die of sorrow.
DORASTE.   Let us both then die of love. But it seems to me that your
            breast sighs with anger, or with jealousy, because I have
            not picked flowers from its garden. I want to make a new
            bouquet of those.]

And indeed the stage direction confirms that he kisses her breast. The lovers' physical intertwining, accompanied by the venerable metaphor of death
for passionate ecstasy, corresponds to what Perdita projects imaginatively
though her similar wish to lavish flowers on Florizel. All in all, the parallel
is compelling, while there is no hint of such eroticized nature-symbolism in
Greene's novel—or its translations.[77]

The intriguing question of Shakespearean influence—it would be the first
known case in France, if it were recognized as such—remains tangential to
my argument. Whatever the facts, Puget's development of the pastoral dimension of his source in a play whose primary thrust appears to be political
makes an important point about dramatic method: it shows up the potential

of such romance, with its established tradition and renewed currency, for enhancing those "miroitements de la fiction théâtrale" ["shimmering visions of the theatrical fiction," quoted above] that keep political meanings in *play*, all the more so by keeping them at a distance. It is in the same perspective that I view Mareschal's adaptation of Sidney's *Arcadia*.

III

This can be done with relative brevity. There is little doubt about Mare-schal's political affiliations and loyalties at the moment when he produced *La cour bergère*, and that moment can be fixed with reasonable precision. Parfaict gives 1638 as the date of the play's performance, which Mareschal presents, in his dedicatory epistle to Robert Sidney, Earl of Leicester—the nephew of the Elizabethan author, currently ambassador to France—as hav-ing been received with great applause;[78] such dating accords with the issuing of the *Privilège* on December 15, 1639, as recorded in the original edition, which also specifies January 2, 1640, as the date printing was completed.[79] By this point, Mareschal was certainly no longer the client of the refractory Gaston d'Orléans, whose librarian he, too, may have been (although the title is likely to have been honorific) around 1632, when the prince was in exile in Lorraine. Mareschal probably numbered among the *cardinalistes* even then, to judge from a surviving letter of state in which Richelieu vouches for his loyalty to the monarchy. At any rate, by 1635, the year of the founding of the French Academy, Mareschal was dedicating his work to loyalists of the cardinal.[80] He may thus be confidently associated with the latter's project of co-opting the adherents of Gaston and the queen mother, such as Beaudoin, too, had been and Puget would continue to be for a few years. Mareschal, it may be noted, had begun his literary career very much like Puget, with a 1625 publication extravagantly celebrating the English marriage.[81] This included a series of sonnets (*La descente des dieux en France* [*The Descent of the Gods into France*]), in which divine spirits address their compliments to members of the royal family—and, tellingly, to the Duke and Duchess of Chevreuse (the volume is dedicated to the former); the queen mother stands out for receiving two addresses (from Juno and Pallas Athena), Gaston for receiving that of an apotheosized Henri IV, who designates him as France's future hope.[82]

Given this background, it is difficult not to see Richelieu as appropriating, through *La cour bergère*, not just an erstwhile partisan of Marie de' Medici, but a specific text that she had commissioned (from Beaudoin), and even an entire genre, that of the pastoral romance, which had been particularly associated with the queen mother and her daughter. Indeed, Henrietta Maria was still actively promoting and practicing the form in London with a variety of political and religious inflections.[83] Mareschal had credentials in the field: he had already composed (probably in 1629 or 1630) a dramatic adaptation of d'Urfé, *L'inconstance de Hylas* [*Hylas's Inconstancy*].[84] Moreover, with his comedy, *Le railleur* [*The Mocker*], produced under Richelieu's auspices in 1635 and published with a dedication to him in 1638, he had recently proved his capacity to deliver barbed quills in dramatic form—with such piquant immediacy, in fact, that performances were halted, apparently under pressure from Anne of Austria's entourage.[85]

To adapt Sidney's *Arcadia* marks a return to the cushioning distance of "fiction théâtrale" in the form not merely of generic pastoral but of a much-admired literary memorial of the recent past associated with an emblematically noble figure, honored by his country and deserving of greater renown in France. This is the perspective that Mareschal hyperbolically promotes in his epistle: Philip Sidney was at once the celebrated author of that "chef-d'œuvre miraculeux qui passe pour l'Helyodore d'Angleterre" ["miraculous masterpiece that counts as the Heliodorus (i.e., the *Æthiopica*) of England"] and an indispensable servant, at the highest level, of his country's interests.[86] (Mareschal refers to Philip's "Roy"—a lapse that might, or might not, have pleased Queen Elizabeth.) Especially as an ambassador, "il a treuvé l'art . . . de se montrer agreable aux Princes étrangers" ["he discovered the art . . . of ingratiating himself with foreign princes"]. He was, in short, the glorious giant in whose footsteps his kinsman is worthily following. The image of Anglo-French relations thereby implied borders on the idyllic. Of course, such fulsomeness goes with the territory of the dedicatory epistle, but a readership in tune with reality might well have seen to what extent the preliminaries of the published text were already engaged in quasi-theatrical fictionalizing—and thereby giving political direction to the play text that follows.

In the first place, Philip Sidney's status as a model would surely have been problematic in the France of Richelieu. Sidney's uncompromising hostility to Catholicism throughout his brief life was notorious, and indeed had been an issue in provoking a translation of the *Arcadia* intended to rival that of Beaudoin.[87] As a young man in Paris he had narrowly escaped the St. Bartholomew's Day Massacre, thanks to the then English ambassador, Francis Walsingham. His closest and most durable French associations were with politically engaged Protestant militants: Hubert Languet and Philippe de Mornay, seigneur du Plessis-Marly. As for Philip's supposed ambassadorial finesse, it had never produced much in the way of practical results, and as far as his interventions in French affairs were concerned, he is likely to have been remembered chiefly for opposing the proposed marriage of Queen Elizabeth with the Duke of Alençon/Anjou.

Robert Sidney continued the family heritage of militant Protestantism and, while in France, made a public display of his religious principles by attending Huguenot services.[88] More immediately to the point for Mareschal's readers, however, would have been his paradoxical involvement—known through Richelieu's spies—in the 1637 intrigues of Marie de' Medici and Anne of Austria in favor of Spain. These schemes, secretly supported by King Charles, and notably by Henrietta Maria, entailed the subversion of the very Anglo-French alliance that Sidney had ostensibly been promoting, but the real target was Richelieu himself. In fact, this makes a clear (if nonetheless nebulous) case of diplomacy pursuing war by other means. There had actually been a conspiracy to assassinate the cardinal in October 1636 (the so-called *complot d'Amiens* [conspiracy of Amiens]) involving the Count of Soissons (Louis de Bourbon) and, most significantly from the present point of view, his cousin Gaston d'Orléans.[89] When it failed, or rather fizzled out, Gaston withdrew to his fiefdom in Blois; Soissons fled to his own and, for a while, took part in Marie de' Medici's negotiations with Spain, which actually led in June 1637 to the signing of a treaty aimed at bringing about Richelieu's downfall. Still, Richelieu soon emerged, yet again, triumphant. A tamed Gaston was once again received at court.[90] And in August of that year, Anne of Austria's secret dealings with Spain exploded sensationally, when Richelieu arrested her valet, Pierre de la Porte, and pressed her into confessing to compromising correspondence.[91] Finally, a major shift in the political dynamic followed in early 1638, with the surprising discovery that Queen Anne was pregnant; she gave birth to the future Louis XIV in September. Gaston was no longer heir to the throne.

Appearing as it did in the wake of these turbulent events, in which Sidney and his political masters (and mistresses) were deeply implicated, Mareschal's effusive dedication takes on a highly ironic, and sternly cautionary, character.[92] And insofar as it constitutes a liminal paratext for the play, staking a special claim to continuity with what follows, attention is directed to the political dimension of the dramatic material, which is considerable. So it is in the *Arcadia* itself, whose multiple intrigues are triggered by a particularly enigmatic oracle that strikes king Basilius with dread, notably for the future of his realm, and leads him to seek refuge in the pastoral world. Questions of succession mingle with the multiple love-plots and are made acute by the ambitious and unscrupulous Cecropia, the king's widowed sister-in-law, whose son Amphialus is finally driven to a despairing death, crushed between her drive for power and his hopeless love for one of the princesses.

These are points on which Mareschal's tragicomedy dwells, and with sensational extravagance, although he claims in his epistle to have swerved from his source only insofar as "la bien-seance et les rigueurs du Theatre n'y contraignissent" ["the decorum and the exigencies of the theater compelled it"].[93] In practice, since he stages a false execution, complete with severed head, and two spectacular deaths, this seems to mean mainly that he has trimmed the abundant extraneous characters and subplots of his source in order to concentrate on what, in his view, are the essentials. As in the novel, the mutual love of the two princes and the two princesses, together with the renewal of fidelity between Bazyle and his queen Gynecie, fulfills the oracle harmlessly and assures the succession (without the complication occasioned in the novel by the king's seeming decease).

For an audience of 1638, or a readership of 1640, the terms in which Mareschal presents the ruthless machinations of Cécropie and her attempts to induce her son Amphyale to abet them, so that he may take the throne of the issue-less Bazyle, could hardly have failed to conjure the intrigues of the incorrigibly rebellious Marie de' Medici and the weaker-willed Gaston. Not only is this material much more diffusely presented in the novel, but the relation in the play between mother and son is evoked through debate that closely echoes contemporary political discourse—to the point where even the modern editor, who generally eschews political interpretation, suggests tentatively that Mareschal might at one point be casting aspersions on Gaston's plots against Richelieu.[94] The opposition is between an unscrupulous thirst for power, on the one hand, and a sense of honor and virtue, on the other. If we take the treatment of Amphyale to be, like the epistle to Sidney, admonitory—a warning to Gaston to behave himself—it makes sense to play up his noble resistance to her blandishments, but also to present him as truly tempted, as is never true of his stalwart original in the *Arcadia*. "Ah! ne me tentez plus" ["Ah, do not tempt me further"], he begs, encouraging her to soliloquize, "J'espere d'amolir un courage obstiné, / Et le porter au thrône où je l'ay destiné" ["I hope to soften an obstinate spirit and to carry him to the throne I have destined for him"].[95] And after their next encounter, she counts him as "gagné" ["won"],[96] since he agrees to have her obtain for him the love of the captive Phyloclée—again, in contrast with the equivalent exchange in the source.[97] As Mareschal presents it, that touch of moral weakness, despite his inherent nobility, feeds into the dynamic that ensures the mutual destruction of mother and son, hence the purging of the evil forces threatening the realm. When Lyzidor (Sidney's Mucedorus) asks, "Quelle fin eut donc leur destinée?" ["What was the fulfillment of their destiny?"], the reply of Zelmane is definitive and resounding: "[c]elle qu'ils meritoient, et qu'ils se sont donnée" ["that which they deserved, and which they gave themselves/each other"].[98]

Sidney's Cecropia is a sadistic and witch-like villainess, addicted to evil for its own sake; Mareschal's Cécropie is mad with the drive for power but keeps her eye unwaveringly on the political ball: "Je changeray l'Etat, c'est dequoy je me vante, / Et de vous couronner encore malgré vous; / Dieux, Destins, Roy, mon Fils, je vous domteray tous" ["I shall change the state—that's what I boast of, and of getting you crowned even despite yourself. Gods, destinies, king, my son—I shall master you all"].[99] And it is explicitly the state, not merely the crown of Bazyle, that Mareschal presents as being in jeopardy. His oracle is very different from Sidney's; the conventional family enigmas of romance prophecy are subordinated to an apocalyptic threat of chaos, which, in Richelieu's France, would have awakened memories and fears of civil war: "Grand Roy, ta fertile Arcadie, / Si dedans quelque temps ton soin n'y remedie, / Arrousera de sang tout ce qu'elle a de fleurs; / On verra ta Maison toute en feu, toute en pleurs" ["Great king, your fertile Arcadia, if you do not care for it with a timely remedy, will pour blood on all its flowers. Your House will be seen all on fire, all in weeping"].[100] Thus, in contrast with the fatalistic passivity imposed on Basilius in the *Arcadia*, this oracle contains a call for action—implicitly, for firm action against the forces of disorder and disruption, such as Richelieu constantly preached through his propaganda spokesmen.[101] Mareschal did not invent the trick of Lyzidor by which the wayward king and his wife are induced to sleep with each other, but it certainly matches the spin he puts on the fable that the return to order at the end should take on such a royal family dimension. France's succession was also, from 1638, assured in this way, and while Gaston would continue to be the inveterate enemy of Richelieu—witness the Cinq-Mars conspiracy of 1642—his (and his mother's) maneuvers could no longer be founded on the same basis of hopeful entitlement.

IV

It makes an intriguing (and suitably inconclusive) coda to this tentative exploration of pastoral passages across the channel to note that 1640 also saw the publication of an English dramatic adaptation of Sidney's romance (seemingly the first "serious" one, as opposed to the fanciful gallimaufry of the perennially popular *Mucedorus* [anon., ca. 1590]). This was *A Pastorall Called the Arcadia*, composed by James Shirley, a Catholic playwright who was patronized by Queen Henrietta Maria and served as house dramatist of her company. The play was entered in the Stationers' Register in 1639; its title page declares that it had been "Acted by her Majesties Servants [i.e.,

Queen Henrietta's men] at the *Phoenix* in *Drury* Lane," so this was presumably before Shirley left for a four-year sojourn in Ireland in 1636.[102] Beyond this, dating the play entails a great deal of conjecture. Paul Addington Ramsay, who has probably studied the question most fully, places the date between 1630 and 1634, with a preference for 1632.[103]

This makes the production of *The Arcadia*, in any case, prior to that of *La cour bergère*, while the publication of the two is virtually contemporary. Given the demonstrable fluidity of French-English exchanges during the period, in both cultural and political terms, might one of these texts constitute a response, even a riposte, to the other? The question is worth asking because the two plays take radically different approaches to the challenge of dramatizing Sidney's novel. Mareschal, as has been seen, claimed that he had adapted his source with the greatest possible fidelity but in fact gives special prominence to the Cecropia/Amphialus plot. Fidelity, as it happens, is also claimed on Shirley's behalf by Ramsay: "the most striking and significant feature . . . is how faithfully Shirley follows his source."[104] Yet what is certainly "most striking" to the comparative reader is that Shirley has wholly suppressed Cecropia, Amphialus, and the action associated with them. At the least, this points to a very different notion of tragicomedy from Mareschal's—one in keeping with John Fletcher's famous definition of the genre as excluding deaths.[105] Such is also consistent with Shirley's gentle treatment, in the venerable English tradition of comic outlaws, of the rebels who intercept the flight of Musidorus and Pamela in act 4. (This episode, which Mareschal ignores, ends with extreme and ruthless violence in the romance.[106]) But whatever the cause, the result is that Shirley's pastoral universe need not be purged of political subversion and intrigue before its love mechanisms can effect the fulfillment of the oracle and the restoration of Basilius to full enjoyment of his kingship (indeed to life itself).

It is possible (although not, of course, obligatory) to figure Mareschal—almost certainly not on his own initiative—as pointedly taking up the romance whose translation Marie de' Medici had commissioned, so as to put particularly biting political teeth into it. He would thus have been infusing with subversive energy a pastoral narrative that her daughter had preferred to see dramatized in idealized, not to say sanitized, form. In that case, might the belated publication of Shirley's play, probably eight years after its staging, effectively constitute a defiant reappropriation of Sidney's *Arcadia*, an indirect affirmation of innocence, moral and political, in the face of the accusatory barbs of Mareschal/Richelieu? Regardless of the facts in this case—which are, of course, irrecoverable—such scenarios would seem to be consistent with the allusive operations of theatrical (and other) intertextuality in the time and place(s) in question. And certainly there is no reason to deny such engagement with reality to a genre whose professed raison d'être is the extremity of its artifice; on the contrary.

Notes

1. The issues of political meaning and authorship are discussed very fully by Sylvie Taussig, Introduction to Europe: Comédie héroïque, attributed to Armand du Plessis, Cardinal de Richelieu, and Jean Desmarets de Saint-Sorlin (Turnhout: Brepols, 2006), 9–189. See also Georges Couton, Richelieu et le théâtre, ed. José Sanchez, introduction by Alain Niderst, 2nd rev. ed. (Paris: Eurédit, 2008), 75–85; and Roland Mousnier, L'homme rouge, ou La vie du cardinal de Richelieu (1585–1642) (Paris: Robert Laffont, 1992), 652–54.

2. See especially Couton, Richelieu, 51–75.

3. Ibid., 51–53.

4. Jean-Marie Constant, Gaston d'Orléans, Prince de la liberté (Paris: Perrin, 2013), 26–29; cf. 192–200.

5. Catherine Guillot and Colette Scherer, eds., Introduction to Mirame, by Jean Desmarets de Saint-Sorlin (Rennes: Presses Universitaires de Rennes, 2010), 16. Cf. Ruth Kleinman, Anne d'Autriche, trans. Ania Ciechanowska (Paris: Fayard, 1993), 213–16, who considers that the resplendent public occasion of the performance, including the presence (under compulsion) of three captive generals of the imperial army, absolves Richelieu of "toute intention malveillante" ["any malicious intention"] (215). The argument can easily be stood on its head. Mousnier appears to me much closer to the mark in detecting "une savante humiliation" ["an erudite humiliation"] and "une vengeance raffinée" ["a refined revenge"] on the cardinal's part (652). All translations are mine unless otherwise noted.

6. See, e.g., Honor Lévi, "Richelieu collectionneur," in Richelieu et la culture: Actes du colloque international en Sorbonne, ed. Roland Mousnier (Paris: Éditions du Centre National de la Recherche Scientifique, 1987), 175–83; Robert Knecht, Richelieu (London: Longman, 1991), 173–74; and the thorough account of Richelieu's polymorphous propaganda by Mousnier, L'homme rouge, 443–507.

7. Couton, Richelieu, 66.

8. Ibid., 75.

9. Jean Puget de la Serre, Pandoste ou La princesse mal-heureuse: Tragédie en prose. Divisee en deux journées (Paris: Nicolas de La Vigne, 1631); André Mareschal, La cour bergère, ou L'Arcadie de Messire Philippe Sidney (Paris: T. Quinet, 1640), which is reproduced in facsimile and used for reference purposes in Lucette Desvignes, ed., La cour bergère ou l'Arcadie de Messire Philippe Sidney, by André Mareschal (Saint-Etienne: Université de Saint-Etienne Institut d'Études de la Renaissance et de l'Âge Classique, 1981), vol. 2. The text can also be found on Gallica at http://gallica.bnf.fr/ark:/12148/bpt6k703696 (accessed July 3, 2014).

10. Jean Puget de la Serre, *Le portrait de Scipion l'Africain, ou L'image de la gloire et de la vertu représentée au naturel dans celle de monseigneur le cardinal duc de Richelieu* (Bordeaux: Guillaume Millanges, 1641), sig. ñ2^v. Scipio Africanus was one of the cardinal's favorite vehicles for projecting his image at this period. The busy Desmarets published his tragicomedy of *Scipion* in 1639 with a dedication to Richelieu, informing him that the author was thereby presenting "la Vertue à la Vertue mesme" ["Virtue to Virtue herself"] (Jean Desmarets de Saint-Sorlin, *Scipion: Tragi-comédie* [Paris: H. Le Gras, 1639], sig. ãijr). Note also the 1642 engraving depicting the two great men together at http://gallica.bnf.fr/ark:/12148/btv1b8403813c.r=richelieu+scipion. langFR (accessed July 3, 2014).

11. These events have been thoroughly documented by historians; see notably Mousnier, *L'homme rouge*, 373–98, who usefully stresses the parallel treatment and response of Gaston d'Orléans. In May 1631 the latter fled from France to Lorraine, where he was welcomed by the duke, "vieil ennnemi du roi de France" ["an old enemy of the king of France"] (396).

12. Françoise Kermina, *Marie de Médicis: Reine, régente et rebelle* (Paris: Librairie Académique Perrin, 1979), 351.

13. Ibid., 354.

14. Jean Puget de la Serre, *Les Amours du Roy, et de la Reine sous le nom de Jupiter et de Junon, avec les magnificences de leurs nopces, ou L'histoire morale de France, soubs le règne de Louys le Juste et Anne d'Austriche: Le tout enrichi d'un grand nombre de figures, etc.* (Paris: Nicolas Bessin et Denis de Cay, 1625).

15. Karen Britland, *Drama at the Courts of Queen Henrietta Maria* (Cambridge, UK: Cambridge University Press, 2006), 28–29.

16. See Knecht, *Richelieu*, 31–32.

17. Puget, *Amours*, 438.

18. See Britland, *Drama*, 173–76. Britland particularly associates Davenant's masque *Lumenalia* with the arrival in England of Marie de Chevreuse, an inveterate plotter against Richelieu, in April 1638, and with the anticipated welcome of Marie de Médicis some six months later. (Cf. Louis Batiffol, *La duchesse de Chevreuse: Une vie d'aventures et d'intrigues sous Louis XIII* [Paris: Hachette, 1913], 180.) There is an indirect connection with Puget through the participation in this masque of Charles, Duke of Vieuville, an ally of Gaston d'Orléans, who had also attended on Marie in Brussels and danced in Puget's *Ballet des princes indiens* (1634). More generally, Britland convincingly establishes the political and religious engagement of Henrietta Maria's theatrical projects, which have long been recognized as informed by her taste for French artistic practices. See, for example, Britland's discussion of Jonson's masque *Chloridia* as a work that "resonates with the events of November 1630" (83). Also notably demonstrated by Britland is the frequency and rapidity of communication across the channel.

On the French influence on the Caroline court, with an emphasis on the philosophical and religious aspects, see also Erica Veevers, *Images of Love and Religion: Queen Henrietta Maria and Court Entertainments* (Cambridge, UK: Cambridge University Press, 1989). Relevant context of a more general kind is further supplied by Lori Humphrey Newcomb, *Reading Popular Romance in Early Modern England* (New York: Columbia University Press, 2002), who extensively documents the diversifying readership of Greene's *Pandosto*; see esp. 77–129 (ch. 2, "Social Things: Commodifying *Pandosto*, 1592–1642"). Newcomb's account of the romance's French translations and adaptations (82–83), however, suffers from some imprecision and fails to recognize Puget's as a provocatively anomalous version; her main source here is Jean-Jules Jusserand, *An Introduction to Shakespeare's "The Winter's Tale"* (Cambridge, MA: Harvard University Press, 1907), xxviii–xxxviii.

19. See the brief summary of Puget's career by Giuliano Ferretti, "Richelieu et les historiographes," in *Les historiographes en Europe de la fin du Moyen Âge à la Révolution*, ed. Chantal Grell (Paris: Presses de l'Université Paris-Sorbonne, 2006), 325–43; 328n15. On the so-called *cardinalistes* placed within Gaston's entourage, see Georges Dethan, *La vie de Gaston d'Orléans* (Paris: Editions de Fallois, 1992), 124–28; and Pierre Gatulle, *Gaston d'Orléans: Entre mécénat et impatience du pouvoir* (Seyssel: Champ Vallon, 2012), 201–3. Gatulle judges it unlikely that Puget was ever Gaston's librarian (239), although he frequented the prince in Brussels during Marie de' Medici's exile there and dedicated the ballet, *Les princes indiens*, to him. According to Gatulle, Puget remained in the entourage of Marie de' Medici until her death in 1642 and returned to France only afterward. This does not account for the comparison of Scipio to Richelieu that Puget produced in 1641 or for the publication of his work by Gaston's printer, beginning in 1642. It is not clear on what authority he is claimed to have been the successor to Mareschal as Gaston's librarian by Claude Kurt Abraham, *Gaston d'Orléans et sa cour* (Chapel Hill, NC: University of North Carolina Press, 1964), 54, but Ferretti more plausibly has him switching his allegiance to Richelieu in 1639, after which he produced an ample series of works in the cardinal's honor, including an *éloge dithyrambique* [dithyrambic panegyric] upon his death (1643).

20. Jean Puget de la Serre, *Thomas Morus, ou Le triomphe de la foy, et de la constance, tragédie en prose* (Paris: A. Courbé, 1642).

21. See Christian Bouyer, *Gaston d'Orléans (1608–1660): Séducteur, frondeur et mécène* (Paris: Albin Michel, 1999), 184–85.

22. Puget, *Thomas Morus*, sig. ãii^v–iii^r; sig. ãii^v.

23. Maupoint, *Bibliothèque des théâtres, contenant le catalogue alphabétique des pièces dramatiques et opéra, le nom des auteurs et le temps de la représentation de ces pièces, avec des anecdotes* (Paris: Chardon, 1733), gives 1630 without further information. The reference to a performance by P. G. Thomas, Introduction to *Greene's "Pandosto" or "Dorastus" and "Fawnia" Being the Original of Shakespeare's "Winter's Tale"* (Oxford: Humphrey Milford, Oxford University Press, 1907), xix, appears to be based on an erroneous interpretation of Mahelot's *Mémoire*, where the reference is rather to a lost *Pandoste* by Alexandre Hardy, dated by the editor prior to 1626. See Laurent Mahelot, *Le Mémoire de Mahelot: Mémoire pour la décoration des pièces qui se représentent par les Comédiens du Roi*, ed. Pierre Pasquier (Paris: Honoré Champion, 2005), 247n144 and 249n145. If Puget's play was performed at all, this would most likely

have been, as with his ballets, for the benefit of Marie de' Medici herself. It is note-worthy that, when the court first traveled to Compiègne in February 1631—the first step toward her confinement—the baggage included theatrical machinery (Kermina, *Marie de Médicis*, 344).

24. The 1631 edition of Nicolas de la Vigne was shared with another Parisian publisher, Pierre Billaine, and there was a pirated reissue in Lyons in 1632 by Claude Larjot and Jean-Aymé Candy. Puget is named on the title pages as "Historiographe de France," as would accord with his identification by Gatulle, *Gaston d'Orléans*, 239, as the *historiographe* of Marie de' Medici, and is not contradicted by the func-tion of "Historiographe de France" attributed to him for the years 1652–1655. See François Fossier, "À propos du titre d'historiographe sous l'ancien régime," *Revue d'histoire moderne et contemporaine* 32 (1985): 361–417, 367; and cf. *Écrivains de théâtre 1600–1649*, ed. Alan Howe, based on analyses by Madeleine Jurgens, foreword by Gérarad Ermisse, preface by Jean Mesnard (Paris: Centre Historique des Archives Nationales, 2005), 140–41, including documents 119–21, in which Puget is also styled "conseiller du roi en ses conseils d'état." Fossier concludes (377–78) that the title of *historiographe*, in whatever form, never had any juridical or institutional value and that, during the seventeenth century, it was accorded to a number of persons of diverse talents and experience essentially for polemical or religious reasons. It is nonetheless suggestive that Puget claimed this title as the queen mother's follower n 1631—and, especially, that no *privilège* appears in any edition of *Pandoste*; in this respect, *Pandoste* is unique among plays first published in that year (see Alain Riffaud, *Répertoire du théâtre français imprimé entre 1630 et 1660* [Geneva: Droz, 2009], 41–42).

25. See Gatulle, *Gaston d'Orléans*, 115–22 ("La guerre des pamphlets" ["The Pam-phlet War"]), and Knecht, *Richelieu*, 54, 178–79.

26. On Richelieu's increasing effectiveness in these spheres over the 1630s, see Knecht, *Richelieu*, 169–89 (ch. 11, "Richelieu as a Propagandist"); cf. Couton, *Riche-lieu*, 13–20.

27. Jean Puget de la Serre, *Pandoste, ou La Princesse malheureuse. Tragédie en prose* (n.p., n.p., n.d), day 1, act 3, 39. For convenience, I cite the digitized text available through Gallica (reference: NUMM 5740362). I have compared the passages cited in the 1631 edition of Nicolas de la Vigne and found no discrepancies. The text is paginated and divided into two "Journées" ["Days"], each comprising five acts, with no indication of scene changes. The citations include the "day," followed by the act number and finally the page number in this edition.

28. Robert Greene, *Histoire tragique de Pandosto, roy de Bohême et de Bellaria, sa femme: Ensemble les amours de Dorastus et de Faunia . . . Le tout premièrement trad. en anglais de la langue bohême [sic], et de nouveau mis en françois par L. Regnault* (Paris: G. Marette, 1615). It seems useful to cite this edition, which is extremely rare, on the premise that it served as Puget's primary, though not exclusive, source. We cannot judge, obviously, whether the playwright might have been influenced by Alexandre Hardy's prior dramatization; nothing indicates that this had been published. The par-allels with Shakespeare that I note seem unlikely to have been anticipated by Hardy.

29. Louis Moreau du Bail, *Le roman d'Albanie et de Sycile* (Paris: Pierre Rocolet, 1626). Apart from shifting the primary locale to Albania and renaming several characters, Du Bail abundantly supplemented Greene's succinct narrative, which he almost certainly adapted from Regnault's version (following, for instance, the latter's change of Trapalonia to Poland), with additional characters and incidents, especially political dealings involving various countries; still, he remained fairly close to his original with regard to the key episodes. Puget notably took from Du Bail the name of his Sicilian king (Agatocles, after Agatocle) and likewise preferred Belaire (Du Bail's Bellaire) to Bellaria, retained from Greene by Regnault; on the other hand, he retained (with a seeming typographical error) the name of Franion (who becomes Orcanò in Du Bail), and, more tellingly, adopted none of Du Bail's additions to Greene's plot. Most suggestive is the fact that Puget, as if profiting from the contradictory identification of Pandoste's kingdom (Bohemia/Albany) in the two French versions, fails to name it at any point. This is highly uncharacteristic of romance narratives and amounts to a clear invitation to imagine events as occurring close to home. Incidentally, the extent to which we are dealing with coterie literary production is suggested by the fact that André Mareschal supplied complementary verses to accompany Du Bail's text.

30. "Celuy" (the masculine pronoun) restricts the symbolic range of Greene's indefinite "that which." The translation's frequent ineptitude is stressed by its first commentator, Henri Potez, "Le premier roman anglais traduit en français," *Revue d'histoire littéraire de la France* 11 (1904): 42–55. Du Bail gives a poetically embellished version of the original specifying "sa fille perduë" ["his lost daughter"] (*Roman*, 211).

31. Regnault, *Histoire tragique de Pandosto*, 52–53.

32. Puget, *Pandoste*, day 1, act 4, 63; repeated day 1, act 5, 77.

33. Robert Greene, *Pandosto. The Triumph of Time*, ed. Stephen Orgel, in *The Winter's Tale*, by William Shakespeare (Oxford: Oxford University Press, 1996), 234–74, 274; subsequent references are to this edition. The expression is omitted from the translations.

34. According to Abraham, Puget had been mocked for the poor quality of his previous prose tragedy *Pyrame* (*Gaston d'Orléans*, 54). This accords with the bitter riposte of the author in his address to the reader in *Pandoste*; the first edition of *Pyrame* appears to date from 1629.

35. On the complex vicissitudes, at least as much commercial as political in origin, associated with the translation of the *Arcadia*, see Albert W. Osborn, *Sir Philip Sidney en France* (1932; fac. repr. Geneva: Slatkine, 1974), 78–91; and Desvignes, Introduction to *La cour bergère ou l'Arcadie de Messire Philippe Sidney*, by André Mareschal, 1: 28–31. A picture emerges of tangled political, religious, and commercial rivalries crisscrossing the channel.

36. Chistian Bouyer, *La duchesse de Chevreuse: L'indomptable et voluptueuse adversaire de Louis XIII* (Paris: Pygmalion/Gérard Watelet, 2002), 47. On the vital role of

the Duke of Chevreuse in managing negotiations for this marriage, so important to the queen mother, see Batiffol, *La duchesse de Chevreuse*, 43–47.

37. Henry Herbert, *The Dramatic Records of Sir Henry Herbert, Master of the Revels, 1623–1673*, ed. Joseph Quincy Adams (New Haven, CT; London: Yale University Press; Humphrey Milford, Oxford University Press, 1917), 51. This was about a month before the sudden and unexpected death (on February 16) of Ludovic Stuart (or Stewart), Duke of Lennox and Richmond, and it would be surprising if there were not French visitors in attendance. The duke was of French origin (the son of Esmé Stuart, James's one-time favorite) and had served as ambassador to France on various occasions.

38. Herbert, *Dramatic Records*, 52; Martin Butler, "*The Fortunate Isles*: Textual Essay," http://universitypublishingonline.org/cambridge/benjonson/k/essays/Fortunate_Isles_textual_essay/1/ (accessed July 3, 2014).

39. Greene, *Pandosto*, 238.

40. William Shakespeare, *The Winter's Tale*, ed. Stephen Orgel (Oxford: Oxford University Press, 1996), 3.2.131.

41. Ibid., 3.2.4.

42. Ibid., 3.2.31.

43. Ibid., 2.3.28; 3.2.173, 205.

44. Puget, *Pandoste*, day 1, act 4, 64.

45. Ibid., day 1, act 5, 79.

46. Ibid., day 2, act 3, 130; day 2, act 4, 147.

47. See Constant, *Gaston d'Orléans*, 21–23. Condemnations of tyranny remained a staple of anti-Richelieu discourse; see Constant, 192–200.

48. Puget, *Pandoste*, day 1, act 3, 50.

49. Shakespeare, *Winter's Tale*, 2.3.8–9; 2.3.3; 2.3.4; 2.3.8.

50. Puget, *Pandoste*, day 1, act 5, 73.

51. Shakespeare, *Winter's Tale*, 2.1.189–93.

52. Puget, *Pandoste*, day 1, act 3, 51.

53. Ibid., day 1, act 5, 74.

54. Shakespeare, *Winter's Tale*, 3.2.89–94.

55. Puget, *Pandoste*, day 1, act 3, 43.

56. Ibid., day 1, act 3, 47.

57. Ibid., day 1, act 4, 64.

58. Shakespeare, *Winter's Tale*, 3.2.64–65.

59. Puget, *Pandoste*, day 1, act 3, 46.

60. Du Bail, *Roman*, 188.

61. Greene, *Pandosto*, 247. For the translations, see Regnault, *Histoire tragique de Pandosto*, 55–56; Du Bail, *Roman*, 208.

62. Shakespeare, *Winter's Tale*, 3.2.44; 3.2.109.

63. Puget, *Pandoste*, day 1, act 3, 43.

64. Ibid., day 1, act 3, 44.

65. Ibid., day 1, act 3, 45.

66. Shakespeare, *Winter's Tale*, 3.2.29–31.

67. Greene, *Pandosto*, 247.

68. Regnault, *Histoire tragique de Pandosto*, 55.

69. Du Bail, *Roman*, 208.

70. It seems possible that both translators, in making the queen an agent, rather than a victim, of spite at this point, may be working from either the 1592 or 1595 edition of Greene's novel, in which "stain spiteful discredit" is corrupted to read "stain spitefully discredit." The reading of 1588 was restored in subsequent editions.

71. There is, then, more to Puget's representation of Flavvye, in my view, than the mere sentimentalizing detected by Newcomb, *Reading Popular Romance*, 83.

72. Puget, *Pandoste*, day 2, act 1, 89.

73. Shakespeare, *Winter's Tale*, 4.4. 114–15.

74. Ibid., 4.4.127–32.

75. Puget, *Pandoste*, day 2 act 2, 109.

76. Ibid., day 2, act 2, 110.

77. In Greene's *Pandosto*, Fawnia is encountered simply making "a garland of such homely flowers as the fields did afford" (257); Regnault, *Histoire tragique de Pandosto*, reduces this still further ("une guirlande de fleurs" [101]), and Du Bail, *Roman*, follows suit (387)—further evidence that he based himself mainly on his French precursor.

78. Claude Parfaict and François Parfaict, *Dictionnaire des théâtres de Paris*, 7 vols. (Paris: Rozet, 1767), 3:277 (under the original title of *Lyzidor*); Mareschal, *La cour bergère*, sig. ãiiir.

79. Mareschal, *La cour bergère*, sig. ãiv^r.

80. On these points, see Lionel Charles Durel, *L'œuvre d'André Mareschal, auteur dramatique, poète et romancier de la période de Louis XIII* (Baltimore, MD; Oxford: Johns Hopkins University Press; Humphrey Milford, Oxford University Press, 1932), 15–16; and Gatulle, *Gaston d'Orléans*, 239.

81. André Mareschal, *Les feux de joye de la France sur l'heureuse alliance d'Angleterre: Et la descente des dieux en France pour honorer la feste de cette alliance* (Paris: B. Martin, 1625).

82. Durel, *André Mareschal*, 14, notes the author's inclusion in a 1626 anthology associated with supporters of Gaston and enemies of Richelieu.

83. See Britland, *Drama*, esp. 35–52, 111–12, and 156–63, where she offers a fascinating (if necessarily inconclusive) discussion of the 1635 English performance of the pastoral *Florimène*, by François Le Métel, seigneur de Boisrobert, another of Richelieu's clients.

84. Durel, *André Mareschal*, 7–8; this was published in 1635.

85. Durel, *André Mareschal*, 86; André Mareschal, *Comédies*, ed. Véronique Lochert (Paris: Classiques Garnier, 2010), 10–12.

86. Mareschal, *La cour bergère*, sig. ãii^v.

87. See Osborn, *Sidney*, 82.

88. My information regarding Robert Sidney's activities comes from Ian Atherton, "Sidney, Robert, Second Earl of Leicester (1595–1677)," in the *Oxford Dictionary of National Biography* (Oxford: Oxford University Press, 2004); online ed. January 2008, http://www.oxforddnb.com/view/article/25525 (accessed July 3, 2014).

89. See Bouyer, *Gaston d'Orléans*, 136–37; Kermina, *Marie de Médicis*, 379; and Knecht, *Richelieu*, 109.

90. Kermina, *Marie de Médicis*, 380.

91. See Batiffol, *La duchesse de Chevreuil*, 140–54; and Kleinman, *Anne d'Autriche*, 177–85. The version of the valet himself may be found in Pierre de la Porte, *Mémoires contenant plusieurs particularités sur les règnes de Louis XIII et Louis XIV 1624–1666* (Clermont-Ferrand: Paléo, 2003), 57–94.

92. Such a reading obviously puts paid to the assumption of Durel, *André Mareschal*, 16, that *La cour bergère* benefited from a virtual English seal of approval through the implication of the ambassador.

93. Mareschal, *La cour bergère*, sig. ãiiiʳ⁻ᵛ.

94. Desvignes, 1: 132, n. to 68, l. 1 (of vol. 2).

95. Mareschal, *La cour bergère*, 3.5, 68; 3.5, 69. Citations of this play refer to act, scene, and page numbers of the 1640 edition.

96. Ibid., 4.1, 78.

97. Cf. Philip Sidney, *The Countess of Pembroke's Arcadia*, ed. Maurice Evans (Harmondsworth, Middlesex: Penguin Books, 1977), 3: 17, 532–34.

98. Mareschal, *La cour bergère*, 5.10, 98.

99. Ibid., 4.1, 77.

100. Ibid., 1.1, 7.

101. See, notably, Knecht, *Richelieu*, 179–82.

102. James Shirley, *A Pastorall Called the Arcadia* (London: J[ohn] D[awson] for John Williams, and F. Eglesfeild, 1640).

103. Paul Addison Ramsay, "*A Pastorall Called the Arcadia* by James Shirley: A Critical Edition" (PhD diss., University of Michigan, 1975), 32.

104. Ramsey, "*Pastorall Called the Arcadia*," 82.

105. John Fletcher, "To the Reader," in *The Faithful Shepherdess*, ed. Cyrus Hoy, *The Dramatic Works in the Beaumont and Fletcher Canon*, gen. ed. Fredson Bowers, 6 vols. (Cambridge, UK: Cambridge University Press, 1966), 3: 497.

106. Sidney, *Arcadia*, 4: 6, 753–63.

Bibliography

Archival Sources

Archives Départementales de la Gironde. 1 B 226. 201a. September 16, 1553.
Archives Départementales de la Gironde. 1 B 158. 93r–96r. May 14, 1555.
Archives de l'État de Genève. Registres du Conseil 41. 142r. July 12, 1546.
Archives de l'État de Genève. Registres du Conseil 43. 67r. April 16, 1548.
Archives de l'État de Genève. Registres du Conseil 44. 58r. April 1, 1549.
Archives de l'État de Genève. Registres du Conseil 48. 101r. August 9, 1554.
Archives de l'État de Genève. Registres du Conseil 54. 35v. January 6, 1558.
Archives de l'État de Genève. Registres du Conseil 54. 220r. June 24, 1558.
Archives de l'État de Genève. Registres du Conseil 56. 224r-v. August 5, 1561.
Archives de l'État de Genève. Registres du Conseil 56. 242r. September 22, 1561.
Archives de l'État de Genève. Registres du Conseil 56. 249r. October 13, 1561.
Archives de l'État de Genève. Registres du Conseil 58. 121r. November 19, 1563.
Archives de l'État de Genève. Registres du Conseil 63. 37r. April 20, 1568.
Archives de l'État de Genève. Mi B 109 p.
Archives de l'État de Genève. Registres du Conseil 56. 249r. October 13, 1561.
Archives de l'État de Genève. Registres du Conseil 48. 101r. August 9, 1554.
Archives Nationales. X2^{a}1394. January 25, 1586.

Primary Sources

Aneau, Barthélemy. *Quintil Horatien*. Lyons, c. 1550.

Aristotle. *The Poetics of Aristotle: Translation and Commentary*. Edited and translated by Stephen Halliwell. Chapel Hill: University of North Carolina Press, 1987.

Badius, Conrad. *Comedie du Pape malade*. In *Théâtre français de la Renaissance: La comedie à l'époque d'Henri II et de Charles IX (1561–1568)*, edited by Enea Balmas and Monica Barsi, 1st series, vol. 7. Florence; Paris: Leo S. Olschki; Presses Universitaires de France, 1986.

Bellone, Etienne. *Les amours de Dalcméon et de Flore, tragédie* [1610]. Rouen: Raphaël du Petit-Val, 1621.

Bèze, Théodore de. *Abraham sacrifiant: Tragédie française*. In *Théâtre français de la Renaissance: La tragédie à l'époque d'Henri II et de Charles IX (1550–1561)*, edited by Patrizia De Capitani, 1st series, vol. 1. Florence; Paris: Leo S. Olschki; Presses Universitaires de France, 1986.

———. *Abrahamus Sacrificans*. Translated by Johann Jakob Barrensi. Geneva: Jacobus Stoer, 1599.

———. *A Tragedie of Abrahams Sacrifice*. Translated by Arthur Golding [1577]. Edited by Malcolm W. Wallace. Toronto: University of Toronto Press, 1906.

Bienvenu, Jacques. *Comedie du Monde malade et mal pensé*. In *Théâtre français de la Renaissance: La comedie à l'époque d'Henri II et de Charles IX (1561–1568)*, edited by Rosalba Guerini, 1st series, vol. 7. Florence; Paris: Leo S. Olschki; Presses Universitaires de France, 1986.

———. *Comedie facetieuse et tres plaisante, du voyage de frère Fecisti en Provence, vers Nostradamus: Pour savoir certaines nouvelles des clefs de Paradis et d'enfer, que le pape avoit perdues*. Nîmes [Geneva?], 1589.

———. *Poesie de l'alliance perpetuelle entre deux nobles et chrestiennes villes franches, Berne et Geneve, faite l'an M.D.LVIII*. [Geneva: Jean Crespin], 1568.

———. *Response au livre d'Artus Desire intitulé: Les grandes chroniques et annales de Passe-Partout*. Geneva: Jacques Berthet, 1558.

———. *Le triomphe de Jesus Christ: Comedie apocalyptique, traduite du latin de Jean Foxus anglois, en rithme françoise, et augmentée d'un petit discours de la maladie de la messe, par Jacques Bienvenu citoyen de Geneve*. Geneva: Jean Bonnefoy, 1562.

Bodin, Jean. *Les six Livres de la Republique de J. Bodin Angevin*. Paris: Jacques du Puys, 1576.

Bonivard, François. *Chroniques de Genève*. 3 vols. Edited by Micheline Tripet. Geneva: Droz, 2001–2012.

Bordier, René. "Grand Bal de la douairière de Billebahaut. Ballet dansé par le Roy au mois de Fevrier 1626." In *Ballets et mascarades de cour de Henri III à Louis XIV (1581–1652)*, edited by M. Paul Lacroix, vol. 3. Geneva: Slatkine Reprints, 1968.

Bourgeois, Louise. *Observations diverses sur la stérilité, perte de fruict, foecondité, accouchements et maladies des femmes et enfants nouveaux naiz*. Paris: Saugrain, 1626.

Boterò, Giovanni. *Della ragione di stato*. Milano: Pacifico Pontio, 1596.

———. *The Reason of State*. Translated by P. J. and D. P. Waley. New Haven, CT: Yale University Press, 1956.

Boulaese, Jean. *Le manuel de l'admirable victoire du corps de Dieu sur l'esprit maling Beelzebub*. Paris: Denis Duval, 1575.

———. *Le miracle de Laon en Launoys representé au vif et escript en latin, françoys, italien, espagnol et allemant*. Cambray: Pierre Lombard, 1566.

———. *Le thresor et entiere histoire de la triomphante victoire du corps de Dieu sur l'esprit maling Beelzebub, obtenuë à Laon l'an mil cinq cens soixante six*. Paris: Nicolas Chesneau, 1578.

Brantôme. *Recueil des dames, poésies et tombeaux*. Edited by Etienne Vaucheret. Paris: Gallimard, 1991.

Calendar of State Papers Foreign, Elizabeth, 1559–1589. 23 vols. [1863–1950]. Edited by Joseph Stevenson et al. http://www.british-history.ac.uk/catalogue.aspx?gid=124&type=3. Accessed July 6, 2014.

Chrestien des Croix, Nicolas. *Amnon et Thamar*. Rouen: Théodore Reinsart, 1608.

———. *Rosemonde ou la vengeance*. Rouen: Théodore Reinsart, 1603.

Corneille, Pierre. *Œuvres complètes*. 3 vols. Edited by Georges Couton. Paris: Gallimard, 1980–1987.

———. *Trois discours sur le poème dramatique* [1660]. Edited by Bénédicte Louvat and Marc Escola. Paris: Flammarion, 1999.

Cotgrave, Randle. *A Dictionarie of the French and English Tongues*. London, 1611.

D'Aubignac, François Hédelin (Abbé). *La pratique du théâtre: Œuvre tres-necessaire a tous ceux qui veulent s'appliquer a la composition des poëmes dramatiques*. Paris: Antoine de Sommaville, 1657.

———. *The Whole Art of the Stage*. Translated by William Aglionby. London, 1684.

D'Aubigné, Agrippa. *Histoire universelle*. 11 vols. Edited by André Thierry. Geneva: Droz, 1987.

De Pibrac, Guy du Faur. *Un essai de propagande à l'étranger au XVIe siècle: L'apologie de la Saint-Barthélemy*. Edited by Alban Cabos. Paris: Edouard Champion, 1922.

Deux sotties jouées à Genève l'une en 1523, sur la Place du Molard, dite sottie à dix personnages, et l'autre en 1524, en la Justice, dite Sottie à neuf personnages. Edited by Francis-Noël Le Roy. Geneva: J. Gay et fils, 1868.

Diderot, Denis. "Les entretiens sur *Le fils naturel*." In *Œuvres complètes*, 7:85–168. Paris: Garnier Frères, 1875.

[Diderot, Denis et al.]. *Encyclopédie, ou Dictionnaire raisonné des sciences, des arts et des métiers*. Vol. 11. Lausanne and Bern, 1782.

Discours au vrai de l'étrange cruauté d'un soldat. Lyon: Antoine Bessy, 1611.

Discours pitoyable de la cruauté et tirannie d'un jeune garçon serviteur, lequel a fait par poison mourir son maistre, maistresse et leurs enfants: Avec plusieurs regrets par luy faits avant son exécution. Rouen: André Chalmenil; Dignent [Dinan]: Robert Recine, [1600?].

Donatus, Aelius. "On Comedy." Translated by O. B. Hardison. In *Classical and Medieval Literary Criticism. Translations and Interpretations*. Edited by Alexander Preminger et al., 305–9. New York: Frederick Ungar Publishing, 1974.

Dorat, Jean. *Magnificentissimi spectaculi a regina regum matre in hortis suburbanis editi*. In *Henrici regis Poloniae invictissimi nuper renunciati gratulationem, descriptio*. Paris: F. Morel, 1573.

Du Bail, Louis Moreau. *Le roman d'Albanie et de Sycile*. Paris: Pierre Rocolet, 1626.

Du Bellay, Joachim. *La deffence et illustration de la langue françoise*. Paris: Arnoul L'Angelier, 1549.

Du Choul, Guillaume. *Discorso della religione antica de Romani*. Lione: Appresso Gvglielmo Rovillio, 1569.

———. *Discours de la religion*. Lyon: Guillaume Rouillé, 1556.

Du Hamel, Jacques. *Acoubar, ou la loyauté trahie*. Rouen: Raphaël du Petit-Val, 1603.

[Du Plessis, Armand, Cardinal de Richelieu, and Jean Desmarets.] *Europe: Comédie héroïque*. Edited by Alain-Gérard Slama and Sylvie Taussig. Turnhout: Brepols, 2006.

Dupleix, Scipion. *Ethique ou philosophie morale*. Chicago: ARTFL Electronic Edition, 2009.

———. *La logique ou art de discourir et raisonner* [1607]. Paris: Fayard, 1984.

Emerson, Ralph Waldo. *Nature*. Boston: James Munroe, 1836.

Factum du procez pendant en la cour entre Pierre et autre Pierre l'Hoste freres demandeurs en reparation de crime d'empoisonnement, suppositions, voleries, faussetés, et suborne-ment de tesmoings. n.p.: n.p., [1626?].

Fletcher, John. *The Dramatic Works in the Beaumont and Fletcher Canon*. 6 vols. Edited by Fredson Bowers et al. Cambridge, UK: Cambridge University Press, 1966.

Fonteny, Jacques de. *Cléophon*. Paris: F. Jacquin, 1600.

———. *Le beau berger*. In *Le bocage d'amour*. Paris: Jean Corrozet, 1615; repr. 1624.

———. *L'eumorphopémie* [Le Beau pasteur]. In *La première partie des ébats poétiques de Jacques de Fonteny contenant une pastorelle du beau pasteur, éclogues, amours, sonets spirituels et autres poésies*. Mont Saint Hilaire:Guillaume Linocier, 1587.

Furetière, Antoine. *Dictionnaire universelle contenant généralement tous les mots françois tant vieux que modernes, et les termes de toutes les sciences et des arts*. Rotterdam, 1690.

Garnier, Robert. *Antigone, ou La pieté*. Edited by Jean-Dominique Beaudin. Paris: Champion, 1997.

———. *Bradamante*. Edited by Raymond Lebègue. Paris: Les Belles Lettres, 1949.

———. *Hippolyte*. In *Théâtre complet*, edited by Jean-Dominique Beaudin, vol. 2. Paris: Classiques Garnier, 2009.

———. *Les Juifves, Hippolyte*. Edited by Raymond Lebègue. Paris: Les Belles Lettres, 2000.

———. *Marc Antoine*. Edited by Jean-Claude Ternaux. Paris: Classiques Garnier, 2010.

———. *Porcie*. Paris: Robert Estienne, 1568.

———. *Porcie*. Edited by Jean-Claude Ternaux. Paris: Champion, 1999.

———. *La Troade, tragédie*. In *Théâtre complet*, edited by Jean-Dominique Beaudin, vol. 5. Paris: Honoré Champion, 1999.

Gentili, Alberico. *De legationibus libri tres* [1594]. Translated by Gordon J. Laing. 2 vols. New York: Oxford University Press, 1924.

Gréban, Arnoul. *Mystère de la Passion*. Edited by Gaston Paris and Gaston Raynaud. Paris: F. Vieweg, 1878.

Greene, Robert. *Pandosto: The Triumph of Time*. In *The Winter's Tale*, by William Shakespeare, edited by Stephen Orgel, 234–74. Oxford: Oxford University Press, 1996.

Greene, Thomas, and Jean Puget de La Serre. *Greene's "Pandosto" or "Dorastus" and "Fawnia" Being the Original of Shakespeare's "Winter's Tale"*. Edited by P. G. Thomas. Oxford: Humphrey Milford, Oxford University Press, 1907.

Gringore, Pierre. *Le jeu du prince des sotz et de mère sotte*. Edited by Alan Hindley. Paris: Champion, 2000.

Hardy, Alexandre. *Alcméon, ou la vengeance féminine*. In *Théâtre de la cruauté et récits sanglants en France (XVIe–XVIIe siècle)*, edited by Christian Biet et al. Paris: Robert Laffont, 2006.

Hegel, Georg Wilhelm Friedrich. *Aesthetics*. Translated by T. M. Knox. Oxford: Clarendon Press, 1998.

Herbert, Henry. *The Dramatic Records of Sir Henry Herbert, Master of the Revels, 1623–1673*. Edited by Joseph Quincy Adams. New Haven, CT; London: Yale University Press; Humphrey Milford, Oxford University Press, 1917.

Hugo, Victor. Préface to *Cromwell, drame* [1827], I–LXIV. Paris: Ambroise Dupont, 1828.

———. "Preface to Cromwell" [1910], in *Prefaces and Prologues to Famous Books*, 39:354–409. Translated by Andrew Motte. New York: Cosimo, 2009.

La Boétie, Etienne de. *Anti-Dictator: The "Discours sur la servitude volontaire"*. Translated by Harry Kurz. New York: Columbia University Press, 1942.

———. *Discours sur la servitude volontaire*. Edited by Malcolm Smith. Geneva: Droz, 2001.

La Calprenède, Gautier de Costes de. *Le mort de Mithridate*. In *Le Théâtre du XVIIIe Siècle*, edited by Jacques Scherer and Jacques Truchet, vol. 2. Paris: Gallimard, 1986.

La Porte, Pierre de. *Mémoires contenant plusieurs particularités sur les règnes de Louis XIII et Louis XIV 1624–1666*. Clermont-Ferrand: Paléo, 2003.

La Taille, Jean de. *Les corrivaus*. In *Commedia del Rinascimento francese*, edited by Giuseppe Macri. Galatina: Editrice Salentina, 1974.

———. *Œuvres*. Vol. 4. Edited by R. de Maulde. Geneva: Slatkine Reprints, 1968.

———. *Tragédies: Saül le Furieux; La Famine ou Les Gabéonites*. Edited by Elliott Forsyth. Paris: STFM, 1998.

Le Coq, Thomas. *Tragedie représentant l'odieus et sanglant meurtre commis par le maudit Cain, à l'encontre de son frere Abel, extraicte du 4. chap. de Genese*. Paris: Nicolas Bonfons, 1580.

Machiavelli, Nicolò. *Discourses on Livy*. Translated by Julia Conaway Bondanella and Peter Bondanella. Oxford: Oxford University Press, 1997.

La magicienne estrangère, tragédie: En laquelle on voit les tirannicques comportemens, origine, entreprises, desseings, sortilleges, arrest, mort et supplice, tant du Marquis d'Ancre que de Leonor Galligay sa femme, avec l'advantureuse rencontre de leurs funestes ombres. Rouen: David Geuffroy et Jacques Besongne, 1617.

Mainfray, Pierre. *La Rhodienne ou la cruauté de Solyman*. Rouen: David du Petit-Val, 1621.

Mairet, Jean. *Sophonisbe*. In *Théâtre du XVIIe siècle*, edited by Jacques Scherer, vol. 1. Paris: Gallimard, 1975.

Mareschal, André. *Comédies*. Edited by Véronique Lochert. Paris: Classiques Garnier, 2010.

———. *La cour bergère, ou L'Arcadie de Messire Philippe Sidney*. Paris: T. Quinet, 1640.

———. *Les feux de joye de la France sur l'heureuse alliance d'Angleterre: Et la descente des dieux en France pour honorer la feste de cette alliance*. Paris: B. Martin, 1625.

Maupoint. *Bibliothèque des théâtres, contenant le catalogue alphabétique des pièces dramatiques et opéra, le nom des auteurs et le temps de la représentation de ces pièces, avec des anecdotes*. Paris: Chardon, 1733.

Le mémoire de Mahelot: Mémoire pour la décoration des pièces qui se représentent par les Comédiens du Roi. Edited by Pierre Pasquier. Paris: Honoré Champion, 2005.

Mercadé, Eustache. *Passion d'Arras*. Edited by Jules-Marie Richard. Arras: Société du Pas-de-Calais, 1893.

Michel, Jean. *Mystère de la Passion*. Edited by Omer Jodogone. Gembloux: J. Duculot, 1959.

Le mistere du siege d'Orleans [ca. 1435]. Edited by François Guessard and Eugène de Certain. Paris: Imprimerie impériale, 1862.

Le mistére du Viel Testament. 6 vols. Edited by James de Rothschild. Paris: Firmin Didot et cie, 1878–1891.

Les recueils collectifs de poésies libres et satiriques publiés depuis 1600 jusqu'à la mort de Théophile (1626). Edited by Frédéric Lachèvre. Paris: Champion, 1914.

Molinet, Jean (?). *Le mystère de Judith et Holofernés: Une édition critique de l'une des parties du "Mistére du Viel Testament"*. Edited by Graham A. Runnalls. Geneva: Droz, 1995.

Monléon. *Thyeste*. Paris: P. Guillemot, 1633.

Montaigne, Michel de. *The Complete Essays of Montaigne*. Translated by Donald Frame. London: Everyman's Library, 2003.

———. *Les essais*. Edited by Pierre Villey and V.-L. Saulnier. Paris: Presses universitaires de France, 1965.

———. *The Essayes or Morall, Politike and Millitarie Discourses of Lord Michaell de Montaigne*. Translated by John Florio. London: Val. Sims, 1603. http://www.luminarium.org/renascence-editions/montaignesearch.html. Accessed July 6, 2014.

Mysère de Saint Remi. Edited by Jelle Koopmans. Geneva: Droz, 1997.

Parfaict, Claude, and François Parfaict. *Dictionnaire des théâtres de Paris*. 7 vols. Paris: Rozet, 1767.

Pasquier, Etienne. *Les lettres*. Paris: Jean Petit-Pas, 1619.

Plato. *Phédon*. Edited by Monique Dixsaut. Paris: GF-Flammarion, 1991.

Postel, Guillaume. *De summopere consyderando miraculo victoriae corporis Christi, quod Lauduni contigit 1566 a creatione mundi anno deque eius fructu Opusculum*. Cambray: Pierre Lombard, 1566.

Puget de La Serre, Jean. *Ballet des princes indiens*. Bruxelles: F. Vivien, 1634.

———. *Les Amours du Roy, et de la Reine sous le nom de Jupiter et de Junon, avec les magnificences de leurs nopces, ou L'histoire morale de France, soubs le règne de Louys le Juste et Anne d'Austriche: Le tout enrichi d'un grand nombre de figures, etc.* Paris: Nicolas Bessin et Denis de Cay, 1625.

———. *Pandoste ou La princesse mal-heureuse: Tragédie en prose; Divisee en deux journées*. Paris: Nicolas de La Vigne, 1631.

———. *Le portrait de Scipion l'Africain, ou l'image de la gloire et de la vertu représentée au naturel dans celle de monseigneur le cardinal duc de Richelieu*. Bordeaux: Guillaume Millanges, 1641.

———. *Thomas Morus, ou Le triomphe de la foy, et de la constance, tragédie en prose*. Paris: A. Courbé, 1642.

Rabelais, François. *The Fourth Book of the Heroic Deeds and Sayings of the Good Pantagruel*. In *The Complete Works of François Rabelais*, translated by Donald Frame Berkeley: University of California Press, 1991.

———. *Gargantua and Pantagruel*. Translated by Michael A. Screech. London: Penguin, 2006.

———. *Le Quart Livre*. Edited with an Introduction by Gérard Defaux. Paris: Livre de Poche, 1994.

———. *Le Quart Livre de Pantagruel (édition dite partielle, de Lyon, 1548)*. Edited by Jean Plattard. Paris: Champion, 1909.

———. *Œuvres complètes*. Edited by Mireille Huchon with François Moreau. Paris: Gallimard, Bibliothèque de la Pléiade, 1994.

Racine, Jean. *Œuvres complètes*. Vol. 1. Edited by Georges Forestier et al. Paris: Gallimard, Bibliothèque de la Pléiade, 1999.

Recueil de sermons joyeux: Édition critique avec introduction, notes et glossaire. Edited by Jelle Koopmans. Geneva: Droz, 1988.

Recueil général de moralités d'expression française. 18 vols. Edited by Jonathan Beck, Estelle Doudet, and Alan Hindley. Paris: Classiques Garnier, 2012–2018.

Recueil général des sotties. 3 vols. Edited by Émile Picot. Paris: Firmin Didot, 1902.

Regnault, L. *Histoire tragique de Pandosto, roy de Bohême et de Bellaria, sa femme: Ensemble les amours de Dorastus et de Faunia . . . Le tout premièrement trad. en anglais de la langue bohême [sic], et de nouveau mis en françois par L. Regnault*. Paris: G. Marette, 1615.

Relations des ambassadeurs vénitiens sur les affaires de la France au XVIe siècle. 2 vols. Edited by Niccolo Tommaseo. Paris: Imprimerie Royale, 1838.

Ronsard, Pierre de. *Œuvres complètes*. 2 vols. Edited by Jean Céard, Daniel Ménager, and Michel Simonin. Paris: Gallimard, 1994.

Rotrou, Jean de. *Bélisaire*. In *Théâtre complet*, edited by Georges Forestier and Marianne Béthery, 1:69–199. Paris: Société des textes français modernes, 1998.

———. *Hercule mourant*. In *Théâtre complet*, edited by Bénédicte Louvat, Dominique Moncond'huy, and Alain Riffaud, vol. 2. Paris : STFM, 1999.

Saint-Sorlin, Jean Desmarets de. *Mirame*. Edited by Catherine Guillot and Colette Scherer. Rennes: Presses Universitaires de Rennes, 2010.

———. *Scipion: Tragi-comédie*. Paris: H. Le Gras, 1639.

Servin, Louis. *Actions notables et plaidoyez de messire Louys Servin, . . . à la fin desquels sont les arrests intervenus sur iceux: Dernière édition . . . Ensemble les plaidoyers de M. A. Robert, Arnault et autres*. Paris: G. Alliot, 1631.

———. *Plaidoyez de Mre Loys Servin*. 4 vols. Paris: J. de Heuquevill, 1603–1613.

Shakespeare, William. *Macbeth*. In *The Norton Shakespeare*, 2nd ed., edited by Jean E. Howard et al. Boston: W. W. Norton, 2008.

———. *The Winter's Tale*. Edited by Stephen Orgel. Oxford: Oxford University Press, 1996.

Shirley, James. *A Pastorall Called the Arcadia*. London: J[ohn] D[awson] for John Williams, and F. Eglesfeild, 1640.

Sidney, Philip. *The Countess of Pembroke's Arcadia*. Edited by Maurice Evans. Harmondsworth, Middlesex: Penguin Books, 1977.

Spenser, Edmund. *The Shepherd's Calendar and Other Poems*. Edited by Philip Henderson. London: Everyman's Library, 1965.

Tallemant des Réaux, Gédéon. *Les Historiettes de Tallemant des Réaux*. 6 vols. Paris: Alphonse Levavasseur, 1834.

Théâtre de la cruauté et récits sanglants en France (XVIe–XVIIe siècle). Edited by Christian Biet et al. Paris: Robert Laffont, 2006.

Théâtre et propagande aux débuts de la Réforme: Six pièces polémiques du Recueil La Vallière. Edited by Jonathan Beck. Geneva: Slatkine, 1986.

De Thou, Jacques-Auguste. *Histoire universelle*. 16 vols. London, 1734.

Tortorel, Jacques, and J. Perrisin. *Graphic History: The Wars, Massacres and Troubles of Tortorel and Perrissin*. Vol. 1. Edited by Philip Benedict. Geneva: Droz, 2007.

Tragédie française d'un more cruel envers son seigneur nommé Riviery, gentilhomme espagnol, sa damoiselle et ses enfants. Rouen: Abraham Cousturier, [ca. 1608].

Tragédies et récits de martyres en France (fin XVIe–début XVIIe siècle). Edited by Christian Biet, Marie-Madeleine Fragonard, et al. Paris: Classiques Garnier, 2009.

Troterel, Pierre. *La vie et sainte Conversion de Guillaume duc d'Aquitaine escrite en Vers, et disposée en actes pour representer sur le theatre*. Rouen: David du Petit-Val, 1632.

———. *Tragédie de sainte Agnès*. Rouen: David du Petit-Val, 1615.

Warner, William. *Albion's England*. London, 1586.

Secondary Sources

Abraham, Claude Kurt. *Gaston d'Orléans et sa cour*. Chapel Hill: University of North Carolina Press, 1964.

Arden, Heather. *Fools' Plays: A Study of Satire in the "Sottie"*. Cambridge, UK: Cambridge University Press, 1980.

Atherton, Ian. "Sidney, Robert, Second Earl of Leicester (1595–1677)." In *Oxford Dictionary of National Biography*. Oxford: Oxford University Press, 2004. http://www.oxforddnb.com/view/article/25525. Last modified January 2008. Accessed July 3, 2014.

Aubailly, Jean-Claude. *Le monologue, le dialogue et la sottie: Essai sur quelques genres dramatiques de la fin du Moyen Age et du début du XVIe siècle*. Paris: Honoré Champion, 1976.

Backus, Irena. *Le miracle de Laon: Le déraisonnable, le raisonable, l'apocalyptique et le politique dans les récits du "Miracle de Laon" (1566–1578)*. Paris: Vrin, 1994.

Bakhtin, Mikhail. *Rabelais and His World*. Translated by Helene Iswolsky. Cambridge, MA: MIT Press, 1968.

Baltrusaitis, Jurgis. *Le Moyen Âge fantastique*. Paris: Colin, 1955.

Bapst, Germain. *Essai sur l'histoire du théâtre, orné de 85 gravures*. Paris: Librairie Hachette, 1893.

Barnavi, Elie. *La Sainte Ligue, le juge et la potence: L'assassinat du président Brisson*. Paris: Hachette, 1985.

Bastien, Pascal. *L'exécution publique à Paris au XVIIe siècle: Une histoire des rituels judiciaires*. Seyssel: Champ Vallon, 2006.

Batiffol, Louis. *La duchesse de Chevreuse: Une vie d'aventures et d'intrigues sous Louis XIII*. Paris: Hachette, 1913.

Beam, Sara. *Laughing Matters: Farce and the Making of Absolutism in France*. Ithaca, NY: Cornell University Press, 2007.

Beck, Jonathan. "De l'endoctrinement des enfants: Les écoliers de la Gestapo antiprotestante d'après le théâtre aux débuts de la Réforme." *Fifteenth-Century Studies* 13 (1988): 471–83.

Benedict, Philip. *Christ's Churches Purely Reformed: A Social History of Calvinism*. New Haven, CT: Yale University Press, 2002.

Benedict, Philip, and Nicolas Fornerod. "Les 2 150 'églises' réformées de France de 1561–1562." *Revue historique* 651 (2009): 529–60.

Bergquist, Peter. Introduction to *The Complete Motets 10: The Four-Language Print for Four and Eight Voices (Munich 1573)*, by Orlando di Lasso. Madison: A-R Editions, 1995.

Berns, Thomas. "'Ô mes conseillers, il n'y a nul conseiller': La politique de l'amitié chez Montaigne." In *Montaigne politique*, edited by Philippe Desan, 57–72. Paris: Honoré Champion, 2006.

Berry, Alice Fiola. *The Charm of Catastrophe: A Study of Rabelais's Quart Livre*. Chapel Hill: University of North Carolina Press, 2000.

Bertens, Johannes Willem. *Literary Theory: The Basics*. 2nd ed. London and New York: Taylor and Francis, 2008.

Biet, Christian. "Le Rouge et le noir, le rose et le vert, ou la pastorale homosexuelle de Jacques de Fonteny (1587)." In *Dissidents, excentriques et marginaux de l'Age clas-*

sique: Autour de Cyrano de Bergerac, edited by Patricia Harry, Alain Mothu, and Philippe Sellier, 265–88. Paris: Champion, 2006.

Biet, Christian, et al., eds. *Théâtre de la cruauté et récits sanglants en France (XVIe–XVIIe siècle)*. Paris: Robert Laffont, 2006.

Biet, Christian, and Marie-Madeleine Fragonard, eds. *Le théâtre, la violence et les arts en Europe (XVIe–XVIIes.)*. *Littératures Classiques* 73 (2011).

Biet, Christian, Marie-Madeleine Fragonard, et al., eds. *Tragédies et récits de martyres en France (fin XVIe–début XVIIe siècle)*. Paris: Classiques Garnier, 2009.

Blanchard, Jean-Marc. "Of Cannibalism and Autobiography." *Modern Language Notes* 93, no. 4 (1978): 654–76.

Blanchard, Jean-Vincent. "*Dies Irae*: Le coup d'Etat de Louis XIII, les pamphlets et l'institution du public." *Littératures Classiques* 68 (2009): 31–42.

Bloemendal, Jan, and Howard B. Norland, ed. *Neo-Latin Drama in Early Modern Europe*. Leiden: Brill, 2013.

Boisson, Didier, and Yves Krumenacker, eds., *La coexistence confessionnelle à l'épreuve: Etudes sur les relations entre Protestants et Catholiques dans la France moderne*. Lyon: Université Jean Moulin Lyon III, 2009.

Bolduc, Benoît, ed. *Texte et représentation: Les arts du spectacle (XVIe s.–XVIIIes.)*. *Texte* 33/34 (2003).

Bonet-Maury, G. "'Le Monde malade et mal pansé' ou la comédie protestante au XVIe siècle." *Bulletin Historique et Littéraire de la Société de l'Histoire de Protestantisme Français* 35, 3rd ser. (1886): 210–24.

Bonnat, René. "Une représentation protestante à Agen, en 1553." *Revue de l'Agenais* 29 (1902): 75–77.

Bordier, Henri Léonard. *Le chansonnier huguenot du XVIe siècle* [1870]. Geneva: Droz, 1969.

Bordier, Jean-Pierre. *Le "Jeu de la Passion": Le message chrétien et le théâtre français (XIIIe–XVIes.)*. Paris: Honoré Champion, 1998.

———. "Satire traditionnelle et polémique moderne dans les moralités et les sotties françaises tardives." In *Satira e beffa nelle commedie europee del Rinascimento*, edited by Maria Doglio Chiabò and Federico Doglio, 109–33. Rome: Torre d'Orfeo, 2002.

Bossy, John. "The Mass as a Social Institution 1200–1700." *Past and Present* 100 (1983): 29–61.

Boughner, Daniel C. *The Braggart in Renaissance Comedy: A Study in Comparative Drama from Aristophanes to Shakespeare*. Minneapolis: University of Minnesota Press, 1954.

Bouhaïk-Gironès, Marie. *Les Clercs de la Basoche et le théâtre politique (Paris, 1420–1550)*. Paris: Honoré Champion, 2007.

Bouhaïk-Gironès, Marie, Jelle Koopmans, and Katell Lavéant, eds. *Le Théâtre polémique français: 1450–1550*. Rennes: Presses Universitaires de Rennes, 2008.

Bourgeon, Jean-Louis. "La Fronde parlementaire à la veille de la Saint-Barthélemy." *Bibliothèque de l'Ecole des Chartes* 148, no. 1 (1990): 17–89.

Bouteille-Meister, Charlotte. "Représenter le présent: Formes et fonctions de 'l'actualité' dans le théâtre d'expression française à l'époque des conflits religieux (1554–1629)." PhD diss. Université Paris Ouest Nanterre, 2011.

Bouteille-Meister, Charlotte, and Kjerstin Aukrust, eds. *Corps sanglants, souffrants et macabres: Représentation de la violence faite aux corps dans les lettres et les arts en Europe XVIe–XVIIe siècles*. Paris: Presses Sorbonne Nouvelle, 2010.

Bouyer, Christian. *Gaston d'Orléans (1608–1660): Séducteur, frondeur et mécène*. Paris: Albin Michel, 1999.

———. *La duchesse de Chevreuse: L'indomptable et voluptueuse adversaire de Louis XIII*. Paris: Pygmalion/Gérard Watelet, 2002.

Bowen, Barbara. *Enter Rabelais Laughing*. Nashville, TN: Vanderbilt University Press, 1998.

———. "Laughing in Rabelais, Laughing with Rabelais." In *The Cambridge Companion to Rabelais*, 31–41. Edited by John O'Brien. Cambridge, UK: Cambridge University Press, 2011.

———. *Les Caractéristiques essentielles de la farce française et leur survivance dans les années 1550–1620*. Urbana: University of Illinois Press, 1964.

Boym, Svetlana. *The Future of Nostalgia*. New York: Basic Books, 2001.

Brereton, Geoffrey. *French Comic Drama from the Sixteenth to the Eighteenth Century*. London: Methuen, 1977.

Britland, Karen. *Drama at the Courts of Queen Henrietta Maria*. Cambridge, UK: Cambridge University Press, 2006.

Bruyer, Tom. *Le Sang et les larmes: Le suicide dans les tragédies profanes de Jean Racine*. Amsterdam: Rodopi, 2012.

Buffat, Marc, ed. *Diderot, l'invention du drame*. Paris: Klincksieck, 2000.

Burgwinkle, Bill, Nicholas Hammand, and Emma Wilson, eds. *Cambridge History of French Literature*. Cambridge, UK: Cambridge Unniveristy Press, 2011.

Buron, Emmanuel. "'Comique' et 'propriété' dans la préface de *L'amoureux repos* de Guillaume des Autels." In *Le lexique métalittéraire français. XIVe-XVIIe siècles*, edited by Michel Jourde and Jean-Charles Monferran, 67–87. Geneva: Droz, 2006.

———, ed. *Lectures de Robert Garnier*. Rennes: Presses universitaires de Rennes, 2000.

Butler, Martin. "*The Fortunate Isles*: Textual Essay." http://universitypublishingon-line.org/cambridge/benjonson/k/essays/Fortunate_Isles_texyual_essay/1/. Accessed July 3, 2014.

Caciola, Nancy. *Discerning Spirits: Divine and Demonic Possession in the Middle Ages*. Ithaca, NY: Cornell University Press, 2004.

Candiard, Céline. "The Reception of Roman Comedy in Early Modern Italy and France." In *A Cambridge Companion to Roman Comedy*, edited by Martin Dinter. Cambridge, UK: Cambridge University Press, forthcoming.

Canova-Green, Marie-Claude. *La politique-spectacle au grand siècle: Les rapports franco-anglais*. Paris: Papers on Seventeenth-Century French Literature, 1993.

Carnel, Marc. "Amour et poison dans l'œuvre de Ronsard." In *Poison et antidote dans l'Europe des XVIe et XVIIe siècles*, edited by Sarah Voinier and Guillaume Winter, 185–99. Arras: Artois Presses Université, 2011.

Carrington, Samuel M. "Censorship and the Medieval Comic Theatre in France." *Rice University Studies in French Literature* 57 (1971): 17–39.

Cavaillé, Fabien. "Alexandre Hardy et le rêve perdu de la Renaissance: Spectacles violents, émotions, concorde civile au début du XVIIe siècle." PhD diss., Université Paris III-Sorbonne Nouvelle, 2009.

——. "Applaudissement universel et ricanements importuns: Représentations de l'assemblée théâtrale de la Querelle du *Cid* à la *Pratique du Théâtre*." In *Concordia discors*, edited by Benoît Bolduc and Henriette Goldwin, 211–21. Tübingen: Günter Narr Verlag, 2011.

——. "Spectacle public, munificence royale et politique de la joie: Le cas du ballet de cour à la ville dans la première moitié su XVIIe siècle (*Le grand bal de la douairière de Billebahaut*, 1626)." *Biblio* 17, no. 193 (2011): 29–42.

Cavaillé, Fabien, and Anne Surgers. "La scénographie du théâtre baroque en France: quand le comédien n'était pas fermé dans une cage." *Cahiers du Dix-septième* 13 (2010): 92–123.

Cave, Terence. "Locating the Early Modern." *Paragraph: A Journal of Modern Critical Theory* 29, no. 1 (2006): 12–26.

——. "Towards a Pre-history of Suspense." In *Retrospectives: Essays in Literature, Poetics and Cultural History*, edited by Neil Kenny and Wes Williams, 158–67. London: Legenda, 2009.

Certeau, Michel de. *L'écriture de l'histoire*. Paris: Gallimard, 1975.

——. "Montaigne's 'Of Cannibals': The savage 'I'." In *Heterologies: Discourse on the Other*, 67–79. Translated by Brian Massumi. Minneapolis: University of Minnesota Press, 1986.

——. *Possession de Loudun*. Paris: Julliard, 1970; re-ed. 2005.

Charpentier, Françoise. "Les débuts de la tragedie heroique: Antoine de Montchrestien (1575–1621)." PhD diss., Université de Lille, 1976 [1981].

——. *Pour une lecture de la tragédie humaniste: Jodelle, Garnier, Montchrestien*. Saint-Etienne: Publications de l'Université Saint-Etienne, 1979.

Chevallier-Micki, Sybile. "Tragédie et théâtre rouennais, 1566–1640. Scénographies de la cruauté." PhD diss., Université Paris Ouest Nanterre, 2013.

Christin, Olivier. *La paix de religion: L'autonomisation de la raison politique au XVIe siècle*. Paris: Seuil, 1997.

Clarke, Jan, Pierre Pasquier, and Henry Phillips, eds. *La Ville en scène en France et en Europe (1552–1709)*. Medeival and Early Modern French Studies 8. Oxford: Peter Lang, 2011.

Closson, Marion. *L'imaginaire démoniaque en France (1550–1560)*. Geneva: Droz, 2000.

Conner, Philip. *Huguenot Heartland: Montauban and Southern French Calvinism During the Wars of Religion*. Aldershot, UK: Ashgate, 2002.

Constant, Jean-Marie. *Gaston d'Orléans, prince de la liberté*. Paris: Perrin, 2013.

Couton, Georges. *Richelieu et le théâtre*. Edited by José Sanchez. Paris: Eurédit, 2008.

Cox, John D. *The Devil and the Sacred in English Drama, 1350–1642*. Cambridge, UK: Cambridge University Press, 2000.

Crane, Susan. *The Performance of Self: Ritual, Clothing, and Identity during the Hundred Years War*. Philadelphia: University of Pennsylvania Press, 2002.

Crouzet, Denis. *La genèse de la Réforme française 1520–1562*. Paris: SEDES, 1996.

———. *Les guerriers de Dieu: La violence au temps des troubles de religion*. 2 vols. Seyssel: Champ Vallon, 1990.

Cvetkovich, Ann. *Depression: A Public Feeling*. Durham, NC: Duke University Press, 2012.

Czepiel, Tomasz M. M. *Music at the Royal Court and Chapel in Poland, c. 1543–1600*. New York: Garland, 1996.

Dabney, Lancaster E. *French Dramatic Literature in the Reign of Henri IV: A Study of the Extant Plays Composed in French between 1589 and 1610*. Austin: University Cooperative Society, 1952.

Dandrey, Patrick. *Les tréteaux de Saturne*. Paris: Klincksieck, 2003.

Daston, Lorraine, and Katherine Park. *Wonders and the Order of Nature, 1150–1750*. Cambridge, MA: MIT Press, 1998.

Daubresse, Sylvie. *Le parlement de Paris, ou, la voix de la raison (1559–1589)*. Geneva: Droz, 2005.

Davis, Natalie Zemon. "Boundaries and the Sense of Self." In *Reconstructing Individualism: Autonomy, Individuality and the Self in Western Thought*, edited by Thomas C. Heller and Christine Brooke-Rose, 53–63. Stanford, CA: Stanford University Press, 1986.

———. *Society and Culture in Early Modern France*. Stanford, CA: Stanford University Press, 1965.

Decsimon, Robert, and Christian Jouhaud. *La France du premier XVIIe siècle: 1594–1661*. Paris: Belin, 1996.

Defaux, Gérard. "Un cannibale en haut de chausses: Montaigne, la différence et la logique de l'identité." *Modern Language Notes* 97, no. 4 (1982): 919–57.

———. *Rabelais agonistes: Du rieur au prophète; Etudes sur "Panatagruel", "Gargantua", "Le Quart Livre"*. Etudes Rabelaisiennes 32. Geneva: Droz, 1997.

Deierkauf-Holsboer, S. Wilma. *Le théâtre de l'Hôtel de Bourgogne*. 2 vols. Paris: Nizet, 1968–1970.

———. *Le théâtre du Marais*. 2 vols. Paris: Nizet, 1954–1958.

Demerson, Guy. "Rabelais et la violence." *Europe* 757 (1992): 67–77.

Derrida, Jacques. *De la grammatologie*. Paris: Minuit, 1967.

Desan, Philippe. *Montaigne: Une biographie politique*. Paris: Odile Jacob, 2014.

———, ed. *Humanism in Crisis: The Decline of the French Renaissance*. Ann Arbor: University of Michigan Press, 1991.

Desprez, Michael. "Les premiers professionnels, ou du comédien à l'acteur. Constitution d'un métier, constitution d'une image, Italie-France, c. 1500–c. 1630." PhD diss., Université Paris-X, 2005.

Desvignes, Lucette, ed. *La cour bergère ou l'Arcadie de Messire Philippe Sidney*, by André Mareschal. Saint-Etienne: Université de Saint-Etienne Institut d'Études de la Renaissance et de l'Âge Classique, 1981.

Dethan, Georges. *La vie de Gaston d'Orléans*. Paris: Editions de Fallois, 1992.

Dewald, Jonathan. *Aristocratic Experience and the Origins of Modern Culture: France, 1570–1715*. Berkeley: University of California Press, 1993.

Didier, Beatrice. *Beaumarchais, ou la passion du drame*. Paris: Presses Universitaires de France, 1994.

Diefendorf, Barbara B. *Beneath the Cross: Catholics and Huguenots in Sixteenth-Century Paris*. New York: Oxford University Press, 1991.

Dixon, C. Scott, Dagmar Freist, and Mark Greengrass, eds., *Living with Religious Diversity in Early Modern Europe*. Farnham, UK: Ashgate, 2009.

Dollimore, Jonathan, and Alan Sinfield, eds. *Political Shakespeare: Essays in Cultural Materialism* [1994], 2nd rev. ed. Manchester, UK: Manchester University Press, 2012.

Dominguez-Vignaud, Véronique. "De la morale à l'esthétique. La danse et le rondeau dans les mystères de la Passion du XVe siècle." In *Le mal et le diable: Leurs figures à la fin du Moyen age*, edited by Nathalie Nabert, 53–77. Paris: Beauchesne, 1996.

Dotoli, Giovanni. *Temps de préfaces: Le débat théâtral en France de Hardy à la Querelle du "Cid"*. Paris: Klincksieck, 1996.

Doumergue, Émile. *Jean Calvin: Les hommes et les choses de son temps*. 7 vols. Lausanne: G. Bridel, 1899–1927.

Duccini, Hélène. *Faire voir, faire croire: L'opinion publique sous Louis XIII*. Seyssel: Champ Vallon, 2003.

Durel, Lionel Charles. *L'œuvre d'André Mareschal, auteur dramatique, poète et romancier de la période de Louis XIII*. Baltimore, MD; Oxford: Johns Hopkins University Press; Humphrey Milford, Oxford University Press, 1932.

Durosoir, Georgie. "Visages contrastés de l'Italie dans les **ballets** de la cour de France dans la première moitié du XVIIe siècle." *Revue De Musicologie* ⁊⁊, no. 2 (1991): 169–78.

Duval, Edwin. *The Design of Rabelais's "Quart Livre de Pantagruel"*. Geneva: Droz, 1998.

Ehrstine, Glenn. *Theater, Culture, and Community in Reformation Bern, 1523–1555*. Leiden: Brill, 2002.

El Kenz, David. *Les bûchers du roi: La culture protestante des martyrs (1523–1572)*. Seyssel: Champ Vallon, 1997.

Enders, Jody. "Of Protestantism, Performativity, and the Threat of Theater." *Mediaevalia: An Interdisciplinary Journal of Medieval Studies Worldwide* 22 (1999): 55–74.

Faguet, Emile. *La tragédie française au XVIe siècle*. Paris: Fontemoing, 1912.

Farge, Arlette. *La vie fragile: Violence, pouvoirs et solidarités à Paris au XVIIIe siècle*. Paris: Hachette, 1986.

Farge, Arlette, and Jacques Revel. *Logiques de la foule: L'affaire des enlèvements d'enfants, Paris 1750*. Paris: Hachette, 1988.

Febvre, Lucien. *Life in Renaissance France.* Translated by Marian Rothstein. Cambridge, MA: Harvard University Press, 1979.

Ferber, Sarah. *Demonic Possession and Exorcism in Early Modern France.* London: Routledge, 2004.

Ferguson, Gary. *Queer (Re)Readings in the French Renaissance: Homosexuality, Gender, Culture.* Aldershot, UK: Ashgate, 2008.

Ferretti, Giuliano. "Richelieu et les historiographes." In *Les historiographes en Europe de la fin du Moyen Age à la Révolution,* edited by Chantal Grell, 325–43. Paris: Presses de l'Université Paris-Sorbonne, 2006.

Floquet, A. "Histoire des Conards de Rouen." *Bibliothèque de l'École des Chartes* 1 (1839): 105–23.

Foa, Jérémie. "Making Peace: The Commissions for Enforcing the Pacification Edicts in the Reign of Charles IX (1560–1574)." *French History* 18 (2004): 256–74.

Ford, Philip, and Andrew Taylor, ed. *The Early Modern Cultures of Neo-Latin Drama.* Leuven: Leuven University Press, 2013.

Forestier, Georges. *La tragédie française: Passions tragiques et règles classiques.* Paris: Armand Colin. 2010.

Fossier, François. "A propos du titre d'historiographe sous l'ancien régime." *Revue d'histoire moderne et contemporaine* 32 (1985): 361–417.

Foucault, Michel. In *Le corps utopique, les hétérotopies,* edited by Daniel Defert. Paris: Lignes, 2009.

———. *Surveiller et punir: Naissance de la prison.* Paris: Gallimard, 1975.

Fragonard, Marie-Madeleine. "Du bon usage politique de la tragédie." *Cahiers Textuel* 18 (1998): 43–56.

———. "Oisiveté et hérésie." In *L'Oisiveté au temps de la Renaissance,* edited by Marie-Thérèse Jones-Davies, 29–50. Paris: Presses de l'Université Paris-Sorbonne, 2002.

Franko, Mark. *Dance as Text: Ideologies of the Baroque Body.* Cambridge, UK: Cambridge University Press, 1993.

———. "Double Bodies: Androgyny and Power in the Performances of Louis XIV." *The Dance Review* 38, no. 4 (Winter 1994): 71–82.

———. "The King Cross-Dressed." In *From the Royal to the Republican Body: Incorporating the Political in Seventeenth- and Eighteenth-Century France,* edited by Sara E. Melzer and Kathryn Norberg, 64–84. Berkeley: University of California Press, 1998.

———. "Majestic Drag: Monarchical Performativity and the King's Body Theatrical." *The Drama Review* 47, no. 2 (Summer 2003): 71–87.

Freccero, Carla. *Queer/Early/Modern.* Durham, NC: Duke University Press, 2006.

Freccero, Carla, and Louise Fradenburg, eds. *Premodern Sexualities.* New York: Routledge, 1996.

Fumaroli, Marc. *Héros et orateurs: Rhétorique et dramaturgie cornéliennes.* Geneva: Droz, 1996.

———. *La diplomatie de l'esprit.* Paris: Hermann, 1994.

———. "Loisirs et loisir." In *Le loisir lettré à l'âge classique,* edited by Marc Fumaroli, Philippe-Joseph Salazar, and Emmanuel Bury, 5–26. Genève: Droz, 1996.

Gabily, Didier-Georges. "Notes traversières" (July 1990–May 1992). http://www
.didiergeorgesgabily.net/miseenscenephedresethippolytes-2.html. Accessed July 3,
2014.

Gambier, Paul. *Au temps des guerres de religion : Le président Barnabé Brisson*. Paris:
Perrin, 1957.

Garnier-Mathez, Isabelle. *L'épithète et la connivence. Écriture concertée chez les évangéliques français (1523–1534)*. Geneva: Droz, 2005.

Gatulle, Pierre. *Gaston d'Orléans: Entre mécénat et impatience du pouvoir*. Seyssel:
Champ Vallon, 2012.

Giavarini, Laurence. "Représentation pastorale et guérison mélancolique au tournant
de la Renaissance: Questions de poétique." *Études Épistémè* 3 (2003): 1–27.

Giraud, Alfred. *La vie et la mort du président Brisson*. Nantes: Imprimerie de
A. Guéraud, 1855.

Godet, Marcel, and Heinrich Türler, eds. *Dictionnaire historique et biographique de
la Suisse*. 8 vols. Neuchâtel: Administration du Dictionnaire historique et biographique de la Suisse, 1921–1933.

Gofflot, L.-V. *Le théâtre au collège du Moyen Age à nos jours*. Paris: Champion, 1907.

Goldberg, Jonathan, ed. *Queering the Renaissance*. Durham, NC: Duke University
Press, 1994.

Gordon, Bruce. *Calvin*. New Haven, CT: Yale University Press, 2009.

Gosselin, Edouard. "Recherches sur les origines et l'histoire du théâtre à Rouen avant
Pierre Corneille." *Revue de la Normandie* 8 (1868): 242–54.

Greenberg, Mitchell. *Baroque Bodies: Psychoanalysis and the Culture of French Absolutism*. Ithaca, NY: Cornell University Press, 2001.

Greenblatt, Stephen. *Renaissance Self-Fashioning: From More to Shakespeare*. Chicago:
University of Chicago Press, 1980.

Greene, Thomas. "Labyrinth Dances in the French and English Renaissance." *Renaissance Quarterly* 54, no. 4 (2001): 1403–66.

Greengrass, Mark. *Governing Passions: Peace and Reform in the French Kingdom,
1576–1585*. Oxford: Oxford University Press, 2007.

Gregory, Brad S. *Salvation at Stake: Christian Martyrdom in Early Modern Europe*.
Cambridge, MA: Harvard University Press, 1999.

Griffin, Robert. *Ludovico Ariosto*. New York: Twayne Publishers, 1974.

Griffiths, Richard M. *The Dramatic Technique of Antoine de Montchrestien*. Oxford:
Clarendon Press, 1970.

Gritsch, Eric W. "Luther on Humor." *Lutheran Quarterly* 18 (2004): 373–86.

Grosse, Christian. *Les rituels de la Cène: Le culte eucharistique réformé à Genève
(XVIe-XVIIe siècles)*. Geneva: Droz, 2008.

Grosse, Christian, and Ruth Stawarz-Luginbühl. "La pastorale (1585) de Simon
Goulart." In *Simon Goulart: Un pasteur aux intérêts vastes comme le monde*, edited
by Olivier Pot, 431–40. Geneva: Droz, 2013.

Guichemerre, Roger. *La comédie avant Molière: 1640–1660*. Paris: Armand Colin,
1972.

Guy-Bray, Stephen. *Homoerotic Space: The Poetics of Loss in Renaissance Literature.* Toronto: University of Toronto Press, 2002.

Habermas, Jürgen. *Between Facts and Norms: Contributions to a Discourse Theory of Law and Democracy.* Translated by William Rehg. Cambridge, MA: MIT Press, 1996.

———. *Structural Transformation of the Public Sphere.* Translated by Thomas Burger with Frederick Lawrence. Cambridge, MA: MIT Press, 1989.

Hallissy, Margaret. *Venomous Woman: Fear of the Female in Literature.* Westport, CT: Greenwood Press, 1987.

Halperin, David. *How to Do the History of Homosexuality.* Chicago: University of Chicago Press, 2002; repr. 2004.

Hampton, Timothy. *Fictions of Embassy: Literature and Diplomacy in Early Modern Europe.* Ithaca, NY: Cornell University Press, 2009.

Hanley, Sarah. *The Lit de Justice of the Kings of France: Constitutional Ideology in Legend, Ritual, and Discourse.* Princeton, NJ: Princeton University Press, 1983.

Hardin, Richard F. "Encountering Plautus in the Renaissance: A Humanist Debate on Comedy." *Renaissance Quarterly* 60, no. 3 (Fall 2007): 789–818.

———. "Menaechmi and the Renaissance of Comedy." *Comparative Drama* 37, nos. 3–4 (2003): 255–74.

Harp, Margaret Broom. *The Portrayal of Community in Rabelais's "Quart Livre".* New York: Peter Lang, 1997.

Harrison, Jane Ellen. *Prolegomena to the Study of Greek Religion.* Cambridge, UK: Cambridge University Press, 1922 [repr. Forgotten Books, 2012].

Hartle, Ann. *Montaigne: Accidental Philosopher.* Cambridge, UK: Cambridge University Press, 2003.

Hayes, E. Bruce. *Rabelais's Radical Farce: Late Medieval Comic Theater and its Function in Rabelais.* Farnham, UK: Ashgate, 2010.

Hayes, Julie Candler. *Identity and Ideology: Diderot, Sade, and the Serious Genre.* Amsterdam: J. Benjamins, 1991.

Helmich, Werner Bernard. *Moralités françaises: Réimpression fac-similé de vingt-deux pièces allégoriques imprimées aux XVe et XVIe siècles.* Geneva: Slatkine, 1980.

Henke, Robert. *Performance and Literature in the Commedia dell'Arte.* Cambridge, UK: Cambridge University Press, 2002.

Herrick, Marvin T. *Comic Theory in the Sixteenth Century* [1950]. Urbana: University of Illinois Press, 1994.

Higman, Francis M. *La diffusion de la Réforme en France: 1520–1565.* Geneva: Labor et Fides, 1992.

———. *The Style of John Calvin in His French Polemical Treatises.* London: Oxford University Press, 1967.

Hoffman, George. "Anatomy of the Mass: Montaigne's 'Cannibals.'" *PMLA* 117, no. 2 (March 2002): 207–21.

Houllemare, Marie. *Politiques de la parole: Le parlement de Paris au XVIe siècle.* Geneva: Droz, 2011.

Howe, Alan, ed. *Écrivains de théâtre 1600–1649*. Paris: Centre Historique des Archives Nationales, 2005.

Ibbett, Katherine. "Pity, Compassion, Commiseration: Theories of Theatrical Relatedness." *Seventeenth-Century French Studies* 30, no. 2 (2008): 196–208.

Jacob, Margaret C. *The Rise of Cosmopolitanism in Early Modern Europe*. Philadelphia: University of Pennsylvania Press, 2006.

The Jewish Encyclopedia. 12 vols. New York: Funk and Wagnalls, 1906.

Jolibert, Bernard. *La commedia dell'arte et son influence en France du XVIe au XVIIIe siècle*. Paris: L'Harmattan, 1999.

Jondorf, Gillian. *French Renaissance Tragedy: The Dramatic Word*. Cambridge, UK: Cambridge University Press, 1990.

Jouanna, Arlette. *La Saint-Barthélemy: Les mystères d'un crime d'état, 24 août 1572*. Paris: Gallimard, 2007.

Jusserand, Jean-Jules. *An Introduction to Shakespeare's "The Winter's Tale"*. Cambridge, MA: Harvard University Press, 1907.

Kantorowicz, Ernst H. *The King's Two Bodies: A Study in Medieval Political Theology*. Princeton, NJ: Princeton University Press, 1957.

Kartun-Blum, Ruth. "'Where Does This Wood in My Hand Come From?' The Binding of Isaac in Modern Hebrew Poetry." *Prooftexts* 8, no. 3 (September 1, 1988): 293–310.

Kenny, Neil. *The Uses of Curiosity in Early Modern France and Germany*. Oxford: Oxford University Press, 2004.

Kermina, Françoise. *Marie de Médicis: Reine, régente et rebelle*. Paris: Librairie Académique Perrin, 1979.

Kettering, Sharon. "Favour and Patronage: Dancers in the Court Ballets of Early Seventeenth-Century France." *Canadian Journal of History* 43 (Winter 2008): 391–415.

Kingdon, Robert M. *Geneva and the Consolidation of the French Protestant Movement, 1564–1572*. Geneva: Droz, 1967.

Kleinman, Ruth. *Anne d'Autriche*. Translated by Ania Ciechanowska. Paris: Fayard, 1993.

Knecht, Robert. J. *Catherine de' Medici*. London: Longman, 1998.

———. *The French Wars of Religion, 1559–1598*. London; New York: Longman, 1989.

———. *Richelieu*. London: Longman, 1991.

———. *The Rise and Fall of Renaissance France*. London: Fontana Press, 1996; repr. 2008.

Knight, Alan E. *Aspects of Genre in Late Medieval French Drama*. Manchester, UK: Manchester University Press, 1983.

Kociszewska, Ewa. "La Pologne, un don maternel de Catherine de Médicis? La cérémonie de la remise du Decretum electionis à Henri de Valois." *Le Moyen Age* 117, no. 3 (2011): 561–75.

———. "War and Seduction in Cybele's Garden: Contextualizing the *Ballet des Polonais*." *Renaissance Quarterly* 65, no. 3 (2012): 809–63.

Koopmans, Jelle. "Genres Theatraux." *Fifteenth-Century Studies* 16 (1990): 131–42.

———. *Le théâtre des exclus au Moyen Age: Hérétiques, sorcières et marginaux.* Paris: Imago, 1997.

———. "'Maistre Françoys Villon, sur ses vieux jours, se retira à Saint-Maixent en Poictou.'" *Cahiers textuel* 35 (2012): 59–69.

Koselleck, Reinhart. *Critique and Crisis: Enlightenment and the Pathogenesis of Modern Society.* Cambridge, MA: MIT Press, 1988.

Krause, Virginia. *Idle pursuits. Literature and "Oisiveté" in the French Renaissance.* Newark: University of Delaware Press, 2003.

Kritzman, Lawrence. *The Rhetoric of Sexuality and the Literature of the French Renaissance.* Cambridge, UK: Cambridge University Press, 1991.

Lacan, Jacques. "Le temps logique et l'assertion de certitude anticipée." In *Ecrits*, 197–214. Paris: Seuil, 1966.

———. "Logical Time and the Assertion of Anticipated Certainty." In *Ecrits*, 161–75. Translated by Bruce Fink. New York: W.W. Norton, 2006.

Lambert, Thomas A. "Cette loi durera guère: inertie religieuse et espoirs catholiques à Genève au temps de la Réforme." *Bulletin de la Société d'Histoire et d'Archéologie de Genève* 23 (1993): 5–24.

Lambert, Thomas A., Isabella M. Watt, Robert M. Kingdon, and Jeffrey R. Watt, eds. *Registres du Consistoire de Genève au temps de Calvin 1542–44.* Vol. 1. Geneva: Droz, 1996.

Lambin, Rosine A. *Femmes de paix: La coexistence religieuse et les dames de la noblesse en France, 1520–1630.* Paris: Harmattan, 2003.

Lancaster, Henry Carrington. *A History of French Dramatic Literature in the Seventeenth Century.* 5 vols. Baltimore, MD; Paris: Johns Hopkins University Press; Les Presses Universitaires, 1929–1942.

Laumonier, Paul. "Deux cents vingt vers inédits de Ronsard: Un gala aux Tuileries (août 1573)." *Revue de la Renaissance* 4 (1903): 201–20.

Lavéant, Kattel. *Un théâtre des frontières: La culture dramatique dans les provinces du Nord aux XVe et XVIe siècles.* Orléans: Paradigme, 2011.

Lavocat, Françoise. "Ut Saltatio poiesis? Danse et ekphrasis à la fin de la Renaissance et à l'âge baroque." In *Ecrire la danse*, edited by Alain Montandon, 55–96. Clermont-Ferrand: Presses Universitaires Blaise Pascal, 1999.

Lawton, Harold W. *Handbook of French Renaissance Dramatic Theory* [1949]. Westport, CT: Greenwood Press, 1972.

Lazard, Madeleine. "Du théâtre médiéval à la comédie du XVIe siècle: continuité et rupture." *Bulletin de l'Association d'Etude sur l'Humanisme, la Réforme et la Renaissance* 44 (1997): 65–78.

———. *La comédie humaniste au seizième siècle et ses personnages.* Paris: Presses universitaires de France, 1978.

Lebègue, Raymond. *Études sur le théâtre français.* 2 vols. Paris: Nizet, 1977–1978.

———. *Le théâtre comique en France de Pathelin à Mélite.* Paris: Hatier, 1972.

———. "Les guerres civiles de Rome et les tragédies de Robert Garnier." In *Actes du colloque Renaissance-Classicisme du Maine*, 283–89. Paris: Nizet, 1975.

———. "Théâtre et politique religieuse en France au XVIe siècle." In *Culture et politique en France à l'époque de l'humanisme et de la Renaissance*, edited by Franco Simone, 427–37. Turin: Academica della Scienze, 1974.

Leblanc, Paulette. *Les écrits théoriques et critiques français des années 1540–1561 sur la tragédie.* Paris: Nizet, 1972.

Lecercle, François, ed. *Réécritures du crime: L'acte sanglant sur la scène (XVIe–XVIIIes.). Littératures Classiques* 67 (2009).

Lecocq, Georges. *Histoire du théâtre en Picardie depuis ses origines jusqu'à la fin du XVIe siècle.* Paris: Menu, 1880.

Le Fur, Didier. *Henri II.* Paris: Tallandier, 2009.

Le Roux, Nicolas. "Guerre civile, entreprises maritimes et identité nobiliaire: Les imaginations de Guy de Lanssac (1544–1622)." *Bibliothèque d'Humanisme et Renaissance* 65, no. 3 (2003): 529–69.

Lestringant, Frank. *André Gide l'inquiéteur: Le ciel sur la terre ou l'inquiétude partagée, 1869–1918.* Vol. 1. Paris: Flammarion, 2011.

———. *Le cannibale: Grandeur et decadence.* Paris: Librairie Académique Perrin, 1994.

———. "L'espace maritime du *Quart Livre*." In *En relisant le Quart Livre de Rabelais*, edited by Nathalie Dauvois and Jean Vignes. *Cahiers textuel* 35 (2012): 29–42.

———. "Garnier." In *Dictionnaire des littératures de langue française.* edited by Jean-Pierre de Beaumarchais, Daniel Couty, and Alain Rey, 869–70 . Paris: Bordas, 1984.

Levack, Brian P. *The Devil Within: Possession and Exorcism in the Christian West.* New Haven, CT: Yale University Press, 2013.

Lévi, Honor. "Richelieu collectionneur." In *Richelieu et la culture: Actes du colloque international en Sorbonne*, edited by Roland Mousnier, 175–83. Paris: Editions du CNRS, 1987.

Longeon, Claude. Introduction to *La farce des Théologastres.* Geneva: Droz, 1989.

Louvat-Molozay, Bénédicte. "Le théâtre protestant et la musique (1550–1586)." In *Par la vue et par l'ouïe. Littérature du Moyen Age et de la Renaissance*, edited by Michèle Gally and Michel Jourde, 135–58. Fontenay Saint Cloud: ENS Editions, 1999.

———. *Théâtre et musique. Dramaturgie de l'insertion musicale dans le théâtre français (1550–1680).* Paris: Honoré Champion, 2002.

Loxley, James. *Performativity.* London and New York: Routledge, 2007.

Lyons, John D. *Kingdom of Disorder: Theory of Tragedy in Classical France.* West Lafayette, IN: Purdue University Press, 1999.

———. "What do We Mean When We Say 'Classique'?" In *Racine et/ou le classicisme*, edited by Ronald Tobin, 497–505. Tübingen: Narr, 2001.

MacDonald, Katherine. *Biography in Early Modern France 1540–1630.* Oxford: Legenda, 2007.

Magnin, Charles. *Histoire des marionnettes en Europe depuis l'Antiquité jusqu'à nos jours.* Paris; Leipzig: Lévy frères; Michelsen, 1882.

Mallinson, Jeffrey. *Faith, Reason, and Revelation in Theodore Beza: 1519–1605*. Oxford: Oxford University Press, 2003.

Manetsch, Scott M. "Pastoral Care East of Eden: The Consistory of Geneva, 1568–82." *Church History* 75 (2006): 274–313.

———. *Theodora Beza and the Quest for Peace in France, 1572–98*. Leiden: Brill, 2000.

Marin, Louis. *Le récit est un piège*. Paris: Éditions de Minuit, 1978.

———. "Théâtralité et pouvoir: Magie, machination, machine; *Médée* de Corneille." In *Le pouvoir de la raison d'état*, edited by Christian Lazzeri and Dominique Reynié, 231–59. Paris: Presses Universitaires de France, 1992.

Marion, Marcel. *Dictionnaire des institutions de la France*. Paris: Picard, 1989.

Marshall, David. *The Surprising Effects of Sympathy. Marivaux, Diderot, Rousseau, and Mary Shelley*. Chicago: University of Chicago Press, 1988.

May, Herbert G., and Bruce Manning Metzger. *The New Oxford Annotated Bible with the Apocrypha*. New York: Oxford University Press, 1973.

Mazouer, Charles. *Le théatre français de la Renaissance*. Paris: Honoré Champion, 2002.

———. *Le théâtre français de l'âge classique (t. 1): Le premier XVIIe siècle*. Paris: Honoré Champion, 2006.

McClure, Ellen. *Sunspots and the Sun King: Sovereignty and Mediation in Seventeenth-Century France*. Urbana: University of Illinois Press, 2006.

McFarlane, Ian D. *A Literary History of France. Renaissance France, 1470–1589*. Vol. 2. London: Ernest Benn Limited, 1974.

McGowan, Margaret. *The Court Ballet of Louis XIII: A Collection of Working Designs for Costumes, 1615–33*. London: Victoria and Albert Museum, 1990.

———. *Dance in the Renaissance: European Fashion, French Obsession*. New Haven, CT: Yale University Press, 2008.

———. *L'art du ballet de cour, 1581–1643*. Paris: Editions du CNRS, 1963.

———. "L'essor du ballet à la cour d'Henri III." In *Henri III, mécène des arts, des sciences et des lettres*, edited by Isabelle de Conihout, Jean-François Maillard, and Guy Poirier, 81–89. Paris: Presses de l'Université Paris-Sorbonne, 2006.

———. "The Presence of Rome in some Plays of Robert Garnier." In *Myth and its Making in the French Theatre*, edited by Edward Freeman et al., 12–19. Cambridge, UK: Cambridge University Press, 1988.

———. *The Vision of Rome in Late Renaissance France*. New Haven, CT: Yale University Press, 2000.

Meere, Michael. "Social Drama, Cultural Pragmatics, and Louis XIII's Performativity: *La victoire du Phébus* (1617)." *The French Review* 84, no. 2 (March 2012): 672–83.

———. "Staging Sanctity: Moral Confusion in Pierre Troterel's *La tragédie de sainte Agnès* (1615)." *L'esprit créateur* 50, no.1 (Spring 2010): 49–61.

———. "Troubling Tragedies: Staging Violence in Early Modern France." PhD diss., University of Virginia, 2009.

———. "Violence, Revenge, and the Stakes of Writing during the French Civil Wars: Simon Belyard's *Le Guysien*." *Romanic Review* 104, nos. 1–2 (2013): 45–64.

Ménager, Daniel. "Montaigne et la magnificence." *Bulletin de la Société des Amis de Montaigne* 7, nos. 29–32 (July–December 1992/January–June 1993): 63–71.

Mentzer, Raymond, ed. *Sin and the Calvinists: Morals Control and the Consistory in the Reformed Tradition*. Kirksville, MO: Sixteenth Century Journal Publishers, 1994.

Merlin, Hélène. *Public et littérature en France au XVIIe siècle*. Paris: Belles Lettres, 1994.

Merlin-Kajman, Hélène. "Indignité comique et public en débat." In *Les querelles dramatiques à l'âge classique*, edited by Emmanuelle Hénin, 97–111. Leuvan: Peeters, 2010.

Meyniel, Corinne. "De la Cène à la scène: La tragédie biblique en France pendant les guerres de religion, 1550–1625." PhD diss., Université Paris Ouest Nanterre, 2010.

Mleynek, Sherryll. "Abraham, Aristotle, and God: The Poetics of Sacrifice." *Journal of the American Academy of Religion* 62, no. 1 (Spring 1994): 107–21.

Mollenauer, Lynn Wood. *Strange Revelations: Magic, Poison, and Sacrilege in Louis XIV's France*. University Park: Pennsylvania State University Press, 2007.

Monter, E. William. "The Consistory of Geneva, 1559–1569." *Bibliothèque d'Humanisme et Renaissance* 38 (1976): 467–84.

Moote, A. Lloyd. *Louis the Just*. Berkeley: University of California Press, 1989.

Morel, Jacques. *Agréables mensonges*. Paris: Klinksieck, 1991.

Moriarty, Michael. "Theory and the Early Modern: Some Notes on a Difficult Relationship." *Paragraph: A Journal of Modern Critical Theory* 29, no. 1 (2006): 1–11.

Mouflard, Marie-Madeleine. *Robert Garnier (1545–90)*. 3 vols. La Roche-sur-Yon [Vendée]: Imprimerie Centrale de l'Ouest, 1961–1964.

Mousnier, Roland. *L'homme rouge, ou La vie du cardinal de Richelieu (1585–1642)*. Paris: Robert Laffont, 1992.

Nagle, Jean. *La civilisation du cœur: Histoire du sentiment politique en France, du XIIe au XIXe siècle*. Paris: Fayard, 1998.

Naphy, William G. *Calvin and the Consolidation of the Genevan Reformation*. Manchester, UK: Manchester University Press, 1994.

Neuschel, Kristen B. *Word of Honor: Interpreting Noble Culture in Sixteenth-Century France*. Ithaca, NY: Cornell University Press, 1989.

Newcomb, Lori Humphrey. *Reading Popular Romance in Early Modern England*. New York: Columbia University Press, 2002.

Noirot, Corinne. "Conjurer le mal: Jean de La Taille et le paradoxe de la tragédie humaniste." *EMF: Studies in Early Modern France* 13 (2010): 121–43.

———. *"Entre deux airs": Style simple et ethos poétique chez Clément Marot et Joachim Du Bellay (1515–1560)*. Paris: Hermann Editeurs, 2013.

———. "French Humanist Comedy during the Wars of Religion: The Familiar and the Strange in Jean de la Taille's *The Rivals (Les corrivaux)*." *Explorations in Renaissance Culture* 39, no. 2 (2014): 128–43.

Noort, Edward, and Eibert J. C. Tigchelaar. *The Sacrifice of Isaac: the Aqedah (Genesis 22) and Its Interpretations*. Leiden: Brill, 2002.

Oberman, Heiko. "Teufelsdreck: Eschatology and Scatology in the 'Old' Luther." *Sixteenth Century Journal* 19 (1988): 435–50.

O'Brien, John, ed. *The Cambridge Companion to Rabelais*. Cambridge, UK: Cambridge University Press, 2011.

O'Brien, John, and Malcolm Quainton, eds. *Distant Voices Still Heard: Contemporary Readings of French Renaissance Literature*. Liverpool, UK: Liverpool University Press, 2000.

Oettinger, Rebecca Wagner. *Music as Propaganda in the German Reformation*. Aldershot, UK: Ashgate, 2001.

O'Hara, Stephanie. "Family Ties: Death by Poison in *La Mort de Mithridate* and *Thyeste*." In *Relations and Relationships in Seventeenth-Century French Literature*, edited by Jennifer Perlmutter, 331–41. Tübingen: Narr Biblio, 2006.

Orgel, Stephen. *The Illusion of Power: Political Theater in the English Renaissance*. Berkeley: University of California Press, 1975.

———, ed. *The Renaissance and the Gods*. New York: Garland Publishing, 1976.

Osborn, Albert W. *Sir Philip Sidney en France* [1932]. Geneva: Slatkine, 1974.

Parker, T. H. L. *Calvin's Preaching*. Edinburgh: T & T Clark, 1992.

Patry, Henri. "La Réforme et le théâtre en Guyenne au XVIe siècle (Agen 1553, Libourne 1555)." *Bulletin Historique et Littéraire de la Société de l'Histoire du Protestantisme Français* 50 (1901): 523–28.

Persels, Jeff. "'The Mass and the Fart Are Sisters': Scatology and Calvinist Rhetoric against the Mass, 1560–63." In *Fecal Matters in Early Modern Literature and Art: Studies in Scatology*, edited by Jeff Persels and Russell Ganim, 38–55. Aldershot, UK: Ashgate, 2004.

———. "The Sorbonnic Trots: Staging the Intestinal Distress of the Roman Catholic Church in French Reform Theater." *Renaissance Quarterly* 56 (2003): 1089–1111.

Petey-Girard, Bruno. *Le Sceptre et la plume: Images du prince protecteur des lettres de la Renaissance au Grand Siècle*. Geneva: Droz, 2010.

Petit de Julleville, Louis. *Histoire du théâtre en France*. Paris: Le Cerf, 1885.

Pettegree, Andrew. *Reformation and the Culture of Persuasion*. Cambridge, UK: Cambridge University Press, 2005.

Phillips-Court, Kristin. *The Perfect Genre: Drama and Painting in Renaissance Italy*. Burlington, VT: Ashgate, 2011.

Picot, Émile. *Les moralités polémiques ou la controverse religieuse dans l'ancien théâtre français* [1887–1906]. Geneva: Slatkine, 1970.

Pineaux, Jacques, ed. *La Polémique protestante contre Ronsard*. 2 vols. Paris: Marcel Didier, 1973.

Pinet, Christopher. "Monks, Priests, and Cuckolds: French Farce and Criticism of the Church from 1500 to 1560." *Stanford French Review* 4 (1980): 453–73.

Poirier, Guy. *L'homosexualité dans l'imaginaire de la Renaissance*. Paris: Honoré Champion, 1996.

Pot, Olivier. *L'inquiétante étrangeté: Montaigne, la pierre, le cannibale, la mélancolie*. Paris: Champion, 1993.

Potez, Henri. "Le premier roman anglais traduit en français." *Revue d'histoire littéraire de la France* 11 (1904): 42–55.

Quinn, Philip L. "Agamemnon and Abraham: The Tragic Dilemma of Kierkegaard's Knight of Faith." *Literature and Theology* 4, no. 2 (July 1990): 181–93.

Racaut, Luc. *Hatred in Print: Catholic Propaganda and Protestant Identity during the French Wars of Religion.* Aldershot, UK: Ashgate, 2002.

Racaut, Luc, and Alex Ryrie, ed. *Moderate Voices in the European Reformation.* Aldershot, UK: Ashgate, 2005.

Ramsay, Paul Addison. "*A Pastorall Called the Arcadia* by James Shirley: A Critical Edition." PhD diss., University of Michigan, 1975.

Ranum, Orest. *Paris in the Age of Absolutism.* Bloomington: Indiana University Press, 1968.

Redouant, René. "Pibrac et la Saint-Barthelémy." *Revue d'histoire littéraire de la France* 26 (1919): 11–35.

Reid, Dylan. "Carnival in Rouen: A History of the Abbaye De Conards." *Sixteenth Century Journal* 32 (2001): 1027–55.

———. "Renaissance Printing and Provincial Culture in Sixteenth-Century Rouen." *University of Toronto Quarterly* 73 (2004): 1011–20.

Reiss, Timothy. *Toward Dramatic Illusion: Theatrical Technique and Meaning from Hardy to Horace.* New Haven, CT: Yale University Press. 1971.

Renaudot, Augustin. *Préréforme et humanisme à Paris pendant les premières guerres d'Italie (1494–1517).* Paris: Champion, 1916.

Renner, Bernd. *Difficile est saturam non scribere: L'Herméneutique de la satire rabelaisienne.* Geneva: Droz, 2007.

Riffaud, Alain. *Répertoire du théâtre français imprimé entre 1630 et 1660.* Geneva: Droz, 2009.

Rigolot, François. *Les langages de Rabelais.* Geneva: Droz, 1972; repr. 1996.

Rivoire, Émile, ed. *Les sources du droit du Canton de Genève.* 4 vols. Arau: H.R. Sauerländer, 1927–1935.

Roach, Joseph. *Cities of the Dead: Circum-Atlantic Performance.* New York: Columbia University Press, 1996.

Roberts, Penny. *Peace and Authority during the French Religious Wars, c. 1560–1600.* New York: Palgave Macmillan, 2013.

Roelker, Nancy Lyman. *One King, One Faith: The Parlement of Paris and The Religious Reformations of the Sixteenth Century.* Berkeley: University of California Press, 1996.

Roper, Lyndal. *Oedipus and the Devil: Witchcraft, Sexuality and Religion in Early Modern Europe.* London: Routledge, 1994.

Rougemont, Martine de. *La vie théâtrale en France au XVIIe siècle.* Paris: Honoré Champion, 2001.

Rousse, Michel. "Une représentation théâtrale à Rouen en 1556." *European Medieval Drama* 7 (2003): 87–115.

Rousset, Jean. *La littérature à l'âge baroque en France.* Paris: José Corti,1953.

Roy, Bruno. "Triboulet, Josseaume et Pathelin à la cour de René d'Anjou." *Le Moyen Français* 7 (1980): 7–56.

Runnalls, Graham. "Les mystères de la Passion en langue française: tentative de classement." *Romania* 114 (1996): 494–506.

———. *Les mystères français imprimés: Une étude sur les rapports entre le théâtre religieux et l'imprimerie à la fin du Moyen Age.* Paris: Honoré Champion, 1999.

Russell, Nicolas, and Hélène Visentin, eds. *French Ceremonial Entries in the Sixteenth Century: Event, Image, Text.* Toronto: Centre for Reformation and Renaissance Studies, 2007.

Sabean, David Warren. "Production of the Self During the Age of Confessionalism." *Central European History* 29 (1996): 1–18.

Scarry, Elaine. *The Body in Pain: The Making and Unmaking of the World.* New York: Oxford University Press, 1985.

Schechner, Richard. *Between Theater and Anthropology.* Philadelphia: University of Pennsylvania Press, 1985.

———. *Performance Theory.* rev. ed. New York and London: Routledge, 2003.

Schweitzer, Zoé. "Une 'héroïne exécrable aux yeux des spectateurs'. Poétique de la violence: *Médée* de la Renaissance aux Lumières (Angleterre, France, Italie)." PhD diss., Université Paris IV-Sorbonne, 2006.

Screech, Michael A. *Rabelais.* London: Duckworth, 1979.

Scribner, Robert W. *For the Sake of Simple Folk: Popular Propaganda for the German Reformation.* Oxford: Clarendon Press, 1994.

Sealy, Robert J. *The Palace Academy of Henri III.* Geneva: Droz, 1981.

Seguin, Jean-Pierre. *L'information en France avant le périodique: 517 canards imprimés entre 1529 et 1631.* Paris: G.-P. Maisonneuve et Larose, 1964.

Shaw, Helen Arnot. "Conrad Badius and the *Comedie du Pape malade.*" PhD diss., University of Pennsylvania, 1934.

Shepardson, Nikki. *Burning Zeal: The Rhetoric of Martyrdom and the Protestant Community in Reformation France.* Bethlehem, PA: Lehigh University Press, 2007.

Siahaan, Poppy. "Did He Break Your Heart Or Your Liver?" In *Culture, Body, and Language: Conceptualizations of Internal Body Organs across Cultures and Languages,* edited by Farzad Sharifian, René Dirven, Jing Yu, and Susanne Niemeier, 45–74. New York: Mouton de Gruyter, 2008.

Sluhovsky, Moshe. *Believe Not Every Spirit: Possession, Mysticism, and Discernment in Early Modern Catholicism.* Chicago: University of Chicago Press, 2007.

Smith, Bruce R. *Homosexual Desire in Shakespeare's England: A Cultural Poetics.* Chicago: University of Chicago Press, 1991; repr. 1994.

Stegmann, André. *L'héroïsme cornélien, genèse et signification.* Vol. 1. Paris: Armand Colin, 1968.

Steiner, George. *Antigones.* Oxford: Clarendon Press, 1984.

Stephens, Walter. *Demon Lovers: Witchcraft, Sex, and the Crisis of Belief.* Chicago: University of Chicago Press, 2002.

Stolberg, Michael. "A Woman Down to Her Bones: The Anatomy of Sexual Difference in the Sixteenth and Early Seventeenth Centuries." *Isis* 94, no. 2 (2003): 274–99.

Stone, Donald Jr. *French Humanist Tragedy: A Reassessment*. Manchester, UK: Manchester University Press, 1974.

Strong, Roy. *Splendor at Court: Renaissance Spectacle and the Theater of Power*. Boston: Houghton Mifflin, 1973.

Sunshine, Glenn S. "French Protestantism on the Eve of St-Bartholomew: The Ecclesiastical Discipline of the French Reformed Churches, 1571–1572." *French History* 4 (1990): 340–77.

Surgers, Anne. "'Estants imitateurs de toute Nature': Analyse des outils de la fiction spatiale du théâtre baroque, à partir des *Galanteries du duc d'Ossonne* de Mairet (1633)." In *L'Age de la Représentation: l'art du spectacle au XVIIe siècle*, edited by Rainer Zaiser, 243–70. Tübingen: Gunter Narr Verlag, 2007.

———. "Logis, portes et fenêtres: le jeu des lieux de mémoire dans le décor du théâtre baroque, une 'caresse pour l'âme et le corps.'" In *La ville en scène en France et en Europe (1552–1709)*, edited by Jan Clarke, Pierre Pasquier, and Henry Phillips, 31–46. Oxford: Peter Lang, 2011.

Symes, Carol. *A Common Stage: Theater and Public Life in Medieval Arras*. Ithaca, NY: Cornell University Press, 2007.

Taschereau, J. A. "Élection et règne de Henri d'Anjou (Henri III) en Pologne (1572–1576)." *Revue rétrospective ou Bibliothèque historique contenant des Mémoires et Document authentiques, inédits et originaux* 4 (1834): 68–71.

Taussig, Michael. *Mimesis and Alterity: A Particular History of the Senses*. New York: Routledge, 1993.

Taylor, Larissa. *Heresy and Orthodoxy in Sixteenth-century Paris: François Le Picart and the Beginnings of the Catholic Reformation*. Leiden: Brill, 1999.

Ternaux, Jean-Claude, ed. *Le théâtre du XVIe siècle et ses modèles*. XVIe Siècle 6 (2010).

Teulade, Anne. *Le saint mis en scène: Un personnage paradoxal*. Paris: Cerf, 2012.

Teyssandier, Bernard et al. *"Le roi hors de page" et autres textes: Une anthologie*. Reims: Épure, 2012.

Thiry, Claude. "Conrad Badius, Jacques Bienvenu et leurs malades." In *Art de lire, art de vivre: Hommage au Professeur Georges Jacques*, edited by Myriam Watthée-Delmotte, 391–99. Paris: Harmattan, 2008.

Thouret, Clotilde. *Seul en scène: Le monologue dans le théâtre européen de la première modernité (Angleterre, Espagne, France, 1580–1640)*. Geneva, Droz, 2010.

Tissier, André. "Sur la notion de 'genre' dans les pièces comiques: De La Farce de 'Pathelin' à La Comédie de 'L'Eugène' de Jodelle." *Littératures Classiques* 27 (1996): 13–24.

Tobin, Ronald W. "*Médée* and the Hercules Tradition of the Early Seventeenth Century." *Romance Notes* 8, no. 1 (1966): 65–69.

Todorov, Tzvetan. "L'être et l'autre: Montaigne." *Yale French Studies* 64 (1983): 113–44.

Tournon, André. "Jeu de massacre. La 'tragique farce' du seigneur de Basché." In *Rabelais-Dionysos: Vin, carnaval, ivresse*, edited by Michel Bideaux, 43–50. Marseille: Jean Lafitte, 1997.

———. *Montaigne: La glose et l'essai*. Lyon: Presses Universitaires de Lyon, 1983.

Turchetti, Mario. "Concorde ou tolerance: Les Moyenneurs à la veille des guerres de religion en France." *Revue de théologie et de philosophie* 118 (1986): 255–67.

———. *Concordia o tolleranza? François Bauduin (1520–1573) et i "Moyenneurs".* Geneva: Droz, 1984.

———. "Religious Concord and Political Tolerance in Sixteenth- and Seventeenth-Century France." *Sixteenth Century Journal* 22 (1991): 15–25.

Turner, Edith. *Communitas: The Anthropology of Collective Joy.* New York: Palgrave Macmillan, 2012.

Turner, Victor. *Dramas, Fields, and Metaphors: Symbolic Action in Human Society.* Ithaca, NY: Cornell University Press, 1974.

———. *The Ritual Process: Structure and Anti-Structure.* London: Routledge and Kegan Paul, 1969.

———. *From Ritual to Theatre: The Human Seriousness of Play.* New York: Performing Arts Journal Publications, 1982.

Usher, Phillip John. *Epic Arts in Renaissance France.* Oxford: Oxford University Press, 2013.

———. "Robert Garnier." *Literary Encyclopedia,* August 2012. http://www.litencyc.com/php/speople.php?rec=true&UID=1691. Accessed June 5, 2013.

———. "Tragedy in the Aftermath of the Saint Bartholomew's Day Massacre: France's First *Phèdre* and the Hope for Peace." *Romance Notes* 52, no. 3 (2012): 255–62.

Vallette, Ludovic. *Étude sur Barnabé Brisson, premier président au Parlement de Paris.* Fontenay-le-Comte: Imprimerie de C. Caurit, 1875.

Veevers, Erica. *Images of Love and Religion: Queen Henrietta Maria and Court Entertainments.* Cambridge, UK: Cambridge University Press, 1989.

Vitez, Antoine. *Écrits sur le théâtre.* Vol. 3. Paris: P.O.L., 1996.

Wagner, Marie-France, and Claire Le Brun-Gouanvic, ed. *Les arts du spectacle au théâtre (1550–1700).* Paris: Honoré Champion, 2001.

———. *Les arts du spectacle dans la ville (1404–1721).* Paris: Champion, 2001.

Walfard, Adrien. "Tragédie, morale et politique dans l'Europe moderne: Le cas César." PhD diss., Université Paris IV-Sorbonne, 2011.

Walker, D. P. *Unclean Spirits: Possession and Exorcism in France and England in the Late Sixteenth and Early Seventeenth Centuries.* Philadelphia: University of Pennsylvania Press, 1981.

Wanegffelen, Thierry. *Ni Rome ni Genève: Des fidèles entre deux chaires en France au XVIe siècle.* Paris: Champion, 1997.

Watt, Jeffrey R. "Women and the Consistory in Calvin's Geneva." *Sixteenth Century Journal* 24 (1993): 429–39.

Weill, Georges. *Les théories sur le pouvoir royal en France pendant les guerres de religion.* Paris: Hachette 1891.

Weinberg, Bernard. "Charles Estienne and Jean de la Taille." *Modern Language Notes* 61 (1946): 262–65.

———. *Critical Prefaces of the French Renaissance* [1950]. New York: AMS Press, 1970.

Weller, Philip. "Lasso, Man of Theater." In *Orlandus Lassus and His Time*, edited by Ignace Bossuyt, Eugeen Schreurs, and Annelies Wouters, 89–127. Leuven: Alamire Foundation, 1995.

Wintroub, Michael. *A Savage Mirror: Power, Identity, and Knowledge in Early Modern France*. Stanford, CA: Stanford University Press, 2006.

Wygant, Amy. *Medea, Magic, and Modernity in France. Stages and Histories, 1553–1797*. Aldershot, UK: Ashgate, 2007.

Yates, Frances. *The Valois Tapestries*. London: Warburg Institute, 1959.

Zanin, Enrica. *Fins tragiques: Poétique et éthique du dénouement dans la tragédie de la première modernité, en Italie, France et Espagne (1550–1650)*. Geneva: Droz, 2014.

Zorach, Rebecca. *Blood, Milk, Ink, Gold: Abundance and Excess in the French Renaissance*. Chicago: University of Chicago Press, 2005.

Index

~

About the Contributors

Sara Beam is associate professor of history at the University of Victoria. She is the author of articles on farce, satire, and violence in early modern Europe, particularly sixteenth-century France and Geneva. Her book *Laughing Matters: Farce and the Making of Absolutism in France* (Cornell University Press, 2007) won the Roland H. Bainton Book Prize for History/Theology.

Christian Biet is professor in performing arts, theatrical and drama aesthetics, and French studies at the University of Paris Ouest-Nanterre-La Défense and the Institut Universitaire de France. He is also regular visiting professor at New York University and Florsheimer Distinguished Fellow at Cardozo Law School, Yeshiva University. A specialist of French and English seventeenth- and eighteenth-century theater, and working on culture, literature, and theater in the early modern period, he has published several articles and books on these topics. His other important research field is law, literature, and theater. In France, he also studies the idea of repertory theater, as a dramaturge, with directors and actors. His current research examines the way theater and the event of theater, spectators included, has been ruled during the early modern period and is ruled today.

Alison Calhoun is assistant professor of French literature at Indiana University, where she specializes in early modern literature and drama. Her first book, *Montaigne and the Lives of the Philosophers: Life Writing and Transversality in the "Essais"* (University of Delaware Press, 2015) situates Montaigne and Diogenes Laertius in the history of life writing from the French Renaissance to the classical age. Her current project explores the mechanics of the passions in the staging and reading of early French opera and ballet as it compares to the concurrent development of the French novel.

Fabien Cavaillé is *maître de conférences* in the Theater and Film Department at the Université de Caen-Basse Normandie. He has edited several plays by Alexandre Hardy and is the author of a forthcoming monograph titled *Alexandre Hardy et le théâtre de ville français au début du XVIIe siècle* (Paris: Classiques Garnier). After studying the links between violence on stage, emotional rhetoric, and political thought at the end of the French civil wars, his current research focuses on two main topics: sentimentalism, peace, and love in tragicomedy and pastoral drama, and the civic use of artistic performance and theatrical scenography during the modern period.

Sybile Chevallier-Micki received her doctorate in the performing arts from the Université Paris Ouest-Nanterre-La Défense with a thesis titled "Tragédies et théâtre rouennais 1566–1640: Scénographies de la cruauté" [Tragedies and theater from Rouen 1566–1640: Stage designs of cruelty]. Her current research aims to uncover the entirety of the provincial corpus of plays from the sixteenth and seventeenth centuries, to study its history, dramaturgy, and stage design. She holds academic appointments in the Performing Arts Department at the Université Paris Ouest-Nanterre-La Défense and in the Theater Studies Department at the Université Sorbonne-Nouvelle-Paris III.

Caroline Gates received her PhD in French from the University of Virginia with a dissertation titled "The Journey Literature of Rabelais, Du Bellay, and Aneau: Visions of Community in Mid-Sixteenth-Century France." She continues to work on travel and the relationship between urban places and notions of community in sixteenth-century French writing. She currently teaches in the Department of Modern Languages at Simmons College in Boston.

Elizabeth Guild lectures in French at the University of Cambridge and is a fellow of Robinson College. Her most recent monograph is *Unsettling Montaigne: Poetics, Ethics and Affect in the Essais and Other Writings* (D. S. Brewer, 2014). She continues to work on Montaigne and is also developing a project on touch in the early modern period.

Richard Hillman is professor at the Université François-Rabelais, Tours, France (Department of English and Centre d'Études Supérieures de la Renaissance-CNRS), specializing in early modern English drama. His monographs include *Self-Speaking in Medieval and Early Modern English Drama: Subjectivity, Discourse and the Stage* (Macmillan, 1997) and three books focusing on links between early modern England and France: *Shakespeare, Marlowe and the Politics of France* (Palgrave, 2002), *French Origins of English Tragedy* (Manchester University Press, 2010), and *French Reflections in the Shakespearean Tragic: Three Case Studies* (Manchester University Press, 2010 and 2012). He has also published verse translations of several French Renaissance plays.

John D. Lyons is commonwealth professor of French at the University of Virginia. He has published widely on sixteenth- and seventeenth-century French literature, thought, and culture. His most recent books include *The Phantom of Chance: From Fortune to Randomness in Seventeenth-Century French Literature* (Edinburgh: Edinburgh University Press, 2011), *Before Imagination: Embodied Thought from Montaigne to Rousseau* (Stanford, CA: Stanford University Press, 2005), and *The Kingdom of Disorder: The Theory of Tragedy in Classical France* (West Lafayette, IN: Purdue University Press, 1999). He is currently working on a book-length project on the poetics of fear.

Andreea Marculescu received her PhD from Johns Hopkins University in 2011 and currently teaches at the University of California, Irvine. She is interested in affect studies and emotions, history of psychiatry, and narratives of mental illnesses in medieval and early modern literature. Andrea has published on the interconnection between medieval theater and the larger fields of medieval demonology and emotions, and she is working on a book manuscript titled *The Return of the Possessed: Piety, Theology, and Personhood in Medieval French Theatre*.

Michael Meere teaches French and European studies at Wesleyan University, where he specializes in early modern French literature, theater, and culture. He has completed a monograph on staged violence in sixteenth-century French tragedy and is directing an international project on William Drummond of Hawthornden and European theater in France at the turn of the seventeenth century. His current research project is a book-length study on the cultural pragmatics of social dramas in French drama during the sixteenth and early seventeenth centuries.

Corinne Noirot, former fellow of the École Normale Supérieure, is associate professor of French at Virginia Tech. Author of *"Entre deux airs": Style simple et* *ethos poétique chez Clément Marot et Joachim Du Bellay* [2011] (Paris: Hermann éditeurs, 2013), she also coedited (with Valérie Dionne) *"Revelations of Character": Ethos and Moral Philosophy in Montaigne* (Cambridge Scholars Publishing, 2007). She is currently preparing a special issue on "Montaigne et la langue" and analyzing the complete works of Jean de la Taille from the perspective of drama as an operative notion in his puzzling yet coherent œuvre.

Stephanie O'Hara is associate professor of French and woman and gender studies at the University of Massachusetts-Dartmouth. She is completing a monograph titled *Poison Onstage and Offstage in Early Modern France* as well as a translation (with Alison Klairmont Lingo) of the first European midwifery treatise written and published by a practicing midwife: Louise Bourgeois's *Diverse Observations Concerning Sterility, Miscarriages, Fertility, Births, and Diseases of Women and Newborn Children* (1st ed., Paris, 1609), to be published by the Toronto Centre for Reformation and Renaissance Studies in the series The Other Voice in Early Modern Europe.

Antónia Szabari is associate professor of French and comparative literature at the University of Southern California. She is the author of *Less Rightly Said: Scandals and Readers in Sixteenth-Century France* (Stanford University Press, 2009) and articles on Montaigne, Luther, Rabelais, Marguerite de Navarre, and Ronsard. She continues to work on the political culture of sixteenth-century France in the form of a book-length project on French-Ottoman diplomacy. In addition, she is cowriting, with Natania Meeker, a monograph on the imaginary plant in early modern science fiction, modern cinema, and art, tentatively titled *The Animated Plant: Vegetal Follies from Early to Late Modernity*.

Phillip John Usher is associate professor of French at New York University. He is the author of *Errance et cohérence: Essai sur la littérature transfrontalière à la Renaissance* (Paris: Classiques Garnier, 2010), of an English translation and scholarly edition of Ronsard's *Franciade* (New York: AMS Press, 2010), and of *Epic Arts in Renaissance France* (Oxford: Oxford University Press, 2014). He has also coedited several volumes, most recently a special issue of *L'Esprit créateur* with Patrick Bray titled *Building the Louvre: Architectures of Politics and Art* (Johns Hopkins University Press, 2014).

Ellen R. Welch is associate professor of French and Francophone studies at the University of North Carolina, Chapel Hill, and author of *A Taste for the Foreign: Worldly Knowledge and Literary Pleasure in Early Modern French Fiction* (University of Delaware Press, 2011). She is currently researching the uses of the performing arts in early modern diplomacy.